AN ANGEL PASSES

HOW THE SEXES BECAME UNDIVIDED

AN ANGEL PASSES

HOW THE SEXES BECAME UNDIVIDED

STUART SCHNEIDERMAN

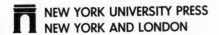
NEW YORK UNIVERSITY PRESS
NEW YORK AND LONDON

Library of Congress Cataloging-in-Publication Data

Schneiderman, Stuart, 1943–
  An angel passes : how the sexes became undivided / Stuart
Schneiderman.
    p. cm.
  Bibliography: p.
  Includes index.
  ISBN 0-8147-7870-4
  1. Angels. 2. Psychoanalysis and religion. I. Title.
BT966.2.S36 1988
235'.3—dc19   87-36465
                                              CIP

Book design by Ken Venezio

For Lila

CONTENTS

AN ANGEL PASSES

HOW THE SEXES BECAME UNDIVIDED

INTRODUCTION

Imagine yourself on the afternoon of a day that you know will end too soon. You are outdoors at the edge of a clearing looking over a field at the patterns figured in the sky. Perhaps you take note of the clouds or of the sunlight's refraction through the air. At some time it may cross your mind that more is going on in the scene than meets your eyes. In fact, it would take an incredible degree of naiveté to believe that all that is is what you see. If this leads you to question what it is that you do not see, you will likely draw upon the reserves of scientific knowledge packed in your brain, and will think immediately that the air over the field is filled with microscopic particles and organisms, with electromagnetic and sound waves, none of which are normally available to sight. What is also reasonably certain, given the place and time and circumstances of history, is that you will not imagine that the clear air of an autumn afternoon is filled with legions of angels. If someone were to come along to suggest such a thing, you would, if you were feeling charitable, consider it to be something of a bad joke. Mixing the realm of "imaginary" entities with that of measurable realities is not, after all, a very serious enterprise.

Have you ever considered that angels want to be taken seriously? Certainly there was a time when they were. Not only is this time beyond our memory, but it is almost inconceivable to the modern mind that anyone would waste time in fruitless and abstract speculation about invisible, immaterial beings who fly through the air carrying divine messages to the race of mortals. The habit of speculating about angels was buried under mounds of derision in the Renaissance, and with the exception of a few daunting neoscholastic spirits, it has remained precisely there. Even those who believe in angels have long since abandoned theorizing about them, to leave them at best to aesthetics and faith.

Of course, there was more to the interest in angels than theoretical speculation. From very early on in Christianity, there was a call to imitate the angels, the better to have what philosophers were later to call clear and distinct ideas, the better to approach and eventually achieve the state of beatitude that is theirs. In the third century A.D. the Alexandrian Origen wrote: "In order that the holy angels of God may be gracious to us and that they may do all they can on our behalf, it is enough that our attitude to God, as far as possible for human nature, should be one of imitating their devotion, since they imitate God, and that our idea of His Son, the Logos, so far as possible should not be in disaccord with the clearer idea which the holy angels have of him, but should be daily progressing towards theirs in clarity and distinctness" (Origen 1980, p. 267). And there were also injunctions against such imitation. Thomas Aquinas is the most significant representative of this tradition: ". . . if man were to have a share in the intellectual light from an angel, it would follow that man as regards his mind would not be made to the image of God Himself, but to the image of the angels, contrary to what is said in *Genesis* . . ." (Aquinas *Concerning Spiritual Creatures* [CSC], p. 118).

Why is it that angels are no longer taken seriously? For all we know this is not even the right question. It may well be that the problem is that the angels no longer take us seriously. Perhaps because once you have tasted of the real thing, you tire easily of imitations. Or perhaps because we humans have developed the tendency to take ourselves so very seriously. To an angel this must be tedious to an extreme. Or it may be that the class of intermediary beings which the Judeo-Christian West has insisted on calling angels are in fact not angels at all.

The gods, demons and genii of pagan antiquity may have initially been seduced by the new identity our religious tradition offered them, only to revert after a time to form. Or else, it is possible that the great minds of the Middle Ages, in their incomparable intellectual energy, their constant flirtation with pagan philosophy, developed theories that persuaded the angels that they were not really angels. Whatever they are, they may have tolerated being called angels only up to a point, finally turning away in dismay. Be this as it may, the reason that you do not take angels seriously and that you believe it is up to you to decide is called the Renaissance. A more or less constant preoccupation of philosophers and theologians through the Middle Ages, the holy angels were one of the casualties of the Renaissance, this despite the fact that their memory lived on immortalized in art. Of course, once it was no longer very acceptable to invoke them, the groundwork was set for some of the more shameless of angel imitators. Also, in their place there was a growing interest, even a hysteria, about the class of fallen angels, those who had originally been the object of pagan worship. Jacob Burckhardt declared that the Renaissance, the great reawakening of the human spirit, the wondrous rebirth of man's sense of his own humanity, had as one of its bases a great eclipse, the eclipse of the world of the supersensible, the place where angels, among others, found a habitation but not a name.

It takes a certain warp of mind to propose at this date and place an effort to recover, not the angels themselves, but whatever it was that so preoccupied the best minds of the Middle Ages in their guise. The best mind of that time, one of the great minds of Western civilization, Thomas Aquinas, was not only passionately interested in angels, but was later dubbed the Angelic Doctor. If we consult only one of Aquinas's works in the field, *The Treatise on Separate Substances,* we find that reflection on the intermediary world of spirits was crucial for Plato and Aristotle, among other luminaries of our civilization. In fact, it was over the status of the Forms or Ideas, themselves inhabiting the world of the supersensible, that Aristotle parted ways with his predecessor. Theoretical sophistication did not inhibit an appreciation of the ministry of angels. No one at the time more fully received that ministry than Francis of Assisi. The crucial episode in his life was receiving the Stigmata through a vision of Christ in the form of a seraph.

A topic that was compelling to the great minds of our civilization ought to interest us, if only because we may sharpen our intelligence in following the workings of theirs. To say that something so fiercely repressed has probably not simply disappeared identifies the author as positively Freudian. A brief glance at the second and third chapters of

Lacan's *The Four Fundamental Concepts of Psychoanalysis* (1973) shows that he saw a clear link between the Freudian unconscious and the different forms of mediators that Christianity took to be angels and devils. Such a linkage comports serious theoretical risks, especially if it leads people to the mistaken belief that the Freudian unconscious is filled with universal meanings or even with affects. Such non-Freudian approaches are consistent in their reference to a metalanguage that would dissipate the veils thrown over understanding by ordinary language, thereby allowing people to see clearly, with insight and awareness. To see, in other words, like the angels.

So my own position is psychoanalytic, and it is best to mention this now since it is hardly self-evident in what follows. What will be self-evident to some readers is that I am hardly an expert on angels. My knowledge comes from research more than from devotion, and the questions that interest me have little to do with faith. While I will devote considerable attention to the ways in which people have tried to be like the angels, you will doubtless notice that this is not an experience that tempts me inordinately. Thus I claim a certain irreverence in regard to the institutional worship of angels, to counterpoint a considerable respect for those whose intelligence attempted to render the angels intelligible and even for those who declared themselves to have accompanied the angels on their flights.

Fortunately, there is a very easy way to connect the angels with contemporary concerns. Angels are mediating spirits, they are messengers who pass between the godhead and the merely mortal; thereby they are agents of communication, and this even before they become theophanies and soulful beings bathing in the eternal bliss promised to the faithful. The world of the angels has to do, at least in part, with communication, and our age has often been called an age of communication or information. Resurgent interest in the fields of semantics, of linguistics, of the philosophy of language represents a return to questions that were of major importance in the Scholastic philosophy of the Middle Ages. A brief excursion through the *Cambridge History of Late Medieval Philosophy*, a compendium organized according to the principles of analytic philosophy, will show how apt the comparison is. The revival of interest in medieval thought demonstrated by two such disparate and influential turn-of-the-century spirits as Charles Sanders Peirce and

Martin Heidegger persuades us of the relevance of medieval philosophical concerns.

Few people who consider themselves intellectuals today feel any particular need for mediation, certainly not between themselves and God. If you ask them why, assuming that they take the question seriously, they might say that God is irrelevant, thank you, or dead, and that they have been much happier since this event was announced. And yet, if Heidegger is correct in reading Nietzsche's statement of the death of God as meaning that the supersensible world of ideas and ideals fell with Him, what is left to mediate between humans and the void created by the death of God (Heidegger 1962, p. 173ff.)? Besides, some would say that this void is God and that God has never been anything else. Of course, a twisted spirit might wish to throw some doubt on such an event, even questioning the place of the "angel" responsible for this modern version of the "annunciation." Doesn't he who takes responsibility for such a de-annunciation promote himself as a member of the community of mediating spirits? The promotion is compounded by his asserting himself to be the angel announcing an apocalyptic end of the world or end of man.

The more obvious reason for the disinterest in mediation is the tendency to idealize immediacy. Why bother with any sort of mediation, any system or code of rules and regulations between man and God, between man and nature, or between man and woman, when immediate knowledge of the other is within our grasp? We have but to reach out and hold it in our hands. Why have recourse to beings whom we cannot touch or hold, beings that are mirages, projections, or even, as Spinoza said, hallucinations, when life is there before us waiting to be plucked? Isn't the refusal to concern oneself with angelic or other forms of supersensible mediators an incontestable sign of sanity and normality? After all, one of the reasons people are so obsessed with the psychosciences is their thirst for an absolute, almost Cartesian certainty about the sanity and normality of their own meager Selfs. It used to be that people wanted to be assured that their souls were going to be saved, were going to see God face-to-face in the afterlife. Nowadays the concern with Self translates a will to be certain that the life one is living is blessed or cursed, that the beings with which one shares this life are angels or devils.

The twin shibboleths of immediacy and intimacy function as powerful ideals, most especially in determining what ought to go on between people who have formed couples. The ideal of the "relationship," as opposed to the mediating relations of kinship, rules many a life. Our point will be that this ideal is a throwback to what had heretofore been considered the province of the angels. People used to believe that we humans require some sort of mediation between ourselves and whatever is out there. This was the price of the Fall of Adam and Eve, the consequence of the presence of a cherub guarding the gates of Eden. We are not allowed, the authors will say, to see God face-to-face. The angels, however, already have an immediate, intimate knowledge of divinity, a knowledge that the faithful will eventually acquire. However, if that time has already come, if the Heavenly City exists in the here and now, then we ourselves are mediating spirits in no need of mediation.

There has been considerable debate about what the angels see when they see God face-to-face, even whether there is anything ultimately to see. What, after all, does it mean to say that God has a face? Some believed that seeing God involved the soul in states of mystical rapture, while others emphasized that angels are intelligences, that their sight was that of the mind. This latter tradition derives from Aristotle through his medieval Arab commentators, primary among whom were Avicenna and Averroës. The greatest Christian author in this tradition was Aquinas. The mystical tradition is Platonic and biblical; its emphasis is on the aesthetic and on the value of feminine experience. Finally it would prevail.

Among the early figures in the mystical tradition were Origen, Gregory of Nyssa, and Gregory of Nazianus. The latter two lived and wrote in the fourth century. In the twelfth century there were, for example, Hugues and Richard of St. Victor and a man considered the dominant churchman of his time, particularly in terms of the ability to wield political power, the formidable Bernard of Clairvaux. It is good to recognize immediately that the mystical tradition is not one of powerless detachment from the world. "For by 1145 . . . St. Bernard of Clairvaux was the most influential figure in all the West. Of course one can dislike this violent, emaciated man; seething with the fury of God, he relentlessly crushed Abélard and lashed out at the Roman Curia with its propensity for temporal glories. But there is no denying that it was Saint Bernard of Clairvaux who launched the Crusades, who counseled and lectured the kings, and who went to Albi to preach against the Albigensian heretics" (Duby 1981, p. 119). Among great women representatives of this tradition were Catherine of Siena in the fourteenth century and Teresa of Avila in the sixteenth.

Yet the figure who dominates the practice, not the theory, of mysticism was obviously Francis of Assisi. "Francis was actually the great hero of Christian history, along with Christ himself, and it is no exaggeration to say that whatever still remains of living Christianity comes directly from Saint Francis" (Duby 1981, p. 143). The most practiced theoretical followers of Francis were Bonaventure in the thirteenth century, John Duns Scotus at the turn of the fourteenth, and William of Ockham in the first half of the fourteenth century. To the latter two, especially Ockham, we are indebted for the notion of intuitive cognition, *notitia intuitiva*, which described the immediate grasp of singular objects without need for any intermediary or mediating thought. Since the modern mind may find it difficult to imagine a situation in which immediate cognition of things as they are in themselves is subject to doubt, we mention that this idea was derived by Duns Scotus from what the angels are now enjoying as they see God face-to-face (in Hyman and Walsh 1984, p. 632).

For immediacy and intimacy nothing approaches the experiences of these representatives of the mystical tradition. Their souls yearned incessantly for the embrace of Christ; they traversed the ranks of the angels in an ever more perfect vision of the light source that Dante placed at the summit of Paradise. Doubtless some of them were blinded in the process, but others, like Bernard of Clairvaux, reached such a level of passionate spiritual conviction that they made it their duty to destroy everyone who did not see what they had seen. Dauntless instigator of crusades, brutal enemy of Peter Abélard, Bernard was one of those who connected the mystical yearnings of the soul with the cult of the Virgin that grew and developed in the Middle Ages. One would be remiss in neglecting to mention the importance of the maternal in this tradition, especially as motherhood became the only acceptable side of femininity.

Not only was the mystical soul considered to be feminine in its lust for Christ's embrace, it had strong tendencies to attack and repress what it considered to be the virile intelligence of people like Peter Abélard. And not merely Abélard. To the list of those attacked by the partisans of the Lady, we add Aristotle and the Arab philosophers, Avicenna and

Averroës, all of whom were a powerful influence on the Angelic Doctor. The *Summa Theologica* may be considered to be the ark of salvation by the modern Church, but just a few years after Aquinas's death, in 1277 to be exact, a considerable number of his ideas were included in a list of positions condemned by the Bishop of Paris, Etienne Tempier. Of course, once Aquinas was canonized around fifty years later, these propositions were no longer considered to be signposts on the road to damnation. Were it not for the political power of Aquinas's Dominican order, much of his work could well have been consigned to oblivion. "The Dominican order reacted against the indictment. Its chapters general of 1309 and 1313 forbade all denial of Thomism within the brotherhood. In 1323 it obtained the canonization of Saint Thomas and used every means, particularly the painted image, to have its justification recognized by all" (Duby 1981, p. 211). Even so the influence of Aristotelian thought was on the wane by the end of the thirteenth century. In the conflict between the mystical and intellectual theological traditions, it was clearly the former that won out, and not just in the world of theology.

John Duns, called Scotus, showed that only a very limited number of dogmatic truths could be based on reason; therefore one should simply believe in the others instead of endeavoring to demonstrate them. It fell to William of Occam, following suit, truly to open the "modern way." His ideas were fundamentally anti-Aristotelian since he believed that concepts were symbols devoid of all reality, that knowledge could only be intuitive and individual, and that the processes of abstract reasoning were consequently useless—whether it was a matter of reaching God or of understanding the world. . . . It was a twofold evasion of the constraints imposed by the Church. By asserting the irrationality of dogma, first of all, it prepared a way toward God which no longer lay through the intellect but through love. It gave free rein to the deep current of mysticism which had irrigated Latin Christendom since Saint Augustine but had been stemmed by the success of Scholasticism and thrust back into the cloister, into Franciscan convents and the small communities of ascetic penitents. (Duby 1981, pp. 211–12)

Those who emerged victorious were clearly on the side of the Lady; they constantly opposed systems of thought that had entered Europe through the patriarchal Arabs and Jews, especially the thought of the pagan Aristotle. Plato and the Neoplatonists, for example, Plotinus and Proclus, were allowed to remain (note the revival of Neoplatonism in the early Renaissance) because their champion was the most venerated figure of the Church past, Augustine of Hippo. Besides, Plotinus, the father of Neoplatonism, had been taught by a Christian, and one could believe that the Word had somehow penetrated his pagan consciousness (Wolfson 1973, p. 12). While Aquinas had denied the idea of the Immaculate Conception of the Virgin by questioning why Christ would have been needed if someone could have been conceived without sin before his birth, Duns Scotus demonstrated that what was later to become dogma was cogent on the grounds that the act through which Mary was conceived could be rendered retroactively free of sin by the power of her son. Thereby was sealed the creation of a type of femininity that had nothing to do with masculine desire, which did not owe existence to anything resembling a phallus. The elevation of such a mother goddess in identification with the Church and the Heavenly Jerusalem has important consequences for the concept and conception of angels. It is consistent with the idea that angels are sexless and are exempt from the constraints of marriage.

Whatever else was going on in Europe at the time, within the world of theology and within the Church there was constituted a moral world to suppress the raging virile world of commerce, politics, and war. Eventually the eternal and essential feminine was to become the moral victor. The version of femininity put forth was not the one promoted by the Greeks through the worship of a goddess like Aphrodite, nor that of the polygamous Arabs who concerned themselves with women's sensual pleasure. The moral superiority of the right kind of women was promoted to cure nothing less than the division of the sexes. This new femininity was modeled on the system of moral values embodied in the Virgin Mother and in the Heavenly City. In fact, it is only under duress that one calls it femininity; the ideal here is maternity.

Its greatest champion had been none other than Augustine. The link between motherhood and sensuality was sundered as Augustine inveighed against the pagan cults to the mother goddess. How could anyone, he wrote, expose his mother to such flagrant obscenity? "For there is something in the natural respect that we have towards our parents that the extreme of infamy cannot wholly destroy; and certainly those very mountebanks would be ashamed to give a rehearsal performance in their homes, before their mothers, of those disgusting verbal and acted obscenities. Yet they performed them in the presence of the Mother of the Gods before an immense audience of spectators of both sexes" (*The City of God* [CG], book 2, chap. 6).

Augustine will be a central figure in our story, and not just because he loved his mother beyond reason. Within the context of his eschatological musings about the Heavenly City Augustine was also profoundly concerned with the inhabitants of that City: their way of life, their enjoyment, felicity, and beatitude. For the moment understand that Augustine brought the angels into the sphere of maternal influence, into a motherly and mothering space. Even as he Christianized Plato he applied his awesome intelligence to making the angels acceptable to Christians. That such a task should be required is telling. Many if not most other religions have various kinds of intermediary beings, be they demons, ghosts, fauns, satyrs, devils, gods, what have you. In Augustine's time there was a system of thought called Gnosticism, some of whose adherents believed that the heavenly angels acted of their own volition, in defiance of God's commands. Marcion believed that it was the angels who created the world to spite God. And pagan myth usually held that the intermediary beings were sexed, that there were male and female varieties, and that they did unseemly and obscene things. (The shadow of such a division was present in alchemical texts.) Such was not acceptable within a world dedicated to the worship of an untouched, undefiled mother. What glory could be expected from the son of such a mother, a man whose values consistently eschewed the virtues pagans associated with masculinity, if the intermediary beings were doing things that Christ did not do himself, if they did not imitate his example?

Primary among the things Christ did not do was father children. To which you may wish to respond that the God of the Old Testament, in contradistinction to the Greek gods, did not do so either (Wolfson 1977, p. 527). It seems that Christ, like his Heavenly Father, was not sexually attracted to women; doubtless this is a source of the general contempt his acolytes have had for women who have wanted to be attractive to men.

In the New Testament, of course, God finally does have a son, but clearly this was not an activity that found great favor in his mind. After all, he only did it once, and this suggests that doing it once soured him on the experience. In any case the erotic antics of the Greek gods were removed from the behavior patterns of the denizens of Jerusalem. Not that women did not offer their love or themselves to Christ, but the Son of Man was impervious to their seductive wiles and feminine enchantments. Witness Mary Magdalene. Of course, he is said to have responded generously to those women whose love was denuded of eroticism, thus that was the most angelic. Odysseus had to have himself tied to a mast to survive the chants of the sirens; no such need in the case of Jesus.

The problem here concerns not Christ himself, but rather the first person of the Trinity, God the Father. In a world defined by the virtues associated with motherhood, what place would there be for a father, be he a Zeus whose amorous exploits were the stuff of myth, legend, and poetry, or a Jehovah of the Old Testament? In a sense he is an embarrassment, and there seems to be an unstated theological requirement that his place be reduced or even eliminated. If there is a direct link between the role of the father and sexual identification, then the way to eliminate the division of the sexes is to reduce and distort the role of the father's desire, his Law, in these formations. So God the Father becomes a point of light in Dante, admittedly not just any point of light, but certainly not one that demonstrates any particularly fatherly characteristics. For an author like John Scotus Erigena, who wrote in the ninth century, it happens that anything we may say of God the Father is a distortion, a limitation on his omnitude. It is striking that the person of the first person of the Trinity is of so little interest in Catholic theology. In effect, we are obliged to await the second half of the fourteenth century for the arrival of Catherine of Siena to find a work, *The Dialogue,* in which God the Father appears on the scene to talk to one of his children. It is probably not an accident that it required a woman to see this, nor that the arrival of the person of the Father takes place in a time of extreme duress, immediately following the unimaginable ravages of the Black Plague. The Black Death first hit Europe in the late 1340s, a point that marks the beginning of the end of the Middle Ages.

What we have roughly labeled the mystical tradition is not the only approach to angels. The fact that angels are messengers yields interesting and important observations about communication. So I propose that these invisible spirits who fly through the air bearing messages have a very close resemblance to spoken words. It happens that the people who spent the most time cogitating the angels were the same who developed the theory of the linguistic sign. In Christian theology the theory of the sign is the subject of Augustine's *De Magistro*. This does not in itself establish that the angels are another way of thinking or writing about language. To find an explicit link we turn to Philo of Alexandria, a Jewish theologian writing in the first century A.D., whose work is considered to be a major influence on Christian thought. Meditating on the dream where Jacob sees angels ascending and descending a ladder to heaven, Philo wrote:

In accordance with this they are represented as ascending and descending: not that God, who is already present in all directions, needs informants, but that it was a boon to us in our sad case to avail ourselves of the services of "words" acting on our behalf as mediators, so great is our awe and shuddering dread of the universal Monarch and the exceeding might of His sovereignty. ... If we consider that which is so called [stairway] in human beings we shall find it to be soul. Its foot is sense-perception, which is as it were the earthly element in it, and its head, the mind which is wholly unalloyed, the heavenly element, as it may be called. Up and down throughout its whole extent are moving incessantly the "words" of God, drawing it up with them when they ascend and disconnecting it with what is mortal, and exhibiting to it the spectacle of the only objects worthy of our gaze; and when they descend not casting it down, for neither does God nor does a divine Word cause harm, but condescending out of love for man and compassion for our race, to be helpers and comrades, that with the healing of their breath they may quicken into new life the soul which is still borne along in the body as in a river. (Philo 5, pp. 373, 375)

I have quoted this at some length to give more than the simple idea that angels were identified as spoken words, as *logoi* in Philo's Greek. Not only does this identify the angels as words, but it also shows the split between the part of language that is available to sense perception and the concept conveyed. In Saussure, we know, the structure of the sign is defined as the split between the signifier, as acoustic image, and the signified, as concept. While we will not follow Saussure in this regard, since we will employ Lacan's distinction between sign and signifier, it is well to note that one of the more contested areas of medieval angelology was whether angels have any material being. Aquinas held that they are immaterial, but this was certainly not agreed upon by everyone.

Philo's Father God is precisely the sort who makes you want to keep your feet on the ground. This Father will want nothing better than to clip your wings, thereby to evoke in your soul considerable praise for the angels that thankfully and gracefully allow you not to see his face. Rapt meditation on the nature of the bliss awaiting you in the afterlife is excluded from such a world as it is excluded from most pre-Christian religions. So it is reasonable that Catholic theology, in which Christ came to fulfill the Law, has little use for the first person of the Trinity, preferring to pray to the second person through the intermediary of his mother. Even the Father God of Catherine of Siena is not a figure to provoke very much anxiety.

If one asserts that the angels at one time represented spoken words, and thus that they are implicated in theories of language and the sign, why does such a theorization get itself tied up with such peculiar creatures? One may certainly question the nature of the sign, the semantic theories of meaning and sense, the problem of reference, the split between signifier and signified, without bringing in the angels. Not only may one do such a thing, one does so often and seemingly without any extensive damage to the theory. What do we gain by hypostatizing spoken words as invisible flying messengers? One essential if paradoxical gain is that we are thereby permitted to visualize the operation of language. This is paradoxical if the angels are merely invisible, but it is less so if we know that angels have on occasion assumed quasi-human form to make appearances to human beings. Man, we might say, is incapable of grasping or being grasped by the functioning of language unless its terms and relations appear in forms that resemble him. This does not necessarily mean that humans project themselves onto the world of language. Making invisible speech into a visible angel may well accomplish just the opposite. It would then provide an account of how the world of words, taken to be abstract, is mapped onto the world of humans—how, in other words, the structure of language intersects with and determines the structure of human relations.

If we follow philosophies of language, both modern and ancient, we see that two questions arise with considerable frequency. Let us assume that the words of a sentence have an independent existence, that they are not simply projections of the human Self or soul. We may then ask what is the nature of the interaction between the components of the sentence, or what is the basis for their cohesion within the sentential unit? The same question may and perhaps ought better to be posed in terms of the two sentences of a dialogue: is it the sentences that interact or the people who relate to each other despite the sentences? Is the interaction of the sentences simply a cover for a more profound relationship between meanings and/or intentions? Our position is that the interaction of the elements of the sentence or sentences defines and determines the interaction of those who deploy them. Sentences, in other words, do not always do what you think they are doing; they do not always ply themselves to your will. Words are not a possession of humans; they have better things to do than to bow down in obedience to any human subject. If they have something like a mind of their own, the question of their desire becomes a matter of urgency. Such are the issues addressed by the positing of a class of intermediary beings. The way these beings are defined—as angels, demons, gods, souls, minds, ideas—will imply a response to the questions we have posed.

One of the constant preoccupations of the contemporary philosophy of language is how, as Hilary Putnam asked, language hooks into the world (Putnam 1984). We will limit the scope of this inquiry for the moment by asking how language hooks into those who speak it. For the fearless theologians of the Middle Ages the question became whether angels interact with humans through acts of copulation; this follows well upon the question of whether they copulate with each other. In the Judeo-Christian tradition, beginning at least with Philo, the idea that God's angels copulate with human women was positively unthinkable. This was, after all, one of the ways that the heavenly angels were distinct from pagan gods and demons, and it was of great importance to preserve this difference. Note that the question concerned copulation between angels and women, and that authors like Philo, who read in Genesis that the sons of God, another name for angels, took the daughters of man as wives, were obliged to say that the angels in question there were manifestly fallen angels. From this there was later to arise, at the end of the fifteenth century, a general European mania about witches, about those women who had unlawful congress with the devils. The female sex was therefore the conduit through which devils could wreak havoc among humans, and this caused no small misogynistic rage among the faithful. On the other side this same female sex, to the extent that it renounced the phallus—which was possessed only by fallen angels—became the pathway to the Heavenly City.

Associating somewhat freely, we find thinly disguised instances of virility in the angels who appear to John in the visions that form the basis for Revelation. They speak with loud voices and sound trumpets, both of which penetrate the listener's body. For the rest of humanity access to the truths of this book must come through a written text . . . read aloud. As the voice says to John: "Write what you see in a book and send it to the seven churches . . ." (Rev. 1:10). The competing claims of speech and writing are manifest in this book and the final judgment falls on the side of Scripture. Whereas in an oral culture the verbal repetition of stories and myths leads to alteration, John specifically promises the worst of punishments for those who do not worship at the altar of Scripture: "I warn every one who hears the words of the prophecy of this book: if any one adds to them, God will add to him the plagues described in this book, and if any one takes away from the words of the book of this prophecy, God will take away his share in the tree of life and in the holy city, which are described in this book" (Rev. 22:18–19). One might even say that the manifestly phallic quality of the voices and trumpets of the angels harks back to pagan sources and that these sources are redeemed by their becoming fixed and immutable in writing. Reading aloud is paying lip service to the speech act. Since the speech act lends itself to translation into terms of sexual difference, speaker and listener being masculine and feminine roles, the religion of the angels had to side with the written over and against the spoken word.

Judeo-Christian angels are not sexed and do not copulate with each other or with human woman. If the act of copulation was not to be invoked to explain how angels interacted with humans, what could be called upon to take its place? Quite simply, the mirror identification of humans and angels. Beginning with the idea of the guardian angel, the heavenly counterpart of each human being, and reaching its apotheosis in the stigmatization of Francis of Assisi, human beings were exhorted to become like the angels, thereby to become in the flesh like the elements of language. Put in these terms this is a strange idea indeed.

What is a lot less strange is the aspiration of people to become like angels. Deriving from monasticism, this hope was lived out in the organization of monasteries and convents, to the point where it eventually spawned heresies in which the crime was wanting to be too angelic. Such an excess of enthusiasm was obviously conditioned by the religious milieu. At times those who promote themselves as holier-than-thou have grasped something that has eluded their more moderate contemporaries. Heresies of the eleventh century are one source of the idea of sexual equality in the abolition of the difference between masculine and feminine (Duby 1982, p. 132). The rejection of sexual difference was founded on "the most radical contempt for the flesh. Blood and sex were repugnant to them. They abstained from eating meat. They were shocked by the wounds in the crucifixion, by the sacrifice in the mass, by the bread that became flesh, the wine that became blood. They wanted no part of marriage. And not merely because they condemned procreation, dreaming of a humanity that would reproduce itself without copulation, as bees were thought to do" (Duby 1982, p. 132). (The asexual reproduction of bees is discussed by Augustine in *On the Trinity*.) These were the "perfect"; they represent the ideal of perfectability based on a shameless imitation of the angel. Duby continued: "The equality of a paradise regained. It is precisely this hope that accounts for the rejection of sexuality. Adam's sin had made copulation necessary, had set the human apart from the angelic. When human beings reached the point of living in total chastity, when, as John the Scot said, 'sex which signifies that which is inferior' had been taken from man, then the earth would once again be joined to heaven" (Duby 1982, p. 133). While we note with considerable interest this expression of the idea of the equality of the sexes, we know that the contemporary versions propose an equality that would be inclusive of copulation and other forms of sexual expression. Of course, heretics did not always make a virtue of consistency either.

For the moment it is more important to remark with Duby that there were close similarities between the "perfect" and the inhabitants of monasteries.

They are reminiscent too of monastic priorities, monasticism having a similar purpose, claiming to attain a higher degree of perfection through an heroic ascesis, through contempt for the world. How are we to distinguish between the monks—who were chaste, who purified themselves through fasting, who humbled themselves through manual labor, who, though not priests, devoted their days to perpetual prayer, who strove indefatigably to become angels—and the exponents of heresy? Was heresy anything other than a fanatical desire at last to cast off the moorings, to bring all Christians within the embrace of a kind of monasticism? What was heresy but the hope of an immense monastery that would suddenly turn into paradise, with the end of the species, the end of procreation, the end of "human beings." (Duby 1982, p. 133)

The belief in angels was not simply an aspect of worship; it influenced human behavior and the way in which human societies were organized. An ideal social organization is, according to this idea, inhabited by beings who are not the same as the beings who inhabit the fallen world. These latter are condemned to remain on either side of the barrier separating the sexes and are obliged to assume an identity as masculine or feminine. The intelligence of monasticism as well as of the "perfect" was to show that the most radical transformation of society produced an equally radical transformation of human beings into angels—no less, but also no more.

In terms of identity this meant simply the replacement of sexual identity by moral identity. Whereas sexual identity and the ethical systems of pagans tended to see the primary division on a horizontal axis, as in the division between right and left, Christianity substituted a vertical division in which the moral became dissociated from the division of the sexes (cf. Le Goff 1984, p. 3). And one might even say that within the Christianized West this division passes for a division of the sexes. This is fundamentally in error, because the moral division of heaven and hell translates a division of sexed and unsexed. Where all humans are unsexed in the sense that their identity is not based on being on either side of a horizontal division, equality reigns. In place of a sexual division there arises a division between the moral and the immoral, the liberated and the unliberated. The world of the angels is far and away the most ambitious attempt in our civilization to establish a world in which identity is not based on sex. It is not merely that the divisions of the fallen world are denounced, but also that a positive existence is dictated for those whose moral worth raises them above such divisions. Within the Christian cosmos moral worth derives from participation in a passion, the Passion of Christ, while in other worlds ethics was based on a code of action. Lacan, for example, asserts that ethics should be defined in terms of whether one acts in accord with one's desire, given that desire is not for a Supreme Good. Lacan's ethical injunction to saying-well implies the accomplishment of an act that produces an effect on a listener. The failure to say things well is not redeemed by the speaker's conviction or his beliefs or his state of well-being. If in the fallen world identity is inseparable from sexual roles, it was required that a new identity be proposed to transcend this division. The requirements for this new identity may well have been inhuman, but this is hardly a reason for believing that they must exist somewhere else.

The Church in the Middle Ages was hardly indifferent to heresy; nor was it calmed by the resemblances between heresy and monasticism. It responded first with the idea that the extension of Heaven to earth was to exist only within the walls of the Church, thus that a barrier existed between good and evil, between the pure and the corrupt; and second with the notion that the angels lived in a world in which there was a hierarchy of moral worth. This suggests an inequality, but it also, and more significantly, lends itself to the idea of moral progress, of a movement of the soul in the direction of greater degrees of moral perfection. In the Middle Ages the hierarchy of the angels was advanced as the prototype of the hierarchy of the church itself (Duby 1982, pp. 133–34). This latter idea was the work of one of the central figures in medieval angelology, Dionysius the Areopagite. The author of works like *The Celestial Hierarchy* and *The Ecclesiastical Hierarchy* claimed the name and the authority of Dionysius, the first Athenian convert of Paul. Discovered in the sixth century, the works were originally dismissed as a fraud. Later their authenticity was promoted by Maximus Confessor and John Scotus Erigena, who translated the work into Latin. Thereon the Areopagite's influence was pervasive in the Middle Ages; his authority was almost canonical. In the Renaissance Erasmus and Luther among others disputed the author's claim to be the Areopagite on stylistic and theological grounds (Nygren 1982, pp. 576–77). At which point one of the major pillars of the discourse on angels crumbled. The incipient Protestant movement, with its distaste for the kind of theoretical speculation represented by the Thomist and Scotist work on angels, delighted in the discovery, used it to discredit Scholasticism's pretense to being Christian, and moved to dismantle the elaborate system of medieval mediators, whether angelic, saintly, or priestly.

But why should anyone have lent any credence to belief in supersensible spirits? Let us try to make contact with the mode of thought that gave substance to angels, not as ministers or messengers but in the sense that angels were taken to be intelligences—minds or spirits. This was the legacy of Aristotle, and it was this aspect of the angelic that drew the most scorn from the Reformation.

Examine the case of a planet, a heavenly body, that is in motion, and whose motion is intelligible to a mind, a human mind. Generally we believe that the planet itself does not have any sort of intelligence that may be acting to move it in a way that is intelligible. Thereby one may assert that a separate intelligence must be moving the planet; otherwise how could its movement be intelligible to a human mind? For Christians this separate intelligence is an angel. The relation between the intelligence and the planet is motion, defined according to the division of mover and moved. For now we leave aside considerations that declare some heavenly bodies to have minds of their own.

It is important to define the distinction between this view and one that bases itself on the Platonic Forms. If there were a Form or Idea of planet existent somewhere somehow, this Form would be the prototype of all planets. Each planet would be an expression or a translation of the Form into sensible terms. The Form would not be taxed with the task of moving the planet; it is intelligible but not a mind or a mover. The purpose of knowledge in this case is to move from the sensible object to the Form, the object being simply a means to an end. The Forms may well exist within the mind of God, as Augustine asserted, but there is little sense that they have any other relation to each other. Their relation to the objects that embody or manifest them is vertical rather than horizontal, as it is in the Aristotelian conception.

Our interest in this problematic is not simply epistemological. The Aristotelian view of minds that move heavenly bodies posits a division that seems to correspond to the division of the sexes. While the soul that moves a human being is united with the body that is moved, when we arrive at the higher heavens the division is more clear. And it is from the principle of division that the concept of the movement of a human or animal body derives its structure. The point for Aristotle was that the mover as mind was in itself unmoved, that movement was in the body. Of course, if the mind was united with a body it would also move once the body was set into motion, but this movement would be only accidental, not necessary. In the case of intelligences that are separate from bodies they may also be moved—not through the movement of a body, but through the action of the first unmoved mover (Wolfson 1973, pp.

4–5). This is a difficult concept, to be elaborated in the course of this volume.

Some authors saw the heavenly bodies united with minds, but for the moment we will limit ourselves to the cases where the separation pertains. What we will argue is that the division of mover and moved maps onto humans in terms of the interaction of the sexes. And we see the principle of this interaction, defined in terms of movement and also of desire, as preferable to those theories that see the sexes as interacting to become united as one. As Aquinas wrote: "The heaven is said to move itself in so far as it is compounded of mover and moved; not by the union of the mover, as the form, with the moved, as the matter, but by contact with the motive power *(per contactum virtutis)* . . ." (ST, part 1, q. 70, art. 3). The Latin word *virtutis* is linked etymologically with the word virtue, and Virtues are one of the class of angels. In Latin it is connected with the word for man, *vir*, and by extension, *virtu* (manliness). Thereby, being an unmoved mover has something to do with masculinity and being moved is related to femininity. One of the problems that then arises is the nature of the contact between an immaterial and a material substance; precisely where and how is the movable touched by an unmoved mover to produce motion? We will leave this open for the time being (but see Wolfson 1973, pp. 48–49).

Aristotle disputed the view that the Platonic Forms preexisted the world of things, to be the model upon which the latter was created. And his dispute was that there was no principle therein to show how the Forms were related to each other and that there was no principle to effect their translation into individual things. Being supersensible, the Forms also tended to lead people to detach themselves from the world of sensible things, to deflect their sight from the visible to the invisible, to be contented with the contemplation of the Form itself. It was through a process of abstraction from particulars that an Aristotelian could arrive at the world of the intelligible and the world of the intelligences. And yet, the knowledge so gained had to be applied, as I see it, to the real and to the requirements of ethical action in it.

To shift focus we will inquire whether the relation between mover and moved may be applied to an analysis of dialogue, where the form of the dialogue is question and answer. Say that the question is an unmoved mover that causes the listener to be moved to answer. It is not the speaker who moves the listener but the question that represents the speaker. Not only the listener is moved, for the answer, passing from the state of unspoken to spoken, will become coupled with the question. The movement of the question from unspoken to spoken is thereby accidental, for once the question is spoken it functions as a mover. The sense of movement here is that the answer is a potential that becomes actualized when the question is spoken. It may well be that the answer is potential knowledge in the listener and that, as is supposed to happen in Socratic dialogue, it is the question that makes the knowledge actual to the listener.

It is one thing to plumb the meaning of a simple declarative sentence, "The cat is on the mat." One may wish to say that there are Ideas of the two terms that exist as universals in the intelligible world and that they are conjoined by the verbal copula and a preposition. One can thereby declare it to be a correct sentence in the English language. The problem arises when you ask what the semantic value of the sentence is when it is pronounced at a time when there is no cat is on the mat. As Donald Davidson has argued, without knowing the situation or context in which the sentence is pronounced, which we translate as knowing what caused it to be pronounced, then you do not know the sense of the sentence.

Place this declarative sentence in a context, as part of a dialogue. Does the sense of the sentence remain the same if it is uttered as a response to each of the following: "Is the cat on the mat?" or "Where is the cat?" or "What is on the mat?" It appears that the coupling of the declarative sentence with a question alters its sense, to the point where we wonder whether it is legitimate to study the sense of the sentence in isolation. Perhaps the purpose of the sentence is not ultimately to convey any sort of meaning or to refer to a world of pure intelligibility that disregards context, dialectic, and phrasing. In Lacan's theory the difference is between the sign, which represents something for someone, and the signifier, which represents a subject for another signifier. We are taking the question and answer as two signifiers and the speaker of the question as the subject who represents himself by the question. The answerer does not then represent himself by his response; the fact that the question is addressed to him does not make him a someone. Signifiers are structured in being paired and have no need of the presence of the subject to provide that structure. The role of the questioner is to provide a provisional connection to the question, before the answer is coupled with it. If the sentence is taken in isolation as representing something like a meaning or a state of affairs for someone then it would have the structure of the sign.

Concerning angels, the question is whether they are signs or signifiers, assuming the distinction we are making here. And you will understand intuitively that in general the angels are considered to be much closer to the structure of the sign; they convey messages that have meaning to various people. If this is the case, the question arises whether they are good or bad angels, whether their message is divine or diabolical. The need to distinguish between the two sorts of angels was of great concern in the Renaissance: see, for example, the *Spiritual Exercises* of Ignatius Loyola. In fact, it is far older; the first text I have found to outline the problem in detail is *The Shepherd*, written by Hermas in the second century A.D. If angels are signifiers, they interact in the way that questions and answers interact; we might even say that they would thereby be coupled, in roughly the way that men and women are. And you can guess that such an activity is excluded from the world of Christian angels. Not that angels are never paired; certainly they are in artistic representation. But the pairing always seems to be on the basis of imaging, as in a mirror, and this is not the sort of coupling that occurs on the level of the signifier.

The sole exception, or what seems to be an exception, is the tendency in Renaissance art to have male and female, even infant angels, in a representation that is far more human than heretofore. What this suggests, to me at least, is that the figures so represented are not angels but rather represent the souls of the blessed, those who will come to inhabit Paradise with the angels and who will have their earthly bodies restored to them after the Last Judgment. Christianity accepted the idea that the bodies so restored are sexed, but this is because they are then beyond Eros.

Our study of angels will necessarily lead us to consider the philosophy of language, especially the semantics of modal statements. Logical modes like possibility, necessity, and contingency were first analyzed by Aristotle, and we will have ample occasion to see how they relate to otherworldly concerns. For the moment, let us examine the question of modes in relation to the analysis of sentential meaning. Using the mode of possibility we will examine part of an extensive debate concerning the function of proper names in relation to possible worlds. Begin with Saul

Kripke's idea that a proper name is a rigid designator, that it has the same referent in all possible worlds or in all counterfactual situations. And consider the objection of David Lewis to the effect that a change in the situation of the referent of the proper name entails a change in the referent itself. In the sentence: "Hubert Humphrey might have been president," the question is whether being or not being president would change the referent of the name Hubert Humphrey. Is the speaker talking about the same Hubert Humphrey when he describes a counterfactual situation in which Humphrey became the president as he is when he makes a statement which is true of Hubert Humphrey? Such is one way of looking at this aspect of the debate.

Kripke's point is that the referent of the proper name is the same no matter what you say about the man, and Lewis proposed that if the situation is altered the referent of the name is a counterpart of the original referent. From this we may understand the rationale for the existence of counterparts of humans in other worlds; within the theological tradition these are called guardian angels.

The idea of rigid designation suggests that the referent of the proper name is unmoved, perhaps because the subject retains his name whether he is elected president or not. Movement and change exist within the world of possibilities, and it is there that desire makes its appearance. Something desired is precisely what one does not have; desire is lack. But if a desired situation must be brought to pass in the real, then that situation must initially be counterfactual. As we locate desire in the movable or possible part of the sentence, here the verb phrase, the question becomes whether the being or referent of the subject phrase, here the proper name, will be altered by the actualization of the possible and desired situation. In a theology where the Word or Verb has primacy over the proper name (*In principio erat Verbum* is the Latin for "In the beginning was the Word") the referent of the proper name is transformed by the power of the Verb and its referent is transported into another world. In a theory where the proper name is an unmoved mover, the primary value is placed on the idea of acting according to one's desire. The world will be altered to correspond to a desired situation, and the idea of adapting oneself to the world as it is will be rejected.

The existence of a guardian angel as your heavenly counterpart and protector would shield you from the obligation of acting on your desire, replacing it with the idea of submitting to the growth and development that occur as your life situation undergoes change. If, according to the principle of plenitude, all possibilities will eventually become actual, there is little interest in reducing the number of possibilities by acting. This principle lends itself to an ethic of acting against desire or temptation, the better to intensify passion. The purified soul thus created will have all of its accrued possibilities rendered actual in the afterlife.

Instead of seeing the distinction between masculine and feminine in terms of active and passive, we therefore propose the distinction between act and potential, or actual and possible. We have thus far taken for granted the linkage between possibility and potential. Certainly this connection has an etymological basis. And yet, the important question arises of whether the link is also functional in Aristotle. In Aristotle there are two senses of possibility: something is possible because it has been actualized and something is possible because it might be actualized (Aristotle *De Interpretatione*, 23a 5–6; in Hintikka 1973, p. 58). And he says that the two uses of the word *dynamaton* are homonymous. One of the senses has to do with the truth of a statement, the other with change or movement. It is only the latter that seems to connect with potentiality. We follow Hintikka here as he quotes a passage from the *Prior Analytics* (34a, 12ff.) to clarify the point: "We must understand the terms 'possible' and 'impossible' with respect not only to generation but also to true statement and attribution, and in all other senses in which the term 'possible' is used; for the same principle will obtain in all of them." Hintikka comments: "Possibility 'with respect to generation' is clearly that variant of the notion of possibility in which being possible presupposes coming-to-be in the sense of changing from potential to actual. Possibility with respect to true statement or to attribution is that sense of the word 'possible' in which a statement's being true at some moment of time suffices to show that it is possible (or a term's being attributable to another at some moment of time suffices to show that the attribution is possible)" (Hintikka 1973, p. 59). This shows that there is cause to connect possibility and potentiality; it does not answer whether there are possibilities or possible worlds that are never and will never be actualized, this in contradiction to the principle of plenitude.

Is the referent of a noun an essence inhering in the object named, or does the meaning of the word exist as an Idea in the supersensible world? This basic difference between Aristotle and Plato is compounded in Aristotle by the addition of modal verbs that offer among other things different dispositions of objects: the object as it is and the object as it might be. Christianity attempted to synthesize the two within the oneness of its own vision. As Henry of Ghent stated in the thirteenth century, "Possible essences, prior to their realization in individual existents, enjoy essential being from all eternity insofar as they are objects of God's knowledge" (in *The Cambridge History of Late Medieval Philosophy* [CHLMP] 1982, p. 403). These possible essences were not taken to be angels, but their location in God's mind, coupled with the time of their essential existence, suggests that they may, even if inadvertently, clarify the question of what angels are about. Whether angels are on the side of the Ideas or whether they are possibilities that have not been actualized is of major theoretical and theological importance. If the angels are something like uncreated possible people, and if they are fundamentally good, why would it be that a God who is good did not create them as people?

Here we see the importance of the idea of creation, especially creation *ex nihilo,* within the Judeo-Christian tradition. A considerable distance exists between God as creator and God as first mover. Rather than create out of nothing, the mover effects movement in what is called the first movable. However much the Judeo-Christian God was assimilated by Scholastics with the Aristotelian first mover, it remains that the idea of creation seems to lend itself more clearly to a metaphysics of Platonic Forms. Augustine was not very far off in calling Plato a near-Christian. For Aristotle God rearranges the parts of a prime matter into new forms; these forms are not the sum of their parts, as atomist philosophers would have it, but once the *telos* of such a recomposition of parts is reached, an essence is disengaged as the intelligible principle of the thing in question. How does this happen? It might happen as things receive names; thus there would be a linkage between an intelligence and a signifier. The intelligible principle of one thing must also apply to others that are the same as it, because the marking of a singular object extends to others of its kind. The thing did not exist in the mind of God as an Idea out of which the world was created or engineered according to plan. Intelligibility does not lead out of the world but permits people to navigate within it, even to modify it. A theory that says that naming a thing marks it and its kind guarantees an intelligibility within human discourse but not beyond it. So the question will be whether human existence can be effectively grounded in a language or whether it must unground itself to find a meaning and enjoyment. A consequence of the incident at Babel was the division of languages, and the introduction of an intermediary level of confusion between man and God. Thereby it was felt that no single commonly spoken language could provide access to divine Ideas, with the exception perhaps of whatever was taken to be God's mother tongue.

Not only was everyday language considered an impediment to communication with the one and only God, but local deities and the rites that were constructed to honor and worship them were also either to be absorbed into the new religion or eliminated entirely. This movement begins with Judaism and is shown in the transformation of the gods of competing tribes into angels whose function was to serve the one and only God. But the idea of a chosen people necessarily implies that there were other peoples whose fate was unenviable. With Christianity the one and only God and his one and only Son establish one religion for everyone, a religion that judges everyone, whether they know it or not. The universalization of the faith may not become actuality in the fallen world, in the world in which the sexes are divided and in which different peoples speak different languages.

For Christians this was not the most immediate requirement; the first task of the new religion was to take over the heavens. The major reason for Christianizing the heavens, converting their inhabitants to the new religion, was to have a space in which the moral vision of the Church had actually arrived at fruition and in which beings found their identity morally instead of sexually. In order to effect the transformation of the heavens, Christianity not only had to remove masculine and feminine traits, which still exist in the early representations of angels, but it was also obliged to do away with the drama, the conflict, the struggle that had characterized the world of pagan deities. These latter qualities are characteristic of a world in which the division of the sexes functions.

The problem was ultimately that the angels thus Christianized became less interesting. The last vestige of interest was philosophical and theological, but even that waned with the close of the Middle Ages, mostly because its greatest adepts were too heavily influenced by Aristotle and Averroës. The effort to reattach the angels to Aristotelian tradition had aimed at reviving interest, but only the sort of interest that could exist under the threat of censorship. When censorship is a clear and present possibility it is best to render one's thought obscure. Under the influence of the dominant Franciscan current, people aspired to become like angels, but Franciscan angels were not so much intelligences as beings of pure affect, burning with love for God, bathing in a supreme beatitude that knows no desire or conflict.

The angels, we have said, were a casualty of the Renaissance and probably also of the Black Death that marks the beginning of the end of the Middle Ages. On the one hand, one might say with Henry Corbin that the angelic theogony was simply too close to basic paganism to have survived forever. Or perhaps once William of Ockham, in the years immediately before the Plague, introduced the principle of parsimony, its application to the legions of heavenly mediators might have led to the thought that since Christ is himself a mediator why bother with several hundred billion more?

These explanations are plausible enough. The only problem is that they see things from the point of view of human being. What, after all, makes us think that this is the only point of view that counts? It may be that the angels reverted to being gods, thereby to take revenge on the Judeo-Christian West in the form of one of the worst plagues mankind has ever known. These gods, after being angelized, were the recipients of the best enjoyment that our religious tradition could offer. Perhaps it was not the right kind, or not enough.

What is interesting here is the idea that the supreme enjoyment experienced by the angels and by the saved may not be sufficient, thus that there may be a surplus enjoyment (what Lacan called a *plus-de-jouir*), which causes them to turn away from the sight of God's face. This is pointed out by Nietzsche in *On the Genealogy of Morals* (first essay, sect. 15). He finds evidence of it in Tertullian and Aquinas. We quote the Angelic Doctor: "Wherefore in order that the happiness of the saints may be more delightful to them and that they may render more copious thanks to God for it, they are allowed to see perfectly the sufferings of the damned" (ST, suppl. q. 94, art. 1). If the vision of God represents an enjoyment than which nothing greater can be conceived, to paraphrase Anselm, then when the saints turn away from God to delight in the vision of the suffering of the damned this gesture tells us that there is still something to be desired.

The worship of only one God, the pagan Celsus wrote, was an error because each god had his area of competence and performance, and the gods who were thus neglected were not likely to sit back and be rendered insipid forever (in Origen 1980, pp. 493–94). In response Origen declared the eucharist to be the proper substitute for sacrifices to local deities. His argument also shows that at the beginning of Christian apologetics the pagan gods were transformed into angels.

Celsus thinks it right to offer the due rites of worship in this life until men are set free from their bonds, as when in accordance with the popular customs one renders the sacrifices to each of the supposed gods in every city. . . . But we say that a man offers worship in this life with the due rites if he remembers who is the Creator, and what things are dear to Him, and if he does everything with regard to what God loves. Again, Celsus does not want us to be ungrateful to the earthly daemons, thinking that we owe them thank-offerings. But we, who have a clear idea of the meaning of thanksgiving (eucharistia), say to the beings who do no good whatever but are on the opposite side, that we behave without any ingratitude when we do not sacrifice to them nor worship them. . . . Therefore we do nothing wrong when we partake of the created things and fail to sacrifice to beings who have not concern with them. But if we see that it is not certain daemons, but angels who have been appointed in charge of the fruits of the earth and the birth of animals, we speak well of them and call them blessed, as they have been entrusted by God with the things beneficial to our race. (Origen 1980, p. 495)

Of course this is persuasive. And yet, the fact that the vast majority of people believes that it is the one and only God and his angels who are in charge of providing all that is good does not necessarily make it so. It is almost as though when Christianity set out to recreate the intermediary beings, it thought that if people on earth were convinced of the truth of its teaching then there would be no more gods. It was tacitly assumed that the nature of those beings was a projection of the human mind. Otherwise, why would it have been necessary to universalize the religion, to scorn the forms of worship that concerned themselves with local deities?

By the time of the Renaissance the belief seemed to be that the divine Message, the incarnate Verb, is best heard without the interference of too many messengers. The Reformation proposed that the Message was writ large in Scripture and that anyone could read it, without any intermediaries, without angels or Church Doctors or priests. Of course, the promotion of Scripture was not exactly a new idea; Western civilization has the characteristic of being based on a single book. The Reformation perceived a risk in questioning and debating the faith. How could the faith become universal if only a dozen monks could understand it? Scholasticism seemed to be introducing something of the specificity of speech, of the dialectic, of oral culture, into a world dominated by the written. Such a world privileges meaning and must revolt against the structure of the signifier. Meditate on Scripture and if your faith is not strong enough to blind you to the contradictions and ambiguities, you will eventually find that the ability to tolerate confusion is a sign of abiding faith. And if you seek an activity to bear witness to your faith, imitate the work of the prophets, the evangelists, the apostles, even Moses himself, and write texts that are clear only to those who have been touched by true belief.

One of the central questions that will track us throughout this work is the relation between the messenger and the message. If angels have to do with the stuff of language, are they signs or signifiers, and is the function of the verbal utterance to convey a meaning, to fix a referent, or to evoke a response in the listener? While we may abstract the world of words and study it in itself, the angels are not just words; they are speakers or users of language. They are not just messages, but they are also messengers. Before concluding that there is something seriously wrong and confused about this, we will say that the world of words, the world of the sentences, cannot be comprised by discussing what goes on among the words, that it is impossible to make sense of the structure of language without finding a place among the words for the speaker of that language. There may be, as Roman Jakobson proposed, an axis of combination and an axis of selection in the construction of a sentence. But do these two axes hold together without a third axis, moving in a different direction, an axis that links speaker and language? No sentence of everyday language is analyzable without its being placed in a dialogue—even if that dialogue is with an angel.

I trust that these preliminary remarks give you a sense of the scope of an inquiry into the world of the angels. I must admit that my own intellectual and practical background is not based in many of the fields that had to be covered, and I therefore required assistance in the pursuit of the research. To those who so ably provided that assistance, David Jacobson and Catherine Colardelle, I, and you, are indebted. Without their mediating efforts I would have remained ignorant of many of the issues discussed and texts referred to.

Also, I wish to acknowledge the considerable support and assistance afforded me by Kitty Moore of New York University Press. Books do not happen of themselves and they do not happen at all if the author relates only to whatever machine he has enlisted to facilitate his enterprise. An enthusiastic editor-reader is essential to the production of a book and Kitty Moore thus deserves great credit for whatever good you may find between these covers.

My experience researching this book was one that perhaps others have shared. The more deeply I examined the issues raised, the more I saw the area that would have to be covered expand. The consequence of this is the length of the present work and also a not very pleasurable awareness of all that has been left out, for reasons of ignorance more than of space. There are dozens of issues raised herein, each of which is the subject of a veritable mountain of literature. I could not and did not peruse it all. Readers who have spent more than a season of their lives with this material may find the omissions glaring or the simplifications compromising.

I have had no wish to exhaust the topic at hand, remaining true to the idea that something ought always be left to desire. This means that the mediating spirits, wherever they are, are opposed to exhaustion, and that their desire is for something other than God.

ONE

RELATIONSHIPS

Not long ago, it seems, people discovered that the path to the Supreme Good was best traveled in tandem. A couple so engaged found its union defined by a word that came to embody all that was positive in human interaction. The word was "relationship." For a time it was in everyone's mouth, not as a spice to give flavor and style, but more like ketchup, applied indiscriminately to all human commerce, generally ruining the taste. It was as though the rules, laws, and conventions of the past no longer pertained, as though we had entered a new era, an era of promise, where things people dreamed of in the past were about to be fulfilled. It may well have been that the words of Christ were coming to pass in our own new world: "for in the resurrected life, men and women do not marry; they are like the angels of God in Heaven" (Matthew 22:29).

It has been quite some time since anyone gave any serious consideration to angels. They are not, after all, central figures in the Bible; they do not belong to the first family of Christianity or Judaism; usually they are intermediaries, messengers or ministers, though at times they act as a choir or chorus. As soon as God gave up speaking directly to mortals and intervening in his person, it was necessary to have a company of angels to pass between him and his creatures. According to Augustine, among others, God never spoke directly to the patriarchs of the Old Testament; so whenever it is said that God spoke this means that angels spoke. He adds that in the New Testament it is not the angels who speak, but the Lord himself through his Word (Augustine *On the Trinity* [OT], book 3, chap. 11). The effect of such an idea is to make the angels more marginal, less necessary as intermediaries or messengers, central only in scenes before the birth of Christ, like the Annunciation. Such implications were later to haunt the West in the form of the Reformation; they were certainly not present in the writings of the Bishop of Hippo.

Eschatological theorizing is one thing; applying its results to the human world quite another. While the first application of the angelic to the human was the creation of monastic communities, this represented the removal of certain special people from the evils of the fallen world; it was not an effort to apply the principles of angelic existence to that world. The latter activity was based from the time of the early Middle Ages on the works of Dionysius the Areopagite. Georges Duby explains: "In the Acts of the Apostles 17:34, it is reported that in Athens Saint Paul converted this Dionysius, to whom he gave instruction. Legitimately, one might imagine Paul expounding to his disciple what he had seen in the third heaven. Hence it was possible to regard Dionysius, recipient of this amazing revelation, as a connoisseur of the other world" (Duby 1982, p. 111). Once the works of Dionysius were translated into Latin in the ninth century by John Scotus Erigena under the patronage of Charles the Bald, they

exerted a prodigious influence in Charles the Bald's entourage. An image of paradise thereby came to be rooted in scholarly imaginations, an image that painters worked to represent figuratively. . . . It helped focus attention on angels, which came to occupy a larger place in pious observances, and assisted Saint Michael in gradually displacing the Savior from the upper chapels to the top level of the porches. It established a peaceful and orderly setting in which eschatological dreams might unfold. For more than a century such dreams were purged of dramatic gestures and histrionic outbursts. Thanks to a knowledge of the works of Dionysius, the Heavenly Jerusalem could truly seem a "vision of peace," a model of that order that kings were being pressed to maintain on earth. (Duby 1982, p. 112)

The influence of Dionysius was no less powerful in theological speculation. A brief glance at Aquinas's *Concerning Spiritual Creatures* shows that time and again the Angelic Doctor invokes the words of Dionysius as definitive and authoritative.

For the moment, however, let us go back in time to third-century Alexandria, to study some early ideas of how the angelic mingled with the human. One of the first Christian authors on this topic, Origen, saw in the angels the ministers of the Church, in the same company as the prophets and the saints. In his commentary on the Song of Songs he identified them with the friends of the bride and bridegroom, of the Church and Christ. Thereby, their role would only be preliminary to a final consummation (Origen 1956, p. 150). In another text he compared the ministry of angels to that of the physician and that of the man offering charity. Here, through metaphor, Origen showed how the angelic functions in human situations.

At the very time of prayer the angels are reminded by the one praying of what he needs, and they accomplish what they are able to do as those who have received a universal order. The following metaphors will be useful with respect to this point and will make my idea acceptable. Imagine that a physician who has his mind set on righteousness comes to a sick man praying for health. And suppose that he knows how the patient may be healed of the disease about which he is praying. It is obvious that he will be moved to heal the man praying, perhaps supposing not in vain that this very thing is God's intention and that God has heard the prayer of the man praying for deliverance from his disease. Or imagine that a man who has more than he needs for life and is generous hears the prayer of a poor man who is making intercession to God for his needs. It is obvious that he will fulfill the requests of the poor man's prayer, and will become a minister of the Father's will. (Origen 1979, p. 103)

Certain human activities, not chosen haphazardly, are elevated to the rank of the angelic. And it is interesting to note that the angelic is identified with the ability to respond to a demand that expresses a need. Angels respond to demands for love when those demands are based on genuine need. The love in question is charitable, it has nothing to do with the erotic or with desire. Many authors raise the question of whether angels are creatures of love or desire, and if of either, of what kind. It is important that one of the essential differences between the Christian angels and the pagan gods and demons is the absence of erotic desire in the former, its presence in the latter. And yet, there are enough writings where Christian angels are said to be desirous of union with God. The use of the term *desire* in such texts is to my mind misleading; the concept of the angelic ministry is more accurately expressed in the above passage from Origen, despite the fact that Origen was much disputed and even reviled by later Christian writers.

Origen was also one of the first Christian authors to introduce the question of whether the soul should model her progress on the being of the angels:

And the soul, pursuing this knowledge of herself, may further ask if there is some other class of beings, whether there are some spirits of the same sort of nature as herself, and other spirits too, that are not as she, but different from her: that is to say, are there not only some other spirits possessing reason as she does herself, but also some lacking reason? And is her nature the same as that of the angels—for it is generally though that one sort of rationality cannot by any means differ from another? And, if she is not such as they by nature, will she, if she be worthy, be made so by grace? Or can she not in any case be made like the angels, if the character and make-up of her nature have not received this form? For one would think it possible for that which has been lost to be restored, but not for that to be bestowed which the Creator did not give in the beginning. (Origen 1956, p. 136)

The introduction of the comparison of the soul to angels has led some to the idea that is is intrinsically good to model one's life and spiritual development on that of the angels. It is also significant that the soul is designated as female.

Beginning around the fourth century A.D. with Gregory of Nazianus and Gregory of Nyssa, extending through Augustine and Dionysius the Areopagite, and reaching an apotheosis in the thirteenth century with Thomas Aquinas, angels came to take on more and more importance, to constitute a world, or better, to constitute the vast majority of the inhabitants of the Heavenly City. For those suffering from anxiety about the immanent Second Coming of Christ, the angels represented the model upon which human relationships had to be based. From the time of Paul Christianity had never been very well disposed to marriage; as is the case with some more modern thinkers, marriage was a compromise entered into by those who were morally inferior and who did not wish to be among the first to enter Heaven. A stronger statement was penned by Gregory of Nyssa in his *Treatise of Virginity*. There he argued throughout that all of the ills and absurdities of life originate in marriage. And most of the ills he lists are experienced by women: the dangers of childbirth, worry about children, the misfortune of widowhood. To renounce marriage was to live the life of the angels.

As Georges Duby has reported, the Church did not take control of the institution of marriage, did not make it a sacrament until the Middle Ages, and even then did so under some duress. The strain was caused not only by the conflicting claims of kings and Church, but also on theological grounds (Duby 1983). The superior path was toward perfection on earth, toward the perfectability of human relationships. This was where the angels became important: they represented the model for the perfect relationship, a relationship that necessarily excluded marriage. The problem was to know what was going on among the angels, and this was not every easy to discern.

According to Aquinas, who seems to have exhausted this among other questions, angels were immaterial, spiritual, self-subsistent forms and intelligences who lived in another world as invisible beings. For a definition he quoted the eighth-century saint John Damascene: "An angel is an intellectual substance, always mobile, free in its will, incorporeal, serving God, receiving immortality in consequence of grace (not by nature)" (in Aquinas CSC, p. 87). Definitions are of course rather dry; they do not impart the splendor and glory of the world of the angels. For a vision of that we turn to Gregory of Nazianus, a fourth-century Church Father. The following long and intricate passage conveys a sense of the expansive prose that was required to sell the angels to the world.

The angel is then called spirit and fire: spirit, as being a creature of the intellectual sphere; fire, as being of a purifying nature; for I know that the same names belong to the first nature. But, relatively to us at least, we must reckon the angelic nature incorporeal, or at any rate as nearly so as possible. Do you see how we get dizzy over this subject, and cannot advance to any point, unless it be as far as this, that we know there are angels and archangels, thrones, dominions, princedoms, powers, splendors, ascents, intelligent powers or intelligences, pure nature and unalloyed, immovable to evil, or scarcely movable; ever circling in chorus around the first cause (or how should we sing their praises?), illuminated thence with the purest illumination, or one in one degree and one in another, proportionally to their nature and rank ... so conformed to beauty and molded that they become secondary lights, and can enlighten others by the overflowings and largesses of the first light? Ministrants of God's will, strong with both inborn and imparted strength, traversing all space, readily present to all at any place through their zeal for ministry and the agility of their nature ... different individuals of them embracing different parts of the world, or appointed over different districts of the universe, as He knows who ordered and distributed it all. Combining all things in one, solely with a view to the consent of the Creator of all things; hymners of the majesty of the Godhead, eternally contemplating the eternal glory, for nothing can be added to that which is full—to him who supplies good to all outside himself—but that there may never be a cessation of blessings of these first natures after God. (in Hardy 1954, pp. 158–59)

Here we see the dizziness of the soul enraptured by the contemplation of the world of the angels. There is light and music, the illuminations and harmonies of a perfect union of the aural and the visual in a love that is constant, perpetual, and blessed. At the same time the angels are assimilated to the Aristotelian intelligences, the unmoved movers who are responsible for the movement of the spheres.

Another text by Gregory of Nazianus gives a sense of how angels relate to each other, and of how humans may do exactly the same. Notice how the angelic and the mental are mixed and mingled here; also how the mental is considered to be of the order of the aesthetic.

But if you will look at what is mental and incorporeal, remember that I in my one personality can contain soul and reason and mind and the Holy Spirit; and before me this world, by which I mean the system of things visible and invisible, contained Father, Son, and Holy Ghost. For such is the nature of intellectual existences, that they can mingle with one another and with bodies, incorporeally and invisibly. For many sounds are comprehended by one ear; and the eyes of many are occupied by the same visible objects, and the smell by odors; nor are the senses narrowed by each other, or crowded out, nor the objects of sense diminished by the multitude of the perceptions. But where is the mind of man or angel so perfect in comparison of the Godhead that the presence of the greater must crowd out the other? (in Hardy 1954, p. 219)

This offers a sense of the kind of relating that may go on between the angels and also between humans raised to the power of the angelic. The vision of Gregory is richer and more vast than what our contemporaries may seek in what they call a relationship, but that may simply be a function of the relative impoverishment of the intellectual and spiritual capacities of our time.

For the implications of these and other similar conceptions of the angelic existence we turn again to Georges Duby. Here is how this existence became translated into the life of the monastery. "The monastic world did not seek to rationalize its faith; instead, it strove to stimulate that faith through the collective wonderment that filled the persons who celebrated mass. It was not concerned with causes, effects, or proofs, only with communicating with the invisible, and believed that nothing led to that goal more directly than the experience of choral liturgy" (Duby 1981, p. 73). This was not the only type of activity that went on in monasteries. There existed a more virile mode of relating connected with the advent of Scholasticism. The contrast is telling:

Inside the monasteries, and even at Saint-Denis, studying was no open-ended exercise. It rested entirely on contemplation, on solitary meditation over a sacred text and on the mind's slow advance over a path marked out with symbols and analogies. In other words, it differed little from prayer and choral singing. But in Chartres, Laon, and Paris, on the contrary, the same dynamic spirit that led businessmen into commercial ventures lured young clergymen into mental conquests. They not only read and meditated, they debated. Masters and students faced each other in verbal jousts—and it was not always the masters who came out victorious. The cathedral schools were lists, the scene of intellectual exploits that were as thrilling as military exploits and, like them, prepared the combatants to take over the world. As a young man, Abélard had distinguished himself in such tournaments. His victories brought him—as to a heroic knight—glory, money, and womanly love. (Duby 1981, p. 114)

While the dominant discourse on angels rejects the clear association of the angelic with such virile pursuits as commerce and jousting, there are nonetheless sufficient significant references to the angels as an army for us to take note. The battle between the good angels, faithful to God, and the bad angels, followers of Satan, was reasonably standard fare. Yet, to the extent that the Heavenly City was maternalized, to the extent that it had a Queen in the Virgin, these references became less important and less imposing. Eventually, too many of the qualities associated with angelic masculinity became connected with devils, and from there it was not too difficult to eliminate them from Jerusalem. It may have been reasonable for the angelic legions of Christ to do battle, but it was never acceptable that these same legions have carnal intercourse with a female being.

For the most part angels were not considered to be divided according to sex. As invisible beings they were bodiless and thus not sexed. So while there are numerous instances of angelic masculinity and even remnants of the divisions that divided the world of pagan gods and goddesses, these should not be considered to be part of the angelic. Angels are undivided and indivisible in the sense of being individuals. If they relate to each other, this can only be a function of their common experience of the same maternal space. It is well and good to consider angels to be sons of God, but if the principle of the division of the sexes is a primary feature of the Law of a father, and if that Law defines relationships in terms of kinship before all else, then this God may ultimately be the Great Mother.

Skipping over several centuries and arriving at Aquinas, we find many of the same questions raised, but without the incessant aspiration to approach the angelic through the aesthetic. Relying for the most part on his incomparable intelligence, Aquinas took the issues one by one, weighed carefully the diverse opinions on each matter, and offered an answer that was intended not only to respond to the requirements of faith, but also to satisfy the intellect. Thus the fact that invisible, incorporeal angels had a tendency to manifest themselves in visible form was for him (and others) a significant question. Aquinas rested his analysis on the idea of the assumption of a body by an angel. He went on to question the differences between the assumed body of an angel and the real body of a human being, explaining that even though some angels took on a visible form to carry a message to a mortal, this visible form did not have the same substance or consistency as human flesh. Angels, he said, have no use for food in their assumed bodies, and if they have generative organs these organs are certainly not used for generation. Angels are pure minds or intelligences and have knowledge as their birthright. This in opposition to humans who may gain equal status with angels in the Heavenly City if they are saints, but who are distinguished for having lived for some time with a corrupt body, and for having used the senses of this body to acquire knowledge.

More to the purpose of defining relations, Aquinas said that angels can communicate with other angels, and that for this they do not need to use speech. They are capable of communicating intelligible content directly without passing through the medium of language. To me this seems closer to telepathy than to empathy. "And by the fact that the concept of the angelic mind is ordered to be made known to another by the will of the angel himself, the concept of one angel is made known to another; and in this way one angel speaks to another; for to speak to another only means to make known the mental concept to another" (Aquinas ST, part 1, q. 107, art. 1). And using this definition of angelic communication, Aquinas could add one to the effect that the true function of human speech should transcend the constraints of natural language. This is hardly an original idea; it worth noting nonetheless. As for the affective link between angels, Aquinas said that it began with love of self, as it does with men. "Consequently both angel and man naturally seek their own good and perfection. This is to love self. Hence angel and man naturally love self, in so far as by natural appetite each desires what is good for self" (Aquinas ST, part 1, q. 60, art. 3). The identification of desire with appetite is questionable, as we will see later; even more questionable is the idea that desire aims toward the good. Ultimately, this is based on the idea that the goal of desire is to reach the Supreme Good. We would say that whatever is loved is elevated to the rank of a supreme good whose function is to annihilate desire by filling it beyond all measure. You may believe that this is an unrealistic goal—and this is not the strongest objection to the idea—but, after all, that is one of the reasons why it is seen to exist in its perfection only among the angels.

Thus both angel and man love God before self: "Consequently, since God is the universal good and under this good both man and angel and all creatures are comprised, because every creature in regard to its entire being naturally belongs to God, it follows that from natural love angel and man alike love God before themselves and with a greater love. Otherwise, if either of them loved self more than God, it would follow that natural love would be perverse and would not be perfected but destroyed by charity" (Aquinas ST, part 1, q. 60, art. 5). What does this tell us about relationships? Not simply that there is something larger than self that is involved in self-to-self relationships. Rather, the dualism that sees relationships as existing between two people or two angels ought to be understood as requiring the aegis of a third party, either God or an ideal, which is in fact the first object of the love that exists between the two people. People only imagine that they are trying to learn to relate to each other; it often happens that people involved in relationships have no idea whatever of what is going on with the other person. Instead, they are each separately trying to respond to the requirements of healthy and wholesome relating, in the hope that if they learn how to relate, that some sort of supernatural charity will descend upon them to render the relationship perfect.

Natural love in an angel is not the same as in a human being. Besides, there is every chance that the term *nature* may be confusing here. Different beings, Aquinas said, have different natures. An angel has an intellectual and not a sensitive nature. His knowledge does not proceed from the intermediary of sense impression, but is purely a function of his mind. "But it is common to every nature to have some inclination; and this is its natural appetite or love. This inclination is found to exist differently in different natures; but in each according to its mode. Consequently in the intellectual nature there is to be found a natural inclination coming from the will; in the sensitive nature, according to the sensitive appetite; but in a nature devoid of knowledge, only according to the tendency of the nature to something. Therefore, since an angel is an intellectual nature, there must be a natural love in his will" (Aquinas ST, part 1, q. 60, art. 1). So one angel will love another angel because he has a nature in common with him. To love another for what you have in common is not the same as to love someone for what divides you. To learn to relate to another is to found love on a common nature; for humans this may be an intellectual nature or else it may be a common affective nature, an affinity of souls. If, in a relationship, you hold the other person's mind in highest value, disregarding whatever it is that designates sexual difference to the senses, then you are closer to what is going on among Aquinas's angels.

But angels are undivided, and one of the reasons for this is that they are beings of love. A simple way of understanding the principle of indivision is to see that their loyalties are consistent and unique. Like the inhabitants of monasteries, whose separation from the outside world removed them from conflicting loyalties, removed them in principle from having to compromise with the evil without, angels represent a principle of oneness as unity. "Now, what is one with a thing, is that thing itself; consequently every thing loves what is one with itself. So, if this be one with it by natural union, it loves it with natural love; but if it be one with it by non-natural union, then it loves it with non-natural love. Thus a man loves his fellow townsmen with a social love, while he loves a blood relation with natural affection, in so far as he is one with him in the principle of natural generation. . . . And so everything loves another which is one with it in species, with a natural affection, in so far as it loves its own species. . . . So then, it must be said that one angel loves another with natural affection, in so far as he is one with him in nature. But so far as he has something else in common with another angel, or differs with him in other respects, he does not love him with natural love" (Aquinas ST, part 1, q. 60, art. 4). There are several important points here. The principle controlling relations between angels is that of union, of unification through the function of will. One intellect or intelligence unites with another naturally because it wills the same. There are no impediments to such a union, no obstacles, and in fact, no desire in the sense of wanting something other than what is conceived in the intellect. Despite the fact that the angel is of an intellectual nature, he unites with another angel with natural affection, with the type of affection that is consistent with an intellectual nature, but only insofar as he has things in common with him. In other words, the tie of natural affection is based on similarity, resemblance, even equality.

Here Aquinas introduced a fundamental distinction between humans and angels that is worth following closely. The difference is simply that human beings tend to love each other because they belong to the same species. Thereby, as he said, they are united for the purpose of reproducing the species, of generating new members. This is a link of blood, and he distinguished it from social ties between inhabitants of the same city. The problem here is that by definition husband and wife are not blood relations; their "union" is contracted socially. Only in the production of children are they joined through blood relations.

To base the idea of relationships solely on a common nature is limiting because it is too general. It excludes everything that is specific to the other individual, everything that differentiates the two of you. Similarly, to found a relationship between undivided self-subsistent beings on self-love incurs the risk of reducing love to narcissism. Thus to extend the idea of relationship between or among angels it is necessary to introduce a difference, not only between angels but between angels and humans. If human love is contaminated by the process of reproduction, and if that process has something to do with belonging to the same species, angels have a more perfect love in not belonging to the same species. Angels, Aquinas said, do not belong to the same species, and therefore their love for their fellows is qualitatively different. The idea that each angel is of a different species, besides being difficult to grasp, was condemned by the Bishop of Paris in 1277.

Be that as it may, here is one definition of the difference. Angels, being of different species, love each other more than can humans. An angel loves another with a love that has universal meaning, not simply meaning within a specific locality. "Consequently, they love one another more if they differ in species, which pertains rather to the perfection of the universe . . . than if they were to agree in species, which would pertain to the private good of a single species" (Aquinas CSC, p. 94). This is hardly a simple idea. The complications inherent in the notion of *species* require considerable elaboration, both here and elsewhere. To begin with the level most easily available to understanding, note that in the animal world "a group of individuals of one species is necessary in order that the specific nature, which cannot be perpetually conserved in one individual being because of its corruptibility, may be conserved in many" (Aquinas CSC, p. 92). No one member of a species contains in itself the perfection of the nature of the species, its specific nature—not in the sense of what may identify it as belonging to the species, but what corresponds to the perfected or ideal type, the *telos,* of the individual beings. Species, then, is among the traits required to specify the nature of a particular object or thing or living being. Gaining knowledge is acquiring the specifying traits in question. These are abstracted from the particular object, but knowledge gained is not knowledge of that particular object. The knowledge is constituted of what may be correctly predicated of a substance. Aside from species the other forms of predicates are genus, difference, property, and accident. These are called universals because each may be predicated of many objects. The species "whiteness" can be applied to many objects, as can the genus "animal," and so on.

Now to the world of higher objects:

But in the higher part of the universe a higher degree of perfection is found, wherein one individual being, such as the sun, is so perfect that it lacks none of the things that pertain to its own species, and hence also the whole matter of the species is contained in one individual being; and the same is true of the other heavenly bodies. Much more so, therefore, this perfection is found in the highest part of created things which is nearer to God, namely, among the angels: that one individual lacks none of the things which pertain to the whole species, and thus there are not several individuals in one species. But God, who is at the summit of perfection, does not agree with any other being, not only in species, but not even in genus, nor in any other universal predicate. (Aquinas CSC, p. 92)

Does this tell us why two beings, each of which is a species in itself, love each other more than two beings who both belong to the same species? Or why people tend to believe that if they become whole, complete, and autonomous as Selfs, that they will thereby be better able to love other whole, complete, autonomous Selfs? The answer may simply be that in the state of perfection and in the bliss that must accompany it, the individual who is a species in himself will not want for anything from the other, will not desire anything from that other, not even to reproduce the species.

What connects the angels, Aquinas wrote, is their not belonging to the same species; rather, it is "the single mode of their relation to beatitude." "As for the order of beatitude, human nature is contrasted with the whole angelic nature, because the whole angelic nature is naturally such as has been produced to attain to beatitude or to fall short of it in one single way, irreparably, namely, right at the first choice; but human nature, in the course of time" (Aquinas CSC, p. 93). The relation to beatitude is not the same as a relation to desire. Beatitude, which we will also have occasion to call enjoyment or, in French, *jouissance,* is something that angels bathe in. It involves complete and perfect self-possession and is consequent on the elimination of any principle of division. Instead of having a division among the angels in which one is mover and the other moved, where their relation comports desire, the experience of enjoyment that results from the angel's seeing God face-to-face is extended to the mode of relation between different angels. There will be attempts to admit desire into the world of the angels and humans, but when it is identified with appetite it becomes a natural function of a being, not a lack. Angels are said to have a desire or an appetite for God, not because of a lack that seeks something that it does not have from someone else, but because this experience of beatitude or enjoyment requires feeding. Certainly relationships, taken as an ideal, are ordered toward beatitude or toward the earthly equivalent, which Leibniz said was happiness.

Medieval thinkers did not reach the level of obtuseness required to believe that the enjoyment of beatitude could be attained interpersonally. For that at least we may be thankful.

Up to now we have avoided many of the difficulties inherent in this concept. A species or specifier is a characteristic of an object that distinguishes it from others while at the same time connecting it with those that share the specifying trait. A species is a predicate; it determines what may be said of a substance, thus what we are permitted to know of the substance. While it is part of the verb phrase, it may be seen as linked to the substantive by the verb, especially where the verb is a copula. The verb phrase would then be composed of the verb and its predicates, and this is analogous to the relation between the Verb, that is, Christ, and the angels. God is the subject, Christ is the verb, and the angels are the predicates or universals. Once this is said, you can see the importance of the debate between nominalism and realism. The nominalists, led by William of Ockham, held that the universals were not real, but were intentions of the human soul. The realists believed that the universals were real and were what was most real. The issue applies or at least may be applied to the existence of angels. But our view is that the angels are in effect neither. The debate between nominalists and realists concerned the status of meanings; for us angels are of the order of the signifier, thus they have the status of symbols. They are not, therefore, universal but are local forms, inseparable from language.

There are a prodigious number of things about which it is correct to predicate roundness or squareness or flatness. If you add edible and redness to roundness you have further delimited the substances you may be talking about. While each universal may be predicated of many substances, it seems fair to say that a combination may end up identifying a particular substance. This idea suggests that a singular substance is the sum of its predicates, and that to know what the substance is it is necessary to know everything that may be predicated of it. Now this leads to two conclusions: first, that the true concept of a substance contains all of its predicates, thus that to know the latter is to know the former; second, that the universals that are correctly predicated of a single substance have some sort of relationship or togetherness. All of which is extremely debatable. For the moment I present things this way in order to render what follows intelligible. This is especially important where Aquinas tried to assimilate the angels to species and by extension to the world of the Platonic forms. Each form, like each angel, is a species in itself. (And note also that Duns Scotus called angels "immaterial forms.") (Duns Scotus 1975, p. 235).

So Aquinas took *human nature* and *whiteness* as species and compared them to angels: "Now if an angel is a simple form set apart from matter, it is impossible even to conceive several angels of one species; because any form whatever, however material and low, if it be set down as abstract either in actual being or in the intellect remains but one form in one species. For let 'whiteness' be understood as subsisting apart from every subject and it will not be possible to posit many whitenesses, since we see that 'this whiteness' does not differ from 'that whiteness' save through the fact that it is in this or in that subject. In similar fashion, if there were an abstract 'human nature,' there would be but one only" (Aquinas CSC, p. 90). The identification of angels with predicable species, with what we may consider to be forms abstracted from their manifestations or instances, points toward important epistemological and semantic problems. A guideline for following the argument is the idea that the meaning of words, especially as it could be abstracted from the particularities of the language in which it was expressed, was considered to be directly linked to "the ontological status—the existence— of things" (Bloch 1986b, p. 85). For the moment note that the angels of Aquinas are here on the side of the predicate, not of the grammatical subject of a sentence. This is not the entirety of his position, since he also saw angels as Aristotelian intelligences, which are separate substances.

We have said that several universals may be predicated of a single subject. Writing in the sixth century, Cassiodorus stated: "For once we have first set down the genus, we then subjoin the species and the other things that are possibly related; then by setting aside the common qualities we make distinctions, continually interpreting differences until we arrive at the proper quality of that which we are examining, its meaning being made definite, as for example: Man is a rational, mortal, biped animal, capable of laughter" (in Bloch 1986b, p. 51). In one sense angels may be seen as emanations proceeding or generated by god, thus a function of god as substance. Their mode of relating with each other would then be a function of their connection with God. While Christ as Verb is connected with God as His Son, the angels are connected in the sense that they are called sons of God. This being given, we ask how these different species relate to each other. The first point is that they are all predicates; all are on the side of the verb phrase. Are all correct predicates of a subject contained within that subject, that is, does the name control or dictate the predicates, or do the predicates in some way subsume the subject, in the sense that it is nothing without them? In either case, the different species relate to each other through their relationship with a superior instance, in this case God. If, however, all predicates are contained within the substantive, this suggests that the substantive has a function that is best considered to be maternal. In fact, one medieval doctor, Alain of Lille, asserted that the noun was in the position of the feminine sex. We will return to this point in a later chapter. The salient point now is that whatever is going on between the subject and its predicates has nothing to do with the division of the sexes, or, as it appears, with any division. To respect the concept of division is to say that the cut between the substantive and its predicates is irreducible, that from a cluster of predicates you cannot get to the substance. The goal of having the predicates of a substance contained within the substance is to heal that division.

Such questions are large and very difficult. Consider the following. If the statement of Cassiodorus is transformed into a question, it will read as follows: What is a rational, mortal, biped animal, capable of laughter? If the group of predicates is sufficiently definite, you are obliged to offer one and only one answer. There is no ambiguity, no equivocation, and also no need to know anything more than the standard and most common meanings of the terms. All of the predicates are contained in the concept of man, but they may also be connected in other combinations to define different substantives. A significant difference is introduced with the following: What walks on four feet in the morning, two feet in the afternoon, and three feet in the evening? Here again the answer is supposed to be man, but the form of the question is a riddle or an enigma. This means that the correct answer is not available to many people, and that there is some uncertainty about why the sphinx is posing the riddle. This aims at the question of the sphinx's desire, and there is the further idea that if the listener is not moved to provide the correct answer he will be moved from the realm of the living to that of the dead. The reasoning involved here requires a grasp of the metaphoric expression of the ages of a man's life. As I have mentioned elsewhere, the answer might just as well be Oedipus. This through the relation of the last syllable of his name with the word for foot. My point here concerns the famous distinction between seeing God face-to-face and seeing through a glass darkly, especially as the latter is often understood as seeing in an enigma. Since seeing God's face is limited to angels, the effort to create a logic that defines out enigmas aims at the human version of angelic intelligence.

To say that what is involved here concerns questions of sexual difference requires a considerable stretching of the imagination. In a divine world where marriage does not exist, where relations are not based on kinship structures that label people according to only one of the two sexes, it seems unnecessary to see relationships as having anything to do with a division of the sexes. And yet, a strange problem arises when we reflect on the fact that angels were thought to move heavenly bodies. Between angels and celestial bodies there is something of a division of the sexes, this through the assimilation of the angels with Aristotle's intelligences. Complicating details are first that for Aristotle some heavenly bodies did have minds, thus were capable of moving themselves, while others did not; and second that all humans have both bodies and minds, thus do not seem to be subject to the same division. Among humans, Aquinas asserted, the soul is united with the body; it is both the mover and the form of the body, and it requires the body to gain knowledge through a process of abstracting from sensible impressions. As concerns movement, a human being is a self-moved mover, with the soul moving the body. The minds that move the heavenly bodies are different for being without sensation and imagination; their functions are to move and to understand (Wolfson 1973, pp. 48–49).

What is involved here is a definition of a division of the sexes in another world, in a world not inhabited by human beings. The problem then concerns how these principles are mapped onto the relations between the sexes, especially where both men and women have both minds and bodies. Certainly it is unacceptable to say that in the division of the sexes men are minds and women bodies. A preferable formulation may be that when it comes to sensual enjoyment, a woman is moved by something outside of herself, a mind that is not her own, to the extent that she allows this to happen, whereas a man as mover causes or produces movement in a woman to the extent that he is not moved by her. I offer this as a preliminary formulation, subject to elaboration.

Whatever the relation between angels and celestial bodies, it is not the same as the relationship between angels. Nor does it correspond to a marriage, because the connection or union between the two is transitory. It "seems incongruous that some angels should be perpetually assigned to some bodies" (Aquinas CSC, p. 76). Whereas a soul is always assigned to the same body, so long as that body is alive, providing both the body's form and its movement, an angel and a celestial body come together only for the purpose of movement (Aquinas CSC, p. 80). Aquinas did not believe that the interaction of angels and celestial bodies served the purpose of the creation of new beings, of generation and corruption, because, following Aristotle, he did not accept that eternal bodies had any need to reproduce themselves to preserve the species.

Neither did he hold that the angels move these bodies simply for the sake of moving them. "One should say then that the movement of the heavens comes from some intelligent substance. For the end of this movement can only be a certain abstract intelligible good, for the sake of which the intelligent substance which moves the heavens does its moving, namely, in order that it may take on a likeness of that good in its working and in order that what is virtually contained in that intelligible good may be made explicit in act; and especially the filling up of the number of the Elect, for whose sake all other things seem to exist" (Aquinas CSC, p. 78). To approach this text we cite the gloss of the translator: "The moving angel, understanding and desiring some higher good (whether God or a higher angel), aims at assimilating himself to that good in his activity, by producing the most perfect movement of his own sphere, that is, the circular, by which movement the process of generation and corruption is carried forward in this sublunar world, particularly the generation and evolution of men, in order that the number of the Elect may be completed" (in Aquinas CSC, p. 78n.).

This passage provides both confirmation of the fact that something of the principle of the division and attraction of the sexes is being written into the heavens, and a sense of the way in which this principle is related to the sexual activity of human beings. Humans copulate to produce other human beings; this is a standard reading of the sexual act within the theological tradition. But the production of new humans is not an end in itself; rather it opens the possibility for the production of souls who will ascend to a place in Heaven, to fill the places left empty by the fall of the rebel angels. In effect, this is what adds the quality of goodness to the sexual activity of humans. Another reading may be that humans ought to follow the principle of the interaction of angels and heavenly bodies and therefore not reproduce at all. Those who were most apt to enter the kingdom of Heaven were, after all, virgins. The refusal to reproduce creates in those who assume it the state of soul in which the soul is most apt to rise to Heaven.

On the other hand the relation between intelligences and heavenly bodies reads generally like an erotic; it concerns desire directly and lends itself to sexual activity in which reproduction is not the goal or the redeeming virtue. This point would have been congenial to the Arab commentators of Aristotle and not to the Angelic Doctor. Here we find alternate readings that each make sense. While our own reading of the existence of a division in the heavens that corresponds to the division of the sexes is in some sense warranted, it seems unlikely that Aquinas or a latter-day Thomist would accept it. Pagans, as opposed to Christians, saw marriage as existing in the heavens; they also saw drama involved in the relations between the sexes. However much Christianity adopted pagan views in identifying the angels with the intelligences and the forms, it did not explicitly accept a sexual division into the world of angels.

The question of the sex of the angels is neither small nor trivial. Here we have seen one way angels are given, consciously or unconsciously, a masculine role. At the same time there are aspects of the masculine role, having and deploying a phallic appendage, which are clearly excluded from God's holy angels. Yet, the angel is consistently assimilated to the functions of the human soul. In some authors the soul is simply another angelic form, having an affective and intellectual side; in others, among them Aquinas, the angel comprises only part of the functions of the human soul, those that concern intelligence and will, while others, which have to do with the uniting of soul with body (e.g., the sensitive side), have no angelic correlate. Not only is the soul, as we have noted, a feminine noun taking a feminine pronoun, but its capacity of becoming married to Christ places it in a distinctly feminine position in relation to God the Son. We have seen this in Origen, and it is also evident in Gregory of Nyssa. To reach her bridegroom the human soul is obliged to follow the Platonic model and put on wings. We must add that the Platonic vision of the soul as charioteer driving across the sky emphasizes the masculine, whereas the Christian soul is feminine. (On the masculinity of the Platonic *psyche* see Kristeva 1983, p. 65.) We will see that cloistered nuns were considered to be one of the most important manifestations of the angelic. Finally, when you examine most medieval visual representations of angels, you will note that their form is usually androgynous. In scenes of the Annunciation, Gabriel is obviously not very virile, and he often appears to have many facial characteristics in common with the Virgin. It is not until the Renaissance that we see woman and children angels in art. According to Berefelt, this means that the interest in angels was on the wane (Berefelt 1968, chap. 7).

Another way of approaching the question of whether angels represent masculine or feminine roles is the following. According to tradition the holy angels are not endowed with phallic appendages. Is the enjoyment or *jouissance* that they experience thereby other than phallic? Are they, for example, phalloi (being what they do not have), or are they endowed with an enjoyment that is beyond the phallus, being of the soul, or being purely affective? If we assume that men experience phallic enjoyment and that women may experience another kind, does the enjoyment experienced by intermediary beings hook into the human body by coming to inhabit the male sexual organ—taken thus as having an enjoyment that is separate from that of the body, because elevated from an organic to a signifying function—or does it communicate with the female body in an experience where sensual enjoyment is not localized but is generalized? My view is that if angels are signifiers, then their enjoyment is phallic. If, however, they are like souls and if their enjoyment consists in their being moved, in their constant mobility, then they are feminine beings whose enjoyment is beyond the phallus. This is the view that is central to the mystical tradition in Christianity.

For the moment we will depart from theological tradition to raise questions of a purely speculative nature. A soul that takes its place in the Heavenly City is not the same as an angel that has always been there. While the soul is, with some consistency, considered to be feminine, the angels are usually represented or thought of in masculine terms. If the soul is feminine then this tells us that the feminine is universal, common to both men and women. Women thereby are in closer touch with this side of human character that aspires to the good. This view is most prevalent in mystical texts. It represents a major shift from the view that something traditionally associated with masculinity, intelligence or mind, is common to both sexes. There masculinity exists in the exclusion of the feminine, and ethical principles would be based on something other than the aspiration toward the good.

We might wonder whether there is any pairing of feminine souls with masculine angels in the afterlife. The answer is clearly that there is not; all Christian souls seek their bridegroom in Christ, not in his angelic imitators, almost as though they were members of the ultimate harem. We know also that Christianity holds a belief in the resurrection of the body, the reunification of the soul with a perfected body at the end of time. And these bodies, being of the same form as a natural body, do have sexual organs. It happens that these organs are not sexually functional; they are there for aesthetic contemplation. The enjoyment experienced by these bodies is therefore feminine; it is an enjoyment of the whole body, not that of one of its separated parts. There is no desire in the resurrected life.

This leads to a curious reflection: is the relationship between the soul and the resurrected body similar to the relation we have discussed between the angel and the celestial body? What would the relationship be between the angels, who will never have a body in the resurrected life, and those company of the blessed who will become resurrected body and soul? Ought we to see the division between angels and the saved as a division of the sexes? If we do so, and if the angels are in a position that is masculine, then the saved must be on the side of the feminine. To the best of my knowledge these issues were not addressed as such by Christian theologians. It was hardly in their interest to write a division of the sexes into the heavens at the end of time. And yet the theories do seem to provide at least some support to such speculations, demonstrating that it is not all that easy to eliminate the division of the sexes. On the side of Christianity, no matter what the constitution of the beings who will come to inhabit the City of God at the end of time it is certain that there will be no erotic desire in the heavens. Commenting on the Song of Songs, Gregory of Nyssa wrote in the fourth century: "So too here the sacred text uses expressions the obvious meaning of which would suggest carnal passion; and yet it does not slip into any improper meaning, but rather uses such words to instruct us by chaste concepts in the life that is divine. And in doing this it shows us that we are no longer to be men, with a nature composed of flesh and blood. Rather, it points to that life we hope to attain at the resurrection of the saints, a life like that of the angels, free from all concupiscence" (Gregory 1979, p. 155).

Continuing, Gregory showed how it will be in the afterlife when the division of the sexes is transcended through the eradication of values most often associated with masculinity—war and capture. The feminine soul will no longer be conquered and captured by the masculine propensity to sin and concupiscence. "After the resurrection, when our bodies will be reunited to our souls, they will be incorruptible; and the carnal passions which disturb us now will not be present in those bodies; we shall enjoy a peaceful equilibrium in which the prudence of the flesh will not make war upon the soul; and there will no longer be that internal warfare wherein sinful passions fight against *the law of the mind*, conquering the soul and taking it captive by sin" (Gregory 1979, p. 155).

The problem with reading a division of the sexes into such a text is that one might just as well believe that the law of the mind or soul, which is promoted against sinful passions, represents a masculine principle that ought to win out over feminine tendencies toward the erotic. There is more than sufficient evidence in the writings of the Church Fathers to show a horror with the erotic tendencies of women. Unfortunately for this reading the flesh is a warrior in the passage; thereby the ordinary association of masculinity with mind and femininity with flesh has been effectively reversed.

What is eliminated, of course, is the masculine. In the resurrected life the division of the sexes does not pertain, having been sundered in the name of a peaceful equilibrium or equality, having been absorbed in a maternal space. Thus women who are virgins or who are identified only as mothers are elevated in value, while those who wish to be attractive to men are attacked with uncommon fury. There is a world, ours, in which the sexes are divided; to renounce such a world is to oppose both masculinity and femininity, or more precisely, to oppose the paternal law that dictates the division in these terms. Clearly enough the Heavenly City abolishes the division of the sexes in the name of their equality, with a bias toward the feminine capacity for moral virtue, especially virginity. Gregory of Nazianus explicitly privileged the moral quality of women: "Oh, feminine nature which has surpassed masculine nature in the fight for salvation, proving that between the two, there is a difference of body, but not of soul" (in Gregory 1966, pp. 502–3n.).

Gregory of Nyssa is of major importance in the effort to define a desire for God that would have nothing to do with concupiscence, with the division of the sexes, with an erotic or dialectical interaction between people. Since his view of desire is not at all the same as the psychoanalytic view we hold to, it is worthwhile to present his at this time. As Daniélou said, for Gregory Eros is simply the most intense form of the Agape (charity) of the gospels (in Gregory 1979, p. 44). What he is essaying is a translation of the erotic into the language of the Heavenly City. For Gregory desire is paradoxical; any experience of its satisfaction leads to a further desire, almost like an appetite that is whetted by whatever taste it receives, never attaining satiety, perhaps because the taste buds are activated by a food that is not substantial but is spiritual. A desire whose realization is unattainable is defined in terms of degrees of satisfaction gained by a progressive knowledge of its object.

The soul, having gone out at the word of her Beloved, looks for Him but does not find Him. . . . In this way she is, in a certain sense, wounded and beaten because of the frustration of what she desires, now that she thinks that her yearning for the Other cannot be fulfilled or satisfied. But the veil of her grief is removed when she learns that the true satisfaction of her desire consists in constantly going on in her quest and never ceasing in her ascent, seeing that every fulfillment of her desire continually generates a further desire for the Transcendent. Thus the veil of her despair is torn away and the bride realizes that she will always discover more and more of the incomprehensible and unhoped for beauty of her Spouse throughout all eternity. Then she is torn by an even more urgent longing, and . . . she communicates to her Beloved the dispositions of her heart, For she has received within her God's special dart, she has been wounded in her heart by the point of faith, she has been mortally wounded by the arrow of love. (Gregory 1979, p. 45)

It is not a mere matter of grammatical gender that the soul is here taken to be feminine. Gregory was providing an important if not major definition of feminine desire, of a desire that is not satisfied with the attainment of its object. It is reasonable to say within this problematic that masculine desire is satisfied with its object, once that object is possessed or captured. If this is true, it is clear that a particular view of the feminine defines the soul's relation to God. The question is not the realization of desire, as it is in psychoanalysis; nor is it the sustaining of desire in the absence of its object, as it is in some erotic techniques. Rather the point here concerns a progressive growth in enjoyment. Things get better and better, there is more and more desire, more and more enjoyment. There is no sense of the soul in bliss turning to sneak a glance at the suffering of the damned. The continual regeneration of desire does not suggest punctual experiences of satisfaction, does not admit of the detumescence of the instrument of erotic desire ("never ceasing in her ascent"), but comprises the body as a whole, transcending sexuality through a yearning for the beauty of her bridegroom.

Clearly this represents an idealization of feminine experience. The problem is that there is something terrifying in the absence of respite, pause, punctuation. The vision may easily become infernal. The soul, discovering the infinity of her bridegroom, is motivated by an increasing knowledge of how unknowable the other really is, thus by an increasing frustration, which she turns into enjoyment. Our question then is whether this represents desire or a demand for love. Does this suggest that women are fundamentally insatiable, that they can never be satisfied?

Does it not collapse desire into a series of demands for an object where the satisfaction of the demand by the provision of the object leads immediately and progressively to a new demand for more? When Gregory says that the true satisfaction is in the quest because the Other is completely unattainable, this means that one turns frustration and despair into enjoyment. There we see that the glorification of the feminine, rendered pristine by its reference to a god instead of to a man, is a formula for the hysterization of the human soul. If we follow Lacan's definition of the hysteric's desire as the desire to have an unsatisfied desire, then on the one hand the realization of this condition in the Gregorian ascent would qualify as a desire, while on the other the soul herself would be constantly thrown back on increasingly urgent demands and plaints.

Certainly this is phallocentric; its center is the arrow and dart of love. The question I pose here is whether the soul's experience of being wounded does not represent something like a psychic trauma. Examine the passage closely and you will see that the soul is initially wounded and frustrated by her impotence to attain her desire. That she later discovers that the wound has been caused by love does not resolve the problem; it simply shifts it to another realm. Having been traumatized by inopportune and unwished for exposure to the phallus, a hysteric may later fall in love with an idealized possessor of said instrument. She may also find satisfaction in the quest for the repetition of the experience, but such satisfaction is hardly desirable. She seeks and achieves progressive states of being fulfilled, of being filled full, but each one leads to a new repetition of her demand. The promise held out to her is one of purification and perfection through a process of psychic growth. The hysteric is a container through whose presence the Beloved Word is perpetually producing and creating angelic states of being. As Gregory said of the angels, created spiritual substance: "The other class of spiritual substance has been brought into being by creation; thus it constantly looks toward the first Cause, and is preserved in existence by a continual participation in transcendent being. Thus, in a certain sense, it is constantly being created, ever changing for the better in its growth in perfection; along these lines no limit can be envisaged, nor can its progressive growth in perfection be limited by any term. In this way, its present state of perfection, no matter how great and perfect it may be, is merely the beginning of a greater and superior stage" (Gregory 1979, p. 65).

The question of how angels relate to human beings is not entirely covered by ideas of imitation and emulation. Angels are also messengers, and the soul that relates to an angelic messenger is in the position of receiving that message. The position of reception is also associated with femininity, but the way in which a woman "relates" to a human messenger is not the same and does not have the same implications as her "relating" to an angelic messenger. The prototypical situation where these issues are raised in Christianity is the scene of the Annunciation. St. Jerome reflected on this question, perhaps inadvertently: "When the angel Gabriel came down to her in man's form, . . . she was filled with terror and consternation and could not reply; for she had never been greeted by a man before. Soon, however, she learned who the messenger was, and spoke to him: she who had been afraid of a man conversed fearlessly with an angel" (Jerome 1980, letter 22, p. 147). So she was having a conversation, or we might better say that she could relate to him. Gabriel's being an angel allows him entrance into the cubicle of the Virgin, and ensures that there is nothing for her to fear—or to desire. Since the actual impregnation of the Virgin is accomplished by the Holy Spirit, the appearance of the angel suggests that the Virgin of herself does not know what has or is happening to her. When Augustine later stated that she was impregnated through the ear, this shows that for him the reception of a message and the activation of reproductive potential are intimately related. Receiving a message in such a context implies the generation of a new meaning in the receiver. And this new meaning is a new being. If anything else were going on the Virgin would have had reason to be afraid.

Reception is also identified with credulousness. The father of John the Baptist, informed of his wife's pregnancy by the same Gabriel, doubts the message and thereby is struck dumb for a time. For speech to be fulfilled, for what is promised to come to pass, what is required of the feminine receptor is belief. As Elizabeth says to Mary: "And blessed is she who believed that there would be a fulfillment of what was spoken to her from the Lord" (Luke 1:45). If these conditions are met the reception of the word bears fruit, leads to the creation of something new. As Christ says in the parable of the sower: "And as for that in the good soil, they are those who, hearing the word, hold it fast in an honest and good heart, and bring forth fruit with patience" (Luke 8:15). The institution of a new concept of listening has it that the model for the concept is the creation of a new being.

As for a word that is neither believed nor understood, yet that moves the listener, there we are not in the realm of seed, but rather in that of the instrument that may or may not bring it. The instrument is the phallus and we call the effect it produces enjoyment. The purpose of the story of the Annunciation is to suggest that whatever is terrifying about an encounter with a phallus has been effectively mitigated. Virginal fears of the instrument of masculine desire are unwarranted and unfounded when the relationship is based on love. Does this not ultimately mean that the virgin in question has been "saved" by her (having a) son from the dire encounter with the phallus? Again, with Augustine, her body remained inviolate not only through her being impregnated but also through her giving birth to Christ. Her experience appears to be narcissistic; Gabriel is her mirror image, and they are in some sense equals. But this needs qualification, because the Virgin is later to be crowned Queen of Heaven. This will place her, the ultimate mother, in a position that is frankly superior to an angel who, according to most theorists on the question, is not even among the highest orders of spiritual creatures.

There may be a masculine side to angelic being, but it is merely the type of masculinity that is tolerated in a world ruled by love. The King and Queen of this world will be a mother and her son, a mother goddess who is unique for never having been touched by a phallic appendage, and a son who will be seen as responding best to prayers offered to his mother. The angels do come to constitute an army, but their fight is for the primary dyad of a mother and a son. Of course, when wars are fought to conquer minds and souls, to universalize the faith, they are far more brutal than are those that concern the maintenance of boundaries, in which rules of warfare are observed. Imagine for a moment applying Gregory of Nyssa's description of the desirous soul aspiring endlessly to an Other that will never be achieved to the conduct of war. No victory, no matter how total, would be total enough.

Concupiscence is not part of the angelic experience, probably because the angels are defined as having it all. What could they want in addition? Wanting for nothing, the angels can only be conceived as desiring more of the same; a desire that would truly be for otherness is excluded from their constitution. To be receptive of love or of grace, both of which are gifts from above, one ought not to be desiring. And one ought certainly not to desire something other than what is given. Libidinous wants among angelic creatures are specifically accorded only to the fallen angels, to the devils, but even they are not beings of desire. Devils and demons suffer essentially from sins like pride and envy. Their relation to sensuality is divided. As Aquinas said: "The demons do not delight in the obscenities of the sins of the flesh, as if they themselves were disposed to carnal pleasures: it is wholly through envy that they take pleasure in all sorts of human sins, so far as these are hindrances to a man's good" (Aquinas ST, part 1, q. 63, art. 2). This is certainly an interesting psychological insight, which might well be extended beyond the world of demons.

Those who believe that a relationship ought to provide a constant source of happiness are basing their thought on a rather angelic conception of human interaction. The same applies for those who hold that the participants in a relationship are both androgynous, or better still, not very well defined as to sexual roles. While there is a certain indefinite quality to such a relationship, it is clear that the structuring principles of marriage do not have a role therein. What goes on between Gabriel and Mary is extramarital. And if the organization of human society according to kinship relations is excluded, so also is the division of the sexes inscribed in those relations. The way to such a reorganization is through reducing the place of the father in favor of that of the mother. This is not only a reduction of one parent's role in favor of the other's. The fundamental relation of husband and wife, so often called the linchpin of the patriarchal system, is excluded from the heavens except when modeled on the relation of mother and son. From the beginning of the monotheistic tradition, God does not have a wife. In place of a symbolic link between husband and wife that excludes an immediate blood-tie, we find in the Christian apotheosis of monotheism the reign of a mother and son—a son as king who makes his mother his queen.

Such a world has no place for masculine desire and always presents such desire in its most unappetizing forms. Angels were called upon in the Judeo-Christian tradition to take the place of the pagan deities, or of the demons the ancients thought of as intermediary between men and the gods. Augustine denied categorically any connection between angels and what the Greeks called demons, but he did allow that what Platonists call gods may well refer to the beings he called angels. The difference is that the demons, comprising what we think of as pagan deities, receive sacrifices and are worshipped with sacred rites, while the angelic multitudes "do not wish that such devout homage should be offered in worship to any being other than the one God, by whom they were created, the God who imparts to them their happiness by granting them a share in his own being" (Augustine CG, book 9, chap. 23). This God may well grant the angels a share in his being, but perhaps he does so in compensation for not granting them mates. The deities who are worshipped by pagans are sexed; not only is it rare that a god not be paired with a goddess, but myth and ritual celebrate the drama of their interactions, the incidences of desire and transgression.

As for relationships, contemporary thought usually sees the link as affective or affectionate. From what we said above we qualify this to say that the right kind of affects are of an intellectual, not a sensitive, nature, meaning that they are neither acquisitive nor violent. This represents the attempt to put into practice a supposed metalanguage of affects that would be universal. Not limited by the constraints of ordinary languages, such a metalanguage would be the basis for a universal human community like that of the Heavenly City. If its rationale is an experience common to all human beings, the privileged experience is usually thought to be that of having been born of a mother. That is what Christ has in common with the rest of the human race; it defines him as human. Such a link is promoted to take the place of a descent through a line of fathers, through a transmission of names. In Luke, for example, the names of John and Jesus are told by the angel. Most particularly in the case of John, those who would have named him in the name of his father Zachariah are overruled by his mother, who names him as the angel commanded.

If Christ represents the fulfillment of the Law in the ending of the line of fathers, a new principle of linkage between heaven and earth or between parent and child must be proposed. This is something like a communication channel between mother and mother, between the Heavenly City and its earthly counterpart, the Mother Church. The idea is exemplified in Augustine, especially in his *City of God*. Therein Augustine divided the human race into "two branches": those who live according to "human standards" and those who follow the will of God. The origin of these two branches may be read either in the myth of the first humans or in that of the fall of the rebel angels (book 15, chap. 1). The City of God contains saints and angels, beings who are freed from sin by the grace of God. But the Heavenly City has an image or counterpart on earth; there is a part of the earthly city that provides an artistic representation of the other city.

One part of the earthly city has been made into an image of the Heavenly City, by symbolizing something other than itself, namely that other City; and for that reason it is a servant. . . . Thus we find in the earthly city a double significance: in one respect it displays its own presence, and in the other it serves by its presence to signify the Heavenly City. But the citizens of the earthly city are produced by a nature which is vitiated by sin, while the citizens of the Heavenly City are brought forth by grace, which sets nature free from sin. . . . This difference is also symbolized in Abraham's two sons: the one, Ishmael, son of the slave named Hagar, was born in the course of nature, whereas the other, Isaac, son of Sarah, the free woman, was born in fulfillment of a promise. (book 15, chap. 2)

What is important here is not only the division of the world into two cities, each of which has a specific moral character; rather it is the fact that the Heavenly City communicates with the earthly through its image there. By communication I mean that the enjoyment of the one is transmitted to the other through a process akin to empathy.

Augustine's version of the birth of Isaac is subject to doubt; some believe that the barrenness of Sarah and the fact that Abraham had passed beyond the age in which he could father children signifies creation through the name, not through grace. It is noteworthy that Isaac was produced in spite of or perhaps because of a biological impossibility. I will leave open the question of whether this is creation *ex nihilo*.

Meantime, Augustine found in the circumstance of Isaac's birth a moral about the type of relationships that pertain in those who share the Heavenly City. "Isaac therefore, who was born as a result of a promise, is rightly interpreted as symbolizing the children of grace, the citizens of the free city, the sharers of eternal peace, who form a community where there is no love of a will that is personal and, as we may say, private, but a love that rejoices in a good that is at once shared by all and unchanging—a love that makes 'one heart' out of many, a love that is the whole-hearted and harmonious obedience of mutual affection" (book 15, chap. 3). Later in this Book 15 Augustine counted the wish to have children, to have a family, as reprehensible, especially in comparison with the idea of producing citizens of the Heavenly City (chap. 23). So it would appear that he opposed relationships to the kind of relations that pertain between members of a family.

In fact, this is what Augustine said when he made of affection the glue that holds society together. He did so in a reflection on incest. Believing in the literal fact that mankind descended from a single set of parents, Augustine reflected that the first marriages were necessarily incestuous. But he did not accept that the function of the Law was to assure what Lévi-Strauss would call an economy in the exchange of women or what Lacan was to call a means to prevent generational confusion. Rather, Augustine saw the system of marriage as based in the idea of expanding the sea of affection. Thus a system of relations that is imposed on humans by the symbolic order is desymbolized and reduced to the need to expand affection. "For affection was given its right importance so that men, for whom social harmony would be advantageous and honourable, should be bound together by ties of various relationships. The aim was that one man should not combine many relationships in his one self, but that those connections should be separated and spread among individuals, and that in this way they should help to bind social life more effectively by involving in their plurality a plurality of persons. 'Father' and 'Father-in-law,' for instance, are names denoting two different relationships. Thus affection stretches over a greater number when each person has one man for father and another for father-in-law" (book 15, chap. 16). Augustine did give equal time to mothers and mothers-in-law. He did not think in terms of a marital exchange, but rather in terms of some law that dictates the expansion of a community of affection. To attribute the prohibition of incest to any masculine principles is inimical to this system of thought.

In the early Christian attacks against pagan deities, writers like Clement of Alexandria and Augustine insisted that pagan gods are fornicating adulterers, rapists, thieves, liars, and so on. The rituals held to honor these gods and goddesses, Augustine noted, are not the kinds of events you would want to take your mother to (CG, book 2, chap. 4). The sins of the gods and goddesses of pagan antiquity exist in a world where masculinity and the values it represents have a place. Instead of seeing the salubrious side to masculine behavior as reason for the articulation of an ethical position in which it is submitted to the rule of intelligence,

Augustine found that it ought not to exist and that its ugly head should be condemned every time it makes an appearance. Certain types of women are condemned by the Fathers of the Church, most especially when they participate in or incite the masculine taste for obscenity, but this should not obscure the fact that the right kind of woman is essential to the Christian world. These are women who, like the angels, avoid coupling, avoid being part of a couple, who are solitary, independent, autonomous beings, whose value is determined by sisterhood, by work, by being part of the enclosed and protected world created by the Mother Church. The condemnation of some kinds of women is a veiled and displaced condemnation of the phallus through whatever is associated with it. A woman, Eve, for whom the phallus and what it represented proved an irresistible attraction, led mankind to perdition. Because of this, salvation had to enter the world through the act of another woman, the Virgin Mary. The same salvation is not offered to the serpent, who will later be crushed under her foot.

The moral division is articulated in the division between human beings and beasts. Evidently there were some who identified the bestial with women, but it is more clear and unambiguous to connect it with the serpent. Women who reject the phallus gain redeeming virtue; the serpent is basically incorrigible. Note well the remarks of Augustine as he responded to the idea of mapping the mind-body split onto the division of the sexes. "Nor does it escape me, that some who before us were eminent defenders of the Catholic faith and expounders of the word of God, while they looked for these two things in one human being, whose entire soul they perceived to be a sort of excellent paradise, asserted that the man was the mind, but that the woman was the bodily sense." ". . . I for my part have not thought that the bodily sense should be taken for the woman, which we see to be common to ourselves and to the beasts; but I have desired to find something which the beasts had not; and I have rather thought the bodily sense should be understood to be the serpent, whom we read to have been more subtle than all the beasts of the field" (*On the Trinity* [OT], book 12, chap. 13). Augustine refused to identify women with the corruption of fallen nature or of sensuality, a position not shared by all of his coreligionists; he reserved the curse of corruption for the serpent. The other beasts share with both men and women bodily sense as "a kind of living power" which must be good because it is of nature.

The serpent, representing the fallen angels, shares with all angels the quality of being a moral absolute. Writing of an angel, Aquinas said: "Accordingly, he is either not fixed upon evil at all, or, if he is fixed on evil, is fixed so immutably" (*Summa Contra Gentiles* [SCG], chap. 55). As for male sexuality, once it is identified with fertility and generation—once, in other words, the phallus is reduced from a symbol to a fertilizing instrument—it finds its own redemption, but in this redemptive state it is cut off from its demonic or mediating function to become subservient to a maternal principle. In the hierarchy of Christian values, this is obviously inferior to the celibate state, the state that most closely corresponds to that of the angels.

Whatever the sex of the angels, their world is feminine, and this is taken to mean maternal. The kind of femininity that has to do with immodesty of dress or behavior, that comprises bodily adornment, the enticement of cosmetics, and other forms of the feminine masquerade, is consistently disparaged. Virginity is highly valued because it appears to be the essence of female virtue, the closest human equivalent to the disembodied and unsexed state of the angels. Christian tradition emphasized the virtue of women because the female body lends itself more readily to the idea of being sexless. You may find it inconsistent that a tradition that takes femininity to be practically equivalent to fertility and motherhood makes such a virtue of lifelong virginity, but this is not so difficult to understand. Both the type of mother Christianity venerates and the virginal girl have this in common: both are untouched by the phallus. That a Virgin become a mother is a singular event. For virgins the Church offered not only sisterhood in the convent but also the possibility of a symbolic or superior motherhood, one that was not defined in terms of phallic power, but rather in terms of identification with another mother.

Where the Judaic tradition had valued especially the production of sons, we find Jerome at the end of the fourth century proclaiming: "I praise wedlock, I praise marriage; but it is because they produce me virgins" (Jerome 1980, letter 22, p. 95). Later he expanded his thought in advising a woman on bringing up her daughter: "Let her be reared in a monstery amid bands of virgins, where she will learn never to take an oath, and to regard a lie as sacrilege. Let her know nothing of the world, but live like the angels; let her be in the flesh and without the flesh, thinking all mankind like herself" (Jerome 1980, letter 107, p. 369).

While sons were important to the Jewish people and probably even to pagans for their ability to transmit a father's name, Christianity in its early days distinguished itself from these competing religious movements by placing value on the production of those who refuse their fathers' name. Christ had put an end to the line of fathers or patriarchs, and thus in a postpatriarchal world, human beings whose lives most closely represented a repudiation of the corruption of the phallus were held in the highest regard.

This should permit us to understand why people on earth can see themselves called upon to model their relationships on what goes on between the angels. The number of people so called upon may vary, and this form of behavior need not be limited to the Church and its monasteries. We may have lost our angels somewhere in time, but it may be that we have done so in order to become angels ourselves.

Seeing relationships as an ideal that embodies the angelic is problematical because for most moderns relationships comport sexuality. How can two people live like angels and still have a sex life? For the moment we disregard the question of whether people in monasteries and convents were as chaste as Jerome would have liked them to be. There is, after all, ample evidence that injunctions to monastic celibacy were often transgressed. This does not, however, respond to the problem. The answer to this conundrum lies in our conception of sexuality. Not all sexuality is the same. Different people engaged in sexual acts may look as if they are doing the same thing while seeing their experience in totally different contexts. We will not belabor the point here; but we should note that there are extensive differences in the way people talk about their sexuality. Some people talk of getting laid and others speak of making love. It is a witness to the power of love, the ability love has to transform and redeem fallen nature, that even the sexual act of carnal intercourse has been brought under its sway.

Beginning perhaps with Augustine, Christianity has a clear idea of sex without desire, exemplified by the coupling of Adam and Eve in Paradise. Augustine began by describing their relationship: "Between man and wife there was a faithful partnership based on love and mutual respect; there was a harmony and a liveliness of mind and body, and an effortless observance of the commandment." A modern thinker musing on marital relationships could not have said it better. Augustine went on to picture carnal relations without desire: "When mankind was in such a state of ease and plenty, blest with such felicity, let us never imagine that it was impossible for the seed of children to be sown without the morbid condition of lust. Instead, the sexual organs would have been brought into activity by the same bidding of the will as controlled the other organs. Then, without feeling the allurement of passion goading him on, the husband would have relaxed on his wife's bosom in tranquillity of mind and with no impairment of his body's integrity" (Augustine CG, book 14, chap. 26). This vision seems clearly to derive from that of a child at its mother's breast. We also note and underscore the wish to make the sexual organs behave just like other organs. Doubtless Augustine was thinking of the male organ, for him the incarnation of lust; its integration in the body is a denial of what psychoanalysis calls castration. The more important point is that sexuality per se is not an obstacle to the type of relationship that pertains in Paradise. Those who make love without desire are thus participating in the heavenly life. This early Christian idea is an important redefinition of sexuality. The Catholic belief that sex ought only to serve the ends of reproduction—or better, the production of virgins—is an effort to make the maternal side predominate over the phallocentric world of the patriarchs and the pagan deities.

These ideas have a direct bearing on the Catholic idea of marriage, especially as it was articulated in the late Middle Ages. Georges Duby has written about the history of the Church's taking control of marriage in the Middle Ages (Duby 1983). One of his central points is that the Church was called upon to protect the interests of women who had been harmed by pagan attitudes toward marriage. Men had taken for themselves the right to repudiate their wives at will, for whatever reason suited them; the usual reason was the failure to produce male heirs. There is also a clear suggestion that the old pagan forms encouraged feminine desire without satisfying it, therefore placing men in a position of constant anxiety about the legitimacy of their progeny.

How did it happen that in the interest of women who were repudiated by their husbands, the Church, led by the monks, decided to make marriage more egalitarian, more in line with what we call a relationship, less connected with the requirement of producing sons? In order to appear to be on the side of women, the Church deeroticized marriage. As Duby noted: "On a symbolical level they were trying to minimize the part played by the nuptials in the ritual of matrimony and to emphasize, by contrast, the part of the procedure that had to do with the union of souls. So they stressed the betrothal, with its according of wills, its mutual consent, its instituting of the 'charity' that was the core of the marital relationship" (Duby 1983, pp. 118–19).

It was not a group of fathers that took control over the institution of marriage. Rather, it was the Mother Church that extended its hegemony to include a ceremony in which flesh could be redeemed, just as it would be at the end of time. Perhaps the most telling sign of the transformation was the replacement of the father by the priest "at the crucial moment of the joining of hands and the giving away of the bride. The earliest record of this decisive change comes from Reims in the second half of the thirteenth century" (Duby 1983, p. 153).

As elsewhere, the ideas of Aquinas are enlightening. A selective examination of his writings about matrimony reveals an attitude that is in manifest propinquity with modern enlightened views. Aquinas declared that friendship ought to exist between husband and wife. And he proposed not only friendship, but even domestic partnership. "Now there seems to be the greatest friendship between husband and wife, for they are united not only in the act of fleshy union, which produces a certain gentle association, even among beasts, but also in the partnership of the whole range of domestic activity" (Aquinas SCG, book 3, chap. 123). On the idea that friendship requires equality and ought not to comport any sort of servitude, Aquinas said: "Besides, friendship consists in an equality. So, if it is not lawful for the wife to have several husbands, since this is contrary to certainty as to offspring, it would not be lawful, on the other hand, for a man to have several wives, for the friendship of wife for husband would not be free but somewhat servile. And this argument is corroborated by experience, for among husbands having plural wives the wives have a status like that of servants. Therefore, if a wife has but one husband and the husband has several wives, the friendship will not be equal on both sides. So, the friendship will not be free, but servile in some way" (Aquinas SCG, book 3, chap. 124). This may sound too good to be true, especially since the attitudes toward women that Aquinas inherited from Aristotle are not of the most enlightened sort. There was no question for him and for other Christian authors that a husband should dominate his wife, that he should be the head of the household. In the passages quoted he seems to be placing himself in opposition to the practice of polygamy, which he would have known about through the writings of the Arab masters. It is important to remark that in Arab writings on sexuality and marriage feminine sexual pleasure was considered of major importance. As Jacquart and Thomasset (1985) showed, the discourse on masculine desire and on the requirement of controlling it in the interest of feminine pleasure entered Western civilization in the Middle Ages through writers who were familiar with life in harems. What the Church instituted as a marital sacrament was not only more egalitarian than polygamy, but it may also have had as one of its purposes the reduction of the erotic side of relations between the sexes. In our times, of course, people see no contradiction between egalitarian relationships and eroticism. Historically, however, the two do not mix well, if at all.

Making of marriage a sacrament must be read in a context where the two feminine roles exemplified in the Virgin and Church are those of mother and bride. The Virgin is not a wife to her husband, at least not in the sense of consummating a marriage. And she is certainly superior to him in the celestial hieararchy. Joseph is, after all, the first husband to relinquish his husbandly prerogatives in favor of his wife's calling or vocation. Does this place one on the path of redeeming the institution of marriage?

So the Catholic view seems at the historical moment we are examining to be that the division of the sexes in the fallen world is the consequence of a moral fault. That moral fault is compounded by entering into a marital exchange that is dominated by a father. This implies a renunciation of the angelic life that the Church offers to both men and women. Since the Church believed therefore that participation in the social determinations of sexual identity was optional, it is reasonable to argue that in place of a sexual identity it has imposed something like a moral identity, where what matters is being on the right side of any moral issue, on the side of the angels in opposition to the devils. A moral identity resembles a commitment to an ideology; it is not a mindless belief in whatever one is told, even though there are situations in which that is what it becomes, but rather it represents the giving over of the mind to the purpose of rationalizing one's moral posture and persuading others to be on the same side. Such a distinction divides the world on other than sexual lines, and thus it has considerable appeal in certain quarters. A division of the sexes does not imply that either one has a monopoly on goodness, and it requires some sort of dialectic between the two because the union of the sexes is excluded. Separated and attracted, the sexes come to exist in a state of constant tension. A moral identity, on the contrary, offers a state of wholeness or unity in which the opposite of oneness is condemned and in which one's moral being becomes self-contained within the City of the Just and Good.

In our time confusion and perplexity surround the notion of a relationship. If the interest in popular psychology is any indication, the population is terribly confused about what it all means. If people seem to be floating in a nebulous area, unable to get their feet on the ground or to get a handle on things, then perhaps the problem lies in the notion they are using to define and articulate their experience; they may be victims of a hybrid concept. Ordinarily, people do or do not get along according to social rules and conventions, the most prominent being the laws of kinship structure. Those who proselytize about relationships have little use for traditional rules and order; they want to go beyond the simple fact that you are related to your parents; they want you to relate to them, as persons, no less. The confusion is between what is involved in relating and what it is to be related. However much the idea of relationship derived from what we call kinship relations, it has come to be separate from and to dominate the latter; this is the legacy of the Christian moral position, represented in medieval thought. The ideal of a relationship posits a transcendent space in which fully human persons, liberated from the constraints imposed by society, can achieve an unreal togetherness, defined as a common soulfulness that is goodness itself. The ideal of becoming fully human persons derives from the Renaissance and the humanist tradition. We should not let it confuse us. When being human is defined as an ideal, it refers to a common human essence, or better, a shared experience of happiness that exists outside the structuring function of social laws and language. Beyond the division of the sexes it corresponds to what hitherto had been reserved for the angels. This move eradicates the difference between humans and angels, but it does so in the name of the perfectibility of human nature; thus the eradication represents a fusion of human and angelic being, with the angelic taking precedence over and even redeeming the human. (We would be remiss if we did not mention here that for some thinkers the common human essence is that of the fallen angels.)

The same sort of redemption exists on the level of the concept. Relating, as any good dictionary will tell you, has to do with kinship. Parents and children are related by the laws of kinship, and this precedes and probably determines any sort of relationship that may or may not develop between them. Since the identity of family members is determined by the places they occupy in the kinship system and by the names that tie them to it, it is more correct to say that they relate primarily through the system of signifiers or symbols than as persons or autonomous individuals. You do not have to do anything or be anything to be related to your parents, your siblings, your aunts, uncles, or cousins. Being related has nothing to do with whether you are a good or bad person. Relations of this sort are dissolved only under extreme duress. The only real choice you have here is forming an alliance with a member of another family through marriage. It is certainly not a general requirement that people who get married and who stay married have a good relationship or that they are or ever were in love. The idea of wedded bliss is a product of Christian history; it performs a specific theological function in bringing the idea of Christian love, *agape* or *caritas,* into the family, thereby extending its dominion. To be consistent, we should add that the ideal of marital bliss is instituted to make desire in marriage difficult or impossible to sustain. Of course, there are marriages where love is always present, and often these are good marriages. From another perspective, Lacan noted one day that there are no longer any marriages that celebrate the excellence and delight of desire. The unfortunate thing is that desire is not on the side of the angels; perhaps even more unfortunate is the fact that it is not on the side of the devils either.

Desire devolves from the structure of the symbol, and thus of relations. The problem is that kinship relations are so contaminated with ideals like those of love and relating that it is extremely difficult to see them outside of the kinds of abuses they seem to generate in our civilization. If the system of kinship relations and the marital exchange has been abused in systematic ways in our civilization, perhaps this is because it has had to compete with an alternate angelic vision that does not permit it to function otherwise. I do not suggest that the kinship system in other contexts is not open to abuse. Kinship systems are systems of subjection, and the modes of subjection do not disregard sex. There is little evidence to suggest that subjection is fair and equitable. One of the sexes has consistently been allowed to ignore its being subject to laws, while the other has generally been burdened by an excessive awareness of its subordinate or subjected position.

The medieval practice of the wholesale repudiation of wives, to which the Church responded by making marriage as a sacrament, is not intrinsic to the marital exchange; it is, however, characteristic of a specific moment in history when the moral vision and power of the Mother Church had not yet asserted themselves in this domain, thereby relegating it to the world of corruption. As Duby noted at the end of his book on this subject: "At the outset, and in the region and in the social group I have chosen to study, Christianity already permeated every nook and cranny of life. But it was a different kind of Christianity. I am sure all those knights feared God, even the greediest and most violent of them, even those inflamed with a desire for women, . . . But, like the heretics, many of them believed with Christ that the Kingdom is not of this world" (Duby 1983, pp. 282–83). Such a thought removes ethical considerations from human behavior and creates the ground where immorality and abuse are licensed by the Mother Church. At the same time it rationalizes the necessity for the Church to expand its hegemony to bring more and more people and more of their activities under its moral domination.

One might be cynical and say that the reason marriage has lasted so long is that it leaves so much to be desired. The kind of satisfaction promised in relationships addresses this problem, proposing the annihilation of desire by tricking it into thinking that it is ultimately a desire for a Supreme Good, a good that is so good it leaves nothing to be desired. This desire for the Supreme Good has nothing to do with erotic desire, represented as it is by the phallus, especially as that phallus is not identical to the male organ it symbolizes and is not subject to the mind's will.

It is useful here to introduce the idea of the symbol and to show what we mean by the assertion that marriage is a symbolic link or pact. By definition, this link exists only where there is no other link, of common blood or common substance. It is noteworthy that the medieval practice of repudiation of wives often sought its rationale in the suspicion of incest, where incest was defined to include a cousin "within the seventh degree of consanguinity, or blood kinship." Duby added: "When spread out over seven generations and linked to the notion of incest, the field of consanguinity was literally beyond measure, with so many people excluded from availability that it was almost impossible to observe the prohibition" (Duby 1983, p. 35). This is an interesting perversion of the incest taboo, one that invoked the taboo to repudiate wives but also made a blood tie coexist with a symbolic tie as often as one wished. The idea of the incest taboo is that these ties should not coexist, though beyond the most obvious objects, mother and sister, the definition of kinship determines what is and is not a blood tie. It would appear that the definition of marriage as the expression of a preexisting link between two people, whether it is a blood tie or an emotional or affective affinity, is a deviant understanding of what a symbol is and what it does.

As is well enough known, the word "symbol" is derived from the Greek *sum-bolen* which means, to throw together. A symbol is a token, one that is split in two pieces, where the matching or throwing together of the pieces produces, in those who use these tokens to represent themselves, recognition of a relation. This occurs even, or most especially, when the two bearers of the symbol have never met before. If you wish to conceive of the token as a card that is cut in two in an irregular way, the crucial point is that each of the pieces of the card will have the same cut. To transpose this onto the practice of marriage as we know it, let us say that the two people joined in marriage have a name in common, a part of each spouse's name is identical. Second, it is the linkage of the two pieces of the token that produces, that is, symbolizes, the link between the people, and not the other way around. In some societies people who have never met each other before are married; through the exchange of vows and the intermingling of names and titles they are connected as kin.

The symbol is not something that represents in public a private relationship or connection; the symbol is a public connection that produces a private connection. The glue that makes and controls the connection is the symbol itself, even when there is some sort of affinity or relationship between the participants. The idea that the two people are connected only through their referring themselves and letting themselves be represented by the symbol is what legislates against their ever achieving the kind of communication we find in the angels. It separates them irrevocably on a certain level, and this separation creates and maintains the conditions in which they desire each other. Thus if there are historical periods where the symbol is called seriously into question, as has happened recently in our history, the fact that people have relationships of whatever quality is not sufficient to hold them together. The joy of their togetherness is mitigated by anxiety about the strength of the ties that bind and despair about the permanence of relationships.

Catholicism was never then very comfortable with the institution of marriage, especially as it represented a system of exchange that ran directly counter to its own structure. If the Church defines the ultimate marriage as that of mother and son, it must at some level oppose women's participation in the marital exchange, in their being exchange objects between men. At the same time it promotes sisterhood in which those who refuse the law of the father are rewarded by being married to the son. That women who did participate should suffer is consistent with this view and perhaps even a consequence of it. When the Church was obliged to accept the institution as part of the fallen world, it promoted reproduction and fertility as redeeming virtues.

The rejection of the marital exchange presided over by father and husband has direct consequences in relation to sexual identification, especially in women. Traditionally, feminine identity is determined by women's participation in the exchange, as Juliet Mitchell asserted, and "not on account of their 'natural' procreative possibilities." And she added: "Lévi-Strauss suggests that there is no theoretical reason why women should not exchange men, but empirically this has never taken place in any human society. Furthermore, if, as is the case, it is empirically proven that it is *always* men who exchange women, then, though the obverse is *hypothetically* possible, there must be available a *theoretical* explanation of why it does not happen" (Mitchell 1975, p. 372).

This idea is critically important. Even though this exchange never happens in human society, it does exist in fantasy and visions. We begin with two instances quoted by Rudolph Bell in his book about saintly anorexics. The first is a vision of Saint Veronica: "I began to undress. That done, I took off the little corset I had and said: 'My Jesus, leave those [your mother's] breasts. Come take milk here from me.' And I offered my breast. He detached from that of the Virgin and attached to mine. Oh God! I cannot find words to tell how I felt at that moment and I do not even recall its effects it caused in me" (Bell 1985, p. 60). Here is a later story concerning Agnes of Montepulciano as Bell recounted it: "After much fervent prayer to Mary, the Blessed Virgin let Agnes hold baby Jesus for a few hours. When Mary wanted the child back Agnes refused, and the two of them engaged in a fierce tug-of-war; although the real mother proved stronger, Agnes did managed to rip a cross from the baby's neck, a relic still venerated by the faithful in Montepulciano. What interests us in this apocryphal tale is its familial implication: Agnes, the bride of Christ, engaged in a struggle for possession of her husband's body against her mother-in-law" (Bell 1985, p. 132).

Bell's last remark is telling; it points beyond the charm value of these stories. Perhaps the theoretical reason why women do not exchange men in marriage is that when they do so the men in question are children, even infants at the breast, while the women in question are identified fundamentally in terms of their motherhood. It permits us to consider the exchange that may or may not take place between the Virgin Mother of God and the Church or soul that is called the bride of Christ. Is the Virgin the mother-in-law of the Church? Is she the mother-in-law of the saintly anorexics who saw the perfect relationship in the mystical marriage with Christ? If it is a patriarchal law that prevents the hypothetical exchange of a man between two women from taking place as a principle of social organization, then perhaps in the resurrected life, this too will come to pass. If this same patriarchal law prohibits first and foremost mother-son incest, then its fulfillment will ensure that the union of Christ and his Virgin bride is thinkable and imaginable by Jerome or Bernard of Clairvaux. If there is no Law, then the marriage of Christ with his Mother is not incestuous. Since there seems in these visions to be no phallus involved, there is nothing to prevent them from taking place.

So there is within the Christian vision the possibility that Mitchell questioned. The Christian answer is that within the fallen and corrupt world this inverted exchange cannot happen, but that in the resurrected life it does take place. The fact that it has never happened does not preclude its occurring at some time in the future; for many people the future is a possibility that has never become actual.

What is called the principle of plenitude asserts that if something is possible then it must become actual at some time in the future. To clarify this it is necessary to examine the idea of possibility. Here is how Hintikka defined the Aristotelian concept of possibility: "There is an assumption concerning the interrelations of time and modality which has undoubtedly played a much more important role in the history of Western thought—in the history of metaphysics, theology, logic, philosophy of nature, and even speculative poetry—than any other assumption conerning their relationships. This is the assumption that *all genuine possibilities* or at least all possibilities of some central and important kind, *are actualized in time*. Any such possibility thus has been, is, or will be realized; it cannot remain unrealized through an infinite stretch of time; in a sense, everything possible will happen in the long run" (Hintikka 1973, p. 94). An example of such thinking is found in the reply of Arnauld to Leibniz on the question of the existence of possible people. To Leibniz's assertion that the real Adam was the actualization of only one of many possible Adams, Arnauld replied: "I acknowledge in good faith that I have no idea of substances purely possible, that is to say, which God will never create. I am inclined to think that these are chimeras which we construct and that whatever we call possible substances, pure possibilities are nothing else than the omnipotence of God who, being a pure act, does not allow of there being a possibility in him" (in Leibniz 1898, p. 97). Not only does Arnauld assert that there are no unactualized possibilities, but he adds, as I read him, that what may appear to us to be an unactualized possible person will be actualized in God. If we were to ask, actualized as what, perhaps the answer is that they become actual angels.

The qualification of the principle of plenitude is that all possibilities will be realized only if their realization does not produce an impossible consequence (Hintikka 1973, p. 208). In order to know whether a possibility will ever come to pass we must know whether its actualization produces any logical contradictions. These ideas explain why those who believed that the City of God was going to be actualized for humanity at some point in the future were required to show that this particular possible world did not contain within itself any logical contradictions. This gives an idea of why Aquinas so belabored questions of logic and why he wanted to render the elements of Christian theology rational. He was not doing it simply to persuade the heathens. If there is going to be a world in which the ideal of relationships will become actual, then there ought to be a way of defining a possible world in which it functions without producing contradictions. Thus it is important to know what is going on among the angels.

To amplify the reasons why there is not going to be anything like a marital exchange between the Marian version of the Great Mother Goddess and another woman we should first ask whether there are any other women, or whether femininity is permitted only as an identification with Her. Marina Warner (1983) emphasized Mary's being alone of all her sex, apart from other women through her position in the Catholic pantheon, apart from other mother goddesses in being untouched by the masculine sex, apart from all human beings by being conceived without sin, apart even from her son in not passing through death. She is not *a* woman, to take a distinction emphasized by Lacan, but rather is Woman. And if there is only one Woman, then one hardly sees how an exchange can take place. According a mother the power to give her son in marriage to another woman involves a contradiction because for such a mother there are no other women. If there is no Law prohibiting incest she will never give him away; her having him makes her whole. This is consistent with the fact that the Church does not permit her sons to marry other women, any more than the Heavenly Jerusalem permits such a thing to her angels. It is as though the Mother Church were saying to her sons, her priests: Thou shalt have no other woman before me. The only morally acceptable feminine role is one that identifies a woman with the Virgin; if not in virginity, then at least in her defining her femininity through motherhood. So the answer to the question of why there is no exchange between a Mother Goddess and an other woman is that there are no other women, certainly none who are worthy of Her son.

According to the Bible, humanity is united in a bond of consanguinity for having one and only mother. According to Augustine, the mother of us all is named Jerusalem, the Heavenly City. And the state of this mother attracts our attention here, especially as it relates directly to the condition and mythology of the angels. Here is how Augustine told the story; I quote it at length to show how some of this ties together, but more importantly, to lead to the fact that Jerusalem is defined as having a gap caused by the fall of the rebel angels.

And so it pleased God, the Creator and Governor of the universe, that, since the whole body of the angels had not fallen into rebellion, the part of them which had fallen should remain in perdition eternally, and that the other part, which had in the rebellion remained steadfastly loyal, should rejoice in the sure and certain knowledge of their eternal happiness; but that, on the other hand, mankind, who constituted the remainder of the intelligent creation, having perished without exception under sin, both original and actual, and the consequent punishments, should be in part restored, and should fill up the gap left in the company of angels. For this is the promise of the saints, that at the resurrection they shall be equal to the angels of God. And thus the Jerusalem which is above, which is the mother of us all, the city of God, shall not be spoiled of any of the number of her citizens, shall perhaps reign over even a more abundant population. ("The Enchiridion," chap. 29)

Our interest in this passage, which represents a central mythic construct, is manifold. First, the gap in the Other, the gap in the Heavenly Jerusalem, is the basis for the desire that people live like angels or become saints. This gap is intolerable; it must be filled. Second, the restoration of the plenitude of Mother Jerusalem, even to an excess of abundance, will necessarily take place as promised. If we were following the principle of plenitude, the past existence of this state would suffice to demonstrate that it was a true possibility. In turn this would make its actualization in the future superfluous. Perhaps this is what led to the thought that human life had another purpose, beyond that of filling in the gaps life by the fall of the angels.

Augustine's vision makes of human beings replacement-angels, as Chenu pointed out. Chenu added that the Renaissance of the twelfth century began with Anselm's finding a purpose for human life that was beyond this function of replacement (Chenu 1976, pp. 52–61). The first glimmerings of Western humanism are found in the idea that the original creation of the Heavenly City was imperfect, thus that the fall of the rebel angels was a further imperfection. In *Cur Deus Homo* Anselm wrote: "If the angels, before any of them fell, existed in that perfect number of which we have spoken, then men were only made to supply the place of the lost angels; and it is plain that their number will not be greater. But if that number were not found in all the angels together, then both the loss and the original deficiency must be made up from men, and more men will be chosen than there were fallen angels. And so we shall say that men were made not only to restore the diminished number, but also to complete the imperfect number" (Anselm 1962, pp. 226–27). This leads easily to the question of how God could have created something imperfect.

Consider how important it is that the angels are not sexed. Whether the gaps in Jerusalem were caused by the fall of Satan and his followers or whether they were there from the beginning, in either case, if the angels were sexed, they would have immediately set out to remedy the situation by reproducing themselves. And if this had happened the place would have grown so full that God would have had no reason to create the human race.

TWO

OF WITCHES AND WOMAN

Christianity teaches that souls are divided in death. Some are consigned to eternal torment, while others are raised to a new life in the City of God. Many are the virtues of those who attain eternal life but no one gains entrance to Jerusalem except through Christ. Those whose only fault was not having heard the Message may suffer less than those who heard and ignored it, but still their petitions will be refused. There are many opinions on what is required of a soul whose fate is to see God. Among them we find the following: living for nothing but being saved, eschewing the goods offered by the fallen world, sacrificing personal happiness in the interest of a better end. Those who have suffered martyrdom for Christ, those who have mortified their flesh or who have renounced the life of the body will receive a reward more glorious than that offered by other religions. They will, on the day of the Last Judgment, receive their bodies in a new and more perfect, even more artistic form. "I am not rash enough to attempt to describe what the movements of such bodies will be in that life, for it is quite beyond the power of my imagination. However, everything there will be lovely in its form, and lovely in its motion and in rest, for anything that is not lovely will be excluded. And we may be sure that where the spirit wills there the body will straightway be; and the spirit will never will anything but what is to bring new beauty to the spirit and the body." So said Augustine, who added that this bodily state will "kindle our rational minds to the praise of the great Artist by the delight afforded by a beauty that satisfies the reason" (CG, book 22, chap. 30).

The division of souls is based on moral worth, according to how well one has loved God. In Catholicism this is inseparable from participation in the rituals of the Mother Church. When identity is moral, having one does not depend directly on the social organization of the fallen world, on being effected or defined by symbolic or social structures. The Church may be surrounded by this world, but its structure is supposed to be the image of the Heavenly City. One's moral being is determined by universal meanings, which are defiled by the passage through a human language. And it is not just being that should not be socially determined; one's acts must necessarily subserve the participation in the passion of Christ. Among the acts that are most clearly condemned is the practice of blood sacrifice: first, because it denies that the Crucifixion occurred to put an end to such abominations; second, because it is addressed to other gods; third, because its purpose is to assure order and harmony in this world, to regulate the affairs of human beings and their dealings with the natural world through an exchange with those who were thought to control them.

Within Christianity moral worth does not hinge on the actions of a singular subject in a delimited context. It is not so much that you commit a sin; it is normal to do so; what matters is whether you accept forgiveness, whether you are sufficiently receptive to the divine instance that lifts you from your evil ways. A more extreme view is it that it does not matter what you do so long as you have the right intentions. Knowledge of such intentions, of their truth, is reserved for God and his inquisitors. It is less important to know what you have done or ought to do than it is to know who you are and what you believe, whether you are with the angels or the devils.

The purpose of dividing, defining, and classifying humans according to the principles of moral identity is to provide a replacement for the sexual identity that is functional in the world of the pagan deities. It may be that the fallen world is divided naturally according to sex. This division is acceptable if it leads to procreative sexuality; if it promotes concupiscence, it is to be condemned. In Christianity, where the inhabitants of the Heavenly City are bodiless angels not considered to be sexed, the division of the sexes can only be a degeneration redeemable either by generative sexual acts or the absence of same.

The horizontal division of the sexes was thus replaced by a vertical division between angels and devils, ultimately between life and death. And yet, it was not so easy to rid the heavens of the division of the sexes. Aside from the fact that the bodies resurrected in the Last Judgment were not neutered, the tendency to see the soul as feminine introduced a second sex into the heavens, to accompany the angels, who at times were defined in masculine terms. If witches were the consorts of devils, why not imagine that the souls of the blessed are paired with the angels? Emile Mâle provided a fine description of the Beatitudes represented at Chartres: "These beautiful maidens are symbols of souls in bliss. The Christian who gazes on their serenity and beauty sees heaven, and forgets this imperfect world. Through them paradise becomes visible, for no man can say of the creators of these noble figures that they were conquered by the greatness of their subject, or lacked power to express eternal bliss" (Mâle 1972, p. 388). This leads us to wonder whether the angels did not from time to time glance at them. In any case, there is an explicit moral superiority granted to certain women in the fallen world, especially to virgins. Following the example of the Virgin, the idealization of virginity may include motherhood so long as it excludes commerce with the phallus. This leads to a division of the female sex into virgins and witches. The difference between the relation of angels with souls and that of witches and devils is not very difficult to see. The souls of the blessed are not coupled with angels; they are like them even to the point where the comparison of souls with angels was eventually to render the angels more feminine than they had been before. While the few angels who are named in the Bible have male names, the gradual reformulation of the nature of angelic being helped these spirits to get in touch with their feminine side—the better to safeguard the virtue of their lovely cohabitants.

Remember that the moral world of the Heavenly City and its earthly counterpart in the Mother Church was not the only reality in the Middle Ages. The placement of female beautitudes on the portals of Chartres did not necessarily define the condition of women in feudal society. Feudal lords were not very moral people in their outward behavior; they did, however, believe that the Church would absolve them of sin and that they would enter into the Kingdom of the Blessed. Alongside the fierce moralism of Holy Mother Church there existed the customs and practice of knighthood and chivalry, representing, among other things, a form of masculine eroticism, not the sort of thing the Church was promoting. Johan Huizinga described this well:

It cannot be brought enough to the fore that the chivalric function found its highest expression in the tournament, and that the tournament was nothing more nor less than the most elegant and most expensively adorned form of those erotic matches whose origins lie not only far outside the sphere of higher culture but also outside that of human culture in general. The essential element in both the tilt and the chivalric vow was the presence of the women under whose eyes the man shed his blood or displayed his bravery and strength. The sexual element was clearly seen and expressed throughout the Middle Ages. From it sprang the whole romanticism of chivalry: the motif of the knight who freed the maiden, of the unknown knight whose unexpected appearance and decisive courage focused all eyes on him, the whole gaily colored setting and sentimental fantasy of the *pas d'armes*. (Huizinga 1984, pp. 87–88).

Chivalry, however, did not have a very easy time of it; it was fundamentally out of touch with the world in which it sought to be actualized. Thus it went, in Huizinga's words, through periods of "emasculation" and "revitalization," finally to die out (Huizinga 1984, p. 89).

If we skip to Kant we not only find a moral division involved in the relation between humans and planets, but we also note that masculinity and femininity are together inferior to both the human and the heavenly. Curiously, Kant saw human beings finding satisfaction only by gazing on those who are inferior. "Human nature occupies as it were the middle rung of the Scale of Being, . . . equally removed from the two extremes. If the contemplation of the most sublime classes of rational creatures, which inhabit Jupiter or Saturn, arouses envy and humiliates him with a sense of his own inferiority, he may again find contentment and satisfaction by turning his gaze upon those lower grades which, in the planets Venus and Mercury, are far below the perfection of human nature" (in Lovejoy 1982, p. 193). No goddess more clearly exemplifies classical femininity than Venus, while Mercury, the Roman version of Hermes, is perhaps less obviously a representative of masculinity. Hermes was the presiding deity of phallic cults, and the phallic objects that marked boundaries in the classical Greek world were called *herms*. The function of the symbol, especially of the cut that the two halves of a token have in common, corresponds well to that of the *herm*. There is little doubt that the qualities represented by the Greek messenger god have nothing to do with the messenger angels.

Hermes is born a liar and a thief; he represents qualities that have no place among the angels. His son Pan was a model for the Christian conception of the devil. For the Greeks, however, Hermes was not a figure of moral evil. In her book *The Fragility of Goodness* Martha Nussbaum called Hermes the god of luck, and her choice of the word "luck" presents us with a concept that seems fundamentally alien to Christian ethics. At the beginning of her book Nussbaum showed how this concept is alien to Kantian ethics, one of the heirs of Christian ethics: ". . . the Kantian believes that there is one domain of value, the domain of moral value, that is altogether immune to the assaults of luck. No matter what happens in the world, the moral value of the good will remains unaffected" (Nussbaum 1986, p. 4). The importance of the concept of luck is that it introduces something outside of the subject, which has an influence on the consequences that result from acts that are ethically correct. You may act ethically and still not achieve what you want to achieve. The concept of luck introduces Otherness, not as an arbitrary and haphazard force, but rather as legislating against any guarantee that ethical action will be well received. In response Christianity posited an Other that does offer such a guarantee in the afterlife. If you act morally in the Christian sense you will ultimately receive the satisfaction of eternal life. You do not enter the Kingdom of Heaven through the agency of luck or through ambiguous mediators. We note therefore Nussbaum's reading of the *Phaedrus,* where she proposed that there is a division at the core of ethical judgments: "For it is both true and false, perhaps, that love is compatible with order, that passion can be passion and still be rational." This conclusion derives from Socrates's reflections on the etymology of the name of Pan. He said that speech "signifies everything *(to pan),* and rolls about and wanders continually, and is double-natured, both true and false" (Nussbaum, p. 233).

Angels are by definition morally unambiguous; their morality is that of a unified subject. For them there was once an occasion in which they might have sinned and in which some did. That having passed, angels are no longer subject to sin. Defined as incapable of sin, they represent a moral ideal which, translated into the human world, becomes an absolute certainty of one's moral rectitude. When you reach this point you are no longer beholden to act on your moral identity. Not only does such a certainty not require testing; it can hardly be appreciated by the corrupted and corruptible creatures of the fallen world. This creates people whose self-righteous moralizing has no use for the consequences of their actions or inactions, or better, who can always find something positive in those consequences. This human version of angelic morality seems to correlate with the views of Peter Abélard. For Abélard the division between intention and action in ethical behavior was to be abolished in favor of the standard of intention or inner motivation that properly could only be known to God himself.

As with other gods, Mercury was transformed by Christianity into an angel—not just any angel, but the angel presiding at the Last Judgment, the angel of death. Emile Mâle wrote:

Throughout the Middle Ages he was held to be the conductor of souls to the other world, the saintly psychogogue. Anxious to divert to St. Michael the worship which the still pagan inhabitants of Roman Gaul paid to Mercury, the Church early endowed the archangel with almost all the attributes of the god. On the ruins of ancient temples of Mercury, built generally on a hill, rose chapels dedicated to St. Michael; ... St. Michael, already the messenger of heaven, became like Mercury the guide of the dead. The funeral role of St. Michael is attested by ancient custom. Cemetery chapels were dedicated to him and the confraternities instituted to bury the dead recognized him as patron. He is sometimes found carved on sepulchral monuments, sometimes on the tombs. ... St. Michael, as we see, is the angel of death, and it is virtue of this that he presides at the Last Judgment. (Mâle 1972, pp. 377–78)

The question of how the moral position of the angels comes to prevail among mortals is linked to the larger issue of what happened to the angels, of why we no longer find them worthy of reflection, meditation, contemplation, or discourse. Since we identify this repression with the Renaissance, we note first that the Renaissance, in humanizing the angels, in making their representations closer to those of human beings, collapsed the distance between human and spiritual beings. Angels were not represented as separate spiritual entities, but rather as the afterlife of those who had previously sojourned on earth. Initially, this was shown in the increasing tendency to form cults to saints and to be obsessed with the presence of devils. There came to exist a closeness, even a communication between the city of God and the societies of men and women. Certainly there was still a strong belief in spiritual beings or creatures, but the good angels ceased to draw much interest, and people began concentrating on devils, on the bad or fallen angels. The angels barely survived the late Middle Ages, mired as it was in mundane issues: in melancholy over the papal schism, in conflict between religious and secular authority, and in the fallout of the Black Death. If they remained alive in the world of art, they were in a sense shadows of themselves, precisely as they became more fully fleshed out. The great age of theological speculation about the angels, which extends through William of Ockham up to the time of the Plague, was replaced by a sterile academic philosophy. The rebirth of the arts was accompanied by an eclipse of theology and philosophy. Of great philosophical minds there are almost none between Ockham and Descartes, a period of almost three centuries.

It is clear that the medieval angels could not coexist with the idealism of Renaissance humanism. While there is much evidence of an increased interest in the classics in the Renaissance—as though the medieval doctors did not immerse themselves in pagan thought—it is more to the point to note that humanism was based theologically on the humanity Christ shared with humans, but not with the angels. The value of being human was affirmed in the fact that Christ became human, he put on human flesh, something the angels could not do. Discussing Nicholas Cusanus or Nicholas de Cusa, who wrote in the early to middle fifteenth century, Cassirer stated: *"The idea of Christ* is invoked as the justification, the religious legitimation, and sanction of the *idea of humanity"* (Cassirer 1972, p. 38). Whereas the Middle Ages were replete with images of the pending apocalypse, after the occurrence of the Black Death (about as close to an apocalypse as anyone would have wanted to see) there was a return to Christ as sole mediator, and ultimately a rejection of the world of other mediating spirits, angels and saints, who were fundamentally impotent before the ravages of the Plague. If we keep in mind that saints were supposed to be able to cure plagues through miracles and that one of the ways the inhabitants of the heavens worked in the fallen world was through miraculous cures, it must have appeared at the time of the Plague that there was something radically wrong with this approach to health. Also, the great minds of the time, the professors at the University of Paris, could find no more helpful solution to the calamity than to say that it had been caused by an unfavorable conjunction of the planets. What had been considered science and the exercise of intelligence could do nothing better than to invoke the specter of bad luck. The position of Nicholas de Cusa is indicative of post-Plague thinking. Appraising it, Hans Blumenberg declared: "The ancient and medieval hierarchical cosmos has lost its reality, and indeed precisely because its mediating function between God and man has been eliminated. The operation of the Divinity streams unhindered and unmediated into the world, and in spite of intensified transcendence is more intensively omnipresent than could be conceived in the shell Cosmos of Scholasticism" (Blumenberg 1985, p. 513).

It is not accurate to say that no angels survived the Plague. The good ones may have begun to vanish, but what did survive and prosper in these times was demonology and witchcraft. Perhaps because the extent of the carnage made it impossible to provide proper burials for the dead, their ghosts were present in the form of fallen angels. On this both Protestants and Catholics found themselves in accord; it was not until the eighteenth century that the persecution of witches ceased. The Renaissance saw in the late fifteenth century the publication of the infamous inquisitors' manual, the *Malleus Maleficarum,* which systematized the persecution of witches throughout Europe and eventually America. The demonic was thus a very active force, while God's angels could excite only yawns.

If we now want to know where the angels went, the answer seems to be that they came down to earth, perhaps to combat the devils who were reigning there unobstructed. The irony is that when the rebel angels were expelled from Heaven, they too fell to earth. The idea of good earthly angels is not new. In the Middle Ages and before some people had tried to model their relationships on what was going on among the angels; thus was born the ideal of perfection. It was not too far from the self-conscious imitation of angels to becoming an angel. The important distinction is between raising oneself up through various means to the level of the angels, thus renouncing the fallen world, and being an angel within a world that has been transformed into a replica of the Heavenly City. One example of the idea of raising oneself to angelhood exists in the late sixth-century monk named Johannes Climacus. "The aim of the monk's efforts is to reach such a rest and apathy as is a reflection of God's own rest. The average man does not attain so high; neither does the ordinary monk, but only he who lives his life in absolute isolation as a hermit, only the real 'hesychast.' He and he alone perfectly represents the life on heaven in his manner of life. He is an angel upon earth" (in Nygren 1982, p. 596).

That some earthly beings could elevate themselves to the ranks of the angelic did not require the arrival of the Apocalypse and universal inquisitorial judgment. How then did the Christian moral position became universalized, to dominate in the world outside of the Church? The people of the time would have thought that only the end of the world could produce such a social transformation, and certainly they had been prepared for it by their religion.

In the thirteenth century the thought of the Last Judgment was a familiar one. Since the Saviour had said, 'Ye shall know neither the day nor the hour,' men believed no doubt that there was some impiety in wishing to guess the date, yet they liked to lend an ear to the prophecies that were current. Joachim of Flora, to whom Dante attributed the prophetic gift, had stated in his Commentary on Jeremiah that the end of the world would come about the year 1200, and St. Hildegarde had prophesied that in 1180 the Last Judgment would be imminent. To Vincent of Beauvais half a century later these predictions still seemed ominous. It was generally admitted that the end of time would be heralded by various signs: the prevalence of crime, the propagation of heresy, the spread of knowledge. More than once the mystics of the thirteenth century—severe judges of their time—believed that the day of wrath was at hand. (Mâle 1972, p. 355)

They did not have too long to wait. People of that time believed that the Plague was a punishment for some horrible offense against God; they saw it as the end of the world, as Armageddon. "In the years following 1348, Florence and Siena were swept by reports of the imminence of a new disaster or the appearance of Anti-Christ. Dire prophecies were uttered. A Franciscan Tertiary . . . proclaimed that new calamities would be wrought by an angry, unappeased God" (Meiss 1973, p. 78). In the time following the Plague people were awaiting the arrival of the angel who was to announce the Apocalypse; they were awaiting a divine emissary bringing the final message. Among those who saw themselves as God's messenger was Christopher Columbus, who thought he was in the process of finding the new world spoken of in the Apocalypse (Delumeau 1978, p. 205). Some people saw in Martin Luther an envoy from Heaven (Delumeau 1978, p. 216). And Vincent Ferrier declared at the beginning of the fifteenth century that he himself was the angel who had come to announce the Last Judgment (Delumeau 1978, pp. 212–13).

It is not easy to see how the angels come to inhabit the earth, or how in the absence of the mediating agency of the good angels people take on their moral face; but the fact that fallen angels were seen to be highly influential through the agency of witches as well as through their own wiles permits us to ask whether the good angels may not have had a similar presence. It would appear that by the time of the Renaissance it was not sufficient to expect that the Church would pardon all sins; rather, a necessity arose for acting morally on this earth, eventually to build a world in which moral action is immune to luck. The embodiment of goodness was the works of saints. The saints were closer to humanity than the angels and provided a sense of immediate experience to which people were able to relate. Cults to the saints were perhaps an intermediary stage on the way to the sanctification of all humanity.

As I see it there are two roles that define how larger numbers human beings became secular angels during and after the Renaissance. The first is the man of science whose knowledge would correspond to that of the angelic intelligences. The second is the spectator in relation to the new modes of artistic representation. The Renaissance artist, I hypothesize, attempted to provide for his spectators a vision that corresponded to the immediate and intuitive cognition of sensible objects. William of Ockham had already stated that this was a form of cognition shared by angels and human beings.

The development of science illustrates the translation of theological abstractions into human terms. There were rumblings of discontent about the angels in the Middle Ages and early Renaissance, but it would take the scientific revolution, especially the discoveries in astronomy, to rid the heavens of angels, thereby promoting the man of science as an earthly angel. Henry Corbin, an unabashed believer in the world of spirits, described this:

Theology would combat all emanationism, claim the creative act as a prerogative of God alone, end the human soul's soliloquy with the Angel Active Intelligence. But the whole cosmology was bound up with angelology. To reject the latter was to shake the foundations of the former. Now, this was precisely what perfectly served the interests of the Copernican revolution. So that we witness an alliance between Christian theology and positive science to the end of annihilating the prerogatives of the Angel and of the world of the Angel in the demiurgy of the cosmos. After that, the angelic world will no longer be necessary by metaphysical necessity; it will be a sort of luxury in the Creation, its existence will be more or less probable. (Corbin 1980, pp. 101–2)

From the time of Bacon, if not before, the Heavenly City had come to be replaced by a nature that was later called upon to provide a model for a new form of human society. Instead of gazing on the angels and the beautitudes, one could gaze into the book of nature, and the knowledge to be gained therein would correspond to the knowledge hitherto possessed only by angels. This knowledge was not the one Aquinas attributed to the angels; it seems to presuppose that the medieval doctors were mistaken in their attribution of Aristotelian science to angels. The new science, gained without reference to intermediary instances or pagan authorities, promoted itself as truer to the observable facts, thus more apt to know the world.

In place of the mystical marriage of Christ and Jerusalem, or the marriage of saintly women with Christ, we find Bacon proposing the marriage of man with nature, with the empirical, with the world of observable facts. Humans were not only allowed to have experience of this nature, but their experience was to be transformed through a careful application of the discoveries of science. As Bacon declared: "And by these means I suppose that I have established forever a true and lawful marriage between the empirical and the rational faculty, the unkind and ill-starred divorce and separation of which has thrown into confusion all the affairs of the human family" (Bacon 1960, p. 14). This is a novel extension of the Church's victory over the institution of marriage.

Bacon's rationale for his attack on the Schoolmen, the doctors of the Middle Ages, was that his knowledge of nature brought him closer to God than did their abstract logical systems. Here is an exemplary passage: "For I am building in the human understanding a true model of the world, such as it is in fact, not such as a man's own reason would have it to be; a thing which cannot be done without a very diligent dissection and anatomy of the world. But I say that those foolish and apish images of worlds which the fancies of men have created in philosophical systems must be utterly scattered to the winds. Be it known then how vast a difference there is . . . between the idols of the human mind and the ideas of the divine. The former are nothing more than arbitrary abstractions; the latter are the Creator's own stamp upon creation, impressed and defined in matter by true and exquisite lines" (Bacon 1960, pp. 113–14). It is well to have such a clear denunciation of the Scholastic enterprise, for it is probably quite similar to what most people in our time think about the world of the angels. And yet, it is also true that the "human" understanding that Bacon so valued was previously the domain of the angels—it was they who had the true knowledge that human reason could only approximate. If we are interested in the new subjectivity that experiences nature and that gains empirical knowledge of it, we will also want to know how angels know; throughout the Middle Ages this was a question of major importance.

The fact that Bacon proclaimed the development of a new science does not mean that he achieved it. Nor does it mean that he defined a form of human subjectivity that would be a functional replacement of the medieval one that derived from pagan sources and was clearly distinguished from the angelic. The credit for defining a new human subject is generally and rightly given to Descartes, and we will examine in a later chapter the extent to which this subject is angelic, to say nothing of being within the grasp of everyone. For the moment it is useful to cite Alexandre Koyré's judgment: "Bacon understood nothing of science." To which he added that the Baconian method concerned the classification of facts, putting them in order, not the application of science to practical problems (Koyré 1968, p. 346). Nevertheless, the very existence of facts and the acknowledgment of their importance does represent a shift in epistemology. For Aquinas there were no facts; when he wanted to know something about nature, he consulted Aristotle. Surely the thought did not cross his mind to consult nature directly. Even his teacher Albert the Great, a man who did engage in experimentation, was far closer to what we would call astrology and magic than what we would call science. The Scholastics did not have the idea that once they gained knowledge they were going to change the world, to create a new world for everyone to live in.

Bacon's criticism was not leveled against God and his City; he thought that the architectonic structure of God's City is revealed to the understanding through the study of nature and that God speaks to men through nature as through a universal language. His criticism was directed against the rampant Aristotelianism of the Middle Ages, the application of logic, not so much to human problems, but rather to speculation about chimera. On the Greeks Bacon had this to say: "Assuredly they have that which is characteristic of boys: they are prompt to prattle but cannot generate; for their wisdom abounds in words but is barren of works" (Bacon 1960, p. 70).

Ridding the heavens of angels involved the subversion of the Aristotelian paradigm of motion. It is not minds or intelligences that move heavenly bodies, Kepler said, but natural forces and powers. In the

Epitome Astronomiae Copernicanae, published in 1618–21, we read the following: "But the celestial movements are not the work of mind but of nature, that is, of the natural powers of the bodies, or else of the soul acting uniformly in accordance with those bodily powers" (in Wolfson 1973, p. 54). The important distinction here between mind and nature yields the idea that in order to ascertain the scientific laws that determine the movement of the celestial bodies it is not necessary to refer to a separate intelligence or mind. Direct access to nature itself provides knowledge for the scientist, providing participation in a knowledge which heretofore had not been part of a mind. Kepler hastened to add that the natural laws were the product of the "Mind of the Creator" (ibid.), but in the absence of mediating spirits separate from natural movement a place is left open for the scientist to know truly what others had mistaken by referring themselves to other minds and by seeking to receive that knowledge from ones they had supposed knowing.

To establish a human angel, it was necessary to eliminate all traces of the influence of Aristotle. Not only the verbal jousting of Scholastic debating tournaments, but also the authority of those teachers whose wisdom was so useless in time of trouble would be rejected. The wicked genie who ruled the Scholastic world, Aristotle himself, had to be reduced in size and importance. It is thus important to appreciate of the stature of Aristotle and his prior influence on scientific inquiry. Among those most responsible for the entry of Aristotle into the West was the Arab commentator Averroës or Ibn Rushd, about whom Julius Weinberg wrote the following:

Ibn Rushd expresses himself on the matter as follows: Aristotle discovered physics, logic, and metaphysics because nothing written on these subjects could be considered a satisfactory foundation of these sciences. Moreover, Aristotle has completed these sciences, for, when his works appeared, men turned away from earlier investigations and no one in fifteen hundred years has been able to add anything to them that is worthy of notice. To find all this in one man is so remarkable that one must consider him almost divine. . . . As Aristotle reached the pinnacle of human intellectual perfection, so is his doctrine the supreme truth. The reason for this is simple: Aristotle discovered both the art of demonstration and the basic premises of the sciences, that is, he found propositions that are necessary, essential, and primary from which, by absolutely certain deductions, the irrefutable conclusions follow. No perception of the senses, therefore, can conflict with these demonstrations. (Weinberg 1967, pp. 129–30)

Given such a reigning genie, there was only limited room for other angelic beings to place themselves in his wake. That many did so is incontestable, and it is equally evident that such knowledge, needing to be acquired from a teacher, was not accessible to very many people. And there was no room for the growth of science if it was all contained in the works of Aristotle.

To move away from such a pedagogical system and toward a more egalitarian one required recourse to something like the innate ideas of Plato, ideas which were in the mind of everyone, even of the unlearned, even of the layman, called by Nicholas de Cusa the *idiota*. At the beginning of *The Layman: About Mind* he provided a stark contrast between the medieval and early Renaissance attitudes. He placed the following words in the mouth of a philosopher: "It is my custom when I visit a man famous for wisdom to be most careful about what troubles me and to bring texts into the discussion and to ask his understanding of them." And the Layman answers in tones that prefigure modern attitudes: "I think that no one can be forced more easily than I to say what he feels. For while I admit that I am an unlearned and unlettered layman I do not fear to answer anything; learned philosophers and men who possess a reputation for knowledge rightly fear a mistake and so deliberate at length. So if you say plainly what you want from me, you will get it directly" (de Cusa 1979, p. 43). Cassirer's summary of de Cusa's views make them sound close to the idea of the marriage of the mind and the natural world. "The human mind, he writes, is a divine seed that comprehends in its simple essence the totality of everything knowable; but in order for the seed to blossom and bear fruit, it must be planted in the soil of the sensible world. The basic character of that 'copulative theology' sought by Cusanus lies in this reconciliation of man and nature, of intellect and sense" (Cassirer 1972, p. 45). If we know that from ancient times angelic beings were called *logoi spermatikoi* [seminal principles] and that Augustine thought (in *On the Trinity*) that angels spent some of their time planting invisible seeds in nature, the connection between this new definition of human knowledge and the angelic will be more clear.

Some people saw the Plague as punishment for excessive interest in pagan thought, coupled with insufficient attention to pure faith. They might also have thought that the excessive faith in miracles and divine intervention had stifled science. If they did not think this, the reason would have been that the task confronting them was to save the faith, to save God. Besides, they had the evidence of texts to tell them that it is the loss of faith that leads to such terrible manifestations of divine wrath. In the 1270s Aquinas is reported to have had a revelation one day that all that he had written was "straw." He stopped writing immediately, only to fall sick and to die several months thereafter. His vision may be compared with an incident that occurred to Jerome centuries before. I do not want to suggest that the same thing happened to Aquinas; the purpose of recounting this incident is to propose one way a man of the Middle Ages might have understood things. He would probably have seen it more as Jerome saw it than as we would. At a time when Jerome was utterly infatuated with reading Cicero he fell gravely ill. As all were preparing for his death he was raised up in a vision to the "Judge's judgment seat." There he proclaimed himself a Christian, only to hear the Judge reply: "Thou liest; thou art a Ciceronian, not a Christian." In the midst of the lashing he was receiving in tandem with the torture of his conscience, Jerome repented and swore never again to read Gentile authors (Jerome 1980, letter 22, pp. 128–29)

There was more to the process of rendering vast numbers of humans more angelic than is comprised in the invention of the scientist. Now we will examine the more mystical side of the enterprise. It is from this side that the new forms of artistic representation and the new conception of the being of the spectator will be derived. Reading Renaissance authors, we gain the impression that the love affair the Schoolmen maintained with logic had drained Christianity of its life, and thereby had made it increasingly difficult for people to relate to Christ. Aquinas had stated explicitly that the purpose of Christ's becoming flesh was to permit people to relate to him; the endless Scholastic debates on arcane points of logic and language seemed to leave little place for the simple Christian act of loving Christ. If we try to reconstruct the spirit of the times, the way the people tried to rebuild their world after a plague that destroyed around one-half of its inhabitants, we must begin with the idea that they believed there was something wrong with their religion or with their behavior, that they had done something to offend God grievously. Perhaps this questioning of their own sin led them inexorably to question the Church itself, especially the hierarchy of the priesthood that it placed between the people and God. Also, the effect of the Plague on the small, closely knit monastic communities was particularly disastrous. After the Plague subsided the Church was hardly in a position to be very selective about the character of those admitted to the orders.

All of this encouraged the growth of mystical tendencies that dispensed with the traditional clergy, seeking to know God directly, thus to live like the angels. Such practices were not embraced by the majority, but they did flourish. Their immediate theological source appears to have been Francis of Assisi and later Franciscans. A fine example is the life of Giovanni Colombini as described by Meiss; Colombini's Sienese successor Catherine will be discussed in a later chapter.

As Colombini and his followers moved about they sang mystical *laudi*. . . . Though the group prayed for long hours, Colombini rejected the mass, citing as predecessors in this respect Mark, Anthony, .and Paul. He was intolerant of intermediation and of formal worship. Like the extreme Spirituals and the Fraticelli [dissident Franciscans], he was opposed to books and learning. A certain Domenico, to whom he had written of mystical love, replied: "I understand clearly by your letter that all sciences, natural, ethical, political, metaphysical, economic, liberal, mechanical . . . are merely a dark cloud over the soul. . . ." Colombini said that he was "burning with the love of the Holy Spirit"; the core of his faith was the conviction that the "fire of love" would renew the world. (Meiss 1973, p. 87)

Those angels who were said to be burning with love were of the highest order, the seraphim; and it was a seraph who appeared to Francis of Assisi to communicate to him the Stigmata of Christ.

Given the failure of Church with its legions of saints and angels, its monks and priests, to say nothing of its great virginal intercessor, to mitigate or control the Plague, people became overwhelmed by their own impotence and their sense of moral cowardice. In such times there is a retreat from the idea of efficacious acts into the turmoil of affective states, be they joyous or sad. The time after the Black Death was characterized, not surprisingly, by a pervasive sense of depression. As Huizinga stated: "At the close of the Middle Ages, a somber melancholy weighs on people's souls. Whether we read a chronicle, a poem, a sermon, a legal document even, the same impression of immense sadness is produced by them all. It would sometimes seem as if this period had been particularly unhappy, as if it had left behind only the memory of violence, of covetousness and mortal hatred, as if it had known no other enjoyment but that of intemperance, of pride and of cruelty" (Huizinga 1954, p. 31). This may be nothing more than a normal mourning process, for certainly there were many dead to be mourned. But it also represents a questioning of the basis of medieval society, a pervasive sense of moral condemnation, particularly addressed to activities controlled by men. This critique of masculine behavior was perhaps extended to the intellectual activities of the Schoolmen, especially their assertions of the primacy of an intellect that was typed masculine and their barring humans from the contemplative or mystical experiences that were typed feminine.

The Black Death did not simply provide a fertile ground for the promotion of mysticism, it also contributed to a search for other knowledge. Before science came to be seen as a new path to salvation, that search led many to experiment with witchcraft and the occult. Philip Ziegler noted: "The terrors of the Black Death drove man to seek a more intense, a more personal relationship with the God who thus scourged him, it led him out of the formal paths of establishment religion and, by only a short remove, tumbled him into the darkest pit of Satanism. The Europeans of the 1350s and 1360s were no more saints or devils than their ancestors, but such emotional disturbance had been generated that they were often within a step of believing themselves one or the other" (Ziegler 1971, p. 277). Jeffrey Russell remarked the great popularity of mysticism in the fourteenth and fifteenth centuries. He made the following important observation: "But the new magical world view of the late fifteenth and sixteenth centuries revived a natural view of the occult and offered occult explanations within a highly sophisticated and coherent intellectual system. Many early modern scientists such as Ficino and Giordano Bruno (c. 1548–1600) were really magicians in this sense. Alchemy, astrology, herbology, and other such subjects formed part of a powerful and respectable intellectual system that into the seventeenth century offered effective opposition to emerging scientific materialism" (Russell 1984, pp. 285, 293). Assuming that these pseudosciences were considered to be aligned with the diabolical, would it not be logical to suggest that the other science, the one we take to be science, was allied with the angelic powers?

Whatever the reason, Scholasticism was eventually overthrown and repressed in the time following the Middle Ages. At a time when the great Scholastic thinkers were canonized and made Doctors of the Church, the authority of the Church, considered to be corrupt, received its most serious challenges. One of the ways it retained its power was to become a leader in the persecution of witches. As Marina Warner has suggested, the Church more and more relinquished the position of intellectual leadership that it had maintained through the Middle Ages. "The Reformation had challenged the virtue of Rome; the Age of Reason questioned something that had never before been doubted—its intelligence. The fountainhead of European culture and knowledge, the curators of world history, were ridiculed as ignorant and credulous. The Counter-Reformation had been a revolt: the Church would prove the Reformers wrong by exceeding them in moral courage; but the assaults that stemmed from rationalism and its legacy and continued from the eighteenth century until the present day did not produce such a muscular response, but a form of acquiescence to their critics . . ." (Warner 1983, p. 312). If medieval Scholasticism represents the Church's claim to intellectual leadership, then the challenge ought also be dated to the Renaissance.

The end of Scholasticism led to a retreat into cults of personal experience, a new love affair with empirical facts, what we now call data, and eventually to numerous efforts to ameliorate the conditions of life, especially political life, in the fallen world. While scientific knowledge is available to fewer people than the mystical and ecstatic modes of worship, the experience of looking at art, especially in Churches and other public places, was a way to extend these modes. Thus, a new style of art was born, but more importantly, a new spectator was created. That new spectator would see things as hitherto only the angels had. Interestingly enough, one of the things that the newly angelic spectator of Renaissance art could see was the sex of Christ. Leo Steinberg has demonstrated this in his book *The Sexuality of Christ in Renaissance Art and in Modern Oblivion* (1983). Also significant is the concentration on Christ as part of what is now called a mother-infant dyad. Steinberg asserted that here for the first time the infant Son of God is represented as having a visible male sexual organ.

Why is such an event so important and in what context ought we to understand it? There are many ways of articulating what the problem was. Here let us propose one. It is clear enough that Christian faith, beginning at least with Augustine, believed that Christ represented the head while the Church represented the body, and that the two would be reunited at the end of time. Christ was the Logos, the incarnate Word, and this role was given dominion over the body. In Aquinas the Incarnation is described in terms that represent a theory of how speech intersects with the body, an idea that has profound significance. This was one way of interpreting the divinity of Christ, but it had the effect of depriving people of the aesthetic enjoyment of contemplating the fleshy form of this divinity. This approach seemed to disincarnate Christ, to make him into a being of pure logic. Not only that, but the minds whose thought was used to find the rationale of the Christian faith were invariably pagan. The Church of Santa Maria Novella in Florence contains a fresco in which Christ is seen as giving the keys to the kingdom to Peter and the book of knowledge to Thomas Aquinas. Not only was Christ disincarnated, but he came to be replaced by Aristotle, a stronger thinker. Not everyone was an Aristotelian, but those who were not were either Neoplatonists, Stoics, or followers of some other exotic and non-Christian philosophy. And it is not so certain that Christian faith can stand up to such scrutiny. I do not mean that the faith cannot be rationalized or rendered reasonable, but rather that the price of such an effort is to prohibit a type of enjoyment that is the well-spring of adherence. If it is simply a question of finding intellectual enjoyment, then why does anyone need the Gospels, except perhaps to provide a challenging series of enigmas? In the Renaissance people seemed to want to stop asking so many questions, to accept matters on faith, as revealed mysteries, as truths that required nothing more than the acquiescence of belief. As a late fifteenth-century author, Brandolini, wrote: "Whereas in earlier times men had to search for the truth and dispute about it, in the Christian era men are to enjoy it" (in Steinberg 1983, p. 9). Later Descartes could assert the following at the end of his third meditation: "For, as faith teaches us that the supreme felicity of the other life consists entirely in the contemplation of the Divine Majesty, thus we experience now a similar meditation, although incomparably less perfect, which makes us enjoy the greatest contentment that we are capable of experiencing in this life" (Descartes 1953, p. 300). While earthly enjoyment does not quite measure up to what awaits us, it is still considered to be of the same kind.

Whatever enjoyment the bouts of intellectual debate and questing provided, at a certain point these pagan philosophical systems seemed to shake the foundations of the faith, and besides, there was an other enjoyment, that of mystical contemplation, of becoming like the angels, of living a moral life. This seems to be so, even if, in a wonderful paradox, the moral life proposed in the Renaissance seemed to have much to do with the life of classical antiquity. In any case, it was far more meaningful to people to discover the enjoyments of living life on earth than it was to speculate on whether two immaterial spiritual beings could be in the same place at the same time.

The term Renaissance is usually defined in terms of a rebirth of culture and learning in civilized Europe. And Renaissance art is radically different from what preceded it, most particularly in its representation of flesh. Suddenly the sight of the body became more positive, more enjoyable, even more appetizing than had hitherto been known in Christendom. This is generally attributed to the renewal of interest in pagan gods. As Jean Seznec stated, the Renaissance restored the pagan gods to their place in heaven (Seznec 1972, p. 23). Perhaps they were restored to that space once it was vacated by the angels who descended upon the earth. The significant question Seznec addressed is whether or not the gods so restored were considered to exist in their pagan splendor or whether they were simply elements in a Christian universe. He believed that at the moment the scale seemed to tip in favor of paganism, the gods were reduced "once more to the status of mere elements in a Christian universe" (Seznec 1972, p. 137). Were the gods restored as objects of worship or as aesthetic objects, newly won converts to the faith? When the Renaissance reverted to something resembling paganism, it did so in a spirit of imitation in the absence of thought that could sustain the social effectiveness of the rites. The interest in the occult and in witchcraft seemed to harken back to pagan times and did make reference to pagan divinities—many of whose names continued to label the planets—but within a Christian world these practices were candidates for suppression. The moral matrix of the faith labeled them evil, and this was not a label that their adherents necessarily disavowed.

There were pageants and other forms of entertainment that also suggested a reversion to pagan ritual, but the culture did not cease for as much to be Christian.

But beneath the gaiety and enthusiasm lurks a stubborn disquiet; just because a "pagan" cult of life is now being professed, with the gods as its incarnation, the need is felt of bringing that cult into line with the spiritual values of Christianity —of reconciling the two worlds. Humanism and art appear, for a brief moment, to have succeeded in accomplishing this result; the Renaissance, in its moment of flowering, is this synthesis—or rather, this fragile harmony. But the equilibrium is disturbed after only a few decades. The sixteenth century, as it advances, is forced to avow the disaccord which it thought had been successfully hidden. An era of crisis and reaction then dawns. The gods no longer arouse the same sentiments. Zeal is succeeded by admiration grown reticent and overscrupulous; intoxication with beauty, by a cold archeological interest, by scholarly study. From being objects of love, the gods are transformed into a subject of study. (Seznec 1972, p. 321)

The previous objects of obsessive scholarly study had been the elements of the Christian faith. A faith that is no longer scrutinized can then become the object of an unmediated belief.

There is more to the Renaissance than a renewed interest in the representation of pagan deities. The period introduced a new way of looking at the central figures of the Christian mythos. Leo Steinberg opened his book on the representation of the sexuality of Christ as follows: "Renaissance art, both north and south of the Alps, produced a large body of devotional imagery in which the genitalia of the Christ Child, or of the dead Christ, receive such demonstrative emphasis that one must recognize an *ostentatio genitalium* comparable to the canonic *ostentatio vulnerum,* the showing forth of the wounds" (1983, p. 1). Since Steinberg is quite clear in situating this body of work within the religious currents of the time, I offer the hypothesis that what is being reborn in the Renaissance is Christ Himself. Thus the renewed emphasis on the miracle of the Incarnation accompanied by the production of delight in the spectator by the vision of a more natural and complete flesh, a flesh that provides more to the eye's appetite, even if that little extra is simply the penile appendage.

Where early Christians had spent their energy claiming the divinity of Christ, where the medieval Doctors had emphasized the Divine Word, and where both had glorified the suffering of the Crucifixion that had redeemed the sins of mankind, the Renaissance developed and cultivated a passion for the flesh, for a flesh that was presented in clearly individuated anatomical details. If the wounds represent redemption, they have been replaced by the unveiled penis as a sign of Incarnation—at the risk of leading people to believe that this is where the Word becomes flesh. It is one thing for the word to become flesh where all of the flesh of Christ is a vestment for the Word; it is quite another to see in the male sexual organ the place where the body is marked by the function of proper naming in circumcision. Bernard of Clairvaux sermonized that Christ abases himself in becoming human; when he allows himself to be circumcised "he descends a thousand times lower still" (in Steinberg 1983, p. 54).

The body's organs are real organs, the artists seem to be saying, thus, that Christ assumed a body of human flesh, this in distinction to the angels who assume bodies that are not of flesh. The suspicion that Christ was an angel had already been proposed by various heretics, and the Christian response was consistently that if the body could bleed it was not angelic (Steinberg 1983, p. 63). Was this distinction sufficient? Francis of Assisi received the Stigmata through the vision of Christ in the form of a seraph. Who would deny that a Christ-like angel had seemed to bleed? Thus the deemphasis of the wounds in favor of the visible penis may well have resonated in a context in which the confusion between Christ and an angel was a problem. It is as though in rendering Christ more human the artists were saying both that Christ was human and also that his body was not the same as those of the angels. So, one irrefutable sign of Christ's humanity, his not being an angel, would have been the existence of a visible penis. This on the assumption that when an angel assumed a human body that body would not have a male sexual organ, an assumption that is open to some question.

It may be the case that the vision afforded by Renaissance artists was not of Christ as people would have seen him alive but rather as his angels saw him then. In medieval art angels are not only ministers at the events of the life of Christ, they are also and often enough witnesses and spectators. If the spectators are angels this would explain the fascination with his flesh; Christ as Word is something the angels were supposed to have known from the day of their creation. Perhaps Renaissance artists are showing what it will be like to see God when no veil of corruption separates the spectator from the visible. If there is no prurient interest in the display of the genitals, as Steinberg argued throughout, this also is characteristic of the resurrected life. When the spectator is transfixed by the scene presented by such works of art, he is in some sense removed from his flesh as he feasts his eyes on the scene before him. While we are considering the spectator to be male, following grammatical convention, it is perhaps not too blasphemous to suggest that the vision of the male sexual organ is more appealing to female spectators. There is no Christian art concerning the theme of the disrobing of the Virgin. The penis of Christ does not make him into a phallic deity; according to Steinberg the opposite pertains. "In this respect Christian culture lies at the furthest remove from cultures whose ritual imagery not only acknowledged the phallus, but empowered it to symbolize something beyond itself. . . ." "The sexual member exhibited by the Christ Child, so far from asserting aggressive virility, concedes instead God's assumption of human weakness . . ." (Steinberg 1983, pp. 45, 47–48).

The Renaissance was a time when many demons and witches were thought to exist throughout Europe. As we consider the iconography that Steinberg studied we should remember that the privileged domain of the influence of witches and devils was the genitalia. The authors of the *Malleus Maleficarum* explained well the work of the fallen angels: "And although they have a thousand ways of doing harm, and have tried ever since their downfall to bring about schisms in the Church, to disable charity, to infect with the gall of envy the sweetness of the acts of the Saints, and in every way to subvert and perturb the human race; yet their power remains confined to the privy parts and the navel. . . . For through the wantonness of the flesh they have much power over men; and in men the source of wantonness lies in the privy parts, since it is from them that the semen falls, just as in women it falls from the navel" (*Malleus Maleficarum* [MM], part 1, q. 3). In this context it is important to note a 1511 woodcut by Hans Baldung Grien, *Holy Family*, in which St. Anne is shown fondling the sex of the infant Christ. At least one scholar of Baldung believed that this gesture denoted for the artist the influence of witchcraft (Steinberg 1983, pp. 6–7). The obsessive association of witchcraft with sexual dysfunctions should alert us to the fact that the portrayal of Christ's sex in the Renaissance, within such a climate of opinion, may well have suggested more than a simple humanity.

Showing the penis of Christ also identifies him as to gender. It would have been simple enough to show the humanation or incarnation of Christ through a more realistic depiction of other bodily organs; the concentration on the penis can point only to the question of gender identity. The appearance of the sexual organ of the infant is the means through which the child is identified as male or female. Certainly, no one would want to say that the existence of a visible penis is an irrefutable sign of being human, especially since a considerable portion of the human race lacks this visible sign. The question here is not of sexual identity, of masculinity and femininity, but rather of anatomical sexual difference. Following Lacan's distinction between penis as organ and phallus as signifier or symbol, the visible presence of a penis does not make of Christ a phallic deity, a Hermes. If Lacan was correct in asserting that the phallus is always veiled, its unveiling, its being shown to be nothing more than an organ or even a bit of flesh, dephallicizes it. Whereas the phallus of Noah was forbidden as an object of sight to his sons, the sex of Christ is most appropriately reduced to an organ since it is not a phallus that had anything to do with fathering children. So the existence of a penis shows that Christ was capable of sexual relations, that his refusal to engage in them was not a sign of incapacity (Steinberg 1983, p. 17).

The question of the intersection or union of signifier and flesh is also central to the theology of the incarnation. In *The Anathemas of the Second Council of Constantinople (Fifth Ecumenical)* (533 A.D.) we read the following: ". . . the ineffable union took place without confusion, neither the Word being changed into the nature of flesh nor the flesh transferred into the nature of the Word—for each remains what it was by nature, even when the union by *hypostasis* has taken place. . . . For when saying that the unique Word was united by *hypostasis,* we do not mean that there was any mixture of the natures with each other, but rather we think of the Word as united with the flesh, each remaining what it is" (in Hardy 1954, pp. 380–81). To follow Lacan's idea that the phallus is a signifier, the veiling of the phallus means that the organ that thus intersects with the signifier loses its nature as organ, functioning as part of a discourse other than that of the body.

The evidence for the representation of Christ with an erect penis adduced by Steinberg is clear enough, and his proposal that erection equals resurrection makes sense within the theological tradition (Steinberg 1983, p. 91), even though as John O'Malley noted in his postscript to the book there is nothing in Catholic theology to correlate with this (in Steinberg 1983, p. 202). Of course there is ample evidence of devils with erections; there are no examples of such a thing in holy angels. Perhaps this is further evidence that Christ is not an angel.

If the requirement existed to demonstrate clearly the gender of Christ there must have been some question about this. If Christ drew his flesh only from his mother, where then would his male sex have come from?

Steinberg's comparison of the showing of the penis with the canonical showing of wounds sustains this idea by proposing the opposition of a masculine and a feminine genital. How long could constant meditation on Christ's wounds, on his vulnerability, continue without someone's noticing that the bleeding wound in Christ's side recalled the female sex? Perhaps this is one of the reasons the bleeding wound was often linked to the idea of a lactating breast (Bynum 1986).

We have stated that the flowering of the visual arts in the Renaissance had as its basis the provision for humans of the enjoyment hitherto reserved for spiritual creatures. It is significant that this should take place in visual arts, which are accessible to a far greater number of people than are the verbal. In comparison with the Gothic art that preceded it, this new art did not require any decoding, it did not need to be read through a system of symbols, it was simply there to be enjoyed. Emile Mâle's description of the conceptual basis for the Gothic would hardly have appealed to Nicholas de Cusa, inventor of *docta ignorantia*, learned or acquired ignorance: "The world therefore may be defined as 'a thought of God realized through the Word.' If this be so then in each being is hidden a divine thought; the world is a book written by the hand of God in which every creature is a word charged with meaning. The ignorant see the forms—the mysterious letters—understanding nothing of their meaning, but the wise pass from the visible to the invisible, and in reading nature read the thoughts of God. True knowledge, then, consists not in the study of things in themselves—the outward forms—but in penetrating to the inner meaning intended for our instruction, for in the words of Honorius of Autun, 'every creature is a shadow of truth and life' " (Mâle 1972, p. 29). Renaissance art was not devoid of symbols endowed with spiritual meaning. The point is rather that by providing an enjoyment of a more naturalistic representation of humanity, their work did not require an effort to read the painting. Steinberg presented a variant of this theme. Speaking of Renaissance artists, he declared: "They did not foresee that the process of demythologizing Christianity would succeed in profaning our vision of their sacred art; so that now, most modern viewers are content to stop at the demythicized image—a human image drawn to all appearances from the natural world, far afield from the mysteries of the Creed" (Steinberg 1983, p. 4).

To follow the fate of the angels after the Middle Ages we are led inexorably to consider demonology and witchcraft, most especially through the *Malleus Maleficarum*. This book, published at the end of the fifteenth century, was written by a pair of Dominican friars, Heinrich Kramer and James Sprenger. It would be difficult to overestimate its deleterious effects, both on the individual women who were tortured and murdered by Malleus-toting inquisitors, and on other women who found their sex to be the object of an unbounded hatred and vilification. While earlier inquisitions concerned witches among other heretics, thus making the hatred of women part of a generalized condemnation of all those who deviated from the faith, the *Malleus Maleficarum* singles out women, not only in particular instances but also as a sex. It is a monument to misogyny, representing the flowering of a new and more vicious strain.

Jean Delumeau questioned the originality of the strain by pointing to a book written in 1330 by a Spanish Franciscan named Alvaro Pelayo and entitled *De Planctu Ecclesiae*. This book was one of the foundations of the early inquisitions, those that concerned witchcraft and heresy, but we cannot give it the same weight as the *Malleus,* if only because the extent of its distribution was far inferior, and its effects thus less global. It is practically unavailable today (Delumeau 1978, p. 317ff.). The Fathers of the Church had expressed on occasion a hatred of women; they did, however, temper their hatred with an idealization of other types of women, those who were virginal and chaste. Perhaps it was the Fathers' love for women that led them to expressions of hatred, for, as Lacan has said, someone who does not know hatred does not know love either (Lacan 1975, pp. 82–84). If this is true, it accounts for the fact that the medieval cults to the Virgin should lead to an unleashing of hatred against other women, against groups for women whose alleged crime was connivance and complicity with phallic devils. As the One Woman, the Virgin does not accept the existence of women as singular beings whose feminine identification does not derive from an identification with her. Up until the end of the Middle Ages the interest in the Virgin and the Heavenly City was based in large part on the theological necessity of repopulating the Heavenly City, thus in the production of angels. After the Plague, however, the matter of repopulating the earth was a more urgent preoccupation, and the sexual act as a natural and thereby good means to this end gained importance as an ideal. Witches were those who interfered with its normal completion; their claims to control nature by invoking malevolent spirits were a major threat at a time when references to the angelic had become problematic and when nature was called upon to provide a more certain path to the mind of God. We have already seen in the discussion of the Baldung woodcut the possibility of a link between the Virgin and the witches. It remains to elaborate that connection, and thereby, through an analysis of the demonic, to clarify what the angels are about.

Kramer and Sprenger were Dominicans; they belonged to the same monastic order as Aquinas. The influence of the Angelic Doctor is present constantly in their work. Certainly they wanted to appeal to the most sound authority, to make it appear that the Church was always misogynistic in the same way that they were. And obviously, the importance given to witches is a sign of women's power, generally defined as a power to do harm, but this must accompany an equal power to do good. Since women were for these authors the Supreme Evil, even more malevolent than devils, it is hardly an irrational leap to say that Woman is the Supreme Good. The difference between a woman, whose plural is women, and Woman, which, being everything, has no plural, is essential to this formulation. "The evils which are perpetrated by modern witches exceed all other sins which God has ever permitted to be done." They added that the enormity of these sins exceeds those of "other worldly crimes," both "the sins of the bad Angels" and those of our "first parents" (MM, Part 1, q. 14). Given this belief, it is justifiable to destroy witches, to exterminate them. Such acts of ritual purification occur in the breach between the necessity to reproduce the species and the necessity to rid the world of eroticism. The assumption was that there could be sex without sin. Obviously this was not quite the image of the resurrected life, though it did represent a step forward in the effort to make the earth more heavenly. During this intermediate stage on the way to the resurrected life sex was allowable under certain conditions in order to fill out the number of the faithful.

Women became witches by engaging in a contract or compact with a devil. This pact was then consummated sexually, in something like a marriage. Women are prone to such acts by what Kramer and Sprenger considered their insatiable sexual appetite. Men have been spared from becoming wizards in such great numbers because Christ "has so far preserved the male sex from so great a crime" (MM, part 1, q. 6). Here we have a flagrant example of a sexual division in which men are entirely mental creatures and women entirely sensual. It is hardly surprising within such a context that women should be chronically unsatisfied. Nor is it surprising to read in the *Malleus* the number of cases in which the effect of witchcraft is to render a man impotent or to cause his sex to disappear. Faced with the power of witches, the phallus becomes the weaker sex.

The book reads almost like a manual in early sexology, its interest in sexual dysfunction being extensive, its pretension to knowledge about such dysfunction being similarly vast. The devil, like an angel, has power over bodies. He may inhibit sexuality in several ways: by preventing the bodies of men and women from approaching each other; by inflaming a man toward a woman and rendering him impotent with another; by disturbing the imagination to make a sexual partner appear to be hideous; by suppressing the vigor of the male sexual organ; and finally, by preventing ejaculation in closing the seminal ducts or else by making it that semen is spent vainly (see part 2, q. 2, chap. 2).

What is perhaps most important, more important even than listing the many ways in which "the venereal act" cannot be accomplished, is the fact that herewith is an explicit doctrine of sexual normality; it is as though the act of conjugal heterosexual intercourse, the kind that produces offspring, were divinely ordained, and thus, any interference with the divine or angelic will in these matters represented the most heinous of crimes. But rather than appeal to angels to guarantee a successful coupling, the activity proposed is a fight against devils through their witches. In the medieval and prior Christian conception, virginity was most valued and heterosexual coupling was part of the curse of the fallen nature, to be overcome when the work of producing children had ended. Here it seems to have been redeemed, but only so long as it is practiced normally and continues to produce children. It seems reasonable to assume that if a subject like sexual normality becomes of compelling interest in a cultural or social climate, then a significant number of people are experiencing sexual difficulties. In another sense the authors, in setting up sexual norms, may also have been trying to forestall the development of erotic arts and practices of the sort that Christianity had long since attempted to excise. The obsessive interest in the successful accomplishment of the sexual act seems to have replaced the obsession with conjugal fidelity that was so common in the Middle Ages.

Retaining a semblance of fidelity with tradition, the authors proposed that the reason that witches destroy unborn or unbaptized children is that these children will not be able to enter the Heavenly City and this will delay the Last Judgment. "For the devil knows that, because of the pain of loss, or original sin, such children are debarred from entering the kingdom of Heaven. And by this means the Last Judgment is delayed, when the devils will be condemned to eternal torture; since the number of the elect is more slowly completed, on the fulfillment of which the world will be consumed" (MM, part 2, q. 1, chap. 13). The problem is that the previous Fathers of the Church who were counseling virginity also thought that they were acting to fill up these empty places. Filling them with virgins is not the same as filling them with a larger number of baptized children. Even though Jerome thought that marriage could produce more virgins his emphasis was on the moral perfection of each individual, not on the production of greater numbers of the faithful. This is clearly a logical problem, and it reflects a change in the Church's position. The interest in reproduction reflects a political decision of consequence. It is almost as though the authors were not so much concerned with the repopulation of the Heavenly City as they were with filling the ranks of the faithful and of repopulating the world, recently deprived of many of its citizens by the Plague. This is an important moment in reproductive politics, a moment in which it was decided that women should produce many children, especially many Catholic children, thus making the strength of the Church correspond, not to the few saints and Doctors, but to the expanding number of Catholics. At the same time this thought had to be rendered consistent with the adoration of virginal chastity prescribed for religious.

We also remark the similarities that exist in the acts of the devils and the acts of the angels. In the first chapter I proposed that there was no marital exchange between a Mother Goddess and another woman because for such a Goddess there are no other women. Here we not only see that witches are the prototypical other women in such a matriarchal world, but also that the function of witchcraft is structurally parallel. The authors of the *Malleus Maleficarum* stated often that women resort to the craft of witches when they have lost a man to another woman. "For men are very often bewitched in this way because they have cast off their former mistresses, who, hoping that they were to be married and being disappointed, so bewitch the men that they cannot copulate with another woman." Perhaps such a man deserves what he receives, but note more carefully the sentence that follows: "And in such a case, according to the opinion of many, the marriage already contracted is annulled, unless, like Our Blessed Lady and St. Joseph, they are willing to live together in holy continence" (MM, part 2, q. 2, chap. 2). This says that the influence of witchcraft may be countered by renouncing sexual intercourse; thus, the intention not to copulate renders the inability to copulate saintly. The problem that the authors confronted here is logical; how can you tell whether abstinence has been produced by a devil or an angel, a witch or the Virgin?

Not only witches render men impotent. It is reported that angels also perform this function, essentially by rendering holy men eunuchs. Tormented by temptation, the Blessed Abbot Equitius prayed to God to relieve him of his phallic affliction: "And when he continuously prayed Almighty God for a remedy against this affliction, an Angel appeared to him one night and seemed to make him an eunuch, and it seemed to him in his vision that all feeling was taken away from his genital organs; and from that time he was such a stranger to temptation as if he had no sex in his body. Behold what benefit there was in that purification; for he was so filled with virtue that, with the help of Almighty God, just as he was preeminent among men, so he afterwards became preeminent over women" (MM, part 2, q. 1). His affliction is obviously phallic, which is consistent with tradition. The deviation lies in the fact that instances of such disinterest in other men are considered in the book to be the work of witches. So how is one to know whether the lack of temptation is the work of devils or angels? Also interesting is the idea that once relieved of the pull of the phallus toward women, this Abbot came to dominate them, probably through the force of his virtue. This is not a very commonly admitted motive for sexual disinterest and impotence in men.

Not to be outdone, Thomas Aquinas had an experience that surely ranks high in the annals of one-up-manship. When Aquinas decided to join the Dominican order his family objected and his brothers kidnapped him and confined him in a fortress for two years. Their strategy was eventually foiled:

Wishing to tempt him, they sent him a seductive and sumptuously adorned harlot. But when the Doctor had looked at her, he ran to the material fire, and snatching up a lighted torch, drove the engine of the fire of lust out of his prison; and prostrating himself in a prayer for the gift of chastity, went to sleep. Two Angels then appeared to him, saying: Behold, at the bidding of God we gird you with a girdle of chastity, which cannot be loosed by any other such temptation; neither can it be acquired by the merits of human virtue, but is given as a gift of God alone. And he felt himself girded, and was aware of the touch of the girdle, and cried out and awaked. And thereafter he felt himself endowed with so great a gift of chastity, that from that time he abhorred all the delights of the flesh, so that he could not even speak to a woman except under compulsion, but was strong in his perfect chastity. (MM, part 2, q. 1)

For those with a more psychoanalytic bent this gives some consistency to the preoccupations of the Angelic Doctor. Otherwise, it is called fighting fire with fire. And we learn here that there is an erotic satisfaction in conversation, that so long as men and women converse with words, even in innocent circumstances, they risk inflaming erotic interest. The gift from God is a gift of love, of *caritas*, and the purpose of this love is to preserve man from the part of his body that responds to fallen women.

Aside from the considerable psychological interest of these texts, they demonstrate the parallel between the actions of angels and those of devils. Both dephallicize, but for different reasons and with different consequences. Angels work on men of God, men whose desire can only exist outside of the Church-sanctioned marriage contract. Witches prevent those whose inferior nature caused them to marry from reproducing, thus preventing them from redeeming their sexuality. The actions of angels are the same as those of the devils, in inverted form. What else can we learn of angels by examining the work of devils? One of the most significant functions of devils and witches is to prevent the birth of offspring. They do this in several ways: by preventing the sexual act from taking place in rendering one or both of the partners incapable of performing it; by preventing the ejaculation of semen, thus making fertilization impossible; by killing a fetus in the womb; and finally, by causing the infant to be stillborn or to die before baptism. Listed this way, these various nefarious acts seem to form something like a hierarchy of evils. It would seem that preventing the sexual act from taking place is not as evil an act as killing a newborn infant. An infant who is killed before being baptized is offered to the Devil, while the infant who would have been conceived from a sexual act that never took place seems not to have suffered the same fate.

The notion of hierarchy was introduced into the culture in reference to angels. So we note that any one of these ways of not producing a child may take place without the influence of devils and witchcraft. Certainly, taking a vow of continence was considered to be a sign of consummate virtue. For the rest, these things do happen naturally, according to nature, and it would be difficult to say within a Catholic theological position that such natural occurrences are anything but signs of the will of God. So I hypothesize that when such things happen naturally what is produced is not of the order of evil, but rather of the order of goodness; thus that the children who are not conceived or who are not born in such circumstances become part of the company of heavenly angels. As Lacan said, those beings who are intermediate between being and not-being are the unborn (See Lacan 1973, chaps. 2 and 3). In the words of Gregory of Nyssa, from the *Treatise on Virginity:* "For in all truth this virgin mother—she who is called sterile by the prophet because of her continence—rejoices to carry in her bosom, by the virtue of the Spirit, these immortal infants" (Gregory 1966, p. 431). One might argue here that by "immortal infants" Gregory does not exactly mean angels; the idea, however, is that in the absence of the conception of human children a woman produces something else.

This tells us why virginity was held in such high esteem, why celibacy was valued above reproduction. Those who held such values, according to my hypothesis, not only expected that the chaste couple would join the angels in heaven, but also that the children that they might have but did not produce would be there too. It is almost as though someone had reasoned as the Greeks that in life the most blessed state is never to have been born, with second best going to dying as soon as possible. What we are proposing then is a system in which reproductive potential, in itself a good, is actualized in the production of spirits when it is not actualized through sexuality. The potential or possible people, the people who might have been born into sin but were not, become angels through another form of actualization in another place. If this is true, the Church has created a world in which the fertility of women is held to be the highest value and in which their monthly loss of reproductive potential is elevated and blessed, transvalued into the production of an angel. What is called "the curse" would then have become a blessing in disguise. So effective is the disguise that there is very little direct evidence of such a thought. Of indirect evidence we note that virginity legislates against any interruption of the menstrual cycle.

You will recall the passage from Augustine quoted at the end of the previous chapter, where he stated that the Heavenly Jerusalem, who will be fulfilled beyond her dreams by the great numbers of angels who will join her after the end of time, was called barren on earth. Would it be too strange to extend this experience to those women who identify with her, who reject femininity and commerce with the phallus to become Woman? The most peculiar piece of evidence for the idea that angels are formed of feminine reproductive potential is offered by Monsignor Giuseppe del Ton, a Vatican prelate, who said in a recent work that the final number of angels is ninety-nine times the total number of people who will have lived on earth by the end of time (in *Paris-Match*, Jan. 2, 1987, p. 11). Could this number approximate the amount of untapped female reproductive potential? Since nine is the number of months required for the gestation of a human child, perhaps doubling it refers to a nongestation.

Evidence concerning the positive value of menstrual blood is extremely rare, nonetheless. It is found mostly in the idea that a woman's blood provides the matter for an embryo, thus that it is redeemed through conception. But this blood, having been attracted to the uterus by copulation, gains thereby, Aquinas said, an impurity, except in the case of the conception of Christ, where the blood is drawn to the right place by other than copulative means. Reading the following texts, you should keep in mind that while a human body has matter, an angel, according to Aquinas, does not have matter but only potential. It is not the matter of menstrual blood that is formed into an angel but rather the potential it represents. "Therefore, it was becoming that Christ's body should be formed not from the flesh and bones of the Virgin, but from her blood, which as yet is not actually a part, but is potentially the whole. . . . Hence, He is said to have taken flesh from the Virgin, not that the matter from which his body was formed was actual flesh, but blood, which is flesh potentially" (ST, part 3, q. 31, art. 5). At the least this suggests that blood is identified as potential; to the extent that it is expelled it is unactualized potential, thus corrupt. Perhaps the blood that is not actualized as a being that can never become flesh. On the question of menstrual blood, Aquinas managed a very neat trick in his discussion of Christ's humanation from a corrupt substance:

But the menstrual blood, the flow of which is subject to monthly periods, has a certain natural impurity of corruption: like other superfluities, which nature does not heed and therefore expels. Of such menstrual blood infected with corruption and repudiated by nature, the conception is not formed; but from a certain secretion of the pure blood which by a process of elimination is prepared for conception, being, as it were, more pure and more perfect than the rest of the blood. Nevertheless, it is tainted with the impurity of lust in the conception of other men: inasmuch as by sexual intercourse this blood is drawn to a place apt for conception. This, however, did not take place in Christ's conception: because this blood was brought together in the Virgin's womb and fashioned into a child by the Holy Ghost. (ST, part 3, q. 31, art. 5)

Perhaps you will not find it excessive to recommend that a similar process could exist in a split between the lost blood of menstruation and the lost potential to reproduce.

Is our hypothesis consistent with the theology about angels? Aquinas declared them to be immaterial, having no matter, but only form. In this he departed from the view of Bonaventure and other Franciscans who said they did have matter and that of Bernard of Clairvaux, who could not conceive them without bodies. Consistent with our view is his idea that angels were created after, not before, the corporeal world (Aquinas ST, part 1, q. 61, art. 3). However, "They were made in a corporeal place in order to show their relationship to corporeal nature, and that they are by their power in touch with bodies" (Aquinas ST, part 1, q. 61, art. 4). Even though angels are immaterial, Aquinas did grant that they have potentiality and act. "Although there is no composition of matter and form in an angel, yet there is act and potentiality. And this can be made evident if we consider the nature of material things, which contain a twofold composition. The first is that of form and matter, whereby the nature is constituted. Such a composite nature is not its own existence; but existence is its act. Hence the nature itself is related to its own existence as potentiality to act. Therefore if there be no matter, and supposing that the form itself subsists without matter, there nevertheless still remains the relation of the form to its very existence, as of potentiality to act" (Aquinas ST, part 1, q. 50, art. 2). Now this is hardly self-evident. He was talking about a form of creation in which there is a composition of matter and form; such a composition would produce a material being, a human being. But he supposed that the form, let us say, of a child, may subsist without its being materialized; it requires an act to make this form exist in the absence of a material composite. This act creates an angel, in our terms, from a possibility that has not been actualized materially.

From these terms a hierarchy can be formed. As Dante learned in Canto 29 of the *Paradiso,* the highest angels are most purely act, while the lower orders are more purely potential. In Canto 32 he also learned that among the company of angels are children, "spirits released from the flesh/ before they could have a true choice." They are there, he was told, through no merit of their own. Finally, in the previous Canto the angels had been compared to a swarm of bees; bees were singled out by Augustine for special mention because, as he saw it, they do not reproduce by sexual intercourse (Augustine OT, book 3, chap. 8). If it is only the lower orders of angels that assume human form, is the unactualized potential they represent a potential birth, while the higher orders represent potential conceptions?

These parallels are not to my knowledge drawn in theology, for a reason that ought to be self-evident. If God is given the will to prevent conception, then why can't his will be enacted through the use of a contraceptive, or through a pregnancy that does not reach its term? Either of these points would undercut the Church's position on abortion and contraception: further, it would seriously question the claims that the Virgin is a fertility goddess, giver of life, health, and fecundity. And finally, in the French countryside, until recently, the common phrase used to describe abortionists was: makers of angels, *faiseuses d'anges.*

The theological question arising from the idea that angels are the forms of unconceived children, or the actuality of unactualized possible children, is whether these angels have been touched by original sin. If there was no conception and no sexual act, would there have been original sin in the beings who had been conceived for not being conceived? This would place the question of the Immaculate Conception in a somewhat different light. If the Virgin Mary was the only woman worthy of giving flesh to the Word because she was not conceived in sin, then the women who give birth to angels (in not giving birth to children) would be assumed to impart to those angels the capacity for sin, since they themselves were conceived in sin. Perhaps this is why angels are lower than Christ in the Heavenly hierarchy and why they are required on one occasion to choose virtue over sin.

The focus on reproductive material leads to an interesting division. Theologians are obliged to condemn masturbation by men because it represents the waste of seed, the misuse of a substance whose natural function is to fecundate. Jacquart and Thomasset note that medieval medicine attempted to preserve male seed and at the same time it favored the expulsion of feminine "liquid" (Jacquart and Thomasset 1985, p. 211). Masturbation in women, however, does not involve such waste and therefore it was countenanced. No less than Albert the Great, Doctor of the Church and saint, counseled the practice of masturbation by women, since he believed that it tempered genital pressures and contributed to their becoming more chaste (in Jacquart and Thomasset 1985, p. 210). As far as female masturbation is concerned, Jean-Louis Flandrin noted that in the Middle Ages theologians considered the following question: "Is it lawful for the wife to achieve an orgasm by fondling herself when her husband has withdrawn before she has made her emission?" And he answered that of the seventeen theologians who considered this question three forbade it and fourteen allowed it (in Ariès and Béjin 1985, p. 119).

It may have taken some time to figure out, but certainly menstruation is a natural process; it does not represent what the theologians might have called a perversion of the will. Thus the natural loss of reproductive material in menstruation cannot be sinful in the sense of being an act of the will, whereas the unnatural waste of semen in male masturbation and even nocturnal emissions must be sinful. If the latter activity is consistently associated with the demonic, with the bestial, why would the former not be associated with the angelic? The medieval attitude was that feminine enjoyment contributed to making the child more beautiful, even though it was not necessary for conception. Otherwise, why would God have created it (ibid., pp. 118–19)? This attitude seems to have changed radically in the Renaissance, when it came to the question of witches copulating with invisible devils, where the act appeared to be solitary. Kramer and Sprenger suggested that this activity produces something like a demonic form. "But with regard to any bystanders, the witches themselves have often been seen lying on their backs in the fields or the woods, naked up to the very navel, and it has been apparent from the disposition of those limbs and members which pertain to the venereal act and orgasm, as also from the agitation of their legs and thighs, that, all invisibly to the bystanders, they have been copulating with Incubus devils; yet sometimes, howbeit this is rare, at the end of the act a very black vapor, of about the stature of a man, rises up into the air from the witch" (MM, part 2, q. 1, chap. 4). Here we have a graphic description of the production of a demonic form. Why would something similar not pertain to the production of an angelic form?

Initially Christianity connected virginal barrenness with the state of Jerusalem. Nothing was more maternal than producing immortal infants, infants who would grow up to be angels. After the Plague the shift in emphasis from the requirement of producing more angels to the production of more Christians led to the identification of women with the Virgin in the sense that she was a mother, that she gave birth to a human child.

I have introduced something like a mythic origin or creation of the angels, admittedly on somewhat scant evidence. We are, however, talking about a religion in which a woman's fertility is clearly sacred and in which worship is offered to a god produced from a woman who not only never engaged in sexual activity but whose own conception was considered to be immaculate. Making angels a function of a maternal space leads to the fact that the vast majority of the holy angels do not have proper names, in marked contrast not only with the pagan gods but more particularly with the angels of Gnosticism and Judaism. It is almost as though the angels provide a myth of the origin and perpetuation of a world inhabited by intelligible meanings.

Angels were understood to be invisible intelligible spirits, and it is consistent with tradition to see them as something like a world of concepts (or conceptions) that preexists their taking on a verbal form that appeals to the senses. For the medieval thinker the question of the angels was linked to questions of a particular semantics in which mental concepts or meanings existed in purified form in their own separate space, and where language existed to signify those concepts. Such a view was inherited from Plato.

We will want to see how the absence of proper names and the function of proper naming tends to throw questions of semantics onto the side of the verb. For the moment note that of the enormous number of angels, only a handful have proper names. Michael, Gabriel, Rafael, and Uriel are clearly exceptions. Since a proper name is given at birth, this supports the link between angels and the unborn. And since the sex of the child is usually not known before birth, the theological belief that immaterial or bodiless beings are not sexed is also consistent. Intermediary beings who are named and sexed may well be the spirits of the dead. Angels, however, are identified with eternal life, and are therefore deprived of their names and their sex. (From early on in Christianity, church councils had strictly forbidden the naming of angels).

The only problem was that saints were, on the authority of Scripture, said to be the equals of the angels. The saints did have names, they had been sexed beings, and they inspired cults that were dangerously close to those of pagan gods.

In the eyes of the thirteenth century the real history of the world was the story of the city of God. . . . But for the Christian of the Middle Ages the saints were not only heroes of history, they were also his intercessors and patrons. There was more than a relic of classical paganism in the honour they received, and they mingled in the lives of men and cities like the indigenous gods of ancient Rome. The Christian received at baptism the name of the saint who was to be his patron and example. These names were not chosen at [random], but were preferably those of ancient local bishops and monks whose relics worked wonders, and many baptismal names, today proper names, point to the native district of the family who bear them. When the child grew up, chose a trade and entered a guild, a new saint welcomed him. If he were a mason he celebrated the feast of St. Thomas the apostle, if a wool carder the feast of St. Blaise, if a tanner the feast of St. Bartholomew. On that occasion he forgot the hard work and the long days, and proud as a knight he walked behind the banner of his patron saint, went to mass with the master and wardens, and later sat at table with them. (Mâle 1972, pp. 268–69)

Saints represent an intermediary stage between the love of angels and the obsession about the presence of devils. The growth in cults of saints at the end of the Middle Ages was in part a reaction to the Plague; saints as intercessors were vouchsafed the ability to cure such things. They also represent a bridge between the concept of angels and that of humanity. "Thus towards the end of the Middle Ages an ultrarealistic conception of all that related to the saints may be noticed in the popular faith" (Huizinga 1954, p. 166). The saints were originally less threatening than angels, because people could relate to them. "The saint, with his clearly outlined figure, his well-known attributes and features as they were painted or carved in the churches, was wholly lacking in mystery. He did not inspire terror as do vague phantoms and the haunting unknown. The dread of the supernatural is due to the undefined character of its phenomena. As soon as they assume a clear-cut shape they are no longer horrible" (Huizinga 1954, p. 168).

Yet the saints became through a dialectical reversal the causes of the ills they were called upon to protect against. "The terrors of the plague called for more than one saintly protector; Saint Sebastian, Saint Roch, Saint Giles, Saint Christopher, Saint Valentine, Saint Adrian, were all honored in this capacity by offices, processions and fraternities. Now here lurked another menace to the purity of the faith. As soon as the thought of the disease, charged with feelings of horror and fear, presented itself to the mind, the thought of the saint sprang up at the same instant. How easily, then, did the saint himself become the object of his fear, so that to him was ascribed the heavenly wrath that unchained the scourge" (Huizinga 1954, p. 173). This shows the risk of referring to angel-equivalents who have proper names. The evocatory power of the name, its signifying presence, tended to supercede the holy meaning, thus to function like a god or demon.

Such a gesture comports serious risks for the Church, especially in its introducing moral equivocation into the world of intermediary beings. It led finally to the reassertion of a cult of the angels at the close of the Middle Ages through the ministry of Jean Gerson. "Too large a part of the living faith had crystallized in the veneration of the saints, and thus there arose a craving for something more spiritual as an object of reverence and a source of protection. In addressing itself to the angel, vaguely conceived and almost formless, piety restored contact with the supernatural and with mystery" (Huizinga 1954, p. 176). When Huizinga added that the cults of the saints were destroyed by Luther a century after Gerson, we should also add that the angels did not fare much better in the Reformation.

I have invoked the idea of the actualization of unactualized potential or possibility, saying that what is not actualized in one place will be in another. The idea of potential or possible beings is perhaps not very clear. It is generally attributed to Leibniz, who asserted in his *Discourse on Metaphysics* that God could have created any one of a number of possible Adams and that he created only one of them. This, as we have already noted, caused no small consternation in the eminent Churchman Antoine Arnauld, who had difficulty conceiving of unactualized possibilities in God. We have already offered a response; it remains to clarify it. One approach is to examine the objection offered by Willard Quine: "Wyman's slum of possibles is a breeding ground for disorderly elements. Take, for instance, the possible fat man in that doorway; and, again, the possible bald man in that doorway. Are they the same possible man, or two possible men? How do we decide? How many possible men are there in that doorway? Are there more possible thin ones than there are fat ones? How many of them are alike? ..." (Quine 1980, p. 4). This is a well-known passage in the field of the philosophy of language. Does it not strike you that some of these questions may be asked of angels? Aquinas, who is usually pictured as both fat and bald (or at least, tonsured), entitled a section of the *Summa Theologica*: "Of the Angels in Relation to Place." In it, perhaps anticipating Quine, he asked the following questions: "Whether an angel is in a place?"; "Whether an angel can be in several places at once?"; "Whether several angels can be at the same time in the same place?" The answers he offered are: 1. that an angel is in a place; 2. that an angel is only in one place at one time; 3. that no two angels can be in the same place at the same time (Aquinas ST, part 1, q. 52).

The skepticism of Quine leads to a consideration of the connection of angels with possible beings from the point of view of semantic theories. The problem simply put is that when we say that John might have gone to China but did not, precisely what are we talking about? The action of going to China has no referent in the real world and does not claim one. To make sense does it need to refer to a possible world in which John is in China, and if this is so is the John who did not go to China the same as the John who is conceived as having gone? Does the predicate "going to China" alter the referent of the proper name? If we say, for example, that John-in-China is different from John-in-Chicago, then we would be siding with those who believe that John stayed in Chicago while his counterpart went to China.

If, however, the proper name has the same referent in all possible worlds, if it is in Kripke's term a rigid designator, then what we say of John does not change who we are talking about; it does not have an effect on the referent. Kripke defines a possible world or a counterfactual situation as one that might have been, that might or would have taken place under certain circumstances, but that did not or has not yet become actual (Kripke 1980, p. 18). (Of course, it may also be a future contingent, as in "John might go to China.") We may understand this in several ways. Some people, for example, have been led to reflect what the world would have been like if there had been no original sin, if mankind had remained in a state of Paradise or a state of Nature. Reflections by Augustine and by John Scotus Erigena about sexuality in the pre-fallen world can be classed in this category. Later thinkers have devoted themselves to rendering this possible world, the world in which Nature had not been corrupted, actual. This involves becoming one's counterpart, the counterpart of oneself that would have existed if the Fall had never taken place, thus becoming an angel on earth. A somewhat different counterpart is the angel one would have become had one not been born. This counterpart is called a guardian angel. The development of a moral being through an accretion of virtuous intentions will lead to the liberation of that being into a new and better possible world. It may even be joined in that place with a possible body, one that is not subject to decay and the ravages of mortality. Thus the soul will ultimately join all those who had the supreme good fortune never to have been born and never to have been named. If, however, the proper name designates rigidly in all possible worlds, the consequence as I see it is that one is obliged to choose which possibilities correspond to one's desire and to act to bring them into reality. To say that the possibilities have some sort of reality produces the consequence of relieving one of the responsibility of choosing which one ought to be rendered real. If John desires to go to China, then just as the proper name designates rigidly, so should going to China come to designate an actual state of affairs for John.

While desire is always counterfactual, not everything that is counterfactual is a desire of the subject about whom it is predicated. For the moment note simply that it is necessary that John be a speaking subject representing himself as "I" in order for him to assume anything of his desire.

Is it possible for there to be no desire, no unactualized possibilities? Is it possible to overcome desire and to escape from sin and death? Is this the meaning of Christian love? Is this what was meant when Aquinas appropriated the first unmoved mover from Aristotle and made God into a being of pure act? If it is the fact of bearing a proper name that brings the subject face-to-face not with God but with possibilities that may or may not represent his desire, then the beings most apt to embody the Christian promise are beings who were never named in the kinship system that imposes ethical obligations in relation to the real.

Among humans, if there were a being who was exempt from sin, untouched by desire even unto the act of its production, then that being would not have to pass through death on the way to Heaven; the possible being that had been created and lived on earth would pass directly into the City of God. This is, of course, the idea of the Assumption of the Virgin, who is, afterall, superior even to her Son for not having died. And while this Lady certainly has a name, if the designating function of the name marks the body, what is the status of the unmarked, virginal body? We will return to this point.

An important conceptual problem here concerns desire. While Protestantism tends to want to eliminate all forms of desire, Catholicism tried to transform them into one desire with which it could live. Desire is a desire for God, a desire for the Good, a desire for perfection, whether it is the perfection of a being or the perfection of a relationship. Thus is desire purified by love. The question remains whether this is still desire, or whether desire has not been reduced to something else that has nothing to do with what was originally desire. If there is a Supreme Good that is ultimately the object of desire, does this not suggest that desire, in seeking this Good, seeks nothing more than its own annihilation as desire? Gregory of Nyssa reasoned that desire never gets there, but there is nonetheless a class of heavenly beings who are fulfilled beyond desire through love. When authors like Origen and Bernard of Clairvaux provided a reading of the highly erotic and suggestive Song of Songs, they transposed the action into the world of the mystical union of Christ and the Church, thereby denuding it of its erotic connotations and perhaps even of its erotic reality.

While the idea of union, of the one God who brooks no competing deities, is consistent with love, it is not clear that it can coexist with desire. If there is only one, what is there to desire? Some writers see God as acting entirely through will, not through desire, because what could God lack or want? Adam may have needed a wife because something was wanting in his life; we may not, within the context of theology, suggest that God created man for the same reason. Nor could God have sent his Son to save mankind because something was lacking to him; he did it, Aquinas said, because he demands satisfaction for the fault of the original parents of mankind (see Aquinas SCG, book 4, chap. 54). This is not the same as to desire something; it is a demand for unconditional love.

And yet, we have seen that Jerusalem, according to Augustine, lacks something: does she desire what she lacks? If Jerusalem desiring does not desire the state of fulfillment that will exist when the Heavenly City has been repopulated, if feminine desire is not satisfied with what religion has promised and offered it, the consequences are terrible to consider. A woman's desire that is not satisfied by heavenly children might direct itself toward God himself. If that desire is erotic it may not be appeased by gazing forever into his holy face. Perhaps this is why Jerusalem inhabits the earth and why she is supposed to descend again in the Apocalypse. If she was barren the first time, maybe the second she was taken to be a witch.

Within the category of things that may be eternally desired because they can never be possessed we find the Oedipal desire of never having been born. It is strictly excluded that any human being ever attain that object of desire. Is it also desirable never to have been named, or if having been named, to act as though the naming had never taken place? The extreme paucity of named angels is unique to Christianity, even among the monotheistic religions. The pagan deities and the dead to whom sacrifices are offered are all named, and once they are named they become part of a family, have relations, and also have desire which they act upon. Christ gains a proper name only when he is born; otherwise he is called the Word, the Verb, the Logos. If Christ, the Son of God, is the Word, why not say that the angels, called sons of God, are words, not as spoken or written, but as mental concepts or words-in-thought? Beginning at least with Augustine, the word-in-thought has priority over the uses of language, as though speech and written language were corrupting influences in the fallen world. But is it plausible to believe that these words or mental concepts constitute a world of beings who do not have names? It is if the angels are the unborn; for it is necessary to be born to be named, to receive a name that enters into social commerce. It is significant that a study of medieval Jewish texts on angels reveals that there are thousands of proper names for the angels. Christian texts of the same period have no more than the handful mentioned in the Bible (Caquot 1971, p. 140).

The theoretical issue is whether the function of proper naming can be reduced to what are called descriptive references, definite descriptions that fix a reference without there being a proper name, and that are substitutable for any proper name. A contemporary version of this point was made by Quine in *From a Logical Point of View:* "Whatever we say with the help of names can be said in a language that shuns names altogether." You may want to know how this is done: "In order to subsume a one-word name or alleged name such as 'Pegasus' under Russell's theory of descriptions, we must, of course, be able first to translate the word into a description. But this is no real restriction. If the notion of Pegasus had been so obscure or so basic a one that no pat translation into a descriptive phrase had offered itself along familiar lines, we could still have availed ourselves of the following artificial and trivial-seeming device: we could have appealed to the *ex hypothesi* unanalyzable attribute of *being Pegasus,* adopting for its expression the verb 'is-Pegasus,' or 'pegasizes.' The noun 'Pegasus' could then be treated as derivative, and identified after all with a description: 'the thing that is-Pegasus,' 'the thing that pegasizes' " (Quine 1980, pp. 7–8, 13).

This suggests that we can identify people through their attributes, through the way in which we describe them. Once you can do that it would be reasonable to say that their moral character and their ability to love provide them with an identity irrespective of the proper name they bear. If we have thereby removed people from identification by a proper name, have we not also removed them from the structuring function of family relations and sexual identity?

To form an idea of how the subject becomes subsumed in the verb phrase or in its predicates, note that Aquinas among others analyzed the relation of God the Father to God the Verb in terms of a sentence's combining a subject and a predicate. He said that the Verb is the image of the one from whom it proceeds: it is coeternal with the Father, it is his equal, it is entirely the expression of the Father, consubstantial with him, and it has been generated by him (Aquinas Op. 3, p. 141). For Aquinas after Augustine the verb is an inner word that grasps a conceived thing in its image and reason; it precedes the clothing of the verb with spoken words ("De Differentia Divini Verbi, et Humani" Aquinas Op. 3, p. 138). The sense of the Greek Logos that is retained here is that of reason, not that of speech.

It would appear from this passage that the Verb is nothing more than the Father rendered intelligible, that there is no difference between the two, thus that the Father is known through knowledge of the Son. Does this affirm the priority of the Father or the priority of the Son, both, or neither? I would argue that this collapse of naming into predication, however much it gives the appearance of privileging the place of the Father, does exactly the opposite. It is not the name that allows us to identify the Father but the meaning embodied in the Son. Concurrently, it eliminates the transmission of a name from the one to the other, and the debt of the Son to his Father, in other words, the central structuring mechanism of the kinship system. In place of this transmission you have a communication of meaning. The harmonious consubstantiality of Father and Son suggests finally that the Heavenly Father may after all have been rendered into a supreme matriarch, Woman, whose presence is signaled in the constant references of a wholeness or fullness that leaves nothing to be desired. As Lacan said: God is Woman rendered whole or Woman rendered into everything [la femme rendue toute] (in Ornicar? 5, 1986, p. 25). And when Lacan said that Woman does not exist, is not everything, he was saying that the function of naming cannot be obliterated on the alter of Woman made, in the expression of Augustine, "mother of us all."

The connection of God with motherhood is not a psychoanalytic invention; it did not arise from a Freudian delirium. That Jesus Christ had maternal qualities even to the point of being identified as a "great mother" was explicitly stated by Anselm of Canterbury in the eleventh century. His "Prayer to St. Paul" contains the following passage.

And you, Jesus, are you not also a mother?
 Are you not the mother who, like a hen,
 gathers her chickens under her wings?
Truly, Lord, you are a mother;
 for both they who are in labour
 and they who are brought forth
 are accepted by you. . . .
 For, longing to bear sons into life,
 you tasted of death,
 and by dying you begot them.
You did this in your own self,
 your servants by your commands and help.
 You as the author, they as the ministers.
 So you, Lord God, are the great mother
 (in Kirshner and Morrison 1986, p. 178).

But what of the father of this son-mother? You may believe that God can engender or create out of nothing, but this makes nothing into the ultimate maternal principles, that about which nothing can truly be predicated, thus that which contains all and no predicates under the term of "Being." One consequence of this reflection in the hands of Gregory of Nyssa is that the nothing out of which God created was God himself (See Wolfson 1973, chap. 11). Following to its logical consequence the idea that God is ineffable and incomprehensible, theologians endowed him with the aura of mystery and Otherness that often surrounds Woman. It was a cold day when they discovered that they had created something very like a witch.

THREE

TALES OF LOVE AND DESIRE

"Words cannot express ..." So often called upon to denote the unspeakable quality of true love, this phrase is a paradox. Love has its heights and depths and lovers will go to great lengths to live their passion. As the phrase suggests, passion is better lived than acted upon. Together the height, depth, and length of love define its capacity or volume, not so much of the love one is giving, but rather of the love one expects to receive. People who are willing to give up everything for love are convinced that love will return the favor, many times over. But if this were their intention their love would be impure, determined by the hope for material or immaterial gain. People tolerate the bleak emptiness of despair because they await a fulfillment beyond all measure, beyond words. Their emptiness is not accompanied by a wanting, because if there is a wanting one is faced with the obligation to seek the desired object, or better, to act to bring about the desired situation. Love would prefer to receive ... charity, if you please. With this kind of love desire is not in question, nor, as Lacan said, is sex. In the absence of desire love becomes an uncontrollable alternation of euphoria and despair. The only good response to the phrase: "Words cannot express ..." is the statement: "What makes you think the words want to express your love?"

There are several different kinds of love. At first, in the Judaic among other traditions there was *nomos,* the love that concerns the obedience and respect accorded to authority. This love implies submissiveness and subjection. "The word *nomos* literally means justice, righteousness, adherence to the law" (Singer 1984a, p. 239). Singer said that more than piety is involved; he saw *nomos* as a paying back in gratitude of what one owes to one's creator (Singer 1984a, p. 247). This is love for a father, and depending on which authority you accept it is more or less absent in the New Testament. If Christ is supposed to have come to fulfill the Law, there would not be much need for *nomos* thereafter.

Next we find the love that constitutes friendship, the Aristotelian *philia.* This love is based on notions such as wishing the best for one's friend and seeing the best in him. It involves obligations, obedience to rules, and a recognition of the moral worth of those who follow those rules. Admittedly, the idea of friendship sounds at first hearing a bit like what is supposed to be involved in a relationship, but this is a misreading. A true relationship does seek a mutuality of affection, but it seeks it outside of all obligations, as a free and spontaneous giving of love regardless of merit. If a relationship is based on Christian love, then the love given is better and more intense precisely as the other person does not merit it.

Through its fusion with Christian love Aristotelian *philia* was transformed and corrupted. You may want to understand *philia* as the basis for the ideals of fellowship and community, and some have suggested that the idea of a mystical marriage between the soul and God derives from this form of love. But friendship in Aristotle derives from the social and political link that determines community; it is not an affectionate tie that precedes social links, but rather one that derives from following the same rules and accepting the same ethical principles. *Philia* covers the affection between members of a family, between husband and wife, and between lovers (Nussbaum 1986, p. 328n.). "Friendship seems too to hold states together, and lawgivers to care more for it than for justice; for unanimity seems to be something like friendship, and this they aim at most of all, and expel faction as their worst enemy; and when men are friends they have no need of justice, while when they are just they need friendship as well, and the truest form of justice is thought to be a friendly quality" (Aristotle *Nichomachean Ethics,* 1155a21–28). This concerns the social fabric and the principles by which people assent to government, not a mystical union that is beyond the law.

Next comes Eros, the Greek god of love, who is probably a stand-in for his mother, Aphrodite. It is significant that Aphrodite, goddess of love among other things, does not lend her name to a form of love. Eros may be divided into two types, the heavenly Eros, which raises the soul upward in the contemplation of the heavenly Forms or Ideas, and the vulgar Eros, which is attached to specific instances of the Form. The division of Eros was proposed by Pausanias in the *Symposium*. He derived it from the division of Aphrodite into two kinds. "We are all aware that there is no Aphrodite or Love-Passion without a Love. True, if that goddess were one, then Love would be one: but since there are two of her, there must needs be two Loves also. Does anyone doubt that she is double? Surely there is the elder, of no mother born, but daughter of Heaven, whence we name her Heavenly; while the younger was the child of Zeus and Dione, and her we call Popular" (Plato 3, pp. 107–9). Popular or vulgar Eros may love a woman for her beauty; heavenly Eros loves the idea of Beauty attained through an ascent of the stages of a hierarchy of values. The problem with Eros is that it seems to be indissolubly connected with desire. Both the beautiful woman and the idea of Beauty are loved because they are desirable. They are not desired because they are lovable. In the *Symposium* Eros is taken to be a neglected god, greatly in need of the praise that Socrates and his companions can bestow upon him (Plato 3, p. 97). Later in this text we are told that he is really a *daimon;* this makes him an intermediary being, one of the forerunners of the Christian angels.

The relation between desire and love is difficult and problematic. Whereas it appears in Plato that what is loved is loved because it is desirable, in Aquinas it is just the opposite. Note especially his assertion that when we desire something this is an expression of our love for self. As with many of our contemporaries in the field of psychotherapy, the basis of his thought is affect: "Again, the principle of every affection is love. For joy and desire are only of a good that is loved, and fear and sadness are only of an evil that is opposed to the good that is loved; and from these all the other affections take their origin. . . . Hence, the things that we want, absolutely and properly we are said to desire, but not to love; rather we love ourselves for whom we want those things: whence it is by accident and improperly that such things are said to be loved. . . . It is therefore apparent from what has been said that, from among our affections, there is none that can properly exist in God save only joy and love; although these are not in God as passions, as they are in us" (Aquinas SCG, bk. 1, chap. 91). While Eros is often translated as Love, as we see in the passage from the *Symposium*, he represents an erotic love that is for us a function of desire. It is to be distinguished from Christian love as charity.

This brings us to the famous *agape*, Christian love, the love that is God himself. As the first epistle of John says: God is *agape* (1 John 4:8). If we follow the Lutheran theologian Anders Nygren here, *agape* is love that descends, that is given spontaneously without thought of ulterior aim or motive, given by God to mankind through Jesus Christ (Nygren 1982, pp. 151ff.). The place to find *agape* is the Crucifixion, and the central passion in Christian tradition is that of Christ on the cross. That God gave the life of his only begotten Son to save mankind is a supreme act of love, as is the decision of Christ to let it happen. This love will redeem and save all those who allow themselves to be touched by it, who allow themselves to receive it. From being something of a minor figure in Greek culture, love through Christ has become God himself, and the fact that our culture today as in the past is infected with the idea of the awesome power of love is a direct consequence of the advent of Christ, his Incarnation, Crucifixion, Ascension, and Resurrection.

From here, if we continue with Nygren, things become rather complicated. As he saw it the history of Christianity before Luther represents a series of failures in the attempt to purify *agape* of Eros. Since Nygren believed that just about everything that rises rises in function of Eros, with the exception of the Ascension of Christ, he found in theology constant evidence of what we shall call erotic tendencies. As Luther put it: "Every false religion is contaminated by libidinous desires. Just keep an eye on sex" (Luther 1967, p. 422). For Nygren these are especially present in the mystical attempt to climb the ladder of the celestial hierarchy, to make oneself worthy of receiving God's love. He argued, peculiarly, that the wish to make oneself meritorious removes from *agape* the quality of spontaneous unmotivated love, reducing it to a question of recognizing peoples' moral worth or value. Thus it would be corrupted not only by Eros, but by *philia* as well. As a Lutheran bishop, he believed that it was only with the advent of Luther that the true meaning of *agape* was revealed. The peculiar aspect of this view of *agape* is that Nygren saw it as constantly corrupted; as though any time it comes into contact with Eros it loses the battle. This would, of course, make *agape* the most feeble of gods, the kind of god that can only exist in inviolate purity, whose virtue is threatened any time the word Eros is pronounced in its vicinity.

Catholic theologians wanted to split Eros, to repress and condemn it when it entailed earthly or sensual desire, the better to harness its more sublime energies in the interest of Christian love. It is as though heavenly Eros was afforded a place among the angels while common or vulgar Eros was classed among the devils. Nygren represented a more puritanical strain; he did not want Christianity to deal with Eros at all, not even in the sense of an adversary requiring repression. This approximates what Lacan called a foreclosure, a permanent rejection, one in which there is no return. Following Freud, Lacan said that when something is foreclosed the effect is of not wanting to know anything about it, which implies having no dealings with it in any form. The consequence is that any encounter with the signifiers of desire becomes the occasion for delusional episodes and worse (Lacan 1966, pp. 558, 577ff.).

Catholic theology maintains greater confidence in the transforming virtue of *agape*. It tends to see it as having the power to separate the sublime from the sensual. Not so with Nygren: he saw the great moment in the interaction of the two loves as what he calls the *caritas* synthesis, articulated by Augustine. The *caritas* synthesis was something like a marriage; it reigned unchallenged until Luther divorced Eros and *agape* in his Reformation. I used these terms because the much celebrated mystical marriage between Christ and the Church was also attacked by Luther; he and his followers sought to take Christ for themselves and leave the Church to the devils. The maternal body of the Church had become so corrupted by the erotic strivings of its members that it was no longer worthy of Luther's love.

In his search for instances where the faith was bewitched, Nygren looked for signs. For him ascent and descent were the clearest signals that we are in the presence of Eros and *agape*. There is an interesting limitation here. It is not so much that Nygren did not find a plethora of examples of things rising; what he did not see is that both of these movements are on a vertical axis. There seems to be no place for the horizontal, to say nothing of a third dimension. The vulgar Eros that Christian tradition consistently opposed does occur on a horizontal axis, as does the Aristotelian friendship that Aquinas attempted to import into the theology of love. Perhaps Catholic theology saw that you cannot have a vertical axis without a horizontal; it is also true that you can have neither without a third dimension to tie them together. Also, it is not very clear why ascent and descent should be taken to be polar opposites in a one dimensional world.

There are certain questions that Nygren could not allow himself to pose, probably because his religion excludes the use of speculative reason in matters of faith and love. It is not that he or other Protestant theologians are unintelligent; they are after all obliged to study all of the corrupted and contaminated theological texts with which they want to have nothing to do. Karl Barth based his position on the reading of Scripture to the exclusion of the questions theology posed before Luther. He followed tradition in attacking the desire manifested in Scholastic questioning. Concerning the angels, he said that the Bible tells us nothing about "the much ventilated question of the nature of angels, whether they are persons, or what is their relationship to the physical world and to space, their number and order, their creation, their original unity, their ensuing division into angels and demons, and many other things which later there was both the desire and a supposed ability to know" (Barth 1960, p. 410). What Nygren did then was to apply a simple and even simplistic scheme to an immensely complex theoretical elaboration of love in order to demonstrate that before Luther all Christians were more or less wrong in their conception of love. It would not be too far from this to assert that Luther represents the second coming of Christ.

To examine Christian love we must begin with the event of Christ. Love is defined as an event, as God's giving the life of his only begotten Son to save mankind. No greater act of charity can, apparently, be conceived or enacted. The consequence of this is that God does not have a lineage, either symbolic or real. People who follow the Jewish religion are descendants of Abraham, they are either direct descendants or affiliated with direct descendants. No one who is a Christian is a descendant of Christ. Thus with Christ we are meant to understand that the line of the fathers, the line of begetting, has stopped. One of the implications of this is that henceforth people are not linked to each other through the Law that determines filiation but rather through love. Another is that Christianity became a proselytizing religion. People become Christians and are implored to do so through experiences of conversion. Not only can anyone do this, but everyone ought to do it; those who refuse are not simply members of a different faith or community; they are condemned to everlasting perdition. So the difference is between linkage through love and linkage through naming. Thus Bernard of Clairvaux, commenting on the Song of Songs, distinguished between the bride's calling her beloved by his name and her appealing to him through love. Only the former is connected with desire. "But take note in the first place how exquisitely she distinguishes spiritual love from carnal desire, when, in her wish to draw her Beloved's attention by her affection rather than by his name, she does not say simply, "whom I love," but "O you whom my soul loves," thereby indicating that her love is spiritual" (Bernard 1983, p. 145).

Here, through one of the most eminent representatives of the mystical tradition, we find an assertion of a feminine side to this charitable love. And there is enough of it for everyone. Among his other statements we find the following: "Here is a further reason why I insist that the breasts of the bride are superior to worldly or carnal love; the numbers who drink of them, however great, cannot exhaust their content; their flow is never suspended, for they draw unceasingly from the inward fountains of charity" (Bernard 1981, p. 60). The problem is that charity was supposedly introduced into history as something between father and son, in the idea of a father who loves his son so much that he cannot allow him to become a father. From this subversion of patriarchal privilege it is not too far to a matricentric world. It was the same Bernard of Clairvaux who took it upon himself to emphasize the maternal virtues of no less than Moses. Admittedly it was not until the twelfth century that the cult of the Virgin had its full flowering, but the logic of its development was perhaps always present in latent form. What was required to bring it forth was some serious philosophical questioning of the faith, questioning animated by the strength of Platonic and Aristotelian philosophy. Perhaps the one and only God was always Woman, and to bring forth this truth an injection of logic and philosophy was required.

Given the growth and development of the cult of the Virgin and other mystical tendencies, it is not implausible that Luther should have appealed to a fear over the feminizing of Christianity and Christ with it. And yet, to see things this way distorts the theoretical questions and misreads the authors. If the love that is central to Christianity is not *nomos* and is not *philia*, if it does not, in other words, base itself on traditional masculine linkage, if it is purely and essentially an affective tie, outside of filiation and naming, then it is probably maternal. In the text above Bernard compared it to a mother's milk. This does not exclude that it descend upon the earth, that it descend into peoples' souls, but those souls, who are supposed to be receptive to the outpouring of divine love, must be infantilized. It is the phallus that ascends, that points upward, and even in a theology as "virile" as that of Nygren this is unspeakable. For Bernard, however, and other Catholic authors, there is a place for a phallus, so long as there is nothing erotic about "the living and active word of God that cuts more keenly than any two-edged sword." And Bernard continued with a fine passage describing divine incest:

"A polished arrow" too is that special love of Christ, which not only pierced Mary's soul but penetrated through and through, so that even the tiniest space of her virginal breast was permeated by love. . . . It transpierced her thus that it might come down even to us, and of that fullness we might all receive. She would thus become the mother of that love whose father is the God who is love; . . . Thus was fulfilled through Mary, who brought forth in visible flesh him whom she conceived invisibly, neither from the flesh nor by means of the flesh. In the process she experienced through her whole being a wound of love that was mighty and sweet; and I would reckon myself happy if at rare moments I felt at least the prick of the point of that sword. (Bernard 1983, pp. 109–10)

It is not the father who copulates with the mother to produce a child, nor does the father marry a woman to become by relation the father of the child they produce; rather it is the son who joins his mother in a sexual act that unifies mother and son, makes them one flesh through love. Is it plausible to say that this is not erotic? If erotic desire exists only in consequence of the incest taboo, then the passage quoted represents the death of Eros, his last stand. The way to be touched by the arrow of Christ's love is, for Bernard, through mother's milk.

Catholic tradition, with its endless musing on the mystical marriage between Christ and the Church, or Christ and the soul, or Christ and his Mother, retains for Christ the masculine position, allocating to the one who is supposed to receive his love, but also to give it, the feminine and maternal role, the feminine identified with the maternal. Once, however, the feminine becomes the maternal, the usual masculine position is that of the eternal son. The Protestant position certainly wanted to separate Christ from the Church and from other matriarchal organizations. But this was immediately extended to eroticism. Making Christ a masculine deity who has nothing to do with feminine eroticism, even when sanitized by being elevated to the sphere of maternity, does not make him more virile. For Nygren the apotheosis of *agape* is Christ hanging on the cross.

Perhaps the reason Protestant ministers are permitted to marry is that having wives is supposed to make them immune to desire. This was Luther's view, as he noted that the requirement of clerical celibacy tended to aggravate desire, not tame it. "When he was quite old, Augustine still complained about nocturnal pollutions. When he was goaded by desire, Jerome beat his breast with stones but was unable to drive the girl from his heart. Francis made snowballs and Benedict lay down on thorns. Bernard macerated his harassed body until it stank horribly. I believe that virgins also have temptations and enticements, but if there are fluxes and pollutions the gift of virginity is no longer there; then the remedy of marriage which God has given should be taken hold of" (Luther 1967, p. 270). Not only was it scandalous that medieval friars often allowed their propensity for lust to get the better of them, but perhaps worse, those who did not sublimated their repressed desires into theoretical constructions.

Eros was feared, but only as he signified the desire of his mother, Aphrodite. And his mother was feared for the reason femininity was always disparaged in Christian history, for its appeal to the phallus. The wiles of feminine women have been considered more dangerous to men than the renunciation of femininity in women who seek economic and social independence. Perhaps Protestantism at some level saw the Mother Church as a new Aphrodite, sustaining erotic desire by forbidding contact with women and by blocking the natural expression of sexuality. It wanted to take Christ from the Church, because the Christ of Bernard and others risked expressing desire for human souls. But without desire neither masculinity nor femininity can receive definition. Without desire masculinity becomes a will to assert that one is not feminine and femininity becomes a will to assert that one is not masculine. Thus are created stereotypical sexual roles that have nothing to do with sexual identification. The interaction of the sexes must then be based on a natural attraction that is normal because it is created by God. As Luther put it: "The longing of a man for a woman is God's creation—that is to say, when nature's sound, not when it's corrupted as it is among Italians and Turks" (Luther 1967, p. 161).

In the passage by Bernard quoted above we might imagine that a Lutheran, and certainly a Puritan theology, would find the imagery offensive, bespeaking a sublimated form of eroticism. My view is that early Christianity did supplant Eros with Christ, and it did so by attributing to the mythic events in Christian tradition elements of the Eros motif. The only way for theologians to assert the fundamental power of the event of Christ was to show that it was capable of absorbing alien elements, of redeeming them, of raising them through love and grace. And if, as Nygren argued, this activity left something of a place for the erotic, perhaps this is something to be thankful for.

In the terms of the present work, the crucial question in the conflict between Christ and Eros is: Who rules the heavens? A fatuous question, we might say, because no one ever believed that Eros had the wherewithal to rule much of anything. His sphere of influence was simply too limited, and he was a *daimon*, not a god. Even if he is considered to be a god, his place is subsidiary to that of his mother, Aphrodite. As Plotinus wrote: "But one must think that there are many Aphrodites in the All, which have come into being in it as spirits along with Love, flowing from an universal Aphrodite, many partial ones depending from that universal one, with their own particular loves—if one assumes, that is, that soul is the mother of love, and Aphrodite is soul, and love is the activity of soul reaching out after good" (Plotinus 3, p. 183).

To understand what is at issue in the question of the structure of the heavens, we reformulate it as: Who rules the unconscious mind? We follow Lacan in saying that the unconscious is structured like a language; this means that there are terms or elements, a syntax or connectives, and a semantics to judge the value of the constructs. The terms are signifiers; the connectives are desire, aggression, and theft or appropriation; and the values are true and false. More or less following Lacan, we identify desire with metonymy on an axis of combination, aggression with metaphor on an axis of substitution, theft and appropriation with enunciation in a third dimension. Signifiers come in pairs, we have said, and thus they are coupled as well as divided. The Law of the Father provides the structuring principle in the prohibition against incest. So some people marry and some are given in marriage, depending on which side they are on in relation to the division of the sexes. Thus we have something that resembles the pantheon of pagan gods; this structure is precisely what does not exist among the world of Christian angels.

The injection of Christ and Christian Love (as a connective) into the heavens produces an effect that resembles repression; some elements of conscious mental life are thrown into the unconscious, not innocently, but to wreak havoc. Their presence attempts to deconstruct the unconscious to render it unreadable and unintelligible. This is what the Apostle said happened with the arrival of Christ in the heavens: "In Paul's opinion, the birth of Christianity accompanied a huge, invisible upheaval among the powers in heaven. This great supernatural revolution was mirrored in an inner change in every believer, an illumination of the knowledge of the glory of God in the face of Jesus Christ" (Lane Fox 1986, pp. 380–81). So instead of beings divided according to sex you find yourself with angels who are undivided and supposedly unsexed. Instead of desire, aggression, and appropriation, you have charity, enjoyment, and self-possession. Rather than have a semantics of propositions in which each is judged true or false according to the Law of the prohibition against incest, you will find a mother and son reigning as king and queen, as bridegroom and bride, undivided, fulfilled, pronouncing one final judgment that will either render it all meaningful or will cast you into eternal insignificance.

To determine who rules the heavens we must return to the angels. They are, after all, the subjects of this ruler; they do his bidding and relate to each other and to us in the terms that the ruler determines. Those who inherited the angels from Old Testament and pagan sources were faced with the task of taking beings who were ruled or defined by their relation to Eros and reconstituting them in function of Christ. The question of who rules the universe, of who rules the heavens, was of obvious importance for people who thought that this place was their final reward. If the God of the heavens also had influence over human life the answer would lead to the formulation of principles of ethical conduct. Thus it is hardly an irrelevant or trivial question. Let us say that Eros and charity represent two alternative principles of connection among the beings who inhabit the intermediate world between humans and gods. All religions seem to recognize such a class of beings, called angels, genii, or demons. If these beings are connected through a principle of attraction or through an alternation of attraction and repulsion, if they are thought to be lacking something in their constitution that leads them to seek it outside of themselves, then the principle of Eros reigns. According to Nygren Christianity owes this view to Plotinus. Plotinus would have established "a sharp dualism between God and matter," and he would have attempted "to establish communication between them by the introduction of a sufficient number of intermediate beings" (Nygren 1982, p. 188). "Plotinus says we must not speak merely of one Eros, but of many. There is one Eros that corresponds with the world-soul, but every individual also has its own special eros; and the relation of the individual eros to the all-embracing Eros is the same as that of the individual soul to the world-soul. Later Neoplatonists much admired this allegory, and there were a number of attempts to imitate it. They play with this idea and gradually the universe is filled with innumerable erotes." In the hands of Proclus this becomes a great chain of love (Nygren 1982, pp. 570–71). Nygren went on to show how this idea influenced the articulation of the hierarchy of angels through Dionysius the Areopagite and how his work influenced medieval conceptions of this intermediate world. What is important for our purposes is the idea that if angels are linked through Eros then the structure of their linkage is that of a chain; they are intertwined or interconnected through an organization of rings. Conceptually, this may represent the idea of a hierarchy, even a chain of command, but it is not the same as representing it through a series of concentric spheres.

Given these two principles, how are we to distinguish them? First, the type of connection involved in a chain seems intuitively to be closer to what happens in copulation. The fact that the angels do not copulate where demons and other forms of intermediary beings do is significant evidence to exclude a linkage through chaining. A correlative question here would be whether those who define copulation in terms of wounding are thinking in terms of chains or of spheres. Second, the idea of concentric spheres is consonant with several of the themes that run through Catholic theology. If the One God is taken to be a point of light that radiates outward, those who are closest to God see this light most clearly; the further away any being or angel is, the more obscure the light he receives. If the elements of a chain are joined one-by-one, the mass of angels is not linked in this way; they are connected by being part of a city, the Heavenly Jerusalem. The idea of an englobing, self-contained, self-satisfied unity, a unifying unity that connects its members through their participation in the divine love, is much closer to the structure of concentric spheres. Thereby Christianized angels are akin to the intelligibles, constituting a world of meanings, originally in the Verb, whereas the pagan gods are more like signifiers, representatives, each being a one that is there for another. This is clearest on the level of the pagan gods when Plotinus declares that gods are intellects and the goddesses who are paired with them are their souls (Plotinus 3, p. 197). The pairing of the two produces a lower order of beings, intelligible spirits. (In Christian angelology gods and spirits would be different orders in the hierarchy of angels.) This production replicates the birth of Eros in Plato's myth from the coupling of Resource or Plenty and Poverty. The difference between this system and that of Christianity is that in Christianity the intelligibles or ideas are always in the mind of God; they are not produced by any pairing of signifiers, nor are they attainable through the function of the signifier. Whereas pagan *erotes* are basically a group of ones, retaining their parentage in the copulation of signifiers, the idea of coupling one angel to another or seeing them as children of gods and goddesses is alien to Christian thought. No Christian would say that the coupling of seraphim or cherubim produces archangels. There is no chain of beings in Jerusalem.

Add to this the fact that the angels are consistently defined as subsisting in a state of unalloyed and perpetual bliss, which leaves nothing to be desired, which by definition can lack nothing, and you find yourself in the world of concentric spheres. Within the Catholic tradition angels are created to render service, not to think or to act of their own desire. Thereby the energy that animates each flows from only one source. Each angel receives that love differently depending on his distance from the source. The more distant he is the less perfect he is. Finally, for angels to be linked as in a chain they would have to have proper names; this would make the principle of their connection paternal rather than maternal, since the proper name is passed on from father to son to grandson in a way that renders the englobing power of maternity irrelevant. A chain of command exists in a masculine ethos. To transform it into degrees of beatific vision is to place it within a feminine space.

We want to elaborate the principle that connects the angels to each other and to humans: whether it be *agape* or Eros, whether it be *agape* as a charity that excludes desire or a charity that encompasses and tames desire. In Christianity the idea that angels are creatures of sensual desire is rejected, and this has raised the issue of whether they can be creatures of desire at all. What is certain is that God is not desire but love. With the Reformation love and desire came to be strictly divided; in one sense this contributed to a clear sense of the division of the sexes, but at the price of there being no way for them to interact erotically.

In the fourteenth century God the Father explained to Catherine of Siena the form of connection pertaining between just souls and angels. Not only is this a wonderful expression of the power of divine love, but it also unifies the just with the saints and angels. The principle of that unification has much in common with what people think of as relationships. God told Catherine:

> By the same principle, those just souls who end in loving charity and are bound by love can no longer grow in virtue once time has passed. But they can forever love with that same affection with which they came to me, and by that measure will it be measured out to them. They desire me forever, and forever they possess me, so their desire is not in vain. They are hungry and satisfied, satisfied yet hungry. . . . Forever they rejoice in love at the sight of me, sharing in that goodness which I have in myself and which I measure out to them according to the measure of love with which they have come to me. They are established in love for me and for their neighbors. And they are all united in general and special love, both of which come from one and the same charity. They rejoice and exult, sharing each other's goodness with loving affection, besides that universal good which they all possess together. They rejoice and exult with the angels, and they find their places among the saints according to the different virtues in which they excelled in the world. (Catherine 1980, pp. 82–83)

Certainly there is a place for desire here, but desire has been made a function of affect, subsumed in loving charity, its edge thereby neutralized. The principle of connection is God's charity, which is universal and totalizing. That neighbors have a positive loving relationship is a function of the love of God. It is what God wills as good.

Also related is the way Bernard identified the bride of the Song of Songs with the bride of Christ. This in itself was standard fare; Bernard took it a step further, albeit a step that had been prefigured in earlier writers, when he identified the bride as Heavenly City with the angelic inhabitants of that city. For the thematic connection of virginal women with the angels this is a central medieval text:

> For if she compares herself to the tents of Kedar because of her body drawn from the earth, why should she not glory in her likeness to heaven because of

the heavenly origin of her soul, especially since her life bears witness to her origin and to the dignity of her nature and her homeland? She adores and worships one God, just like the angels; she loves Christ above all things, just like the angels; she is chaste just like the angels, and that in the flesh of a fallen race, in a frail body that the angels do not have. But she seeks and savors the things that they enjoy, not the things that are on the earth. What can be a clearer sign of her heavenly origin than that she retains a natural likeness to it in the land of unlikeness, than that as an exile on earth she enjoys the glory of the celibate life, than that she lives like an angel in an animal body? (Bernard 1983, pp. 78–79)

The key to the passage is not the refrain "just like the angels," but rather the fact that the experience described herein is one of enjoyment, not of desire. This is the promise and premise of Christian love. We must note that this and other exhortations to women to identify with angels gave rise in the fourteenth and fifteenth centuries to a wave of anorexia among pious young women who renounced the food grown by the earth to delight and savor the food of the angels. The first of these was Catherine of Siena (see Bell 1985). Finally, the identification of the city that englobes the angels with the angels themselves, their participation in the same light and love source, seems to point to the structure of concentric spheres.

The experience of angelic enjoyment legislates against desire. This enjoyment, proper to angels, derives from the direct vision of God, from seeing God face-to-face, as many authors assert. This experience of enjoyment has not prevented Catholic authors like Gregory of Nyssa from postulating a hierarchy of desire or from defining desire as coexisting with this enjoyment. We have already said that the use of the word desire in such a context is a misnomer; beings who seek perfection and complete fulfillment in God's love are not desiring; they are demanding satisfaction. The reason for this is that by our definition desire does not seek satisfaction; desire, Lacan asserted, desires recognition; it desires the Other's desire and is constituted originally as that Other's desire. To say that desire seeks complete fulfillment means that it desires its own annihilation. And this it cannot do; it can, however, demand satisfaction in the wish that satisfaction annul the desire.

As far as God's desire is concerned, it is questionable that such a thing exists. God wills, he does not lack. Since he is defined as a plenitude, he can lack nothing. As far as God's attitude to the sin, original or otherwise, of mankind, Aquinas described it in terms to which we have already alluded. "Christ had to suffer death not only to give an example of holding death in contempt out of love of the truth, but also to wash away the sins of others. This indeed took place when He who was without sin willed to suffer the penalty due to sin that He might take on Himself the penalty due to others, and make satisfaction for others. And although the grace of God suffices by itself for the remission of sins, . . . nonetheless in the remission of sin something is required on the part of him whose sin is remitted: namely, that he satisfy the one offended. And since other men were unable to do this for themselves, Christ did this for all by suffering a voluntary death out of charity" (Aquinas SCG, book 4, chap. 55). God is the offended party and the offense requires satisfaction, satisfaction that can be offered only by his Son. And yet, it says in the epistle of John that God gave his only begotten Son. So he also acted through charity, thus love, because the only way for him to show mankind how to satisfy his demand for love was to make the most grandiose gesture of love imaginable and then to require of humans a response in kind. The Crucifixion marks the moment in which God was cured of his inability to love.

Like the angels, man is directed toward the enjoyment of God in love and this love comes to rule desire. "Again, since man's perfect beatitude consists in the enjoyment of divinity, man's love had to be disposed toward a desire for the enjoyment of divinity, as we see that there is naturally in man a desire of beatitude. But the desire to enjoy anything is caused by love of that thing. Nothing, of course, so induces us to love one as the experience of his love for us. But God's love for men could be demonstrated to man in no way more effective than this: He willed to be united to man in person, for it is proper to love to unite the lover with the beloved so far as possible. Therefore, it was necessary for man tending to perfect beatitude that God become man" (Aquinas SCG, book 4, chap. 54). This summarizes several of the points we have been making. First, desire is defined as a desire for enjoyment or for beatitude, fulfilled in the enjoyment of God. Second, the mutuality and reciprocity of desires is called love. Third, man wants to enjoy and he wants beatitude because he loves. To these points we add that the beings who represent and who live this perfected state are angels. The angels participate in degrees of perfection, in a hierarchy of perfection, but this does not mean that they experience desire in our sense of the term.

The contrast with the desire that Plotinus saw in the class of intermediate spirits is stark. And Plotinus understood the importance of rejecting the idea of angelic satisfaction to maintain desire. Note the emphasis he placed on the deficiency of his *daimons*. His meditation derives from the Platonic myth that declares the parents of Eros to be Poverty and Plenty or Resource:

And Love [Eros] is like a "sting" without resources in his own nature; therefore, even when he attains his object he is without resources again; he cannot be satisfied because the mixed thing cannot be; only that is truly satisfied which has already attained full satisfaction in its own nature; but Love because of his intimate deficiency is impelled to longing, and even if he is for the moment satisfied, he does not hold what he has received, since his powerlessness comes from his deficiency, but his ability to provide for himself from his rational nature. But one must consider that the whole race of spirits *(daimonion)* is like this and comes from parents of this kind; for every spirit is able to provide himself with that to which he is ordered, and impelled by desire for it, and akin to Love in this way too, and is like him, too, in not being satisfied but impelled by desire for one of the partial things he regards as goods. (Plotinus 3, pp. 192–93)

While Christian authors sometimes use the term desire when they talk of angels, they do not talk of the deficiencies of angels, nor do they talk about the inability of angels to achieve other than momentary satisfaction. Also, the direction of the desire of Eros for partial things that he regards as goods contradicts the idea that the only desire of value is the one for the Supreme Good, the desire for divinity. With partial things we are in the world of desire, whether through the psychoanalytic theory of the partial object or through the idea that the fetish object is the prototype of the object that causes desire.

Here again Catholicism has effected an important transformation whose purpose is to recuperate this structure in the interest of love. The Church has retained partial objects in the form of relics, not to cause or provoke desire but rather to promote life, health, wholeness, even fertility. It is not an erotic body that has the most value, but a healthy one. As Marina Warner wrote:

The dynamic holiness of icons and relics did not just stir the soul to the contemplation of higher things, they also physically communicated the properties of their subject or owner. Images were alive, and so they could breathe life into the dying. Mary's peculiar qualities of bodily and spiritual integrity made her the supreme medium of healing and rendering whole again, and her shrines have always been thronged, since early Christian times, when, according to a tenth-century legend, the Empress Zoë had been cured by touching the girdle preserved in the Chalkoprateia church. . . . By the high middle ages, no scruple about the Virgin's assumed body impeded the discovery and veneration of physical relics. Whereas the Byzantines had concentrated in clothes the Virgin wore, western Christians revered her hair, her milk, and even her nail parings, which were kept in a red satin purse at Poitou. (Warner 1983, pp. 293–94)

However much Christian authors were influenced by Neoplatonism and other pagan philosophy, they have in the matter of love effected a decisive repression of its pagan sources, even to the point of doing fairly constant battle with the return of the repressed. This repression is not the kind of foreclosure recommended by Nygren; the repressed is not rejected but is transformed: since desire taken to be concupiscence was considered to be the path to sin and death, the partial objects that cause it are made into life-giving and life-sustaining substances, affording participation in the charity that is supposed to give rise to eternal life and resurrected heavenly bodies.

How they did this will next retain our attention. One central area in which the transvaluation of pagan values took place was the reinterpretation of Scripture. Within the field of literary studies much is made of the importance of reading texts, often to the chagrin of outsiders who have no idea why such an activity is as important as scholars claim. But when we turn to the tradition of biblical exegesis we see that from the advent of Christ, this was a central arena in which the new religion wanted to establish itself and to make war on other religions. The technique used by Christian authors, especially the anagogical or allegorical reading, was pagan. Seznec traced it to Stoic authors who "undertook at times to discover spiritual significance in the figures and even in the names of the gods, and moral lessons in their adventures" (Seznec 1972, p. 84). We also see it unambiguously in the writings of the Jewish theologian Philo of Alexandria.

Christianity altered the content of the moral meanings derived, simply by placing the event of Jesus Christ at the center of all readings of the Bible. This led to the use of what Erich Auerbach has called figural reading of Scripture. "Figural interpretation establishes a connection between two events or persons, the first of which signifies not only itself but also the second, while the second encompasses or fulfills the first. The two poles of the figure are separate in time, but both, being real events or figures, are within time, within the stream of historical life. Only the understanding of the two persons or events is a spiritual act, but this spiritual act deals with concrete events whether past, present, or future, and not with concepts or abstractions; these are quite secondary, since promise and fulfillment are real historical events, which have either happened in the incarnation of the Word, or will happen in the second coming" (Auerbach 1984, p. 53).

The first requirement of the new religion was to demonstrate that Jesus Christ was who he and his followers said he was. There were and still are people who do not believe that Christ was the Messiah. The way of proving this was to show that Christ in his person and in the events of his life fulfilled the Old Testament prophecies of the coming of the Messiah. It was necessary to show that Christ was the unique referent who fulfilled or satisfied the predictions; that he was the predicate to end all predicates. And not only that he had come or that he would come again, but also that he had always been there. As Auerbach said:

For every future model, though incomplete as history, is already fulfilled in God and has existed from all eternity in His providence. The figures in which He cloaked it, and the incarnation in which He revealed its meaning, are therefore prophecies of something that has always been, but which will remain veiled for men until the day when they behold the Saviour *revelata facie,* with the senses as well as in spirit. Thus the figures are not only tentative; they are also the tentative form of something eternal and timeless; they point not only to the concrete future, but also to something that always has been and always will be; they point to something which is in need of interpretation, which will indeed be fulfilled in the concrete figure, but which is at all times present, fulfilled in God's providence, which knows no difference of time. (Auerbach 1984, p. 59)

Here the horizontality implied in the correlation of two events in figural interpretation is subsumed under a vertical reference to the timelessness of the realities played out therein.

It also seems to have been necessary to show that there was one and only one reading of Scripture, only one truth. The reader who did not grasp it or agree with it was himself at fault. This meant that the book of the Old Testament was thus closed. Christ was its ultimate meaning, and it was best not to seek other meanings, lest God be sorely offended. To say that Christ was the ultimate meaning, the meaning to end all meanings, suggests a parallel with the idea that Christ was the ultimate lover, the one to whom all feminine souls offered their love, from whom they all hoped to receive love—not because this would bring them to desire, but rather because it would release them from said desire and also from the seeming servitude to other gods who might be its object. The God who had just recently overcome his inability to love was best not tested; anyone who offers such a supreme gift of charity reacts badly if his gift is not well received.

How then to show that Christ was in fact always present, there from the beginning? Jews did not read the Old Testament in quite this way, because the idea that Jesus was there beside God in the beginning is not in Genesis; it is in the Gospel of John. Therefore, it was necessary to reread the Old Testament recursively to reveal the invisible hand or presence of Christ throughout. To say that Christ is present is also to say that Christian love is in evidence. And since the primary dyad is Christ and his Mother, this required a shift in emphasis from the paternal to the maternal. This requires something of a transformation, and one of the ways it was done, by Gregory of Nyssa, for example, was to say that patriarchs like Abraham and Moses were feminine mystics. If the mystic is one who sees God directly, if Moses saw God, and if the soul that has this experience is feminine, then it follows. . . . A text by the incomparable Bernard of Clairvaux makes Moses into the ultimate representative of maternal love: "Clearly he speaks as a mother for whom there is no delight or happiness that is not shared by her children. For instance, if a wealthy man should say to a poverty stricken woman: 'Come and join me at dinner, but better leave outside the child in your arms, his crying will only disturb us,' do you think she would do it? Would she not rather choose to fast than to put away the child so dear to her and dine alone with the rich man? Hence Moses was resolved not to go alone to join in his Master's happiness, while those people to whom he clung as a mother, with all a mother's affection despite their restlessness and ingratitude, remained outside" (Bernard 1981, p. 80). Here is another example of *agape* and additionally a precursor of what psychoanalysis calls affect theory. Just as post-Freudian psychoanalysis revised and reread Freud in order to recenter the theory on the mother, so did Christianity rewrite the Old Testament. The difference is that the theologians knew that what they were doing was religion; psychoanalysts who find the mother-infant dyad at the center of everything think that they are scientists.

One of the most striking and significant Christian reinterpretations concerns the erotic poem called the Song of Songs. The story of the nuptials of Solomon and his bride had been subject to interpretation by

Jewish authors who read the bride as the representation of the chosen people, of Israel. Christian authors changed this to make the bride into the Church and the bridegroom into Christ. Of these authors, one of the first to provide a systematic reading of the text was Origen of Alexandria in the third century. While he was not the first to do so, he is probably the most important source for the tradition of anagogical reading of the Bible. The purpose of such a reading, especially important when the text in question is explicitly erotic, is to show that the immediate sense of the story is simply a means to gain access to spiritual realities. The terminology of desire is through this reading raised up by love. Origen stated: "But if any man who lives only after the flesh should approach it, to such a one the reading of this Scripture will be the occasion of no small hazard and danger. For he, not knowing how to hear love's language in purity and with chaste ears, will twist the whole manner of his hearing of it away from the inner spiritual man and on to the outward and carnal; and he will be turned away from the spirit to the flesh, and will foster carnal desires in himself, and it will seem to be the Divine Scriptures that are thus urging and egging him on to fleshly lust" (Origen 1956, p. 22). (The surviving version of Origen's text is not the original Greek but a Latin translation, apparently loose, prepared a few centuries after the original.) Be that as it may, there is a tone of fanaticism and horror at the risks in misreading Scripture. Origen himself was sufficiently horrified at such a possibility to have castrated himself in a fit of piety, the better to immunize himself against Eros.

Origen's reading moves from the visible or sensible world to the invisible and hidden, from the letter of the text and the images it evokes to a meaning that is structurally isomorphic, that corresponds point for point.

Paul the apostle teaches us that the invisible things of God are understood by means of things that are visible, and that the things that are not seen are beheld through their relationship and likeness to things seen. He thus shows that this visible world teaches us about that which is invisible, and that this earthly scene contains certain patterns of things heavenly. ... But this relationship does not obtain only with creatures; the Divine Scripture itself is written with wisdom of a similar sort. Because of certain mystical and hidden things the people is visibly led forth from the terrestrial Egypt and journeys through the desert, where there was a biting serpent, and a scorpion, and thirst, and where all the other happenings took place that are recorded. All these events, as we have said, have the aspects and likenesses of certain hidden things. (Origen 1956, pp. 218, 223)

The vertical division of the letter of the text from its meaning is also applied to the division of body and soul, of outer and inner being. Strangely, the reading proposed by Origen is based on the idea that the terms used in the text are "homonyms." "The thing we want to demonstrate about these things is that the Divine Scriptures make use of homonyms; that is to say, they use identical terms for describing different things. And they even go so far as to call the members of the outer man by the same names as the parts and dispositions of the inner man; and not only are the same terms employed, but the things themselves are compared with one another" (Origen 1956, pp. 25–26). It is clear enough that the reading presupposes the metaphoricity of the text; more important for the moment is the use of the concept of homonym. For if we had wanted to know how the spiritual world is connected with the corruptible world of the senses, then the answer lies in the function of the homonym in which a word simultaneously has two meanings.

At the least Origen's idea of a homonym is not the usual one. A homonym is a word that has two unrelated meanings; it would be more accurate to call it a phonetic accident. "Bark" is a homonym, and this does not imply that the bark of a tree is the visible manifestation of a dog's bark. Origen's idea was that a word that has a concrete referent, like "body," also an invisible referent that is the true one. The latter exists in the supersensory world.

We have already mentioned that Origen saw the souls involved in the love of the Word as having the same nature as the angels. The type of anagogic reading offered by him and others is parallel to the dual nature of the angelic spirits. Angels may assume human bodies, but the visible form is consistently taken to be metaphoric of a more spiritual and invisible reality that is proper to them.

The requirement to translate from the visible body of the text to the invisible world of meanings derives within Christianity from Christ. The descent of the Word into human flesh was a rendering visible and palpable of an invisible reality. Readings that ascend in the opposite direction place the reader in touch with a world that is supposed to be more real than the real.

The significant point is that the Word does not gain a sensible representation through a word or words; rather the Word has as its sensible form the flesh of Christ. By extension Scripture would have the status of an assumed body, not a body of flesh but one that resembles it, which shares its appearance but not its reality. One example is the illuminated manuscript, another, the love-letter. A love-letter incites a special reading, not only by its wording, but also by the appearance of the words on the page. In a world where God never speaks directly to humans, where he always interposes angels, and where the only thing that matters is participating in charity, would you not look for signs of that love? You might well be led to read them into a text.

This involves a special practice of reading where the reader's look must be aware of the visible form of the writing. The graphic image will be one of the paths to finding hidden meanings. It also engages an appreciation for the beauty of the written word, taken as an object of aesthetic contemplation. Obviously, this does not limit itself to the written page; it extends to the relation between the spectator and the work of art.

The radiant light of God shines through concentric spheres to produce different aesthetic forms. A good example is that of the stained glass window, especially those in the great cathedrals of the Middle Ages. Whereas in other religions the human body is marked or scarred or circumcised, and where this action represents something like receiving a name, Christianity rejects these pagan practices and substitutes something like an identification with the visual representation of celestial realities. This happens only through the power of love. Francis of Assisi received the Stigmata of Christ by identifying with a vision of a seraph representing the form of Christ, not through the intervention of any cutting instrument. And, Catherine of Siena received her invisible Stigmata through a vision of the Crucifixion, this through the intermediary of her knowledge of the paintings of the stigmatization of Francis (See Meiss 1973, Chap. 5).

The importance of visual form for making the connection between heaven and earth is evident in the idea of the resurrection of the body. The resurrected body in Christian tradition was a body given over to aesthetic contemplation, a body of beauty, and from this body all evidence of desire or Eros, especially masculine desire, was subtracted. Certainly, this idea has had a large influence on aesthetics in the Western world. Whereas beauty for Plato first excited erotic interest as a quality much prized in those to whom one was attracted, the Christian conception of beauty, based as it is on another form of love, reviles any erotic component. We may even suggest that the Platonic idea that desire is desire for the idea of Beauty represents a purification of desire and not a precursor of Christian love. Commenting on the opinion that the female sex is a defect that will be removed in the Resurrection, Augustine declared: "Thus while all defects will be removed from those bodies, their essential nature will be preserved. Now a woman's sex is not a defect; it is natural. And in the resurrection it will be free of the necessity of intercourse and childbirth. However, the female organs will not subserve their former use; they will be part of a new beauty, which will not excite the lust of the beholder—there will be no lust in that life—but will arouse the praises of God for his wisdom and compassion, in that he not only created out of nothing but freed from corruption that which he had created" (Augustine CG, book 22, chap. 17).

These points converge in the idea that love is metaphor. The transforming power of charity, its ability to transport from one space to another, from the space of the erotic to the aesthetic space of love, operates through the becoming flesh of the insensible Word. Christ is considered to be the mediator of the transformation, which occurs only in a maternal space. The identification of the Church with the soul, with the Virgin Mother, and with the Heavenly City, all of them being at one time the bride of Christ, all identified with each other as concentric spheres, is proposed as completing and fulfilling the work of love. It is not difficult to identify scriptural metaphors or even metaphors that become flesh. One has but to recall the miracles performed by Christ, represented by phrases like the following: The blind see, the deaf hear, the lame walk. Perhaps these are the simplest of metaphors, in which there is a contradiction between the attributes of the subject and those of the predicate. As such they border on oxymorons. What better place to see the predominance of the verb and the way in which the verb transforms the subject? More significantly, when the metaphor becomes reality, this eliminates the figurative meaning of the sentence. If the verb were not primary we could understand the sentence "The blind see" as describing the prophetic powers of a blind Tiresias. That of course would preserve a dialectical tension, much as the Platonic Eros does, and such was not the goal of Christianity.

Since the sacrifice of Christ had as one of its purposes the putting an end to blood sacrifice, this practice, consistently identified with masculinity, is transformed through the influence of Christian love into a metaphoric, invisible equivalent. Augustine explained it clearly: "God does not want the sacrifice of a slaughtered animal, but he desires the sacrifice of a broken heart. . . . And the reason why they had to be changed, at the fitting and predestined time, was to prevent the belief that those things were objects of desire to God himself, or at least were acceptable gifts from us to him, and to make us realize that what God required was that which they signified" (CG, book 10, chap. 5). It is not simply the passage from one world to another; in the passage something is lost and that is the erotic or masculine element. Augustine articulated this by writing that the signifying becomes erased in the interest of the hidden, invisible signified. "Thus the visible sacrifice is the sacrament, the sacred sign, of the invisible sacrifice." Later in the same chapter he showed how the transformation from desire to love represents an accession to beauty. "If then the body, which the soul employs as a subordinate, like a servant or tool, is a sacrifice, when it is offered to God for good and right employment, how much more does the soul itself become a sacrifice when it offers itself to God, so that it may be kindled by the fire of love, and may lose the 'form' of worldly desire, and may be 're-formed' by submission to God as to the unchangeable 'form,' thus become acceptable to God because of what it received from his beauty" (CG, book 10, chaps. 5 and 6).

What then makes of love a metaphor? And what is it in the operation that permits people to believe that the world can thus be transformed? To say that love is a metaphor is not to limit ourselves to verbal metaphors; what retains our interest is the way people become metaphors, the way they come to live as though they were parts of speech. If the Law is simply transgressed, the action affirms the existence of the Law. Fulfilling the Law implies a movement into language, as though what is forbidden elsewhere is the rule therein.

To introduce the idea of metaphor we propose Roman Jakobson's now classical analysis of sentence construction (in Jakobson and Halle 1956). Jakobson postulated two axes of sentence construction: a vertical axis of selection and a horizontal axis of combination. When a word is chosen for inclusion in a sentence it is selected from among several terms with similar meaning. Since only one term is chosen at a time, the axis of selection is considered to be vertical. The word is then combined with others in a sentence. If a noun is chosen it is combined with a verb and so on along a horizontal axis. The combined words are contiguous to each other in the sentence. You will notice immediately that the advantage for us lies in the division along horizontal and vertical lines; if the authors we have been discussing are right, then love pertains to the vertical axis.

We read in Jakobson that metaphor is formed in relation to the vertical axis of selection. Whereas the substitution of similar or synonymous terms on this axis preserves semantic structure in the sense that each synonymous sentence is true or false in relation to the same world, metaphor results from the substitution of a dissimilar or discordant term, a term that is disjointed from the rest of the sentence. The new sense does not lie in the same world as that of the simple declarative sentence. It is important to note, as Lacan said, that the only way of identifying the deleted term is through the fact that it has left a trace of its passage in the rest of the sentence (Lacan 1966, p. 507). Take a metaphor proposed by Lacan as exemplary: Love is a pebble laughing in the sunshine. This is a metaphor because pebbles do not laugh. The pebble's attribute of inanimate contradicts the animation of laughter. Or we may use the idea of Cohen and Margalit that the most obvious semantic variables of the word pebble are effaced and only less obvious ones are called upon to make the pebble metaphoric (Cohen and Margalit 1972, p. 735). Here the variable concerning the shining pebble might be its radiance compared to the radiance of someone laughing. In addition to saying that a semantic variable is present or is created in the word pebble, it is also correct to say that the pebble is substituted for whoever is laughing. The term designating the lover or the beloved has been removed from the sentence, and the only indication of his presence is the laugh; in his place we find a pebble that represents his seeing his own laughter in a most trivial object. The triviality of the object is the occasion for showing the transforming power of love; love can elevate worthless objects to significance. The usefulness of Cohen and Margalit's analysis does not obviate the fact that there is a further aspect of metaphor to which we gain access through Jakobson as taken up by Lacan (See Lacan's essay "The Agency of the Letter," in his *Ecrits*, 1966).

We hypothesize that when a metaphor is constructed the first act is the removal of a word from a declarative sentence. This creates a hole or gap in the sentence. One may decide to restore the semantic integrity of the sentence by substituting a synonym for the missing term, or else one may decide to block the reassertion of that integrity by introducing a discordant element. The new word makes a metaphor by functioning as a bridge (Cf. the idea that Christ is a bridge in Catherine of Siena's *The Dialogue*). It does not close the hole so much as make manifest its creation. The metaphor subverts the meaning of the declarative sentence and creates a meaning that cannot be restated as such, a meaning that does not refer to facts as they may exist in the world we call real or actual. Note also that the activity has two parts; one might reasonably consider them to be ascendent and descendent. The sentence is no longer pulled down by the requirement of referring to a state of affairs but is elevated to posit a meaning existing elsewhere.

Following Lacan in his unpublished seminar on transference, we say that in love there are two roles, that of the lover and that of the beloved. At first one person is loving and the other is loved. What we call falling in love occurs when the person who is loved finds that he loves the person who loves him. Thus a substitution takes place: instead of being loved one finds oneself loving. One of the terms has fallen away— perhaps this gives the sense of falling in love—and another takes its place; the person who now loves feels himself elevated to a new position; idem for the person who is now loved. It is as though the lovers were identified with the terms that represent them in a declarative sentence, then to undergo what happens to the terms when the sentence becomes a metaphor. It is not a question of role reversal. When the beloved learns to love, he does not thereby cease to be loved.

The experience is often called ecstasy or rapture; its transcendent quality is often praised. Those who are involved are moved, in both senses of the term; they have been transported from one place to another. And this is consistent with the fact that the Greek word from which we receive "metaphor" is *metapherein,* to transport.

A classic example of falling in love occurs for Alcibiades as recounted in the *Symposium*. Nussbaum wrote that Alcibiades had "spent much of his young life" in the role of one who is loved and unmoved. This describes someone who is "closed and self-absorbed," "a beautiful creature without pressing needs of his own." Nussbaum's description of Alcibiades in love demonstrates that when the beloved learns to love he retains the position of loving and also that when a metaphor is constructed a gap or opening is created in the sentence: ". . . the experience of love is felt as a sudden openness and at the same time an overwhelming desire to open" (Nussbaum 1986, p. 188). In contrast to charity, the love of Alcibiades for Socrates is erotic and interested.

Christian readings of the Old Testament want to accentuate the fact that the people therein love God and that God, their beloved, does not love them in return. He may have made a pact with the Jewish people, but this is not the same as sacrificing the life of his only Son. With the advent of Christ the God who was loved becomes loving and everyone may then become his beloved; they may now receive for the first time an infusion of divine love. The sign that God has opened up is that Christ bleeds on the cross. The love in question demands reciprocity; it would not tolerate an interpretation aiming at a desire within the demand. This is because what God sacrificed in allowing his only Son to be crucified was his desire, in the sense that a father's desire is for a lineage. Not only does God, having learned to love, demand love, but he must guarantee that this will satisfy him and also that he will satisfy the one who offers it. God has shown his love by making a sacrifice for you; if you make a similar sacrifice the accounts will be balanced and eternal bliss will be yours.

It is possible to base an erotic practice on the frustration of demands for love. In our civilization the relevant instance was courtly love. A callow youth with a somewhat poetic spirit solicits the love of a lady. She, being master of the game, believes that his demand is impure and she imposes trials on him. She requires that he prove himself, that he show, not how much he loves her, but how badly he wants her. She does not give charity and does not expect it from him. What she wants is to bring the youth to desire, to want her. The attitude of worship and adoration present in his initial entreaties is what she wants to cure him of. Courtly love was something like a therapeutic of *agape*; not surprisingly, it was suppressed by the Church.

We have already noted that miracles are translations of metaphors into reality. That a virgin become pregnant and give birth to a son is a metaphor that has come to life. This makes it an otherworldly event. The reason this one occurred on earth was to prophesy a world in which others will become real; the one event provides the path to the others. Christianity demands that one accept such metaphors as real. To the extent that you believe you are offering your love. It is excluded that such metaphors be subject to interpretation. Virgin birth means what it says and the religion will allow no place for interpretations that will give it a more conventional sense or that will attempt to resolve the metaphor. If you should ever let your mind think that perhaps she was not a virgin, and that the angel was her lover in disguise, then you either are suffering from an inability to love or have read too much Boccaccio.

What is involved in Virgin birth is not an obscure meaning of the word virgin; rather, it is a contradiction in terms. This contradiction demands love in the form of belief. In order for the metaphor to mean what is says there must exist a concrete referent that surpasses the limitations of language, that places us beyond language and human logic. This is not of the same order as the pebble laughing in the sunlight. There we questioned the intention of the speaker of the sentence, seeing in the metaphor an expression of the experience of love. In order for the metaphor to be functional linguistically the listener should know that the speaker is not referring to a fact, but rather that the metaphor reflects back on the speaker himself. The metaphor does not demand of the listener that he believe that pebbles laugh; if that were the case the division of speaker and listener would collapse into a referential delirium.

In effect, the role of metaphor in language is to extend the range of the meanings of words, to add meanings. Rather than there being a fixed number of meanings for a word or a combination of words, their use in metaphoric expressions legislates against the idea that a particular expression means one and only one thing. Things are different when it comes to living metaphors. The metaphor of the Virgin Birth has only one referent, and this tells us that where language does not hook into the world through the function of proper naming then something else will come to substitute for that function. The difference is that where proper naming tends to mark or cut the human body, especially the male body, the miraculous realization of a metaphor in Christianity is supposed to heal it.

Cohen and Margalit have recommended that metaphor functions to create new meanings for words and phrases. They saw within language "an infinite potential for new metaphor," where new metaphors come to replace old or dead ones. These latter lose their metaphoric edge through overuse or banality. We have already shown that the world of angels was assimilated to the world of meanings; here we will test that idea.

In the beginning there was language; apparently it did not take a long time to be created. The words had meanings, and perhaps, as many people have believed, these meanings were the true ones, the ones that were most intimate with nature. People were speaking God's mother tongue. And yet, somehow or other people made mistakes in their use of language, not always unintentionally, making meanings that were local rather than universal. These new meanings then took on a life of their own, and since they were not universals they were considered to have fallen from the sphere of true meaning to sow falsehood and disbelief. The mistakes were at times metaphors and therefore God, in order to bring humanity back to the world of universal meanings, created his own metaphor, not a simple linguistic expression that could serve in the commerce of the fallen world, but a metaphor in flesh and blood. And he told people to eat it. Through this process God proposed to cure people of their detachment from meaning, from their propensity to lie, their playing with metaphor, and most especially of their foolish tendency to refer to people by their proper names. Not only did those names perpetuate the power of the patriarchy, but they did not have a meaning. Proper names were radically untranslatable into God's mother tongue. Why do you need a name when you can have a guardian angel?

Positing a universal world of meanings leads easily enough to the reflection that this world must correspond in some way with what is called nature. We remember that Lévi-Strauss in *The Elementary Structures of Kinship* defined the natural as the universal. This suggests that a world of universal meanings posits a common experience of the natural world or of the constancy of the natural world, taken to be created by God. This helps to explain why the world of the angels is a maternal space. It is as though in using language man separated himself from the natural world and from his own experience of it. Anything that is named or spoken of is immediately contaminated; we do not see it directly but rather through our linguistic apparatus. Similarly, any child born is immediately named in the name of his father; thus is he torn from his original attachment to his mother. This sustains our argument that it is only the unborn who are fit to become angels, and that they share in the highest beatitude for never having been submitted to the patriarchal function of naming. Meanings, then, corresponding to what Augustine called the words within the mind, are conceived or begotten. For a meaning to be true it must give us knowledge of things, thereby providing a concept that is true, that participates in what he called the divine truth. This is not what happens when a child is begotten; it corresponds more to what we have supposed happens when an angel is begotten. Giving birth to the word then becomes synonymous with speech, and we find that the process of maternity is the model upon which Augustine based his theory of speech. Note how love is the key to this process: "We behold, then, by the sight of the mind, in that eternal truth from which all things temporal are made, the form according to which we are, and according to which we do anything by true and right reason, either in ourselves, or in things corporeal; and we have the true knowledge of things, thence conceived, as it were as a word within us, and by speaking we beget it from within; nor by being born does it depart from us. . . . Now a word is born, when, being thought out, it pleases us either to the effect of sinning, or to that of doing right. Therefore love, as it were a mean, conjoins our word and the mind from which it is conceived and without any confusion binds itself as a third with them, in an incorporeal embrace" (OT, book 9, chaps. 7 and 8). We add that love here is *caritas*, distinguished in the same chapter from desire as *cupiditas*.

It is plausible, even Nietzschean, to assert that desire has not fared well from its experience of Christian love. Certainly, our way of reading the Platonic dialogues that are supposed to form the basis for the concept of desire is colored if not distorted by the lens of charity.

To get our bearings we quote the comments of a scholar of Greek religion concerning Eros and his mother, Aphrodite. This will provide a frame for our study of Plato and will also show why sensuality is significant, even crucial, to this particular view of love and desire. Walter Burkert commented: "Aphrodite's sphere of activity is immediately and sensibly apparent: the joyous consummation of sexuality. Aphrodisia, *aphrodisiazein* as a verb, denotes quite simply the act of love, and in the *Odyssey,* the name for the goddess is already used in the same sense. The old abstract noun for sexual desire, *eros,* which is masculine by grammatical gender, becomes the god Eros, the son of Aphrodite; Yearning, *Himeros,* often stands by his side; both are portrayed as winged youths and later also as child putti" (Burkert 1985, p. 152). Eros is one of the winged figures upon which the form of the angels is based.

Let us look at the *Philebus,* a dialogue specifically about pleasure, about the pleasure that gives us the word *hedonistic.* Socrates' definition of desire (epithumia) serves adequately as an introduction. Comparing desire to hunger or thirst, Socrates makes the simple point that one who is hungry feels empty and then desires to be filled. "The man, then, who is empty desires, as it appears, the opposite of what he feels; for, being empty, he longs to be filled" (Plato 8, p. 285). The initial point is that desire is the opposite of feeling. Across more than two millennia this remark retains its relevance. Why then is desire the opposite of feeling or affection? Precisely because if desire is for a state other than the state that you feel at the moment, then it cannot be through a deeper understanding of feelings that you will get any closer to your desire. Socrates says that it is only through memory, through the soul, that one can conceive of a state of fullness when in fact one's truest feeling is simply one of emptiness. From this he draws some startling conclusions: "This argument declares that we have no bodily desire . . . because it shows that the endeavour of every living being is always towards the opposite of the actual conditions of the body. . . . And the argument, by showing that memory is that which leads us towards the objects of desire, has proved that all the impulse, the desire, and the ruling principle of every living being are of the soul" (Plato 8, pp. 286–87). Is it not then consistent that a religion that promotes the resurrection of a body that has nothing to do with the erotic should oppose desire in the name of affections? And is it not also clear that the soul in such a religion must be transformed into a being that loves bodies, bodies taken to be aesthetic, not erotic objects?

Instead of saying that desire is for a state of fullness, we alter the formula in asserting that desire aims at a scene, a situation—dinner at your favorite restaurant—rather than the state of repletion and satiety that follows the meal. Desire, Lacan often emphasized, is in another scene, a scene that is other to the one you are living. This does not mean that there is no object involved; an object may cause desire but that does not necessarily mean that the desire is for the object. In psychoanalytic theory it is often said that the child desires his mother, that he has a desire for her as an object. To this Lacan offered the corrective that what is in question is the mother's desire, what she wants. At first the child will attempt to be what she lacks; in this way he seeks a communion based on affect beyond words. When Freud asserted the central importance of a child's recognition of his mother's castration, he meant to signal first the separation between mother and child effected by the intervention of the father's Law prohibiting incest and second, the mother's turning to the father, her desiring something other than what the child can offer.

Take the story of Hamlet as Lacan discussed it in his seminar on desire and its interpretation (in *Ornicar?* 24, 25, 26–7; 1981–83). Examining the question of why Hamlet is incapable of revenging his father's murder, Lacan asked not whether Hamlet desires his mother, but rather, what is his mother's desire? It is not a question of Hamlet's not knowing what he wants but instead his doubts concern knowing what she wants. In the famous scene in his mother's bedchamber we find the expression of his horror over the possibility that what his mother wants is precisely the situation that presently pertains in Denmark, that her desire is for the lubricious Claudius. Impossible as it is for Hamlet to conceive, this implies his father's failure.

Hamlet is trapped by the ghost's command because it does not simply say to murder Claudius but it adds, as an afterthought, that no harm should come to Queen Gertrude. As long as Hamlet accepts this condition he is incapable of performing the one action that he ought to do. Were Hamlet to assume a desire as his, that desire, consonant with the command of the ghost, would be for a situation that is radically different from the one that pertains in Denmark. Hamlet has an obligation to modify the world as he finds it; instead, he tries to find a place for himself within in. Thereby he becomes a being of affect, even to the point of competing with Laertes over whose affects are stronger.

Hamlet is not entirely incapable of assuming a desire. His problem is that he can assume it only when the situation that would be created by action in accord with it is impossible. Thus Hamlet desires Ophelia most when she is dead. Lacan has suggested that one line represents most clearly Hamlet desiring. As he jumps into Ophelia's grave, the prince shouts: "It is I, Hamlet the Dane" (in *Ornicar?* 24, 1981, p. 31). We stated that the requirement of connecting oneself as I with one's proper name has something to do with assuming a desire and acting upon it. Hamlet's statement shows us how this happens. A proper name refers to you whether you are present or absent; it refers to you in the third person. The subject's I is not identical with the referent of the name; it is in apposition to it. The relation is not one of substitution but of contiguity.

It is one thing to be designated by a name and quite another to bind oneself to it by one's own act. In psychoanalytic terms the assumption of one's name as one's own corresponds to the mythic act of patricide. If the intention of the patricidal act is to become free of the constraint of the Law, it is singularly ineffective. In fact, it produces exactly the opposite effect, as Freud pointed out in *Totem and Taboo*. It is one thing for someone named Hamlet to be designated as required to carry out an act; it is quite another for a subject to accept that he is the one who must act. It is one thing for us to speak of the possibilities that confront John; it is quite another for John to accept that those are his possibilities. This does not make him the agent of the possibilities; rather it makes him an agent whose act can translate some of those possibilities into the real.

A child is born into the discourse of his parents, their desires for him are predicated of his name: parents speak of their wishes for their child or the possibilities they want to be his. These possibilities do not become his until he accepts that the name he has through the agency of his father —the paternal function comports naming—is his own. This involves his acting against the person occupying the paternal position; what makes the name designate him rigidly is not the intention of the person who has named, but rather a law of language, most clearly operative when it is not attributed to a person.

In a girl's development things happen somewhat differently. Certainly, the act of assuming a proper name as one's own is operative, but when we arrive at the point where mother and daughter are separated through the agency of the Law prohibiting incest, the girl has a lesser tendency to repair her mother's loss with her being. She accepts that something has been taken from her mother because she believes that it will be given to her. Freud saw the resolution of the female Oedipus complex in the girl's wish to be given a child by her father. Thus she will attempt to be the object of her father's desire. This dynamic provides an excellent illustration of the limitation of seeing desire in terms of acquiring an object. Under normal circumstances what the father wants to give his daughter is not a child; he wants to give her. . . away. Here the analogy between desire and appetite falls short. The father's desire to give his daughter away is realized only in his not having her, but rather in her occupying another place with another man. If desire is confused with appetite, the desire to give a daughter away will appear to be a desire satisfiable only in being unsatisfied. When this happens, the daughter may identify with her father's desire and seek to construct for herself a desire that is chronically unsatisfied, no matter what objects it obtains. Such is the case of the hysteric, as Lacan has theorized it (Lacan 1966, pp. 620–21).

The preeminent Platonic text on love and desire is the *Symposium*. It is not a very easy matter to do justice to this text in the brief span that we can devote to it. The *Symposium* recounts the event of a banquet or drinking party given to honor the dramaturgical prowess of one Agathon, who has just won a prize for one of his plays. Being an attractive boy, Agathon has become the object of the amorous interest of Socrates, and this interest has been reciprocated. The dialogue is organized around a series of speeches: each of the convivants is called upon in turn to discourse to Eros, a god who has become wanting in praise. From the standpoint of the Christian tradition the speech that seems to bear the most weight is that of Socrates himself. Of course, in this speech Socrates does not speak in his own name; he says he is recounting the lessons that a Mantinean woman named Diotima taught him. Many people believe that Diotima is really presenting the views of Socrates himself; it is equally plausible that the master ironist has chosen to speak through Diotima so that his audience would believe her views to be his when in fact they are not.

Diotima's conclusion is worth quoting because it contains the idea of the ascending ladder of Eros. Some Christian authors have compared this ladder, through which one ascends to Beauty, with one Jacob saw, on which angels were ascending and descending. The idea of ascending a ladder was later to become the model for the mystical ascent through which the soul was to become angelic and to reach God. In any case, Diotima concludes: "Beginning from obvious beauties he must for the sake of that highest beauty be ever climbing aloft, as on the rungs of a ladder, from one to two and from two to all beautiful bodies; from personal beauty he proceeds to beautiful observances, from observance to beautiful learning, and from learning at last to that particular study which is concerned with the beautiful itself and that alone; so that in the end he comes to know the essence of beauty" (Plato 3, p. 207).

How seriously are we to take this? It is certainly not the last word of the dialogue. Is it the truth about desire or half of it? Here desire finds its ultimate object, but this represents at once an escape from the "bondage to luck" and a "longing for an end to longing." One would arrive at a "world in which erotic activity, as we know it, will not exist" (Nussbaum 1986, pp. 181, 183). It is one thing to attain this world; quite another to desire it. So long as it is unattainable it will continue to remain desirable. Perhaps the speech of Diotima represents the condition of a woman's desire. As such, its juxtaposition with that of Alcibiades shows the extent to which men and women are at cross-purposes when it comes to desire. The text leaves us with the question of whether the speech represents the views of Socrates. At the very least, if this theory is his, he does not articulate it in his own name. In order for the ascent up the ladder of beauty to represent a desire, its completion must be interdicted by the intervention of a male figure. We might even say that the speech is so true that its effect is to evoke or produce precisely the male whose role is to make of it a lie. Enter Alcibiades.

Immediately as Socrates finishes his speech, there is a knocking at the gate and the appearance of an inebriated crasher named Alcibiades. Bearing signs of Aphrodite and Dionysus, acting more like the latter than the former (Nussbaum 1986, pp. 193–94), Alcibiades, within the dramatic context, is Eros arriving at his own party. It is useful here to remind ourselves who Alcibiades was, as this would have been well-known by Plato's contemporaries. Alcibiades was one of the most important political and military figures of his time. And yet, as a result of an unfortunate incident where he mutilated statues honoring the god Hermes, he spent much of his life as a man without a country, a high-class beggar, selling military secrets for a home and security. His sexual prowess is not merely based on his well-known unconsummated affair with Socrates; he also managed when in Sparta to seduce the Queen of Sparta and to beget a child. Such was public knowledge at the time and did not endear Alcibiades to the King of Sparta, who was eventually to have him killed. So Alcibiades was flamboyant, outrageous, insolent, and arrogant. As Plutarch described him: "In the midst of this display of statesmanship, eloquence, cleverness, and exalted ambition, Alcibiades lived a life of prodigious luxury, drunkenness, debauchery, and insolence. . . . He had a golden shield made for him, which was emblazoned not with any ancestral device, but with the figure of Eros armed with a thunderbolt" (Plutarch *Lives,* p. 16) To say that Alcibiades represented Eros incarnate is not entirely inappropriate.

Informed of the requirement to speak in praise of Eros, Alcibiades demurs. He prefers to praise Socrates, averring that Socrates cannot tolerate hearing someone else praised in his company. And Alcibiades launches into a passionate declaration of his love for Socrates, issuing a demand for that love. Rather than speak of love, Alcibiades shows himself loving. That there is desire in the speech is manifest; the problem will be to know what that desire is. If, as Lacan said, desire is interpretation, our access to Alcibiades' desire comes through the interpretation offered by Socrates. Since Lacan said that this interpretation corresponds well to the structure of psychoanalytic interpretation, we will examine it closely. The interpretation bears on the context as well as the content of the utterance; it reveals the fact that this most passionately offered declaration of love is a deceit, a ruse, an example of cunning.

Alcibiades' love is not lacking in affect. "As for myself, gentlemen, were it not that I might appear to be absolutely tipsy, I would have affirmed on oath all the strange effects I personally have felt from his words, and still feel even now. For when I hear him I am worse than any wild fanatic; I find my heart leaping and my tears gushing forth at the sound of his speech, and I see great numbers of other people having the same experience" (Plato 3, p. 221). Here he places himself as listener; and yet all the time he is himself speaking. His positioning himself as feminine in relation to Socrates, his bearing witness to the effect speech produces on him, should not obscure the fact that by speaking himself he is trying to produce a certain effect on his listeners. As we have noted, desire is in opposition to feeling, and that opposition is dialectical. That his desire is masculine is revealed by the fact that his wanting Socrates derives from a vision of something that corresponds well to what we have been calling partial objects, and which now we may call the kind of fetish objects that cause desire. Lacan believed that the following passage was exemplary for showing the structure of what he called the object causing desire: "Whether anyone else has caught him in a serious moment and opened him, and seen the images (agalmata) inside, I know not; but I saw them one day, and thought them so divine and golden, so perfectly fair and wondrous, that I simply had to do as Socrates bade me" (Plato 3, pp. 224–25). The afterthought of these images causes the desire of Alcibiades. That desire is not directed to the goal of possessing the agalmata; rather, it concerns the enactment of a series of scenes, each of which approximates his desire without ever realizing it.

Alcibiades asserts in the most open and exhibitionistic way that his love for Socrates was unrequited; that it was an exercise in which the hoped for enjoyment was never granted. His frustration leads him to make his public display. Or so he seems to think. Socrates, of course, thinks otherwise, and as soon as Alcibiades finishes he offers an interpretation, not one that reveals a hidden meaning, but rather one that effects a dialectical reversal. Socrates is not fooled by the stratagem or ruse, made persuasive by so much affect. "I believe you are sober, Alcibiades; else you would never have enfolded yourself so charmingly all about, trying to screen from sight the object in all this talk, nor would you have put it in as a mere incident at the end. The true object of all you have said was to stir up a quarrel between me and Agathon: for you think you must keep me as your undivided lover, and Agathon as the undivided object of your love" (Plato 3, p. 241). In making a grandiose declaration of love for Socrates, Alcibiades was in effect trying to seduce Agathon, the true object of his amorous interest: his desire was not addressed to the one to whom he spoke, but rather to the one seated beside him, the one contiguous to Socrates. Desire is then a displacement; whatever is demanded is not what is desired. One always desires someone or something else, someone or something connected to the object of passion or of pathos. The difference between Alcibiades and most analysands is that the latter do not accept as readily as the former the gesture that seems to deprive them of their pathos to put them on the road to their desire.

Note also that Socrates defines the desire of Alcibiades as a scene different from the scene that exists in actuality and also different from whatever it is that Alcibiades is recounting from memory. So perhaps it is not simply memory as a function of the soul that determines desire. Alcibiades' desire exists in his vision of a different linkage of three people; the principle of this linkage has nothing to do with charity and is in opposition to his deeply felt affects. There is a sense of another world in which the desired situation exists. This is not the same as finding the meaning of a metaphor, and certainly not the same as finding that the meaning of all metaphors is love.

The reversal, reorganization, or relinking of terms takes place on a horizontal axis that Jakobson called that of combination. Notions like displacement and deferral, associated with desire, are also conceptualized on such an axis. The figure of speech that mines most effectively the resources of this axis is metonymy. According to the *American Heritage*

Dictionary, metonymy is a figure of speech in which an idea is evoked by means of a term designating some associated notion. One may talk of war by speaking of swords or of authority by evoking scepters. Through metonymy something is designated without being named because the close connection of two terms makes it possible to evoke both by naming only one. There is no substitution, because war and swords coexist without any problem as connected terms. Metonymy is an alternate way of naming things. We have seen it in the strategy of Alcibiades; in professing his love for Socrates he was in fact attempting to seduce Agathon, seated next to Socrates.

If metaphor has something to do with the succession of proper names that establishes a lineage, as between father and son, then metonymy represents or even embodies the desire to name. It does this by pointing to the lack of a name. Kripke has argued persuasively that descriptions of people do not function as substitute proper names, that the name is not reducible to the description or to the qualities we associate with the person. The expression "the author of the *Symposium*" does not function in the same way as the proper name Plato does. And yet, if we are within the function of metonymy we may well posit that the two can exist in apposition and that the phrase "the author of the *Symposium*" will normally evoke for the reader the proper name Plato. This does not mean that the one is a substitute for the other. It is as though one were forming a question: Who is the author of the *Symposium*? and someone were to answer: "Plato." The point is that the answer does not erase or swallow up the question; it coexists with it dialectically. In the context of the speech of Alcibiades its analysis assumes that the connection between Socrates and "the beloved of Alcibiades" is tenuous, that the proper name is something like a decoy, not in the sense that it does not designate Socrates, but rather in the sense that "the beloved of Alcibiades" is someone other than Socrates, someone who is named only in passing and who is never named with that description. Metonymy is used because Alcibiades does not want to name his beloved directly.

If a metonymic expression is used in place of a proper name, then it happens in psychoanalysis that the purpose of such a trope is to lure the analyst into providing the name. Generally it is best not to respond to such a lure, since the analyst is not privileged to know what the name is or why the analysand refuses to pronounce it. Metonymy may certainly be used figuratively, and then there is no reason to believe that the person who uses this or an other trope is repressed or neurotic. And yet there are cases or situations where the refusal to name is systematic, where attributing a proper name to a being, even a supreme being, or calling him by it is forbidden. This might indicate that all of the names that are used to designate in place of the proper name are metonyms designed to direct desire toward the unnamed Other. How else to be Other than to have a name that cannot be used to fix a referent? Another interpretation offers itself here. Could we not say that the Other who is not named, whose name cannot be pronounced, is the God who is metaphor, who therefore is love? Such questions have been at the heart of major theological debates. For our purposes a group of intermediary beings lacking proper names are beings of love, not of Eros. In such a world the purpose of interpretation is to gain access to meanings, not to find the occluded proper names. When desire is functional the purpose of interpretation is to permit access to a repressed name or a repressed signifier.

If the signifier is the phonetic material of language, as it was defined by Saussure, then the inability to pronounce a name or word may be symptomatic in relation to whatever resonances the sounds of the name or word may have, whatever associations may be connected with the resonant sounds. It may also be symptomatic of a will to retain a person in the context of whatever meanings are attributed to him, especially insofar as they permit the subject to retain his sense of himself as meaningful and unnamed, as meaningfully unnamed. So interpretation in psychoanalysis does not provide a meaning, does not show that the analyst has understood what he has heard, and does not expect the patient to agree with or confirm the interpretation. It does not propose an anagogic reading by providing an allegory that takes place in a different sphere, be it the sphere of weaning, toilet training, or other aspects of infantile development. What it does provide is a restructuring of the connections between the elements of discourse, showing that the analyst has not heard what is meant, but rather is listening to what has been effectively pronounced. The analyst, in interpreting, assumes that something of the analysand's desire is involved in the speech act itself, taken within its context. He interprets from the position that has been attributed to him in the transference. Since his love is considered to be the answer to all of the analysand's questions, this is one thing that he, like Socrates, does not offer. Nor does he accept the offer of love from the patient. To respond to the patient's demand for love would place the analyst as sympathetic, empathic, understanding—one who knows the meaning even before the sentence has been pronounced, one who makes the pronunciation of the sentence superfluous to the more immediate affective link.

These ancient quarrels about angels and demons still persist within the world of psychoanalysis. Most psychoanalysts formed outside of the school of Lacan have never heard of desire; nor does it enter into their theoretical or clinical work. They are, as it were, with the angels, only they do not know it.

Whether we are looking at these things from the point of view of theology or from the point of view of psychoanalysis, there remains a question we have still not addressed directly, the question of sexuality. Probably it was most pressing in Chapter 1, especially since angels, whose society is the ultimate basis for the cult of relationships, do not have sexual relations as we know them. From the present chapter it should be clear that whether or not angels have a sex life, or better, whether or not people who are modeling their relationships on the angelic mode of being do, the angelic company knows nothing of Eros.

Is there sex without desire, is the situation imagined to have been that of the parents of the human race reproducible among mortals? To fashion an idea of what was going on in Paradise we turn again to Augustine in *The City of God*. These passages recount a tale of love and desire. On Adam and Eve Augustine said:

The pair lived in a partnership of unalloyed felicity; their love for God and for each other was undisturbed. This love was the source of immense gladness, since the beloved object was always at hand for their enjoyment. There was a serene avoidance of sin; and as long as this continued, there was no encroachment of any kind of evil, from any quarter, to bring them sadness. Or should it have been that they desired to lay hands on the forbidden tree, so as to eat its fruit, but that they were afraid of dying? In that case both desire and fear was already disturbing them, even in that place. But never let us imagine that this should have happened where there was no sin of any kind. For it must be a sin to desire what the Law of God forbids . . . (CG, book 14, chap. 10)

And after stating that "lust is the general name for desire of every kind" (CG, book 14, chap. 15), he went on to suggest that in Paradise the sexual organs were subservient to the will, just as other parts of the body, other members, are in fact. "Then (had there been no sin) the man would have sowed the seed and the woman would have conceived the child when their sexual organs had been aroused by the will, at the appropriate time and in the necessary degree, and had not been excited by lust" (CG, book 14, chap. 24). The disobedience of the phallus, in particular, becomes the model for the rebel angels, while the other parts of the body, in their happy obedience to the commands of the will, are models of the heavenly host.

So, is there sex without desire? In effect, this has been one of the great wagers of our time, which informs the work of sexologists and the better part of the mental health profession. The sexologists, with their excessive emphasis on orgasm, discovered one day that many of the people they had cured of sexual dysfunction no longer had any desire for sexual relations. Touted at the time of its discovery as a setback for sex therapy, this may have been the secret goal of the treatment: to cure people of their desire, thus to bring them to taste the fruits of paradise on earth. Such a state of affairs would have been foreign to the Christian world view; in the latter the idea of lacking a propensity to sin is barely conceivable. Even saints are tempted, and we remember that Aquinas had to wear a sash to keep the lust of his flesh in tow. So the idea of using scientific knowledge about sexuality to make sexuality into a function of love represents the application of the Christian love ethic to life among mortals. It is in this direction that the commentary of Foucault seems to lead. This latest effort to bring the City of God into being on earth has been yet another effort to save Christ, not so much through the intermediary of the organizations and institutions that function in his name, but through an application of the meaning of his life. That meaning is love. Most people, even the most irreligious, believe in love, at times more than in life itself. It requires a certain amount of conceit for them to think that they do not thereby believe in God.

FOUR

THE SEX OF THE ANGELS

In the fifty-first question of the first part of the *Summa Theologica* Thomas Aquinas addressed the issue of the angelic body. He did so in three articles: The first article asks "whether the angels have bodies naturally united to them?" to which he answered that they do not. The second asks "whether angels assume bodies?" to which he answered that they do. The third asks "whether the angels exercise functions of life in the bodies assumed?" to which he answered that they do not. In these articles the greatest of medieval angelologists attempted to resolve the problematic issue of the assumed bodies of angels. In the course of his discussion he was obliged to address the question of the sex of the angels. The problems are textual; angels are described in certain ways in Scripture, they are seen engaged in various activities, among which are eating and copulating. And yet angels are not human beings, they do not have bodies subjected to Original Sin. Thus the question became one of semantics. What is the sense of a text in which it is said that the angel eats? Is it a metaphor; or does it refer to an order of being that is possible, but not the same as what we experience within the confines of our empirical existence?

The theological difficulty was to reconcile these texts with the articles of faith and with the moral universe that the Judeo-Christian tradition was attempting to impose on the human race. From the time that Philo of Alexandria commented on a text in Genesis in which it is recounted that the sons of God—also known as angels—took as wives the daughters of men—also known as human women—it seems to have been an article of faith that God's holy angels could not be taxed with such acts. The agents of this work could only be the fallen angels or fallen angelic humans. This view was taken up by Augustine and formed a part of Aquinas's response to the question of the angelic body. The issues surrounding the sex of the angels loom large. If the division of the sexes does not exist among the angels, then perhaps it is nonessential for humans. Nonessential means that humans are not required to identify themselves according to sex. If they grant relevance to this aspect of fallen nature, they are aligning themselves with the fallen angels. Thus Christian children are all baptized; whether this is a ritual cleansing or nostalgia for the womb, the ritual does not divide the sexes. Ritual circumcision obviously does and it implies a relation to being named that does not function in baptism.

Lacan has stated that the signifier enters the world through sex (Lacan 1973, p. 138); this implies that the question of how language comes to function in the world, how it hooks into the world, to use the phrase of Hilary Putnam, is addressed through an appreciation of the sexual division of the human race. Language hooks into its speakers in dividing them. If one part of the answer concerns the connection between naming and cutting the body, the other relates to the sexual commerce between devils and witches. Given that the opposite number to witches, virgins, cannot engage in such intercourse, the interaction between God's own angels and the human world is more difficult to conceptualize and ultimately appears more tenuous and more doubtful.

As for the other natural function that seems to be presented hand-in-hand with the sexual—nourishment—the authors are in general agreement that in their assumed bodies angels seem to be eating (but are not) something that is in fact food. In the City of God they eat the food that is proper to that place. On earth, however, they are placing various forms of nourishment in their assumed bodies, but since there is no way for digestion to happen, this nourishment has to be expelled in the same form that it entered. Such considerations are important in trying to define the sense of sentences that concern angels. They are also of interest when we are dealing with people who adopt the angelic attitude toward food—that is, anorexics and bulimics. Many religions adopt ritual fasting as a means of atonement and purification; it is quite another story when this extends beyond the observance of a rite and becomes a way of life. To what extent is the passage from a ritual fasting to an eating disorder sustained or even encouraged by exhortations to emulate the life of the angels? Where copulation between angels and humans is excluded, is this the only way to maintain contact between the two worlds?

These issues are linked to another one, raised in the questions on the angelic body. And that concerns the translation from the invisible to the visible world. The problematic nature of the angelic body, the assumed body that presents itself to the senses while retaining a quality of the ephemeral in its absence of bodily function, leads us to consider it to be a point of intersection between the visible and the invisible. As such it may remind us of dreams and fantasies, even of hallucinated images; it lends itself to a reflection on Freud's interpretation of dreams, in which he notes the necessity for dreams to present thoughts and messages in pictorial form. The Freudian emphasis on the fact that dreams are coded would place them within the context of Gothic art, at least as Emile Mâle defined its resource. The difference is that the coding of the sculptures on a Gothic cathedral seeks a visual representation of eternal truths; the figures point beyond themselves to an unambiguous message. The encoding of a dream, however, is a function of the fundamental equivocation of the signifier as representation. The signifier is not an extraneous element introduced to make something sensible to a fallen race; rather it is something like a boundary marker, a *herm*, which is restored to its place by interpretation. Its function is to divide, not to bring about any sort of coalescence or unification. In Freud the pictorial script of dreams does not translate back into an invisible world of meanings. Rather, it is resolved into something invisible in the sense of being of the order of spoken language.

Once the idea of an assumed angelic body is proposed we are obliged to note that Christ also had an assumed body, but that his was subject to natural functions and to the death that is the fate of such bodies. As we have seen, this puts Christ and the angels in some sort of competition. Aquinas noted clearly that there is not in the Incarnation a unification of body and Word; rather the Word puts on a body in the sense of vesting itself with a corporeal envelope. The fact that a body is assumed does not necessarily mean that it is a mirage. In the contemporary usage of the idea of assuming we find the idea of an assumed identity, a masking of features and/or name. Both the assumed body of the angel and the assumed body of Christ are falsifications of the being of each. Such is the theological assumption. And we ought not to ignore the fact that the body of the Virgin is assumed into heaven without having to pass through death. This assumption is the reverse of what happens to Christ and the angels; it prefigures the resurrection of the body.

Let us begin on these issues with the reasoning Aquinas proposed (ST, part 1, q. 51). The angel, he said in the first article, is an intellectual substance, and it is not intrinsic to an intellectual substance to have a body; some have bodies and some do not. Those that are united naturally and necessarily to bodies are human beings; those that are "quite separated from bodies" are angels. To have a body is a sign of imperfection; in having a body a human being does not have a "fullness of knowledge" as a part of his own nature. He does not know in and of himself; rather, he acquires knowledge through sensible things, which he perceives with bodily senses. To go from sensation to knowledge a human must abstract from the intermediary form of a phantasmatic image of the sensible thing. This mode of knowledge distinguishes man from angel, although this is not the only way in which humans know. So, having or not having a body is first an epistemological issue, whose interesting consequence is that angels are defined as not having to have any interaction with the world. Explicit in the angel's way of gaining knowledge is a separation of mind from body. This tells us that having a real body would serve no useful purpose for an angel; he puts on a body only for another. The body he assumes for another is limited in its functioning to the benefit it will bring to its human interlocutor.

An angel is a perfectly intellectual substance that has no need to acquire knowledge from things. Regarding human knowledge, the following qualification is offered. Aquinas said later that the human soul, while being naturally united with the body, may gain understanding either through sensible things or through intelligible objects; these latter are separated from things. "The soul, therefore, when united to the body, consistently with that mode of existence, has a mode of understanding, by turning to corporeal phantasms, which are in corporeal organs; but when it is separated from the body, it has a mode of understanding, by turning to simply intelligible objects, as is proper to other separate substances" (ST, part 1, q. 89, art. 1). The source of the intelligible objects is God, taken to be a light source; the further the intellectual substance or soul is from the source, the greater the contact with sensible things. "This will appear if we consider that every intellectual substance possesses intellective power by the influence of the Divine light, which is one and simple in its first principle, and the farther off intellectual creatures are from the first principle so much the more is the light divided and diversified, as is the case with the lines radiating from the centre of a circle" (ibid.). The higher the order of the angels the more simple its understanding. The higher orders have concepts that are more universal than the lower. The same hierarchy pertains in the human race. "We can see this to a certain extent in man, for those who are of weaker intellect fail to acquire perfect knowledge through the universal conceptions of those who have a better understanding, unless things are explained to them singly and in detail" (ibid.). Thus, there exists a hierarchy of meanings or concepts moving from the most particular to the most universal, and also a hierarchy of beings determined by quality of understanding.

To return to Question 51, the second article introduces the idea of assumed bodies. Angels do not have bodies, but they may assume them in order to communicate with human beings. "Angels need an assumed body, not for themselves, but on our account; that by conversing familiarly with men they may give evidence of that intellectual companionship which men expect to have with them in the life to come." Curiously enough this suggests something very like what we have been calling a relationship; intellectual companionship would surely include affective companionship. What needs to be clarified here is the idea of an assumed body, a body not naturally united to the intellectual substance, but taken on for a purpose that has nothing to do with the substance itself. This assumption is a purely selfless act. The first point Aquinas made is that these assumed bodies are not imaginary; they are not apparitions that are beheld only by a single individual. When an angel assumes a body it is said to be beheld by everyone; this means that angels are a social reality that is beheld through the faculty of vision.

What then distinguishes an assumed body from a real one? The answer is that the faculties of an assumed body are representations of intelligible properties; they do not function as bodily faculties. "For as in the Sacred Scripture the properties of intelligible things are set forth by the likenesses of things sensible, in the same way by Divine power sensible bodies are so fashioned by angels as fittingly to represent the intelligible properties of an angel" (ST, part 1, q. 51, art. 2). This refers evidently to the anagogic readings of Scripture, as examined above. In the third article Aquinas expanded this point: "Sensation is entirely a vital function. Consequently it can in no way be said that angels perceive through the organs of their assumed bodies. Yet such bodies are not fashioned in vain; for they are not fashioned for the purpose of sensation through them, but to this end, that by such bodily organs the spiritual powers of the angels may be made manifest; just as by the eye the power of the angel's knowledge is pointed out, and other powers by the other members, as Dionysius [the Areopagite] teaches." While a real body may serve a purpose other than the representation of spiritual realities, the assumed bodies of angels, deprived of sensation and perception, serve only to point beyond themselves to spiritual things. The function of representation here is that of the sign and not of the signifier. The sign represents something for someone; this corresponds well to what Aquinas was defining here. The signifier represents a subject for another signifier; such is not the case in this text.

Let us say that you wish to communicate some meaning to another person. To do so you are required to clothe that meaning in sensible form, for example, in a sentence. If the sentence is like a body, then it would be most angelic as it points most clearly to the meaning that is communicated, least angelic the more its sensible form attracts the attention of your listener. Or we may say that the sentence is least angelic, less of an assumed body, where it is equivocal. If the form of the sentence accentuates the sounds, through punning, then the body would not be assumed. Also if the sounds interact among themselves, thereby to obscure the more universal meaning, the body is again not assumed. For Aquinas the sounds of speech are what language has in common with all other sounds, even sounds made by soulless things; thus the sounds of speech that convey intelligible meaning draw the least attention to themselves, the most attention to the meaning. Fortunately, Aquinas remarked on the faculty of speech to draw an analogy with the difference between assumed and real bodies: "Some functions of living subjects have something in common with other operations; just as speech, which is the function of a living creature, agrees with other sounds of inanimate things, in so far as it is sound; and walking agrees with other movements, in so far as it is movement" (ibid.). It is important in this context that the sounds of speech have a distinct phonetic structure, discovered by linguists to be knowable through binary opposition, and that this phonetic structure is not the same as that of inanimate things.

If speech is considered to have something in common with natural sounds, then Aquinas would deny that angels speak. "Properly speaking, angels do not talk through their assumed bodies; yet there is a semblance of speech, in so far as they fashion sounds in the air like to human voices" (ibid.). Here again the question is to distinguish speech from its semblance. Are we justified in saying that there are human beings who fashion sounds in the air and do not speak? Ordinarily, we would think we are referring to people who speak to say nothing, who engage in idle chatter or meaningless bantering. Such an activity, however, would hardly be fitting of angels. It is more consistent to say that angelic speech points most clearly to meanings that are to be communicated; there is no dialectic within such speech and no chance of misinterpretation. "External speech, made by the voice, is a necessity for us on account of the obstacle of the body. Hence it does not befit an angel; but only interior speech belongs to him, and this includes not only the interior speech by mental concept, but also its being ordered to another's knowledge by the will. So the tongue of the angel is called metaphorically the angel's power, whereby he manifests his mental concept" (ST, part 1, q. 107, art. 1). Does this say that angelic communication has more in common with writing than with speech? The predominant importance of sight in angelic experience points in this direction. And where the body is not an obstacle to be penetrated by a voice and by sounds, perhaps communication can involve an integral transmission of concepts. Lacan, for example, often noted that it is only with writing that anything is transmitted integrally from one person to another.

Aquinas also addressed the issue of angelic nutrition. He said that "eating involves the taking of food convertible into the substance of the eater. . . . But the food taken by angels was neither changed into the assumed body, nor was the body of such a nature that food could be changed into it; consequently, it was not a true eating, but figurative of spiritual eating. This is what the angel said to Tobias: *When I was with you, I seemed to eat and drink; but I use an invisible meat and drink*" ST, part 1, q. 51, art. 3).

The connection between speaking and eating had long been established, from various Scriptural passages (see Deuteronomy 8:3) in which men are said to be fed by the word of God, and among the Fathers of the Church by Tertullian, who asserted that the shift from the function of eating and drinking to that of speaking represented what would happen to the body in its ultimate resurrection (Tertullian 1980, chap. 61). Of course, it makes a difference whether one does not eat to receive words or whether one does not eat to speak words. And it is quite something else to eat one's words.

This confusion suggests that it is not obvious to the unconscious how it happens that words enter the ear to exist the mouth. Among those with eating disorders, people who eat and force themselves to vomit offer a nice representation of how the substance of food is prevented from changing into the substance of the body. But this is also a parody of the speech act, based on the unconscious assumption that the place where words enter is the place from which they exit. This symptom is a visualization of an invisible process. From the idea of the assumed body of the angels, we may now examine how someone who aspires to their company takes her own body to be nothing more than assumed. This woman died at the age of thirty-three while nourishing herself exclusively with communion wafers.

We are referring to Catherine of Siena; one whose anorexia was eventually considered a sign of her piety. There are many ways she could have been informed of how angels eat, but she would probably have been aware of the teaching of Aquinas. Catherine was a Dominican religious living in the second half of the fourteenth century. Aquinas himself was noted for his enormous appetite; he was anything but an anorexic. The idea of coupling Thomas Aquinas and Catherine of Siena must appear somewhat strange. And yet they represent two different approaches to the same theological question, and these approaches may well be considered masculine and feminine. In relation to the unsexed angels there are two traditions, one that approaches the issue through the means of intelligence, the other through the affective side of the soul. Perhaps these two represent the division of the sexes, or at least one version of it. The first promotes the activity of the mind and leaves the body to its devices; the second requires studied imitation of angelic being. In some way Catherine represents, through the witness of her body and the witness of her speech, the translation into practice of theories produced by eminent theologians. It is one thing to understand what an author meant by a statement; it is of equal if not more importance to know how his statements were understood and how they translated, not into action, but into passion.

Using these ideas as an approach to anorexia yields an important clinical point, which was emphasized by Lacan. It was not true that Catherine of Siena was not eating; she was eating, but what she was eating was not real food, it was invisible spiritual food. Similarly, while she had no appetite or desire for food, she was consumed by what she called a "holy desire" for spiritual nourishment. This is hardly synonymous with what Rudolph Bell labeled "holy anorexia." Her phrase does not necessarily point to what psychiatry labels as illness. There ought to be a distinction between sainthood and anorexia; what have we accomplished in reducing a Catherine to a category of people who will never achieve sainthood? Perhaps Catherine was suffering from an excessive emulation of angelic being; but why should she not have done so when virgins had long been considered the most angelic humans? What made her different from the ordinary anorexic was that her fasting was inscribed in the structure of religious ritual and observance. It was not an individual event, but became part of a social organization. If there is room for a critique of anorexia in this context, it should be directed toward a theological system that encouraged and sustained the emulation of angelic being. An epidemic of eating disorders, a situation where many young women imitate the affective experience of one, calls our attention to a type of identification that is sustained by a group.

Catherine was not only affected by Aquinas's teachings; the example of the founder of the Franciscan order also exerted an influence. We know that Catherine, like Francis of Assisi, received the Stigmata of Christ, the difference being that hers were invisible. We read in Bonaventure's biography of Francis a passage that links angelic being with fasting. "He was joined in a bond of inseparable love to the angels who burn with a marvelous fire to be rapt out of themselves into God and to inflame the souls of the elect. Out of the devotion to the angels he used to spend the forty days after the Assumption of the glorious Virgin in fasting and continual prayer" (Bonaventure 1978, p. 264). If we accept that Catherine wanted be what she called an "earthly angel," and that she succeeded in becoming a saint, why not say that anorexics are failed angels? Perhaps it is in failing that they have a chance of surviving. The distinction might be understood in the context of Lacan's analysis of anorexia, to which we alluded above. Anorexics do eat, Lacan said, only what they eat is nothing. In our terms the difference between eating spiritual food and eating nothing draws the distinction between saints and failed angels.

Some passages from Catherine's writings will elaborate these points. In the first place note that the translation of a real body into an assumed body is the basis for her spiritual quest. The following text is an excellent example of the metaphoric transposition of the concerns of the body onto the activities of the soul. God the Father explained these things to Catherine in *The Dialogue*:

She eats the food of souls for my honor at the table of the most holy cross. In no other way and at no other table can it be eaten perfectly and in truth. And she chews it (for otherwise she could not digest it) with hatred and love, the two rows of teeth in the mouth of holy desire. There she takes this food and chews it with hatred for herself and love for virtue in herself and in others. Every sort of assault—derision, insult, slander, reproach, endless persecutions, hunger and thirst, cold and heat, pain-filled longing and tears and sweat for the salvation of souls—she chews them all for my honor as she bears with her neighbors and supports them. And after she has chewed them she tastes the flavor, savoring the fruit of her labor and the delight of this food of souls, enjoying its taste in the fire of charity for me and her neighbors. And so this food reaches the stomach (that is, the heart), which has been prepared by desire and hunger for souls to receive it willingly, with heartfelt charity and affection for others. She delights in it and chews it over and over in such a way that she lets go of her delicacy about her bodily life in order to be able to eat this food at the table of the cross, the table of the teaching of Christ crucified. (Catherine 1980, pp. 140–41)

In the lines that immediately precede these the connection between eating and speaking, which is central to the structure of eating disorders, is made manifest. "The mouth speaks with its tongue and tastes flavors. . . . So it is with the soul. First she speaks to me with the tongue of holy and constant prayer that is in the mouth of her holy desire. This tongue has an external and interior language. Interiorly, the soul offers me tender loving desires for the salvation of souls. Externally, she proclaims the teaching of my Truth, admonishing, advising, testifying, without any fear for the pain the world may please to afflict on her" (Catherine 1980, p. 140).

The beginning of a spiritual quest is marked by a purge of the soul, which is analogous to a bodily one. "They begin to empty their soul's house of filth when free choice sends them the message of fear of punishment. ... It is just like a man who, once he has purged his stomach and vomited out the bile, has an appetite for food. So these souls wait for the hand of free choice to offer them lovingly the food of virtue, for as soon as it is offered they are eager to eat it" (Catherine 1980, p. 177). And in this state the soul will eat: "If you follow this truth you will have the life of grace and never die of hunger, for the Word has himself become your food" (Catherine 1980, p. 67). (Obviously this echoes the biblical passages to which we have already alluded.) The soul becomes angelic by eating the right kind of food: "Dearest daughter, contemplate the marvelous state of the soul who receives this bread of life, this food of angels, as she ought" (Catherine 1980, p. 211). This state comports enjoyment: "But after the soul has let go of the body's heaviness, her will is filled. She longed to see me and now she sees me, and in that vision is blessedness. Seeing me she knows me. Knowing me she loves me. Loving me she enjoys me, the supreme eternal Good. This enjoyment fills and satisfies her will, her longing to see me and to know me. She longs for what she possesses and possesses what she longs for, and, as I have told you, her desire knows no pain, nor her satisfaction any boredom" (Catherine 1980, p. 92). She is equal to the angels in enjoyment: "This is that superb state in which the soul even while still mortal shares the enjoyment of the immortals. In fact, she often attains such union that she hardly knows whether she is in the body or out. She tastes the pledge of eternal life through her union with me as well as because her own will is dead. It is by that death that she realizes her union with me, and in no other way could she perfectly accomplish that" (Catherine 1980, p. 158).

I argued at some length and with some pains in Chapter 2 that after the Black Death the angels became less interesting to people, first because they were replaced by devils, and second because they had descended to earth. Therefore, it is important that these ideas are expressed explicitly in *The Dialogue,* which was written by one who ministered to the sick and dying during one of the outbreaks of Plague, one of the few walking through Siena during that time (Meiss 1973, p. 88). God tells Catherine that the body of the Church has been corrupted by ministers who are acting as devils, and she, devout daughter, would bear witness to this truth with her body. "Woe, woe, to their wretched lives! For what the gentle Word, my only-begotten Son, won with such suffering on the wood of the most holy cross they spend on prostitutes. They devour the souls who were bought with Christ's blood, eating them up in so many ways, and feeding their own children with what belongs to the poor. O you temples of the devil! I appointed you to be earthly angels in this life, but you are devils who have taken up the devils' work" (Catherine 1980, pp. 232–33). That Catherine herself was of the company of these earthly angels seems beyond doubt. It would not have been fitting for her to claim such a rank and privilege; but in the minds of her contemporaries, especially those who imitated her, such was surely the case. The point is that if it was no longer possible to be an earthly angel within the Church, then it was necessary to be one outside of it, in the world. This is not necessarily what Catherine would have wished; it was imposed by the corruption of the clergy.

These denunciations do not represent what some pretend to see as a revolt against patriarchal authority. In the first place, the power of the clergy was seriously compromised during Catherine's time; the pope had taken up residence in Avignon and his authority was gravely contested by local princes. Certainly Catherine preached virtue to popes; her goal, however, was explicitly to restore them to positions of virile authority. She wanted the papacy returned to Rome, and her influence is shown in the comment by Kirshner and Morrison that Gregory XI did do so in 1377 at her behest. He died promptly thereafter (Kirshner and Morrison 1986, p. 423). She wrote to Gregory XI: "I want to see you a forceful man, fearless and without earthly love for yourself or for any being related to you by blood. . . . Since He has given you authority and you have accepted it, you must use your virtue and your power. If you are not willing to use them, you should have refused what you took on. . . ." And she wrote to Urban VI: "Most Holy Father, God has placed you as a shepherd over all his sheep of the Christian religion. . . . He has placed you in an age in which there is more wickedness among the clergy than during long ages past, both within the body of the holy church and in the universal body of all the Christian religion. This is why it is absolutely necessary that you be firmly founded in perfect charity and [hold fast to] the pearl of justice, in the way I have said. . . . Then like a true knight and a just shepherd, you will chastise with virility, uprooting vice and planting virtue, and preparing yourself to lay down your life if need be" (in Kirshner and Morrison 1986, pp. 424, 427). Surrounded by men who are incompetent or inept, Catherine is looking for one who will not fail her. A real man is defined as one who will do what she says, who will obey her command. The search for male authority in such women is explicit, but it is also doomed to fail. This kind of structure, most evident in hysteria, is not a revolt against paternal authority; rather, it manifests a father's having failed his daughter—either by being abusive or by being disinterested.

The denunciation of corruption among the clergy becomes therefore a call for authority, a higher and more perfect authority, one that just happens to speak through Catherine. God the Father spoke directly to Catherine. This may or may not be unique in Church history, but it is certainly uncommon, bordering on heresy. As Meiss explained: "The essential conviction of mysticism that the soul was capable of a direct experience of God was only one short but fateful step from the belief that the soul could attain so high a degree of spirituality that it might dispense with the intermediation of the Church and its orders. ... Opponents of Catherine within the Church, many of them jealous of her growing influence, attacked as sheer vanity her assertions of direct knowledge of God, her visions, and her consequent assurance of evangelical mission" (Meiss 1973, p. 104). Since God was supposed to speak through his Son and his angels, Catherine's taking herself to be God's mouthpiece identified her first with the angels and ultimately with Christ.

A popular misconception about anorexics is that they are demonstrating an exaggerated participation in society's ideal of the svelt feminine figure, that they do not eat because they want to attract men. This is patent nonsense; the state at which the anorexic arrives, when she feels herself slim, not only does not incite masculine desire and libido; it has the opposite effect. Add to emaciation the trials and scourges of flagellation and other forms of chastisement and you create a female body fully given over to love of God, which demonstrates this by the fact that no human male could possibly find such a body sexually attractive.

Certainly, not every young woman suffering an eating disorder arrives at this state. It is sufficient to know that this is what she aspires to. If she is also an aspiring saint, and if she risks being accused of witchcraft, perhaps the state of her body will bear witness to a thorough absence of commerce with phallic devils. Any phallus would be refused, and not because the sexual act places her in a position that resembles eating. The anorexic's anxiety about copulation and penetration concerns the fantasy that in the sexual act she will be eaten. Consequently, in not eating, she allows her body to consume itself. This provides a perfectly autonomous enjoyment, independent of all external agency. When desire is purified by being transposed onto a spiritual body it becomes cointensive with enjoyment.

Quite naturally this leads us to the question of the sex of the angels, or, to the problem of the commerce between angels and women. More specifically, the question was whether angels in their assumed bodies exercise a sexual function. Aquinas raised the issue through a biblical text (ST, part 1, q. 51, art. 3). He replied to it by referring to a commentary of Augustine in *The City of God*. To begin let us note the passage from Genesis 6:1–4, as translated in the Anchor Bible. Alternate translations are included in brackets. "Now when men began to increase on earth and daughters were born to them, the divine beings [sons of God or angels of God] saw how beautiful were the human daughters and took as their wives any of them they liked. Then Yahweh said, 'My spirit shall not shield man forever, since he is but flesh; let the time allowed him be one hundred and twenty years.' It was then that the Nephilim [a race of giants] appeared on earth—as well as later—after the divine beings [sons of God or angels of God] had united with [came to or cohabited with] human daughters to whom they bore children. Those were the heroes of old, men of renown."

To reply Aquinas quoted Augustine and shifted the reference immediately to the question of whether fallen angels copulate with women. The first point is that sexual commerce between devils and women does happen. This is relevant because devils, being fallen angels, are of the same material or substance as the holy angels. If the one has sexual commerce, why not the other? Augustine commented:

Nevertheless it is the testimony of Scripture (which tells us nothing but the truth) that angels appeared to men in bodies of such a kind that they could not only be seen but also touched. Besides this, it is widely reported that Silvani and Pans, commonly called incubi, have often behaved improperly towards women, lusting after them and achieving intercourse with them. These reports are confirmed by many people, either from their own experience or from the accounts of the experience of others, whose reliability there is no occasion to doubt. Then there is the story that certain demons, whom the Gauls call Dusii, constantly and successfully attempt this indecency. This is asserted by so many witnesses of such a character that it would seem an impertinence to deny it. Hence I would not venture a conclusive statement of the question whether some spirits with bodies of air (an element which even when set in motion by a fan is felt by the bodily sense of touch) can also experience this lust and so can mate, in whatever way they can, with women, who feel their embraces. (CG, book 15, chap. 23)

One thing that immediately strikes a modern reader is Augustine's belief not only that Scripture always tells the truth: those who have testified to experiencing sexual intercourse with demons were also for him being entirely truthful. Thus, when it comes to a matter of this urgency, women and/or their confessors are always truthful. Compare this with Freud's doubts about the veracity of the accounts of his first hysterical patients. Considering how many women asserted that they had been sexually molested by their fathers, Freud came to believe that some had fantasized the events. This does not make them less truthful, nor does it deny that these things do happen. Even if an event has happened, what remains of it is the phantasm, the image formed in the mind; and it is not so obvious that the best way of dealing with that phantasm is to anchor it in some real event. The phantasm is known or ignored according to principles that come from other than the world of empirical realities. Otherwise the simple remembering of the event and the knowledge that its reality is accepted by others would be therapeutic.

Had Freud's patients, for example, asserted that they had been molested by demons, would he have had occasion to doubt their truthfulness? Perhaps not, since his idea that these acts may have been phantasmatic would have accorded perfectly with the idea that the agents of seduction had been demons. It is incorrect to assume that Freud was accusing his patients of fabulation. His point, as clarified by Lacan, was that the truth to which they bore witness was not factual or empirical. Note also the following: Freud in his first theorization of psychoanalysis declared that phantasies were the visual representation of things heard. Is it too hard to imagine that a girl may be molested metaphorically, that she may be touched corporally by the speech of an Other, perhaps more particularly, by the voice of an Other that penetrates her. (It is from Augustine that we have the idea that the Virgin was impregnated through the ear.) That this Other be her father is certainly possible, and if we extend the function of paternity to others besides biological fathers, it may be more than possible. Thus the truth of the phantasm corresponds well to something that has happened; yet the experience need not be explicitly sexual. Perhaps Freud, despite himself, was pointing to the fact that the reduction of the sexual to the genital is a masculine bias; that for women or for beings who approach sexuality from a feminine position sexuality can never be merely genital. Does this not tell us something in addition about the bodies of angels? Augustine called them bodies of air, from which Aquinas concluded that they are like clouds—incorrectly, because speech also is a movement of the air that touches people. Perhaps certain forms of speech are experienced as embraces; such embraces may well produce effects, whether offspring or symptoms. Is it the voice behind or within the words that produces the effect, or is it the phonetic materiality of the language that is responsible? Perhaps the agent is simply the invisible insensible meaning—to the extent that it is visualized. The latter example refers to the communication of holy angels, whereas anything that is produced in a listener by the play of the signifying chain, by its phonetic structure is on the side of the devils.

The idea that the angels who couple with the daughters of men in Genesis are actually devils dates at least to Philo of Alexandria. "These are the evil ones who, cloaking themselves under the name of angels, know not the daughters of right reason, the sciences and virtues, but court the pleasures which are born of men, pleasures mortal as their parents—pleasures endowed not with the true beauty, which the mind alone can discern, but with the false comeliness, by which the senses are deceived" (Philo 2, p. 455). For Philo it is perfectly appropriate that good angels couple with something, namely knowledge and virtue. Later, it appears, angels and the daughters of right reason will become so thoroughly undivided that they will not need to couple.

Augustine too did not believe that Genesis 6:1–4 refers to angels. His commentary is not cited by Aquinas in addressing the issue. Augustine's paraphrase of the biblical text was: "Thus the sons of God were captivated by love for the daughters of men, and in order to enjoy them as wives, they abandoned the godly behavior they had maintained in the holy community and lapsed into the morality of earth-born society" (CG, book 15, chap. 22). Augustine continued that by "sons of God" or "angels of God" we are to understand the sons of Seth. This is not insignificant, for Augustine not only did not consider that the sons of God were angels, but he collapsed the distinction between humans and angels by setting up a group of angelic humans whose corruption and fall derived from their attraction to female beauty. Thus the reference of the biblical text is to human beings, not to holy angels. Of the latter there is no suggestion of such activity.

The production of the coupling of fallen angelic humans with women would eventually be destroyed in the Flood. The theological problem is that Augustine, having identified the sons of Seth as angels, went on to speak of those angelic humans who did not fall, who were not tempted by the daughters of men. These earthly angels ". . . begot children for God, not for themselves; that means that the lust for coition was not their master, but it was a servant, subordinate to duty for procreation. They did not procreate children to found a family to minister to their pride but to produce citizens for the City of God, so that they, as angels of God, could give their children this message: that they must put their hope in God . . ." (CG, book 15, chap. 23). This represents the type of sexual congress that Augustine saw as having taken place before the Fall; it excludes both masculine sexual desire and the concerns of kinship. So despite the Fall, the kind of sexual union preferred by Christianity persisted when men were sufficiently angelic. The term angel then seems to be used to mean any servant or messenger of God, not necessarily a heavenly being or spirit. "Now these sons of God were not angels of God in such a way that they were not also human beings as some people suppose" (ibid.). Among other things this confirms the fact that thinking of relationships in angelic terms need not exclude sexuality. And the Augustinian view also seems to presuppose that angels are male; there is no sense of there being female angels, daughters of God.

Aquinas introduced the question of angelic sexuality with the lines from Genesis. He did not, however, respond by citing the exposition from Augustine. Perhaps he believed that Augustine, commenting on Genesis, had simply avoided the issue, addressing it fully only in his remarks about copulation between devils and women. Otherwise, it may have been unthinkable for the Angelic Doctor that angelic humans engage in such acts no matter what the redeeming intention. Aquinas's concern was with the composition of the angelic body, and to the extent that sex was in question he was obliged to refer to the fallen angels. "Still if some are occasionally begotten from demons, it is not from the seed of such demons, nor from their assumed bodies, but from the seed of men taken for that purpose; as when the demon assumes first the form of a woman and afterwards of a man; just as they take the seed of other things for other generating purposes, as Augustine says (*De Trin.* iii), so that the person born is not the child of a demon but of a man" (ST, part 1, q. 51, art. 3). Just as an angelic body cannot eat because it is incapable of digesting food, so such a body cannot produce semen. And yet there are women who assert themselves to have been impregnated by demons, and, following Augustine, it would be impudent to doubt their testimony.

Aquinas declared that the same demon may first assume the form of a woman—this would be a succubus—to extract by some means or other seed from a man, then to change into the form of a man—an incubus—to deposit this seed in a woman's womb. Following this reflection, the authors of the *Malleus Maleficarum* provided an answer sought by Freud, as mentioned in a letter to Fliess (letter of Jan. 24, 1897). The question was: why do witches say that the semen of devils is cold? The answer is: because the demons have had to carry it some distance from the man from whom it was stolen to the woman who is to receive it. In such a transit the fertilizing substance loses heat.

Not only are demons sexed, but they can change from one to the other. The angels of God are of neither sex so long as they remain in Heaven. Remember that the pudenda are properly the province of demons, not of the holy angels. Second, it is interesting that Aquinas here seems to identify fatherhood with the man whose body has provided the semen that has impregnated a woman. (In the fuller version of his idea on the subject of fatherhood Aquinas presented a triple paternal function: the father accounts for the child's individuality, a celestial body makes it belong to the human species, an angel provides the aptitude of matter to accept the rational soul, the alliance of matter and mind [Jacquart and Thomasset 1985, pp. 80–81].) Third, as representatives of masculinity, the demons are thieves. Might there not be in this attribution a veiled reference to the pagan deity who, like the angels, was also a messenger, an intermediary between the worlds of the living and the dead? After all, Hermes was not just a messenger, he was a thief and a liar, as is clear from the Homeric hymn. As for the modus operandi of the thieving demons, we will hypothesize that it has something to do with a problem that Luther declared, around a century and a half after Aquinas, to be the bane of monastic life. "Almost every night the brothers were bothered by them, so that they didn't dare celebrate mass the next day. But when a large number of masses that had been imposed on us and appointed for us had to be omitted on account of our own refusal, it became public, and the prior conceded that anybody at all could and should celebrate mass, even if he had nocturnal pollutions. Phew! All the monasteries and convents ought to be dismantled on account of these shameful pollutions alone. . . . Dear God, protect us from such abomination; let us remain in the holy estate of matrimony, where thou dost wink at our infirmity" (Luther 1967, p. 295). This gives an insight into why Luther wanted the clergy to marry; he is a long way from the injunction that it is better to marry than to burn.

With the angels the question is not desire but enjoyment. And here we find a significant division. Consistently throughout Christian theology the angels are granted the enjoyment that devolves from seeing God face-to-face. This is the enjoyment promised to the soul that attains an angelic state, and it is clear that there is supposed to be no better enjoyment. As far as a soul is concerned, this enjoyment is feminine, in part because the soul that experiences it is often referred to as "she," in part because this enjoyment is experienced by one who is married to Christ, and in part because ever since Tiresias it has been common knowledge that women's enjoyment, whether or not you consider it sexual, is superior to that of men. The angel whose entire being is inflamed with love of God is a model for feminine enjoyment, especially if we consider that masculine enjoyment is specific to an organ. Many authors have no real problem with attributing feminine enjoyment to angels. With Aquinas, however, the question that arises is whether there is a masculine enjoyment for a disembodied spirit. And his view seems to be that the intellectual enjoyment experienced by an angel is virile, because this enjoyment is located in a being that is separated from a body. Rather than say that it is phallic, we will call it encephallic. The enjoyment of intellectual labor seems clearly to be different from that of the soul in a state of mystical rapture. And perhaps it is not surprising that Aquinas should hold such an idea, given the influence of Aristotle and his Arab commentators. Their world had a place for virility. If there is a sense of masculine enjoyment in Aquinas's angels, it appears to be an inheritance from non-Christian sources.

It is false to think that Catholicism has cast scorn on feminine enjoyment, whatever its attitudes toward the feminine sex. Witness the advice of Jerome to a virgin named Eustochium: "Christ, Jerome explained to a girl, was the supreme 'opener' of virgins: 'when sleep overtakes you ... your Lover will come behind the wall, thrust his hand through the opening and caress your belly ... you will start up, trembling all over, and you will cry, "I am wounded with love *[Vulnerata caritatis ego sum.]*' '" (in Lane Fox 1986, p. 371; Jerome, letter 22, p. 109). Another victory for charity! Certainly this suggests, as we saw in a previous text of Albert the Great, that some eminent Church authorities were not overtly opposed to manual stimulation of the female sex for the purpose of producing enjoyment. And yet, we ought not think that this represents a copulation, nor that there is any phallic enjoyment. Charity here means giving pleasure while not taking any. There may be some voyeuristic enjoyment involved for the male who thus abuses virgins in their sleep, but phallic enjoyment is not mentioned.

Immediately prior to these lines Jerome defined the type of communication taking place between the virgin and her bridegroom: "If you pray, you are speaking to your Spouse: if you read, He is speaking to you." True speech passes in silence. The French language gives us the idiom: *un ange passe,* whose translation is the title of this book. This refers to a spontaneous moment of silence occurring in the midst of a conversation. The pronouncing of the phrase functions to break the silence. Are we now to assume, as many contemporaries will think gleefully, that the virgin is dispossessed of the act of writing? Did Jerome recoil in horror at the subversive force of a virgin with a pen in her hand? Not for a moment. In the same letter he told Eustochium: "You too may be perhaps the Lord's mother. 'Take thee a great new roll and write in it with the pen of a man who is swiftly carrying off the spoils' [Isaiah 8:1]. ... And he whose name just before you had inscribed upon the tablet of your heart, and had written with speedy pen upon its new surface, after He has recovered the spoils of the enemies and has stripped principalities and powers [Colossians 1:15], nailing them to His cross, He having been conceived grows to manhood, and as He becomes older regards you not as His mother but as His bride" (Letter 22, pp. 147–9). So much for the Law. Let the reign of deconstruction begin.

What then of the other kind, the masculine enjoyment and desire? One would be hard put to find a discourse on masculine desire in the writings of the Fathers, except in the endless admonitions against the subtle cunning of the serpent. Other than that, masculine sexuality is for the most part given over to the work of fertility; it is a fertilizing instrument. Otherwise it is considered to be necessary to the health of the body through the regulation of a balance of various fluids (Jacquart and Thomasset 1985, p. 109). In either case its proper deployment is thought to be in the interests of life; its attachment to death or its mediating function between the living and dead has been sundered. Phallic enjoyment as distinct from feminine enjoyment is localized, it is situated in an organ, not in a body, and not in a soul. But this part of the body may be conceptualized as detachable from the body proper. We have said that the phallus is a part of the body that functions as something other than an organ. Thus, with its experience of enjoyment it is called back to its origin.

The phallus is also a signifier of desire, and it is noteworthy that the discourse concerning the control and mastery of this desire in the interest of producing sexual enjoyment in both partners, especially in the female partner, is not integral to Christian tradition. It was imported from the Arab East, the product of a polygamous society (Jacquart and Thomasset 1985, pp. 257–8). R. H. Van Gulik described the reasoning behind practices aiming at semen retention in China: "Here then are two fundamental notions that Chinese sexual literature never fails to advance. The first is that a man's semen is his most precious possession, the source not only of his health, but of his life itself; any emission of semen will diminish this vital force, unless it is compensated by the acquisition of an equivalent quality of feminine *yin* essence. The second is that a man should give to a woman a complete satisfaction each time that he couples with her, but that he should only allow himself an orgasm under certain prescribed occasions" (in Jacquart and Thomasset 1985, pp. 133–34). Someone might have arrived at a similar ethic by following arguments about angels and semen. If no angelic body produces its own semen, and if such a body may copulate with a woman, would it be able to ejaculate? Chinese erotic technique places masculine desire in opposition to masculine enjoyment, as though the two were in some sense exclusive. It also gives primary value to the requirement of balancing the accounts, maintaining the structure, as far as enjoyment is concerned. In the Christian West the question would be whether semen retention is a form of contraception, and thus contrary to natural law.

It is not so much because desire is counter to the natural function of procreation that it is condemned; rather, the obsession with procreation in the worship of fertility is a reaction against masculine desire and the phallus. Within these Eastern cultures it is the man who holds the key to sexual pleasure for both partners. According to Jacquart and Thomasset, the originality of Western eroticism is that it is the woman who is the master of pleasures (p. 134).

The Westernized version of the virtue of semen retention was promoted by those who were influenced by Arab philosophers. Their point of view was that abstinence promoted the ability to produce philosophy. In one sense, then, the erotic has simply been transferred upward into the functioning of the intellect, unless you believe that the phallus is in fact a separate intelligence. The life of Peter Abélard is evidence that the practice of Scholastic philosophy did not have the effect of dampening sexual desire.

Within theology, masculine desire is most often posited through what appears to be its sublimated form; it exists through the exercise of an intermediary function, rarely if ever designated as phallic, usually called by the name of the intellect. The connection does not require Freud; it was stated explicitly by the authors of the time. Albert the Great was able to argue that seminal fluid derived especially from the brain, with which it had in common the qualities of whiteness, softness, and wetness. Thus he was able to conclude that "coitus empties especially the brain" (Jacquart and Thomasset 1985, p. 78). If the brain is like a testicle, then the intellect is a phallus.

The recourse to intellect exists where some theologians, of whom Aquinas was the most eminent, decided that the ultimate in enjoyment, that of seeing God face-to-face, was forbidden to humans. Those who are prohibited from seeing God face-to-face, who are constrained to see only through a glass darkly, or in an enigma, posed for themselves the task of clarifying things through the activity of the intellect. The knowledge thereby gleaned was not thought to be the same as that gained by the face-to-face encounter promoted by the mystics. Therefore the enjoyment was not thought to come from direct contact with God, but rather with the fullest exercise of the intellectual function. While the rapture of mystics is an experience of body and soul beyond intelligence, the enjoyment experienced by the mind in its exercise of intelligence occurs at the expense of the body. Thus the split of mind and body, the process by which the mind abstracts from sensible things to reach ultimate realities in the form that they present themselves to it, is a model of masculine desire—of the transformation of an organ into a signifier or separate intelligence. And it is also required that there be sensible objects, fetish objects, to cause this desire.

So we have two kinds of enjoyment, the one the enjoyment of mystics, the other the enjoyment of intellectuals. Unfortunately, rather than seeing the two as contiguous, theologians tended to make the issue an either/or proposition. Roughly speaking, the division of the two was represented in late medieval monasticism by the division of Franciscans and Dominicans. Beginning with Francis of Assisi, moving through Bonaventure and even Duns Scotus, the Franciscans believed that the enjoyment of divinity, the soul's union with God, could be attained by people who were sufficiently angelic in their being. (The basic idea was that whereas the Bible had said that one could not look at God and live, mystical experience afforded a metaphoric death.) While the quality of mind of the great Franciscans was in no way lacking in brilliance, the Minorities for the most part taught by the example of their lives, in imitation of Christ and the angels. They were the monks with whom people could relate affectively. Of these Francis was the most exemplary.

Aquinas represented the other side, which believed that such an enjoyment was impossible. He defined angels as intellectual substances whose vision of God represented an immediate grasp of intelligibles. A human being could approach the angelic understanding only through the function of the intellect, to the detriment of sensory perception. To this Duns Scotus and William of Ockham replied that an angel could have an immediate cognitive knowledge of things, by which they meant that there existed an immediate experience of things in the world, an experience not mediated by intellect or by the categories of Aristotelian philosophy. To say that one has a satisfying experience of an object is not at all the same as to say that one must abstract from the sense impression of that object to know its concept or principle. Obviously it will make a difference to the object whether it is the cause of desire or the object of an immediate intuitive cognition.

The two types of enjoyment are two approaches to knowing the truth. They represent alternate approaches to meaning; the problem they pose may be considered to be epistemological, but it also points to semantics. The goal of the work of the Thomist intelligence is not to have an immediate intuitive cognition of things but to go beyond the particular to the intelligible. "For, since the perfection of the intellect is what is true, in the order of intelligible objects, that object which is a purely formal intelligible will be true itself. And this characteristic applies only to God, for since the true is consequent on being, that alone is its own truth which is its own being. . . . So, other intelligible subsistents do not exist as pure forms in the order of intelligible beings, but as possessors of a form in some subject. In fact, each of them is a true thing, but not truth, just as each is a being but not the very act of being" (Aquinas SCG, book 3, chap. 51). On the question of the ultimate felicity, Aquinas was quite clear about what it consists in: "Also, quite apparent in this conclusion is the fact that ultimate felicity is to be sought in nothing other than an operation of the intellect, since no desire carries on to such sublime heights as the desire to understand the truth. Indeed, all our desires for pleasure, or other things of this sort that are craved by men, can be satisfied with other things, but the aforementioned desire does not rest until it reaches God, the highest point of reference for, and the maker of, things" (SCG, book 3, chap. 50). The chapter titles of this third book tell us that felicity does not consist in pleasures of the flesh, honors, glory, riches, worldly power, goods of the body, the senses, acts of the moral virtues, prudence, or the operation of art. What is important here is that knowledge of truth can be gained only through the functioning of the intellect and that this represents a masculine approach to felicity. The other modes of felicity are aspects of the pleasures of the body. Might we suggest that the angel as separate intelligence is a phallus that assumes a body, most often a male body, in order not to frighten off a womanly truth? The question is whether the truth that is grasped through the agency of the intellect is the same as the one that is grasped by immediate intuitive cognition.

Among the Franciscans, the contemporary of Aquinas most clearly considered his competitor is Bonaventure. Both were nominated as cardinals at the same moment, though only Bonaventure came to occupy the position; Aquinas died on route to the investiture. A reading of Bonaventure will demonstrate clearly the difference from Aquinas. In the Prologue to the *Itinerarium mentis in Deum* (The Soul's Journey into God), Bonaventure stated: "I ask you, then, to weigh the writer's intention rather than his work, the meaning of his words rather than his uncultivated style, truth rather than beauty, the exercise of affection rather than erudition of the intellect" (Bonaventure 1978, p. 56). Or at the end of the same work: "In this passing over, if it is to be perfect, all intellectual activities must be left behind and the height of our affection must be totally transferred and transformed into God" (p. 113). It is not that Bonaventure disparaged the intellectual faculties; he believed that they are passed over, in his phrase, through the contemplation of Christ: ". . . when finally in the sixth stage our mind reaches that point where it contemplates in the First and Supreme Principle and in the *mediator of God and men,* Jesus Christ, those things whose likenesses can in no way be found in creatures and which surpass all penetration of the human intellect, it now remains for our mind, by contemplating these things, to transcend and pass over not only this sense world but even itself" (p. 111). For Bonaventure the ecstatic transfer of affection is beyond the intellect; it requires, however, intellectual activity to arrive at the point where mind can be passed over. We may turn to him for a statement concerning the grasp of meaning, and of truth. "The intellect can be said truly to comprehend the meaning of propositions when it knows with certitude that they are true. To know this is really to know because the intellect cannot be deceived in this kind of comprehension. For it knows that this truth cannot be otherwise; therefore, it knows that this truth is unchangeable" (Bonaventure 1978, p. 82). Happily, Bonaventure provided a clear summary of the ascending order of meanings. We quote at length to demonstrate the movement from beings to Being, among other things.

The function of the intellective faculty consists in understanding the meaning of terms, propositions and inferences. Now, the intellect grasps the meaning of terms when it comprehends in a definition what a thing is. But definitions are constructed by using more universal terms; and are defined by more universal terms until we come to the highest and most universal. Consequently, unless these latter are known, the less universal cannot be grasped in a definition. Unless we know what being per se is, we cannot fully know the definition of any particular substance. We cannot know being per se unless we also know its properties, which are: one, true, good. Now, being can be considered as incomplete or complete, as imperfect or perfect, as being in potency or being in act, qualified being or unqualified, partial being or total being, transient being or permanent being, being through another or being through itself, being mixed with nonbeing or pure being, dependent being or absolute being, posterior being or prior being, changeable being or unchangeable being, simple being or composite being. Since privations and defects can in no way be known except through something positive, our intellect does not come to the point of understanding any created being by a full analysis unless it is aided by a knowledge of the Being which is most pure, most actual, most complete and absolute, which is unqualified and Eternal Being, in which are the principles of all things and their purity. (Bonaventure 1978, pp. 81–82)

The place that Bonaventure wished to reach represents the annihilation of opposites in the Oneness of God. The state is seen obscurely and at a distance in this passage. As with Francis, the ultimate unity occurs through identification with an image, "For if an image is an expressed likeness, when our mind contemplates in Christ the Son of God, who is the image of the invisible God by nature, our humanity, so wonderfully exalted, so ineffably united, when at the same time it sees united the first and the last, the highest and the lowest . . . ." (Bonaventure 1978, p. 108).

This unity of Christ and man is not quite what Aquinas sought. Bonaventure was asserting the value of sensory faculties as providing a way to God because sensible objects are emblematic of the divine perfection. For Aquinas such a movement was impossible; for him the path of sensory illumination was corrupted by the image of things that we maintain in our minds, by what he called phantasms. And Aquinas wanted to abstract intelligible truth from the phantasm. There is no sense in his thought that phantasms or sensible objects are formed in the image of divine forms.

Through creatures Bonaventure saw the path open to God. "These creatures, I say, are exemplars, or rather exemplifications presented to souls still untrained and immersed in sensible things so that through sensible things which they see they will be carried over to intelligible things which they do not see as though signs to what is signified" (Bonaventure 1978, p. 76). Thus his quest is a seeking after the signified, the intelligble things that lead to the vision of God. The creatures as signs will ultimately fall away in the ecstatic contemplation of divinity. This process is described as the movement from the contemplation of color to the contemplation of light itself, which is being and good. "Strange, then, is the blindness of the intellect, which does not consider that which it sees first and without which it can know nothing. The eye, concentrating on differences of color, does not see the very light by which it sees other things; and if it does see this light, it does not advert to it. In the same way, the mind's eye, concentrating on particular and universal being, does not advert to being itself, which is beyond every genus, even though it comes to our minds first and through it we know other things" (Bonaventure 1978, p. 96). The Being of God is absolute, pure, simple, actual, perfect, and one. It knows no opposites; thus it represents the transcendence of dialectics. Ultimately it will not be through the activity of the intellect that the soul grasps the oneness of being itself. Rather, it will be in the surpassing of the division between intellect and truth; the intellect affords glimpses of the true, but the truth in itself can only be grasped immediately, intuitively, by seeing it and by becoming it. This is a function of piety and faith more than it is of learning.

The identification of humans and angels had long been a major theological issue; it was perhaps most present to people of the thirteenth century through the extraordinary story of the stigmatization of Francis of Assisi. This goes beyond imitation and emulation to attain a unification of Francis with the image of Christ in the seraph. The fact that the seraph is fused with the image of Christ provides the intermediary step to the experience of Francis. It is as though mystical marriage to Christ was not quite close enough, or else that it was not fitting for a man to entertain such Bernardine yearnings overtly. So Francis took things one step further. Bonaventure wrote: "Jesus Christ crucified always *rested like a bundle of myrrh in the bosom* of Francis's soul (Cant. 1:12), and he longed to be totally transformed into him by the fire of ecstatic love" (Bonaventure 1978, p. 263). Of course, Francis ultimately got his wish.

By the Seraphic ardor of his desires, he was being borne aloft into God; and by his sweet compassion he was being transformed into him who chose to be crucified because of the excess of his love. On a certain morning about the feast of the Exaltation of the Cross, while Francis was praying on the mountainside, he saw a Seraph with six fiery and shining wings descend from the height of heaven. And when in swift flight the Seraph had reached a spot in the air near the man of God, there appeared between the wings the figure of a man crucified, with his hands and feet extended in the form of a cross and fastened to a cross. ... Eventually he understood by a revelation from the Lord that divine providence had shown him this vision so that, as Christ's lover, he might learn in advance that he was to be totally transformed into the likeness of Christ crucified, not by the martyrdom of his flesh, but by the fire of his love consuming his soul. (Bonaventure 1978, pp. 305–6)

Does this not tell us something of the power of love and the fact that love must be reciprocated for there to be what we call a falling in love? The interesting point is the identification or unification involved here. The identification takes place basically on the level of marks on the body, marks visible to those who are permitted to witness them. The marks are a sign anticipating the total transformation to come. Here we have an angel, one of the highest order, assuming not the body of an ordinary mortal, but the body of Christ crucified, and doing so in order to present a vision or an image that will transform the body of the beholder. Is this simply an identification in a mirror?

The problem with the idea of mirror identification is that one does not in the mirror stage, as Lacan stated, identify with particular traits of the body; one seeks an image of a connected body in the mirror and one identifies with the body's wholeness, as represented by the image. This is quite different from the appropriation of identifying traits from another person. But even this is inaccurate; appropriation is a masculine activity and Francis was identifying with the Passion of Christ, his femininity (cf. Bynum 1986). There is in effect no sense that Francis was appropriating anything; he was in the position of receiving the Stigmata. And even if it makes sense to see things in terms of mirrors, it is not possible to analyze the phenomenon entirely from the point of view of the imaginary. Do the Stigmata then represent a hysterical identification, a psychosomatic phenomenon, or even something that might have been self-inflicted in a dissociated state? In any case, Bonaventure did not attribute the Stigmata entirely to an identification; he added an interesting passage asserting that it was "the finger of the living God" which "engraved" the marks in "the members" of Francis's body; he said this to distinguish and compare these marks with the inscription of the Law on the tablets carried down from Sinai by Moses (Bonaventure 1978, p. 307). What better representation could we find of the difference between the Judaic Law and its Christian fulfillment? We can extend the comparison and say that the marking of the flesh in the Jewish tradition is called circumcision, a practice that early Christians rejected. Circumcision was a practice that was obviously limited to males; it represented the transmission of the Law through a line of fathers. Christ did not have a son to keep his name alive; therefore the transmission of his Passion to his children had to take place by other, nonsexist means. The stigmatization is not comparable to the scarification practiced in ritual circumcision. Yet, there is a sense that Francis thereby became a privileged son of Christ. He seemed to provide through his example an alternate to the kinship system.

The Stigmata are not wounds of the sort that a warrior would receive; they are not marks of valor. The transpiercing of the male body suggests its feminization through love, its reception of the greatest love that is supposed to have existed. Thus it represents the assertion of the essential femininity of all human bodies taken as flesh, their fundamental, ineradicable link with a mother. This appears to be where the dephallicization leads. Note well the description Bonaventure offered of the wound in Francis's side. The wounds in his hands and feet were accompanied by visible nails; the wound in his side had no visible, present cause—might we not think of it as vaginal? (As it happens, the wound in Christ's side was often compared to a mother's lactating breast [Bynum 1986]. Perhaps this represents the substitution of a visible trait for an invisible non-trait.) Bonaventure described the corpse of Francis: "His limbs were so supple and soft to the touch that they seemed to have regained the tenderness of childhood and to be adorned with clear signs of his innocence. The nails appeared black against his shining skin, and the wound in his side was red *like a rose* in springtime . . . so that it is no wonder the onlookers were amazed and overjoyed at the sight of so varied and miraculous beauty. His sons were weeping at the loss of so loveable a father but were filled with no little joy as they kissed on his body the seal-marks of the supreme King. This unprecedented miracle turned their grief into joy and transported into amazement their attempts at comprehending it" (Bonaventure 1978, p. 323). Certainly this is amazing, but not for the reasons invoked by Bonaventure. On the one side we have the reference to Francis as father of the Franciscan order, coupled with the reference to Christ as King, another representation of paternity. On the other we have the wound that was passed from the one to the other, which will not be retransmitted, and which is described in terms that liken it to a female sexual organ. This reads like an exemplary instance of identity confusion, of a confusion of the sexes, with their division healed, we might say, in one body and one event. This does not make of him an androgynous figure. Those who believe would doubtless say that with Francis the question is not one of sexuality. They would say that the signs we read of the two sexes are not there to show that Francis is androgynous; rather, they are confused because the experience is beyond the division of the sexes. Basically, I would agree, with the qualification that this places us in the world of a mother and an infant. The soft, supple, tender, innocent body may well be that of a child, a presexual child in the arms of a mother. We are, in effect, beyond the phallus. Given the aphallic nature of the angels, Christianity was obliged to propose another means of communication between the divine and human worlds. The question is, at what price?

If Francis represents an enjoyment beyond the phallus, then Christ must also represent it; Francis would then be a means of recalling the truth of the Crucifixion, the truth of the Passion of Christ, especially as it represents the demand to worship the feminine side of experience; the feminine enjoyment is supposed to be intensified by being linked indissolubly with suffering. Christ and Francis represent a passing over, as Bonaventure called it, to the feminine side, because masculine enjoyment is inadequate.

"Despite," Lacan said in referring to male mystics, "not what I call their phallus, despite what encumbers them in its place, they perceive, they experience the idea that there must be an enjoyment that is beyond" (Lacan 1975, p. 70). Masculine enjoyment is inadequate because it is not everything, and not only that, in the world of enjoyment it is inferior. Women, of course, were obliged to pay dearly for this adoration of their sex. And besides, without the testimony of women themselves, how are we to know that this version of feminine experience promoted by male mystics is true?

It is hardly surprising that women like Catherine of Siena were glorified (as well as condemned) in their time and after it. People were eager to have the direct testimony of her and her sisters-in-ecstasy because their experience would provide witness of the truth of the experience of the males who aspired to their condition. As we noted, Catherine of Siena was second to no one in her identification with Christ.

And yet, Catherine also participated fully in the tradition of the mystical marriage to Christ; that marriage does not take place through a Francis-like identification. Nor does it take place in full view, on a hill. Here is one version of it:

One day she suddenly went out of the house and out of Siena by the Porta di Sant' Ansano to a region where she thought there were certain dells and caves almost hidden from the eyes of men; there she entered into one, and finding herself in a place where she could neither be seen nor heard, she kneeled on the ground, and in a transport of overwhelming love called the mother of Christ, and with a childlike simplicity asked her to give to her in marriage her son Jesus; and praying thus she felt herself raised somewhat from the ground into the air, and presently there appeared to her the Virgin Mary with her son in her arms, and giving the young girl a ring he took her as his spouse and then suddenly disappeared; and she found herself set back on earth and she returned to Siena and to her home. (quoted in Meiss 1973, p. 111)

Here we find the theme of the mother of a bridegroom giving her son in marriage to another woman. Perhaps it is only when the masculine prerogative of exchanging women in marriage is reversed that it is acceptable for a woman to engage in a mystical marriage with Christ.

The sense of feminine enjoyment lies in the experience of levitation. What distinguishes this experience from that of Francis and other male mystics is the idea of being given a ring. If we read the stigmatum of Francis as identifying the feminine sex as a visible wound, Catherine becomes a woman, gains access to femininity, through an object that represents this sex as an openness that is not produced by a violation. According to Leo Steinberg, Catherine claimed that her wedding ring was the foreskin of Jesus, the relic of relics, which was supposed to exist in several churches in Europe. He noted that at the time the question of whether the body of Christ retrieved its foreskin in the Resurrection was a question of theological actuality (Steinberg 1983, p. 159). With Catherine of Siena we see an effort to restore to Christ something of his virility. And this is consistent with the vision and the work of Bernard. Whether or not the wound on Francis's body has something to do with the female genitalia, it is certainly not, when taken as the essential beauty of a rose, a sign of virility.

It would appear that the experiences of feminine enjoyment proposed and promoted by mystics have nothing to do with the phallus. If this means that the enjoyment is not phallic in the sense of being localized, then we may concur. The problem is whether they occur through an identification of passions, thus beyond the division of the sexes, or whether there must be a phallic element present and in opposition. The former would be the case in the stigmatization of Francis, except for one element, the finger of God, which Bonaventure said inscribed the Stigmata. In the case of the mystical marriage of Catherine of Siena, the foreskin as ring functions as a phallus in a subtle way. We may say with some assurance that these experiences do not require the presence of a man. But the absence of a man does not seem to exclude commerce with a phallus. What seems to be gained in the absence of a man is the ability in the person having the experience to disregard precisely what is happening. As Lacan suggested, perhaps knowing that something is happening and not knowing what it is is the basis for mystical rapture.

The theological problem is that if a woman through some sort of spiritual copulation with an angel were to achieve an experience of mystical ecstasy, and if angels are defined as not having a phallic appendage, then how would one not know that these women are not engaging in commerce with the devil? And yet, if the experience requires something phallic—something to get a handle on—then the idea of an identification with a feminized Christ, with the Passion of Christ crucified, becomes questionable. To say that the experience requires something phallic, we must show what happens when a phallus is not present. And that situation will be most evident in those eating disorders that are most frankly pathological.

The question of the commerce between angels and women changes fundamentally when we turn to a woman author. Here this commerce resembles a sexual encounter, though it is clear that for Teresa of Avila her experience is not sexual. The following lines are the basis for the famous sculpture by Bernini, and Lacan referred to them as an exemplary expression of feminine enjoyment. Whatever the parallels with other experiences of mystics, it is not proposed as an identification with the experience of anyone else. And when Teresa asks that others have the same experience she prays to the God who gave it to her to give it to them. This text dates from the 1560s, thus around two centuries after Catherine of Siena. Teresa wrote:

It pleased the Lord that I should sometimes see the following vision. I would see beside me, on my left hand, an angel in bodily form—a type of vision which I am not in the habit of seeing, except very rarely. Though I often see representations of angels, my visions of them are of the type which I first mentioned. It pleased the Lord that I should see this angel in the following way. He was not tall, but short, and very beautiful, his face so aflame that he appeared to be one of the highest types of angel who seem to be all afire. They must be those who are called cherubim: they do not tell me their names but I am well aware that there is a great difference between certain angels and others, and between these and others still, of a kind that I could not possibly explain. In his hands I saw a long golden spear and at the end of the iron tip I seemed to see a point of fire. With this he seemed to pierce my heart several times so that it penetrated to my entrails. When he drew it out, I thought he was drawing them out with it, and he left me completely afire with a great love for God. The pain was so sharp that it made me utter several moans; and so excessive was the sweetness caused me by this intense pain that one can never wish to lose it, nor will one's soul be content with anything less than God. It is not bodily pain, but spiritual, though the body has a share in it—indeed a great share. So sweet are the colloquies of love which pass between the soul and God that if anyone thinks I am lying I beseech God, in His goodness, to give him the same experience. (Teresa of Avila 1960, pp. 274–75)

The passage is justly famous, because it shows us what happens when an angel is granted a phallic attribute. The love between the soul and God is no longer conceptualized as some sort of unifying experience; it is a colloquy. Thereby, it is incorrect to say that a man may be defined as having something in sexual surplus and a woman as being characterized by a sexual lack, the two canceling each other out in a corporeal fusion. The function of the phallic spear is not to fill the saint's body and soul, but rather to create an opening therein. And there is no sense that this is other than a unique experience; Teresa is not receiving someone else's wound or opening or pain or enjoyment. In this it has more in common with Catherine's receiving the ring of her bridegroom than it does with the stigmatization of Francis.

It is significant that the enjoyment experienced by Teresa was so intense that she concluded that no real man could possibly content her. Having had this she will be content with nothing less. From this passage among others Lacan concluded in Encore that feminine enjoyment requires an experience of something Other than a real man, that its agent cannot be simply a human being. If we understand Teresa as providing the truth of feminine sexual enjoyment, we may also say that her renunciation of men represents a love of the truth in retreat from desire. As opposed to an angel a man will always leave something to be desired.

One of the issues addressed by a juxtaposition of the experience of Teresa with that of Francis is feminine sexual identification. Does a girl become a woman by identifying with another woman, her mother, a role model, or does this experience require the intervention of something phallic, in the sense of a symbolic phallus? It would appear that the stigmatization of Francis argues for the former, whereas the ecstasy of Teresa asserts the latter. You might understand the first as proposing the identification of one wound with another, or better, the attribution of significance to one wound in relation to another. This assumes that the feminine sex is a specific trait gained through identification with another being who has the same trait. Teresa is providing something of a corrective to the shameless emulation of feminine experience indulged in by male mystics. Her femininity is not the same as the one they were seeking, because hers is a woman's while theirs, typified in Francis, was supposed to be universal to humans.

What creates an opening in the body of Teresa is the phallic spear; it is not some part of her own body that serves this function. Imagine that you want to create a hole in a sphere; you may even add that you want to create a hole that does not make the sphere a container. The shape of a container has more in common with a uterus, and it is a good idea to avoid identifying feminine sexuality with the uterus; such a hypothesis leads quickly to hysteria, and besides, there is no question of the cherub's spear depositing anything inside the body of Teresa. So, to create an opening and not a container, what you should do is simply to attach a handle to the sphere, roughly as one would attach a handle to a tea cup. This permits you to hold the cup, or to keep things in control. Since the opening is a void and not a trait, there is no chance that a woman will acquire one through identification with another woman. As far as human anatomy is concerned, the male sexual organ seems particularly apt to function as just such a handle—topologically speaking. What does not seem apt to function in this way is the much-touted clitoris. For all its many virtues and for all the importance it has in female sexual experience, the clitoris does not lend itself to functioning like a handle. Anatomy has its place here, but that place should not obscure the fact that our introduction of this problematic in terms of Teresa's experience is designed to make clear that the experience through which a girl becomes a woman, in which a feminine identification is established, does not necessarily require a human male; it does, however, seem to require the introduction of an extraneous, phallic element. Feminine identification is not determined by a woman's identification with another woman, whereas masculine identification is determined by a man's adoption of the traits of masculinity he finds in and appropriates from another man. The effort to define feminine identification in the same terms as masculine characterizes the experience of Francis of Assisi, and therefore it gives access to neither in attempting to merge both. Nor does it make such a claim; what it claims is an absolute moral identity.

We have been blithely assuming that the spear that penetrates Teresa is phallic, and for a post-Freudian time this is almost a given. In a sense it is unjust, for it avoids the question of whether she experiences it that way. As Lacan said, she knows that something is happening, but she does not know what it is (Lacan 1975, p. 71). Teresa does not believe that her experience is sexual, and she does not see herself as fornicating with a cherub. If she thought such a thing, the angel would be a devil and she would be a witch. Accepting Teresa's terms, we learn the following: For a woman sex is never just sex, and there are times when it isn't sex at all. To say that it is, to say that what is going on here is simply a function of sexual frustration, is a masculine prejudice. Our statement may be qualified if we add that for a woman sex may be just sex if she approaches it from a masculine position. If she approaches it from a feminine position there is always something else going on, and this something else usually escapes her. There is a point in the experience, Lacan suggested, when she is absent to herself, when she gives up control, when she lets herself go (Lacan 1975, p. 36).

One of the salient characteristics of this experience of feminine enjoyment, a characteristic we saw in Catherine's levitation, is that the body as a whole is transported or transferred in the ecstasy or rapture. You might consider this an experience of letting go or of letting oneself be carried somewhere. It may be summarized by the idea that in this kind of enjoyment the body and soul are moved—thus the constant references to the movement of the soul in its ascent to God, which takes place as the soul and body become more and more angelic. If the angel is a material being, as was asserted by Bonaventure and other Franciscans, then its experience of enjoyment is closer to that of the mystics. The Thomist immaterial angel as separate intellectual substance has an enjoyment that has more in common with the phallic.

The question raised here concerns the mode of communication between the intermediate world of angels and the fallen world of humans. In the case of Francis of Assisi and to a lesser extent Catherine of Siena, there is a communication through identification of one sort or an other; what is of primary importance is the similarity of the two in an affective communion that reads, in the case of Catherine, like an identification with a work of visual art. This mode is a simulated femininity; it is an attempt at a response to the question of feminine identification without any reference to a phallus. Teresa represents a different communication in which there is no identification between her and the cherub, nor is there any attempt to attain such a thing; her femininity is gained in opposition to a being that is other to her, that is above her, and that deploys his spear to create an opening in her body. Femininity is better served by such a colloquy.

In discussing Teresa's ecstasy, we avoided making womanhood a function of the uterus. The question does, however, deserve some serious consideration. With the uterus we are in a space defined as a container, having the characteristics of being full or empty. On the contrary, the opening in the center of the ring is decidedly not a container; when you put a ring on your finger you do not say that it contains your finger or that it has passed from emptiness to fullness. Those who think of the feminine sex as containing something will often talk about how their lives are empty or else how at other times they feel fulfilled. Such considerations lead invariably to the idea that womanhood is definitively confirmed by pregnancy. There is a sense in which pregnancy is redemptive in transforming eroticism into reproduction, the latter taken as natural. The acceptance of the presence of a man in the process, considered to be a compromise with fallen nature, may ultimately be redeemed by childbirth. To erase any final trace of Eros the phallus must next be transformed from a weapon that creates an opening into an organ whose function is contained in the activity of depositing seed. As opposed to the angels who were seen as showering the world with *spermatikoi logoi,* seminal principles, Teresa's cherub does not penetrate her to deposit something meaningful in her body.

So we have two opposing concepts of feminine sexuality, and the most telling example of the conflict between them is seen in women with eating disorders. There the body proper becomes the battleground where the two opposing forces exhaust themselves and the woman. The patient whose testimony we will examine is discussed by Robert Lindner in his book *The Fifty-Minute Hour* (1982). Her name is Laura. What she describes in the passage we will quote is called an acting out. Having been failed by her father, and perhaps also by her analyst, Laura is one for whom femininity has become a question. Not one that she articulates, perhaps because there was never anyone to hear it, but one that is posed elsewhere, in actions. Cut off from the social articulation of her femininity, Laura does unequal battle with her sex:

I think it begins with a feeling of emptiness inside. Something, I don't know what to call it, starts to ache; something right in the center of me feels as if it's opening up, spreading apart maybe. It's like a hole in my vitals appears. Then the emptiness starts to throb—at first, softly like a fluttering pulse. For a little while, that's all that happens. But then the pulsing turns into a regular beat; and the beat gets stronger and stronger. The hole gets bigger and bigger. Soon I feel as if there's nothing to me but a vast, yawning space surrounded by skin that grabs convulsively at nothingness. The beating gets louder. The sensation changes from an ache to a hurt, a pounding hurt. The feeling of emptiness becomes agony. In a short while there's nothing of me, of Laura, but an immense drumming vacuum. . . . The moment I become aware of the hole opening inside I'm terrified. I want to fill it. I have to. So I start to eat. I eat and eat—everything, anything I can find to put in my mouth. It doesn't matter what it is, so long as it's food and can be swallowed. It's as if I'm in a race with the emptiness. As it grows so does my hunger. But it's not really hunger, you see. It's a frenzy, a fit, something automatic and uncontrollable. I want to stop it, but I can't. If I try to, the hole gets bigger, I become idiot with terror, I feel as if I'm going to become nothing, become the emptiness—get swallowed by it. So I've got to eat. (Lindner 1982, p. 119)

This represents what we will call the darker side of the female orgasm. As such, it is a worthy counterpoint to the ecstasy of Teresa of Avila. In the throbbing and fluttering pulse there is evidence of something that corresponds to the role of the clitoris in orgasm. This pulse is ineffective in providing a boundary for the experience, a handle with which Laura can got a hold on things. Without a handle the hole that opens in her risks expanding to engulf her. The only way she can attempt to assert control is to treat the hole as the mouth of a container. Therefore she tries to fill it. But if it is something like the hole in the center of a ring, there is no way to fill it; nothing gives her a sense of satisfaction, and the experience will often end in exhaustion. The fact that she follows her binges with self-induced vomiting is another way of showing that the digestive tube is not a hole but is a container. A further way in Laura's case is her simulating pregnancy.

It is reasonably clear that in eating disorders food is used for a purpose that removes it from the normal function of nourishment. My hypothesis is that it comes to function as a means of posing the question of the speech act, first from the point of view of what happens when one speaks and second from the point of view of the satisfaction to be derived therefrom. Young women with eating disorders have an acute sense of the effect of speech on the human body. The problem is that it simply does not make sense that these invisible, airy things called words can produce such a profound effect on them. Thus they concretize the speech act through a solitary ritual of which they are usually the only witnesses.

Eating and speaking are related directly and dialectically. First, they both engage the mouth, though the mouth that eats and the mouth that speaks are not the same. Second, the substance that enters the mouth, food, moves in an opposite direction from the substances that exit the mouth, words. In an eating disorder the two will often get mixed up. If the woman forces herself to vomit, or to spit out her food, she will correlatively eat her words—not all of them, but most especially those that name, those that are called substantives and proper names. As with any form of hysteria, the accent is placed on the verb or on the predicate, and it is with this that the young women will identify. It is not an accident that such disorders tend to afflict young women, since they consider themselves as in some sense nameless; they await the Other who will offer them a name and an identity. But since no man can be equal to their demand, they attempt to become feminine by identifying with other women. They wish to become women by sharing experiences that are unique to their sex.

For them the act of speaking is reduced to an affair of the voice. Either they are voiceless, awaiting the voice of an other, or else they are all voice, speaking too loudly, having identified with the other whose voice has at times molested them. The enjoyment of the speech act is radically missing; speech seems insufficient to their needs or emotions; it seems too frail or flimsy to sustain the weight that their inner life may call upon it to bear. When they do speak they are constantly leaving gaps in the discourse, leaving terms unspecified or undefined; they do not say much of anything; rather they signify by their speech their openness to the word that they expect to receive, even to the point of demanding it, either in word or deed. This shows us an excess of femininity, defiant and unsatisfied, because after all there is nothing that an ordinary man can say that will adequately respond to the demand. If they enter into commerce with a diety, this may well rescue them from the eating dissorder, to turn them into saints. Since they define their being as beyond naming, the arrival of a man who does want to give his name will be met with scorn, derision, or flight.

If not by a name, they, as hysterics, will be marked by a verb. Only this will provide the fullness of meaning that responds to the question of what it is to be a woman. And the answer will always be posed in terms of pregnancy, whether real or imagined. To be receptive means to be fertile—and to be unmarked. Even if the hysteric has a sense that her sex is an opening, her attitude will be that it ought to be closed. Being pregnant represents precisely such a cloture, a self-enclosure around something that renders her sexual identity meaningful.

The proper name marks the male body by cutting round its sex. And it marks the female body through the instrumentality of the phallus in the act of defloration. A God whose name is a verb may also come to mark the female body in the production of conversion symptoms. These invisible stigmata, transmitted from the body of a son who will not become a father, are resolved only when the desperate search for meaning yields to the agency of the signifier.

The question is after all how language affects human beings, how it hooks into human subjects, how it touches and changes their animal bodies into something else. One way is through proper naming, the functioning of the Law prohibiting incest, and the deployment of the signifier to represent the subject for another signifier. But this way divides the sexes irrevocably and it ensures that you will never become an angel. So the rule of the Name was replaced by that of the Verb, to the point where God no longer had a name but became the verb to end all verbalizing, all predication—Being. When it is not a copula the verb "to be" is the universal predicate, the predicate that combines with any substantive, that may be predicated of the largest number of substantives truthfully. Of course it does not say anything about them, but then again, what more can be said of this God except that He is? It would appear that the function of the copula—since "to be" may also be used in this way—becomes subsumed under the supreme Being, which simply is. When Christ became flesh the verb came to act as copula, making Christ's flesh God's predicate. Through Christ God is connected to human flesh in a descent. Through Christ the faithful are supposed to be able to ascend to Being itself, the Being that does not of itself require any flesh, that is predictable of everything, the meaning of everything, saying nothing. Unnamed and unnameable, God is the Great Mother from which all meaningful being flows, especially as She is beyond language.

For Duns Scotus, Bréhier told us, being is a univocal term that has the same meaning no matter what it is applied to (Bréhier 1971, p. 333). Or as Duns Scotus wrote: "It can be said that God is conceived not only in a concept by analogy with the concept of a creature, which concept is altogether different from that which is said of a creature, but in some concept univocal to Himself and a creature. . . . every intellect certain about one concept and doubtful about different ones has a concept of that of which it is certain which is different from the concepts about which it is doubtful. But the subject includes the predicate and the intellect of the wayfarer can be certain of something (God) that it is being while at the same time doubting whether that is finite or infinite, created or uncreated being" (in Hyman and Walsh 1984, p. 603–4). While we may doubt the kind of being different creatures have, we can be certain that they are and that they share being univocally with God. For the subject to include the predicate, we should say that Being is.

The subject of which things may or not be predicated with certainty is "being," a nominalized verb. This is not, of course, a simple issue. To follow the arcane Scotus a bit further, we discover that "ultimate differentiae" pose a particular problem for being (in Hyman and Walsh 1984, p. 617). Does, in other words, the concept of difference subvert the presence of being? This would say that the assertions that being is finite and that being is infinite do not show the concept of being as univocal, because finitude and infinity do not have the same sort of being. And the problem would, significantly, be the same if we were to reverse the order and say that finitude is and infinity is. Is the verb the same, does it have the same meaning, in the two cases? It would be a problem if the predicate to end all predicates were to be influenced or modified by a predicate. Scotus attempted to extricate himself with the following: "And yet, despite this, I say that being is the primary object of our intellect, since a two-fold primacy concurs in it, namely, the primacies of commonness and virtuality. For everything intrinsically intelligible either essentially includes the characteristic or includes it virtually. For all genera and species, as well as individuals, and all the essential parts of genera, and uncreated being, include being definitionally. All ultimate differentiae are included in some of these essentially or definitionally. . . . Therefore, those to which being is not definitionally univocal are included in those to which it is thus univocal" (in Hyman and Walsh 1984, p. 618). Being, in other words, swallows difference by a principle of inclusion. The finite may not be in the same way as the infinite is, but to the extent that finitude is intelligible it must be included within a univocal concept of being. And it does not seem to matter whether being is on the side of the subject or the predicate, since in the absence of proper naming there is no referential function.

To make being a name or a subject is to show the power the verb has to define and determine the name of the subject. This differs from the Old Testament God, who most certainly has a name, who has several proper names by which he is referred to, but whose real name cannot be spoken or written. Faced with this prohibition, Christianity decided that God did not have a proper name, but rather a proper verb—Being. Far from being unspeakable, it was speech itself, meaningful speech, independent of naming. Not that God was unnamed; the same fate awaited all deities, universally. Not only do all humans have the same source, derive from the same matrix, but Christianity took things one step further in saying that not only all humans but God himself was of woman born. It was not surprising to find that the angels were then redefined to be consonant with a maternal space. Faced with the multiplicity of languages and cultures, Christianity attempted to provide one meaning for them all, one God who would render them all true, so long as that God was accepted as truth.

It is interesting and curious that the difference between the sexes was not obliterated forasmuch. We see it in different medieval conceptions of the enjoyment to be obtained from alternate ways of approaching the angels. Seemingly while no one was looking, it crept into the division between different monastic orders, between different conceptions of enjoyment. But if Christianity had not succeeded in abolishing the difference between the sexes, then perhaps the Doctors of the Middle Ages had made an error in their reflections and calculations. Perhaps what they had taken to be the work of God had really been the work of some trickster, a genie who had escaped the general angelification of the intermediary world. Such was to be, roughly speaking, the reflection of Descartes, and we emphasize the fact that the *malin génie* (wicked genie) so justly celebrated by commentators on his thought is one of the very few genii mentioned in Christian civilization. While Descartes did not give a name to his genie, we suggest that since Descartes represents one of the ways out of Scholasticism, since Scholasticism had found one of its richest resources in the works of Arab philosophers, since in the Moslem religion there are so many genies or djinns that the use of the word in itself suggests Islam, given all of this it appears that the wicked genie of Descartes was none other than Aristotle.

FIVE

FATHERS AND SELFS

Writing at the beginning of our century, Martin Heidegger remarked in medieval thinkers "the preponderance of the idea of authority and the great esteem in which all Tradition was held." The medieval thinker, he added, had "a way of giving himself over absolutely and of plunging with ardor into what past knowledge delivered to his appetite" (Heidegger 1970, p. 29). The wording here gives us a sense of the desire with which these intellectuals approached their work. This desire was sustained by its direction toward Otherness; these people did not seek in their own minds luminous thoughts; they repaired to the work of others, their predecessors and contemporaries in a movement that afforded full recognition of a filiation, passing from generation to generation. Thus, unstated, something like a family structure persisted, with the place of paternal authority increasingly occupied by Aristotle. Because Aristotle stated that the male sexual organ "has both tendons and cartilage, which permits it to contract itself or to extend itself and to fill itself with air," Albert the Great, who knew otherwise, was obliged to declare that said penile appendage contained "cartilage, but not really real cartilage, but rather ligaments whose hardness is close to that of cartilage" (in Jacquart and Thomasset 1985, pp. 53–54).

It is significant that the precondition of this desire was the fact that the medieval thinker did not have what Heidegger called a possession of Self. This he defined as: "the subject's liberation in relation to his link to his surroundings, his confirmation in his own life" (Heidegger 1970, p. 30). For most European philosophers the key moment in the movement toward the possession of Self was Descartes's discovery of the *cogito*, the "I think" that represented a subjective grounding impervious to the systematic and methodological doubt to which all other thought succumbed. Moreover, the "I think" permitted the inference that "I am"; that a thinking thing, an "I" whose nature was to think, could affirm its existence merely as a consequence of its thought.

A gesture of such revolutionary import, a moment so crucial to the history of philosophy, was presented to Descartes in a series of dreams, which had been predicted to him by a genie. He asserted at the time that "the human mind had no part in it" (in Maritain 1932, p. 7). If we can show that the mind that ultimately takes possession of itself is not human but angelic, then we will be back with our subject.

We have no reason to doubt that Descartes took possession of Self, and not only for himself; our question will bear on the price of this gesture, the cost in desire. The Self may well have been liberated from the weight of whatever was exterior to it, be it physical objects or Greek philosophers, and it may have been more than willing to have this experience in the spirit of sacrifice to gain a better and more perfect end. Ethically, it is pertinent to ask whether something that can be given away with the sense of joy that we associate with liberation ought really to be sacrificed—whether, in other words, this sense of freedom, freedom from and freedom to, is not ultimately duplicitous, bespeaking an ethical failure of major proportions. Certainly the accompanying sense of acquired self-enjoyment does not constitute a demonstration of ethical value. And we should want to know what is retained when Otherness is sacrificed in the interest of Self; it may well be that the enjoyment derives from the sense that by giving up something that seems to be of little value, one has placed something much more important in a position where its protection appears to be absolute, impregnable.

The Cartesian enterprise is based fundamentally in appropriation: first, through the supposition that any idea appropriated from another can never fully and absolutely belong to Self; second, through the moral and epistemological necessity for Self to grasp itself, to appropriate itself as thinking in its act of thinking. Basing itself in appropriation, in the gesture of total innocence in relation to the wish to appropriate the ideas of any other, in the inability to accept the least trace of what Harold Bloom has called "the anxiety of influence," the Cartesian method arrives at appropriating the only thing that no one could possibly reproach it for appropriating: the Self.

Since we have previously linked the idea of appropriation with speech and enunciation, we should remark with Lacan that the Cartesian "I think therefore I am" is gained only when Descartes pronounces it or thinks it to himself (Lacan 1973, p. 128). As Descartes wrote in the *Meditations:* ". . . let him [the wicked genie] deceive me as much as he wants, he will never make me be nothing, so long as I think of being something. . . . finally we must conclude and hold for constant this proposition: *I am, I exist,* is necessarily true each time that I pronounce it, or that I conceive it in my mind" (Descartes 1953, p. 275). Lacan continued that the Cartesian *cogito* is a homunculus, an aborted fetus, the kind of little man placed inside of a human being to govern him, to direct the chariot (Lacan 1973, p. 129). Are we very far here from the function of the angel?

It would be a relatively simple matter if the issue were the choice between the acceptance of authority and the possession of Self. People could simply choose up sides and argue if the uncertainty about whether one's experience is really one's own is worth the advantages that accrue to the mind that refers itself to other authorities. Unembarrassed by personal experience or by the worry that it may not be theirs, the medieval Scholastics are known for the extent of their theoretical prowess, the application of their intellectual gifts. And yet they arrived at such a level of abstraction that after a time only a precious albeit happy few had any idea of what they were disputing. Not only did they abstract thought from the real world, but some believed that they had succeeded in abstracting people from the real faith in Christ. Since the medieval thinker most identified with unintelligible abstraction is Duns Scotus, it makes sense that Heidegger would attempt to revive his theories in particular, by relating them to the philosophy of language and the theories of intentionality elaborated by his teacher Husserl. For Heidegger the two currents were not necessarily contradictory; a proper appreciation of Scholasticism would show that its abstractions could be adequately grounded in the subjective experience of speech. And the point of intersection of the two was Heidegger's acceptance of the standard idea that speech expresses thoughts that are originally formed in the mind. One of the ironies of this affair is that Heidegger wrote about Duns Scotus in order to establish his place as the most powerful of the medieval Scholastics. To do so he included an extensive commentary of the *Speculative Grammar,* attributed at the time to Scotus but later shown to be the work of another author, Thomas of Erfurt.

Merging Cartesian subjectivity with Scholasticism is like putting the mind and the body together again. As you may know, Descartes was obliged to disconnect them in the interest of gaining access to subjective certainty. Once he had acquired this form of self-possession he was faced with the problem of how to reunite the body with the liberated mind. This he argued at some length, for a specific and for us very significant reason. If the union of body and mind is merely accidental and not necessary, he said, the mind or soul that inhabits the body would be an angel (letter to Regius, Jan. 1642, in Gilson 1984, p. 246). Whether or not you believe that Descartes was successful, it is useful to note the conclusion drawn by Saul Kripke at the end of an analysis of the effort to link mind and body through the identity thesis: "In sum, the correspondence between a brain state and a mental state seems to have a certain obvious element of contingency." The reason lies in "the possibility, or apparent possibility, of a physical state without the corresponding mental state. The reverse possibility, the mental state (pain) without the physical state (C-fiber stimulation), also presents problems for the identity theorists which cannot be resolved by appeal to the analogy of heat and molecular motion" (Kripke 1980 p. 154). Significantly, Kripke is aware that Descartes gained access to a Self by seeing it in angelic form, as a spirit, and this he rejected for reasons that we may or may not find persuasive. "If we had a clear idea of the soul or the mind as an independent, subsistent, spiritual entity, why should it have to have any necessary connection with particular material objects such as a particular sperm or a particular egg? A convinced dualist may think that my views on sperms and eggs beg the question against Descartes. I would tend to argue the other way; the fact that it is hard to imagine me coming from a sperm and egg different from my actual origins seems to me to indicate that we have no such clear conception of a soul or self" (Kripke 1980, 155n.) We will leave aside the tale of the sperm and the egg, except to note that finding a way out of Cartesian dualism seems for Kripke to have something to do with sexual difference, or more explicitly, with reproductive material.

Descartes's denial of the connection between the thinking thing and an angel suggests that the connection was at least thinkable. Yet there is scholarly precedent for making the connection. Remembering that Descartes believed in innate ideas, and that this notion derives from Plato, we are better placed to understand the following. In a book on the connections between Cartesianism and Scholasticism, Gilson commented on Aquinas's view of the necessary union of mind and body in humans; he asserted that this position answers Plato's error of pretending to discover that there are innate ideas in the human soul. Speaking of Plato and by implication Descartes, Gilson said: "His reasoning presumes always that man is an intelligence pure as an angel, or that he enjoys in this life the beatific vision that God reserves for his elect" (Gilson 1984, p. 12). A philosopher with a less theological bent, Martial Gueroult, argued persuasively and at length that the *cogito* is a pure intelligence, an intellectual nature, arrived at through the exclusion from the soul of other functions like imagination and the senses (Gueroult 1968a, vol. 1, chap. 3, sects. 2, 4) And Jacques Maritain, in his *Three Reformers,* accused Descartes of the sin of angelism, of mistaking people for angels and thus of leading people away from the true faith into confusion and error. While there is merit in his point that Descartes's formulation of subjectivity is angelic, the mixture of that idea with a theological polemic whose purpose is to denounce the enterprise and to urge us to return to the Scholasticism fails to see the value of the new philosophy (Maritain 1934, p. 53ff.). It also fails to address the flaws in the Scholastic system that led to the requirement for self-possession. Furthermore, Maritain did not appreciate the extent to which Descartes reformulated Christian theological arguments. When Maritain asserted that Descartes promoted himself as "the unique 'Engineer' of the modern city of intelligences," he not only failed to note that this is an eminently Christian goal, but also that Descartes did not promote himself, but rather his method or reason as the agency that would effect the desired transformation (Maritain 1932, p. 20).

Note well the distinction between Aquinas and Descartes on the place of Reason. Hiram Caton summarized it: "The key premise of St. Thomas's argument is the fallibility of reason, which is admitted by most of antiquity except in regard to logical truths. Descartes seems to have concluded that the autonomy of reason could be reestablished if an argument were discovered which showed the infallibility of reason—its immutable, unshakable certainty—after conceding all and more than theology might urge against reason" (Caton 1973, p. 122). So while we agree that the Cartesian subject is an angel, we more willingly follow the opinion of Kojève that Descartes represents the explicit beginning of a truly Christian philosophy, a philosophy unencumbered by pagan influences (Kojève 1973, p. 482).

If it is reasonable to assume with Gilson that Aquinas is Descartes's adversary, then we arrive at the following idea. Like the cherubim guarding the gates of Eden, Aquinas erected a barrier that prohibited humans from seeing God directly. But if we know God only through intermediaries, how can we know with certainty that those intermediaries are angels and not demons? It is within such a problematic, if we are to believe Gilson, that Descartes proposed first to gain absolute certainty on a subjective level, and from there to move to a cognitive certainty about God. We should repeat here that there were views other than Aquinas's on the feasibility of seeing God directly. The mystical tradition represented by Bonaventure, among others, asserted the contrary. While fully accepting the idea that seeing God face-to-face was impossible for living humans, Bonaventure introduced the idea of a metaphoric death that accompanied the mystical vision of God.

Let us place Descartes the adversary of Aquinas within this mystical tradition. As Caton wrote: "Although it is known that the *Meditations* simulate the mode of Loyola's *Spiritual Exercises* and other writings of that genre, little attention is paid to this significant fact. The last stage of the doubt and the refutation by the Cogito is certainly a moment of high drama, which deserves study in light of the religious antecedents to which the *Meditations* are known to refer" (Caton 1973, p. 123). The goal of the mystical project seems in most cases to be a loss of Self, whereas the Cartesian center is a Self that is entirely present to itself. One might well argue that the mystics, after an experience of loss of Self, finished by regaining a more pure and more perfect Self, but still the difference should be taken seriously.

And so Descartes several centuries later suggested that perhaps what we have been taught, what constitutes accepted knowledge, was planted in us by a genie to trick or deceive us. If such an eventuality is possible, then, he asserted, we may have no absolute certainty about anything that has come to us from without. Caton offered an example of a thought process that would lead to the restoration of the Logos as Reason; in previous times the most certain way of distinguishing devils from angels was Christ and his cross. "By propounding his doubts, Descartes, the evil demon, so to speak, assumes the shape of a good angel: 'You can doubt the truths of mathematics and the existence of the world, my friend. Do you deny it? Well come and look, I will show you that it is quite easy. You believe in God and all his miracles; and that the legions of Satan are spreading lies and deceit everywhere. You believe these things. Why then do you not admit that you are helpless against these infernal powers? What basis has your prideful confidence in things that seem evident to you, when all the while you believe that reason is weak and mendacious?' " (Caton 1973, pp. 123–4). We ought also to remember that events in the Renaissance, particularly the increasing belief in devils, had opened the problematic of doubt for the culture at large. One of the most important sections of the *Malleus Maleficarum* dealt with knowing the truth about what the women accused of witch-craft had experienced. It is significant that in a time when torture was used to extract confessions Descartes proposed physical pain as one of the demonstrations of the union of body and soul.

To arrive at the *cogito* Descartes was obliged to separate mind from body; is this a metaphoric death of the sort proposed by the mystics? If it is, then Descartes was providing a logical and rational basis for mystical experience. The *cogito* is the consequence first of a logical process of destruction or deconstruction whose basis, Hintikka has asserted, is to be found in algebraic operations (Hintikka 1978, p. 82). In addition, Hintikka has argued that the *cogito*, as intuitive self-percep-tion, as what Descartes called "a simple act of mental vision," corre-sponds to what philosophers call a performative act, an act that is existentially self-validating or self-verifying. Hintikka emphasized the logic of the act of enunciation. It is absurd for someone to pronounce the statement "I don't exist," since the first person pronoun always refers to the one who is speaking (Hintikka 1962, passim). The question that arises is, who is listening to this enunciation? The immediate answer Descartes gave is that God is listening, and not only that, but that God is a type of ideal listener who is the guarantor of the truth of the *I am*. Thus Hintikka added that as much as "I don't exist" is absurd and self-defeating, so is the enunciation "You don't exist," because if it is true then there is no one to whom it can be addressed (Hintikka 1962, p. 19).

Of course the soul of the mystic arrives at a state of loss in which it is enraptured by the vision of God. As we have seen, this implies a transcendence of the intellect. So while the Cartesian project seems to follow the path of mysticism, it does not when it takes possession of itself arrive at the same conclusion. The place it arrives at is closer to an angel, according to Aquinas, which in fact does have a possession of Self as pure intelligence. Of course, if it had followed a Thomist epistemology it would never have become an angel. As Aquinas wrote: "For the human intellect, although it can know itself, does take the first beginning of its knowledge from without, because it cannot understand without a phantasm. . . . There is therefore a more perfect intellectual life in the angels. In them the intellect does not proceed to self-knowledge from anything exterior but knows itself through itself" (Aquinas SCG, book 4, chap. 11). We add that for Aquinas the intelligence of an angel is not its being, since its being is a participation in the Supreme Being (SCG, book 2, chap. 52).

Let us now examine the argument that leads to the postulation of a wicked genie. Descartes began the first meditation: "Now then that my mind is free from all cares, and that I have procured an assured retreat into a peaceful solitude, I will apply myself seriously and freely to destroying generally all of my old opinions" (Descartes 1953, p. 268). You might wonder whether he thinks he is in a monastery or in some other place to which we all will retire in peaceful solitude and in which our old opinions will no longer be anything but dross. The sense of freedom translates a will, not to create, but to destroy. How else is the mind to show that it is truly free from things that have entered it from without?

First Descartes doubted whatever he had learned through the senses; however true this learning appeared to be it was also true that he had had the experience of being deceived by his senses. Therefore, he concluded, "it is prudent never to trust entirely those who have deceived us once" (Descartes 1953, p. 269). Of course, he was talking about "those" senses, but this phrase has a slightly different resonance, one that may well refer to people who deceive in love or in marriage. The French word *tromper,* used here and in relation to the genie, is the same as the one used for a spouse who cheats in a marriage. While this question was probably not in Descartes's consciousness, we will exercise some theoretical license and say that one way of reading this distinction between doubt and certainty may have to do with kinship. A child's knowledge of who his parents are is split; we consider generally that the link between mother and child is certain because based on observation, while that of father and child is subject to doubt because based on the mother's word. Of course, the child's knowledge of who his mother is, while certain to some, is not certain to him through observation; he must rely on someone's word.

Descartes did not raise these questions, and for a good reason. If subjectivity is based on kinship, this would account only for one's body, taken as the product of the copulation of one's parents. "As for my parents, from whom it seems that I derive my birth, even if everything that I was ever able to believe of them is true, this does not in any case make it that they conserve me, nor that they have made and produced me in so far as I am a thing that thinks, since they have only placed some dispositions in this matter in which I judge that I, that is, my mind, which alone I now take to be myself, finds itself enclosed . . ." (Descartes 1953, p. 299). This is a very curious way of looking at kinship relations; it tells us that the subject is a pure mind trapped in a body, perhaps seeking liberation, but also that kinship has been reduced to biology, thereby to be eliminated from consideration. According to George Nakhnikian, the body "is conceived as an inactive, a passive thing, that cannot act, that can only be acted upon, and is such that if it moves at all it moves only because something 'foreign to itself' sets it in motion" (Nakhnikian 1978, pp. 256–57). This places the body on the side of the maternal or the material, to leave for mind the more active functions.

Certainly the subject owes his corporeal existence to his parents; and it is significant that Descartes recognizes debt only in material or maternal terms. These are the ones we said are most certain. Conveniently, he forgets that his parents, through the paternal function, also give him a name. About this there is doubt, and Descartes occludes it. If the mind has no body, what is there to receive the mark of the proper name? It is not so much that it is difficult to establish a Self without reference to a body, but how is one to have an I without having a name? The necessity for self-possession perhaps derives from the failure to recognize that the

I identifies a subject in apposition to the proper name. This failure is not particular to Descartes; it would appear to be endemic to a system of thought that bases itself on the Verb.

The Self designated by "I" is certainly metaphysical, and one may delimit it through thought, as Descartes did. He said that of the attributes of the soul the only one that cannot be detached from it is thinking. It is worth noting that when Descartes listed some of these attributes, they are all verbal infinitives: *se nourrir, marcher, sentir, penser* (Descartes 1953, pp. 276–77). Or as Nakhnikian stated: "As conceived by Descartes; the ego or any cogito is '[a] thing which thinks. What is a thing which thinks? It is a thing which doubts, understands, conceives, affirms, denies, wills, refuses, which also imagines and feels.' Note that every one of these items is conceived to be an action. The words are verbs" (Nakhnikian 1978, p. 256). They are also all either intransitive or rendered thus. They participate in the function of the verb "to be" as attribute of existence and disregard the function of "to be" as copula.

To return to our argument, it is not sufficient for Descartes's demonstration to doubt only the evidence of the senses. He was therefore obliged to introduce the hypothesis of the wicked genie, which extends doubt to cover "the intrinsic objective value of clear and distinct ideas" (Gueroult 1968a, p. 41). If the value of such ideas lies in their being guaranteed by God, then in order to extend doubt to them what must be put into question is what one considers to be God. Here is the way Descartes articulated it.

> I will thus suppose that there is—not a true God that is the supreme source of truth—but a certain wicked genie, no less clever and deceitful than powerful, who has employed all of his effort to deceive me. I will think that the sky, the air, the earth, colors, figures, sounds and all of the external things that we see, are nothing but illusions and deceptions that he uses to trick my credulity. I will consider myself as having no hands, no eyes, no flesh, no blood, as having no senses, but believing falsely that I have all these things. I will remain obstinately attached to this thought; and if, by this means, it is not in my power to attain knowledge of any truth, at least it is within my power to suspend my judgment. This is why I will scrupulously take care not to accept any falsity in my beliefs, and I will prepare my mind so well for all the ruses of this great deceiver that, however powerful and clever he may be, he will never be able to impose anything on me. (Descartes 1953, p. 272)

And the deceit may extend to arithmetic and geometry, to ancient and ordinary opinions, any and all of which may be false, especially as they have been received from an authority or teacher (Descartes 1953, pp. 270–71).

Or, as Freud said: "A man who doubts his own love may, or rather *must*, doubt every lesser thing" (Freud *Standard Edition* [SE] Vol. 10, p. 241). Descartes did not mention love specifically, but is there not a sense of deception, of taking the beloved to be someone else, lying behind the hypothesis of the wicked genie? The love in question here is the love of God, which may be directed to a false deity, to one whose perversity extends even to what "I" holds to be most certain. The limit to the deception is the "I think," which can be held with absolute certainty even if there is a wicked genie up there. So Descartes concluded that the "I think" must be the path to God and that it must be guaranteed by a true God. At some level Descartes was trying to save God from the Scholastics which would not have been inconsistent with a wish to save his Self.

Gueroult emphasized that the hypothesis of the wicked genie is founded in reason: if God is omnipotent, why is it not possible for him to produce falsehood? Why would there be a restriction on his will and his liberty? Gueroult responded: "God certainly could have freely created other truths than those which are given as such, for he would then have created other beings; but he could not create the deception which is neither another truth nor another being, but which is rather non-being and the annihilation of truth, for these are excluded from creation by a Supreme Being" (Gueroult 1968a, p. 47). These lines echo the reasoning of Duns Scotus discussed at the end of Chapter 4.

The genie is the spirit that renders all beliefs false, or better, all beliefs but one act of intuitive self-cognition. No less than God, the genie is taken to be a creature of will, of a perverse and single-minded will to deceive, from which deception we imagine that he draws enjoyment. And yet, when Descartes refused the imposition of false beliefs did he not, in saying no, reveal the genie as desiring? If the genie did nothing but impose beliefs on Descartes without any obstacle, and if this were his intention, his will would be his act. It is when the genie cannot impose his will that he becomes desiring, and it is at this point that Descartes thought that he had escaped the genie.

If the wicked genie is a being of desire, in contrast, a true God is a being without desire. Like the holy angels and those who aspire to the angelic condition, God is perfect. As such he guarantees a desire that would be a function of the thinking subject—thus the necessity to discard the genie when he comes to represent a desiring Other. The following passage makes clear that the methodical doubt is linked with an unquestioned subjective desire. "For how would it be possible for me to know that I doubt and that I desire, that is, that something in me is lacking and that I am not entirely perfect, if I did not have in me any idea of a being more perfect that my own, in comparison with which I would know the defects of my nature?" (Descartes 1953, p. 294). And at the end of the same meditation he added: "From which it is sufficiently evident that he [God] cannot be a deceiver, because the light of nature teaches us that deception depends necessarily on some defect" (Descartes 1953, p. 300). If the wicked genie represents a figure of the Otherness of desire, his rejection by Descartes is consistent with theological tradition.

What is the nature of this desire that is connected with the methodical doubt, but, apparently does not fall before it? The answer is not very complicated: the desire we are confronted with here is a desire for perfection. If we see desire as outside of the subject, then the desire of Descartes is a desire for a God who does not desire. Lacking desire, God comes to represent perfect self-possession, as do his angels. If you possess the only thing that has value, the thing whose lack renders you desiring, then you will cease to desire. That the thing you lack is Self must appear to be a strange idea. But if this is what you are to come to possess, evidently you must have lacked it at the start. A better way of expressing this is to say that you were originally alienated from your Self, as least in the sense that you did not know what it was or where to find it, and that you eventually are reunited with it and know yourself to be it. You had thought, in other words, that your being a human subject involved a union of mind and body. All the while your Self was somewhere else, in the world of pure intelligences. When you go out of your body and reject everything that has ever been put in your mind you will find this Self. If God is perfect and does not desire, this deductive process cannot correspond to God's desire. In answer to Descartes's question of how he can know that he desires except in contrast to a perfect being who does not desire, I would say that he desires in function of the genie whose will is not accomplished. Descartes knows imperfection because he sees it in the wicked genie.

Descartes's rejection of the idea that the thinking subject is an angel was based on the necessary link between mind and body. We have noted with Kripke that this is doubtful at best. Still, we are required to provide a more substantive demonstration of the point that the thinking subject is angelic. Descartes saw that the separation of mind and body lends itself to the idea that the mind taken to be a thinking thing or cognitive substance is an angel. To counter this he proposed that after their separation mind and body were unified in a problematic union. This idea requires attention, but we are obliged to note that if Descartes had united mind and body as persuasively as he separated them, then there would be no mind-body problem today. In the following passage note the relative uncertainty Descartes exhibited on this question: "And although perhaps (or rather, certainly, as I will soon show) I have a body to which I am very narrowly conjoined; nevertheless, because on the one hand I have a clear and distinct idea of myself, in so far as I am only a thinking thing without extension, and that on the other I have a distinct idea of the body, in so far as it is only an extended thing that does not think, it is certain that this 'I,' that is, my soul, by which I am what I am, is entirely and veritably distinct from my body, and that it can be or exist without it" (Descartes 1953, p. 324). To resolve this problem he invoked the authority of nature, especially as manifested in affective states of pain, hunger, and thirst. Remark, however, that he considered the union of mind and body a source of confusion. The figure of the ship's pilot in the following section represents a role that we will see later as that of an angel.

Nature teaches me also by these feelings of pain, hunger, thirst, etc. that I am not merely lodged in my body, as a pilot in his ship, but, beyond that, that I am very closely conjoined with it, so confused and mixed with it, that I compose something like a single whole [*un seul tout*] with it. For if that was not the case, when my body is wounded I who am only a thinking thing would not feel pain, but I would perceive this wound only through understanding, as a pilot perceives through sight when something is broken on his vessel; and when my body needs to drink and to eat, I would simply know that itself, without being averted by confused feelings of hunger and thirst. For in effect all of these feelings of hunger, thirst, and pain, etc. are nothing other than certain confused ways of thinking which derive from and depend on the union and apparent mixing of the mind with the body. (Descartes 1953, p. 326).

We juxtapose this text with the following from the letter to Regius, January 1642, to which we have already alluded. The occasion for this letter was a remark by Regius that the connection of mind and body was accidental. Descartes replied: "We perceive that the sensation of pain as well as the others are not pure thoughts of the soul distinct from the body, but confused perceptions of the soul really united to the body: for if an angel found itself in the body of a man, he would not have our sensations, he would only perceive the movements caused by exterior objects, and would thereby be distinguished from a true man." As Gilson commented, an angel, being purely intellectual cognition, would know the movements of the particles of the body that have been wounded, and he would dissociate the extended particles and submit them to the laws of mechanics to follow their action along the nerves, and so on (Gilson 1984, pp. 246–7). The interesting point is not so much that Descartes did not think that the mind is an angel inhabiting a body, but rather that this picture of what would happen if such were the case corresponds well to branches of scientific inquiry, as though scientific thought were angelic. The case is not whether Descartes was right or wrong about what happens to the body when it is wounded, but rather that the separation of mind from body, opening the possibility to consider the body purely as extended substance—extended means that it has dimensions in space—is one of the bases for modern scientific inquiry. The means by which Descartes proposed the study of extension were geometric. This seems to say that once the heavens are rid of intelligent beings they can be studied astronomically as pure extension, thus yielding scientific knowledge of them. The question that arises here is whether this scientific knowledge represents the knowledge that angels have. Perhaps it is closer to the knowledge of angels than is Aristotelian logic.

The problem Descartes faced was that nature is sometimes deceptive to the mind; thus he argued at some length that a man with dropsy feels thirst but ought not to follow what nature teaches and drink, since that would be injurious to his health. However, the man of science, here the physician, knows how to read nature correctly; and this seems to suggest that nature may be deceptive, but not for the scientific intelligence. This is consistent with Descartes's idea that this scientific intelligence does not proceed from physical objects producing sensations and phantasms to move then to the predicates that describe those objects. Rather it begins with an idea, and when it arrives at clarity and distinctness on the level of the idea it goes out to find the object in the real that necessarily corresponds to that idea. The ideas are not caused to exist in the mind by physical objects; rather, the impressions made by physical objects tend to cloud the inherent clarity of thought. The connection of clear and distinct ideas with whatever exists in the world is guaranteed by the existence of God. It was through the demonstration of the fact that the idea of an infinite and perfect being must necessarily have been transmitted to the mind by such a being that Descartes could conclude that the link between ideas and objects is true and not deceptive (see Meditation 3, and also Gueroult 1968a, pp. 179ff.).

In the third meditation, Descartes attempted to prove the existence of God. And yet, such a proof would hardly be part of the mental activity of an angel, nor would it be required if there were in the mind an intuitive cognition of God that was worthy of certainty. Also, Descartes stated clearly enough that even with his frailties and imperfections he was capable of having an idea of the infinite perfection of God, which then could not have generated from his mind alone. How then, given this evidence, do we connect the *cogito* with the mind of an angel? First the imperfections of the philosopher's mind are what render it necessary for him to effect a proof of the existence of God. These imperfections are not merely the fact that the mind has been enclosed in an imperfect body; the mind has also been corrupted by questions about the existence of God, and it must address these questions in order to eliminate them, not in order to persuade itself that God exists. When Descartes asked whether his own mind, through its progress in actualizing its potential, might ever arrive at the state of God, and when he answered that while God is purely actual there will always be unactualized potentials in his mind, this does not disqualify him from being angelic; it simply marks the clear distinction between being an angel and being God.

Once Descartes had gotten beyond the false opinions of others, he recognized that it is through the faculty by which he conceived of himself that he knew himself to be the image of God. This rejoins the view of Aquinas where it is through his natural knowledge of himself that the angel knows God. It is significant that the process of transmission of the idea of God is specular and that it concerns an impression: "For since God's image is impressed on the very nature of the angel in his essence, the angel knows God in as much as he is the image of God. Yet he does not behold God's essence; because no created likeness is sufficient to represent the Divine essence. Such knowledge then approaches rather to the specular kind; because the angelic nature is itself a kind of mirror representing the divine image" (Aquinas ST, part 1, q. 56, art. 3). Descartes knew, in the sense of cognizance *(connaissance)*, that God actually possesses in himself everything that Descartes aspired to in thinking that God possesses them. God is God because He effectively, actually, and infinitely enjoys this possession (Descartes 1953, p. 300). If the wicked genie is an imperfect being, a being of desire, God is not a wicked genie because He is pure, absolute, and unmitigated enjoyment. The condition that makes the *cogito* a form of self-possession is the existence of a God who does not desire anything of his subject. The question we must reiterate here is whether this God can be anything like a father, whether God is not in fact identified here again with Woman rendered whole, thus lacking desire.

Having established that his own idea of perfection could have been placed in him only by a perfect creature, Descartes concluded, based on what he called natural light, that God cannot be a deceiver (Descartes 1953, p. 300). Is this another way of saying that God cannot be a father? It appears that "natural light" is necessary if one is to see things clearly and distinctly. At the least this keeps things in the realm of the specular and the aesthetic. And from the natural light of his own mind Descartes moves to the source of this light in its unreflected form, the "immense light" that is God and whose "incomparable beauty" he could then consider, admire, and adore.

Gilson has demonstrated in detail the distance between Descartes and Aquinas on the question of human intellection (Gilson 1984, chap. 1); such an approach requires an additional proposition, that the model for the mind in Descartes is the angelic, not the human, intelligence of the Scholastics. Descartes began by leaving to the side the question of the relation of such a mind to the human body. He rejected the idea of gaining knowledge through preexistent objects that produce phantasms in the mind. ". . . it was not by a certain and premeditated judgment that I believed that there were things outside of myself, and different from my being, which, through my sense organs, or by some other means, sent to me their ideas or images, and impressed on me their resemblances" (Descartes 1953, p. 289). So much for Thomist epistemology. On the other hand, angels do not gain knowledge through sensible things in the world, but rather their ideas of species derive from the divine intelligence that created them. Through the truth of their ideas they may arrive at knowledge of sensible things in the world, just like Descartes.

Aquinas stated that the human soul is radically different from the angelic intelligence. The soul is so closely connected with the body that it can only seek its perfection from and through bodies:

The lower spiritual substances—that is, souls, have a nature akin to a body, in so far as they are the forms of bodies: and consequently from their very mode of existence it behooves them to seek their intelligible perfection from bodies and through bodies; otherwise they would be united with bodies to no purpose. On the other hand, the higher substances—that is, the angels—are utterly free from bodies, and subsist immaterially and in their own intelligible nature; consequently they attain their intelligible perfection through an intelligible outpouring, whereby they received from God the species of things known, together with their intellectual nature. ... There are images of creatures in the angel's mind, not, indeed derived from creatures, but from God, Who is the cause of creatures, and in Whom the likenesses of creatures first exist. (Aquinas ST, part 1, q. 55, art. 2).

And Aquinas added in the first and second articles of Question 57 that through their knowledge of species angels can know singular material things, but that to gain such knowledge they do not have to pass through the process of abstracting from the phantasm. The preexisting ideas in their minds make things intelligible to them, and they know singular things through their mental power. Finally, he declared that angels do not have discursive knowledge, that is to say, that they do not learn or acquire knowledge.

So, likewise, the lower, namely, the human, intellects obtain their perfection in the knowledge of truth by a kind of movement and discursive intellectual operation; that is to say, as they advance from one known thing to another. But if from the knowledge of a known principle they were straightway to perceive as known all its consequent conclusions, then there would be no discursive process at all. Such is the condition of the angels, because in all the truths which they know naturally, they at once behold all things whatsoever that can be known in them. Therefore they are called *intellectual beings:* because even with ourselves the things which are instantly grasped by the mind are said to be understood (*intelligi*) ... But human souls which acquire knowledge of truth by the discursive method are called *rational;* and this comes of the feebleness of their intellectual light. For if they possessed the fullness of intellectual light, like the angels, then in the first aspect of principles they would at once comprehend their whole range, by perceiving whatever could be reasoned out from them. (Aquinas, ST, part 1, q. 58, art. 3).

In order to reach this point Descartes was obliged to deconstruct what he had learned from teachers. His approach represents something like a negative epistemology. Unburdened by discourse, by the dialectic of speaker and listener, the mind will discover itself to be angelic and will find within itself, not only first principles, but "whatever could be reasoned from them."

On the topic of the ideas that exist in the mind, Descartes, while protesting about the imperfections of his knowledge, had no doubt whatsoever that ideas had been placed in his mind by God. Their acquisition corresponds to a remembering or retrieval of ideas that were all placed there at once. There is no sense that this knowledge is acquired discursively.

... as I apply my attention a little, I conceive an infinity of particularities concerning numbers, figures, movements, and other similar things, whose truth makes itself so evidently apparent and which accords so well with my nature, that when I begin to discover them, it does not seem to me that I discover something new, but rather that I remember what I already knew before, that is, that I apperceive things which were already in my mind, even though I had not yet turned my thought toward them. And what I find to be more important here is that I find in myself an infinity of ideas about certain things, which cannot be assumed to be of pure nothingness, even though perhaps they have no existence outside of my thought. . . ." (Descartes 1953, pp. 310–11)

The doctrine of innate ideas has a distinctly Platonic ring. For good reason Gilson underscored the point that the identification with angels had a Platonic origin. Angels have innate ideas as well as what is called knowledge of things in the Word; it is through innate ideas that they have knowledge of things as they are. These kinds of knowledge are distinguished as morning and evening knowledge. In Descartes knowledge of things in the Word would correspond to knowledge of Self in the *cogito*, perhaps even including the method that gives access to it. Knowledge of extended things in the world would be a function of the sort of innate ideas possessed by angels. Aquinas drew the following distinction: "As in the ordinary day, morning is the beginning, and evening the close of day, so, their knowledge of the primordial being of things is called morning knowledge; and this is according as things exist in the Word. But their knowledge of the very being of the thing created, as it stands in its own nature, is termed evening knowledge; because the being of things flows from the Word as from a kind of primordial principle; and this flow is terminated in the being which they have in themselves" (ST, part 1, q. 58, art. 6). And also,

... the evening knowledge is that by which the angels know things in their proper nature. This cannot be understood as if they drew their knowledge from the proper nature of things. ... because ... the angels do not draw their knowledge from things. It follows, then, that when we say *in their proper nature* we refer to the aspect of the thing known in so far as it is an object of knowledge; that is to say, that the evening knowledge is in the angels in so far as they know the being of things which those things have in their own nature. Now they know this through a twofold medium, namely, by innate ideas, or by the forms of things existing in the Word. For by beholding the Word, they knew not merely the being of things as existing in the Word, but the being as possessed by the things themselves. ... (Aquinas ST, part 1, q. 58, art. 7)

Angels have innate ideas through which they know the being of things as they exist of themselves. What is primary, however, is knowledge of things in the Word or the Verb. If what is primary in Descartes is the subject's self-identification as a thinking thing, and if this knowledge is prior to any knowledge of things, does this not tell us that in the first combination of a nominative form, thing, with a verbal participle, thinking, it is the verb that predominates, that specifies, while the subject is taken to be the more general, more lacking in definition?

According to Augustine, God the Father is the artisan and God the Son is his know-how. Does this not suggest that the idea of "method" or the practice of this method of hyperbolic doubt through meditation is a translation of the idea of the Word as know-how? And since this is primordial to the recuperation of innate ideas, does this not give us something like the distinction in time represented by morning and evening knowledge? Certainly no angel is required to apply the method to erroneous opinions. The discovery of a method corresponds to the discovery within the mind of the principle of knowledge in the Word.

Since discursive knowledge may also be gained through teaching, Descartes had to rid himself of the need to be subject to the authority of these masters. Through the intermediary of his method he attempted to circumvent the appeal to the authority of wicked genii. Descartes was proposing that placing one's faith in God promotes intellectual activity, even more than does placing one's trust in Aristotle. If it is necessary to overturn Scholasticism, it is also necessary to show that people who engage in intellectual activity without recognizing Aristotle as their patron can think as well as those who do. Descartes seemed to say that while Aristotle may well be the father through whose influence one arrives at the best in human cognition, the mind functions optimally in a different mode, in which God himself is taken to be the guarantor of the truth of thought. Descartes's idea that God is a worker who imprints his mark on the being he has created is reminiscent of Augustine's notion of God the Father as artisan. So when Descartes wrote of the idea of God being imprinted on him, he added that the mark need not be different from the work itself; thereby, he came a bit closer to the angel's idea of God. Declaring that God has produced him in God's image and semblance, Descartes continued: "I conceive this resemblance by the same faculty by which I conceive myself" (Descartes 1953, pp. 299–300).

The advantage in redefining the human subject as an angel ought to be clear. There is a gain or expansion of knowledge and an assurance that this knowledge, once gained, belongs to the knower. If this process has anything to do with mystical experience, its addition of the idea of self-possession overcomes the inconvenient aspect of mystical ecstasy, that is to say its sense of a loss of self-possession and self-control. Whereas the soul of the mystic was consistently defined as feminine, Descartes seems to have eliminated sexual difference from the experience. Perhaps the reason behind the separation of mind and body is to posit a mind that transcends the division of the sexes. Aquinas had said that we should want to understand how "Socrates knows," because this is the normal form of the sentence. We do not say that the mind of Socrates knows. It is not so much that knowledge is acquired for Aquinas through the intermediary of the phantasm and is inseparable from the body, but rather that the identity of the knower, the name of the I, requires a body for its inscription. To say that the I knows does not tell us whose I it is. And since it could be the I of anyone, that anyone is not marked according to sex. The body that is added to that I may be sexed, but its connection is tenuous and does not establish the identity of the knower.

Even this gesture is not sufficient, because the division of the sexes in terms of minds and bodies or minds and souls is present in many Christian texts, a vestige of their pagan ancestry. To break down this division Descartes was obliged to modify the element of desire and its dialectic; this is what connects the two in their division. Certainly, these gestures are prefigured in theology; they are a goal toward which it had constantly been moving. As is usual, the way to subvert desire is through the assertion of will.

In the following passage Descartes stated clearly on the one hand that God did not make him an angel, one of "the most noble and most perfect beings," but that he could achieve through the force of his will a state that at least approaches the angelic. The only difference is that angels are born that way and Descartes had to make himself that way. Is there a better expression of the denial of all references to parents? His constant intellectual effort is to counter, to negate whatever in his mind is human. His being an angel is something that God might have made him, in another possible world.

> I see nevertheless that it would have been easy for God to make it so that I never make mistakes, even though I remained free and with limited knowledge, by giving to my intellect a clear and distinct intelligence of all the things about which I should ever deliberate or else if he merely had so profoundly engraved in my memory the resolution never to judge anything unless I conceived it clearly and distinctly that I might never forget it. . . . I have no right to complain if God, in having put me in the world, did not want to place me in the ranks of the noblest and most perfect beings; even so I have reason to be contented because . . . he at least left within my power the other way which is to retain firmly the resolution never to pass judgment on things whose truth is not clearly known to me. For even though I remark this weak point in my nature, which is that I cannot attach my mind continually to the same thought, I can nevertheless, by an attentive and oft-repeated meditation, so strongly imprint this in my memory that I never fail to remember it each time that I need to, and to acquire thereby the habit of not erring. (Descartes 1953, pp. 308–9)

No other passage shows so clearly not only the aspiration to being an angel but also the sense of having acquired that state, not through desire, but through the force of intellectual willpower. I find it extraordinary that it is said to be most truly acquired when it becomes a habit.

Descartes's statement needs simply to be juxtaposed to the following from Aquinas: ". . . there can be neither deception nor falsehood in the angel's knowledge . . ." He continued that angels do not understand through the operations of composition and division, what philosophers now call synthesis and analysis, but through seeing directly the essence of the thing. For if they do they may accidentally fall into error. Their way of avoiding error is through the exercise of will: ". . . owing to their upright will, from their knowing the nature of every creature, the good angels form no judgments as to the nature of qualities therein, save under the Divine ordinance; hence there can be no error or falsehood in them." We also remark that if the essence of the thing is the referent of the name of that thing, this knowledge of the essence has a semantic consequence, in terms of what may or may not properly be predicated of the thing. And it is here that the Cartesian subject differs from the angels about whom Aquinas said: ". . . through [the knowledge of the] essence of a thing they know everything that can be said regarding it. Now it is quite evident that the quiddity of a thing can be a source of knowledge with regard to everything belonging to such thing, or excluded from it; but not of what may be dependent on God's supernatural ordinance" (Aquinas ST, Part 1, q. 58, art. 5). Through this idea of supernatural qualities of things Aquinas covered exceptional behaviors of things, of the sort that might happen through divine and miraculous intervention. Knowing everything that may properly be predicated of the thing seems to suggest knowing the truth value of analytic statements. We are perhaps stretching things too far to say that what is covered by supernatural intervention is synthetic statements, statements. where something is predicated of a thing that is not of its essence.

The Cartesian subject does not concern itself with such saying. Its one saying, *cogito ergo sum*, suffices. The terms do not support predicates; they are pure verbs, and do not participate in the function of the copula. Perhaps Descartes recognized that in the division of subject and predicate something of the division of the sexes remained. So he was obliged to eliminate not only the parental or paternal function of proper naming, but also that of whatever could be predicated of a subject or substantive.

To denounce Descartes for having committed some sort of sin is ultimately not satisfactory. Descartes confronted an important epistemological problem that, as Gilson asserted, he inherited from the Scholastics. For Aquinas sensible objects produce phantasms in the mind through the intermediary of bodily sensations. From these phantasms the intellect may abstract an intelligible species or specifier and gain knowledge. The intellect is divided into active and potential functions; initially it is a potential or receptive organ, later it receives intelligible ideas that the active intellect connects with phantasms. The intellect does not by nature contain any species; originally it has what Aquinas called seeds of knowledge (Praeexistunt in nobis quaedam scientiarum semina) (in Gilson 1984, p. 14). When it receives species this potentiality is activated in the same way as the sensitive soul is activated by the action of objects on the senses. The mind has both intellectual and sensitive potentials, which are activated by different means. It is not, however, all that clear how an image in the mind becomes connected with an intelligible idea. This seems to require the act of the intellect in matching an idea with an image.

The key to this process is the phantasm; on the one hand it yields to the abstract species and on the other it is a sensible image in the mind. The phantasm has therefore a dual nature, which may be thought of as corresponding to the intellectual and sensitive sides of the human being, thus as the coupling of feminine and masculine principles. We may also say that the individual is born with two potentials, both of which are received from a mother, and gains knowledge when these are activated by the injection from the outside of two things that are typed masculine. It would appear from this analysis that the subject is said to gain knowledge that belongs to him because the process by which it is gained repeats the process by which he was created.

The phantasm is the juncture of mind and body, but only to the extent that the body is taken to be a sensible organ receiving impressions from without. Gilson defined the Thomist concept of the phantasm as follows: "A spiritual being, but representative of the individuating material conditions of the object, full of the *species intelligibilis* that it contains potentially and that only the agent intellect will render intelligible in act, the *phantasm* is thus placed between matter and spirit, at this mysterious limit where the soul enters into contact with things without ceasing to be itself" (Gilson 1984, p. 23). Here is the problem; Gilson declared that the fault in this conception is the failure to explain the mechanism whereby the sensible object is received by the sense, the difficulty to understand the passage from the object to the organ of sensation, the problem of its penetration into the organ (Gilson 1984, p. 24).

Descartes himself criticized the notion of the phantasm in his *Optics*. His intention was to sunder the idea of the resemblance between the picture of an object we have in the mind and the object itself. A picture, he said, may be produced by things other than the object itself; it may be produced by words or signs that in no way resemble the pictures they evoke in the mind (Descartes 1953, pp. 203–4). His objection bears on how images enter the mind, though the fact that an image may be evoked by a word does mean that the image could not have been formed unless it had previously entered the mind's set of stock images. When the image of an object is produced in the mind, how does it happen that something of the object made its way into the mind? Or did it? Does the image belong to the mind, the object, both, or neither? Even if the aspect of the external object that intrudes in the psyche activates a potential within the psyche, why is the activated potential thought to be the image of the object? To what extend do we believe that there is a kinship between the external object and the image in the mind, rather than that the true kinship exists between the containing body and the image produced therein?

Even if you resolve these problems to your satisfaction, how does it happen that the phantasm is intelligible, how does it become connected with an idea? Why is it necessary to have an intermediary instance between sense perception and knowledge, especially when an image in the mind may be caused by something other than an object and may mean something other than the intelligible species of the image. The phantasm appears to be as much an obstacle to knowledge as its promoter. Cartesian epistemology offers clear and distinct ideas whose value is independent of any external agent. And without any intermediaries these ideas permit the thinking subject not just to know an object when he sees it or to know what people are talking about, but to change and to move nature himself, to alter its composition, to become its master. If this subject is an angel, then its alteration of nature based on proven scientific principles will be for the good. We are not here in the presence of a mind that functions to modify the real in order to bring it into accord with its desire. Such an ethic implies a rearrangement of elements in the real. And it would be strictly localized; it would not pretend to create from nothing something that has never existed or to destroy things to demonstrate one's ownership of them. Descartes intended to provide knowledge of nature and thus power over it. It is good to say that the purpose of the Cartesian project is to create a knowing subject outside of the division of the sexes, but as we will see this subject is in fact paired with a nature taken to be unknowing. So the division of the sexes, eliminated from the commerce of human beings among themselves, has been simply displaced into another area.

If the problem did not concern the acquisition of images of objects but rather the acquisition of language, things would be simpler. There a teacher is required, and that teacher must be external to the speaking subject. Whatever potential the human mind has for speech must be activated by the process of receiving language from someone else. This still leaves open the question, how is it that the speaker comes to acquire language? Language, after all, is never the possession of a speaker. And what does it mean for a speaker to acquire language? The Cartesian response is that the subject enlists language to express his innate ideas freely and creatively. If this is so the ideal verbal communication exists when language is transparent, when it in no way distorts meaning. It also assumes a listener who understands perfectly what is intended. Further, it must posit that the language does not ideally do anything other than what the speaker wants it to do.

Aquinas, we have said, argued that the union of mind and body is a given, for otherwise we would say that the mind of Socrates knows this or that instead of saying that Socrates knows (Gilson 1984, p. 11, Aquinas ST, part 1, q. 76, art. 1). What makes it that Socrates knows is the phantasm as epistemological intermediary. Note with Gilson that the phantasm is neither material nor intelligible. If it were material it would be the object itself instead of its representation; if it were intelligible it would be of a different order from the sensed object (Gilson 1984, p. 22). The key to the system of Aquinas is that the intellect abstracts from the phantasm of a particular object to gain knowledge of the species and other universals. A physical object, a horse, produces an image of itself in the mind through the sensitive faculty of the soul. This image in itself tells you nothing of what you see; it is a configuration of form and color; you do not yet know that it is a member of the species of horses, nor do you know that it is classified under the more general category of animal. In order to effect this transformation, the soul requires an illumination that falls from above through the function of the agent intellect. It is convenient within such a system that there be angelic messengers who we might imagine as called upon to provide the meanings of experience (Gilson 1984, p. 23). If this is true, then the angels as carriers of meanings would be obliged to have a sensible form, but one that is subordinated or even transparent to the meaning conveyed. Angels could not equivocate or deceive. If ideas are innate in the mind, as Descartes said, there is no need for a world full of spiritual beings to carry them to us.

Aquinas's theory depends on the hypothesis that before things were created they already existed as ideas in the mind of God and the angels, that they were created according to the divine plan. The phantasm is retained to determine the fact that it is a human being who has acquired knowledge; and that knowledge is necessarily less perfect than the knowledge of the angels, because it requires the activation of the senses for its acquisition. One problem here is that the system seems to move in the direction of increasing degrees of abstraction. Assuming that one abstracts from the flower in the field to gain a knowledge of the universals that define that flower, how does one see a singular flower as anything other than an instance of those universals? Knowledge may therefore comprise the essence of the flower and it may permit the subject to identify a flower when he sees it. He knows what a flower is, he knows one when he sees one, and he knows how to speak of flowers. But does this allow him to know a singular flower? The role of the singular flower seems limited to providing sense impressions from which a phantasm is formed. From there a process of abstraction yields knowledge. But how do we get back to the singular flower, or do we? There is a sense in which for Aquinas the question is irrelevant, or the product of a defective intelligence. Why would anyone want to know a flower? The response of Duns Scotus and especially William of Ockham was that through an act of intuitive cognition the subject could know a singular object, in some sense to enter into its singularity. For Scotus the question concerns knowing the "thisness," the "haecceity" of a thing. For these Franciscans the question is one of enjoyment; to know a singular thing is to enjoy it fully. Such enjoyment seems excluded for Aquinas, who, as we have said, barred face-to-face encounters in the interest of sustaining desire. The enjoyment of a Thomist seems to be "encephallic," and this effectively excludes the enjoyment of a singular object. This correlates in an interesting fashion with a statement of Lacan to the effect that a man never enjoys a woman's body because in the sexual act his own phallic enjoyment functions as an obstacle (Lacan 1975, p. 13). Of course, one has the impression that Aquinas renounced commerce with singular objects as he renounced conversation with individual women. Lacan was not pointing in the direction of such a renunciation, but rather toward the tension between attempting to grasp the singularity of a woman and being prevented from doing so. For Lacan there is a return through an image in the mind to the translation of that image into reality. In psychoanalytic theory the phantasm or phantasy has a dual nature. When it is tormenting it ought to be a rendered intelligible; its intelligibility is grasped only when the desire it manifests is articulated. It also has the function of presenting to the mind a desire, a counterfactual situation that may be translated into reality. In that sense it sustains desire. This is certainly not what Aquinas was talking about when he developed his theory of the phantasm, but we are struck by the resemblance as well as by the difference.

There are several other things to note here. The word phantasm is intimately related to the word phantom, and both are linked to the idea of deception. The dictionary tells us that the two are almost synonymous. The phantasm, as Aquinas noted, is the remembered image of the sensible object. So phantasms are ghosts, and the question arises of why they are produced when they are produced. The ghostlike quality of the phantasm, its ability to deceive, throws into doubt its connection with an object as well as with an idea. Here we remember that for Socrates such mental images were realizations of desire; they do not point to the gaining of knowledge, but rather to the appropriation of desire.

Freud stated clearly in his early work (and the point is certainly crucial to the interpretation of dreams) that what psychoanalysis calls a phantasy is in fact not a representation of objects in the world but a visualization of a verbal message. This is one reason why they are analyzable through being told in words in psychoanalysis. The idea that we ought to want to gain knowledge of things in the world or that we ought to want to make use of things to gain knowledge of species and other universals may well represent a failure to read the phantasm to gain access to desire. This would place the epistemological project in doubt, or better, it would tend to show that gaining knowledge in and of the world corresponds to a form of cognitive beatitude. In preserving the function of the phantasm, Aquinas was more willing to grapple with desire than was Descartes. Perhaps Descartes saw that the association of phantasm with deception made it an uncertain path to knowledge of things in the world, and that the active intellect might at some point try to interpret it. The Cartesian project represents a further purification of enjoyment through the elimination of the supporting desire. The world of extended bodies in Descartes yields nothing of desire, either the desire of man or of God. The analysis that leads the mind to clear and distinct ideas presupposes that love exists between ideas and physical objects, because otherwise there would be no reason for the one to have anything to do with the other. And that love is contaminated by questions concerning why you want to know, or better, what is the desire enacted in a will to know. The problem with the phantasm is that you end up not knowing the thing, but rather the idea of the thing. Descartes, through his innate ideas, began with the ideas and gained thereby direct access to things. He had to know them because he would not have been contented simply to know about them. We have argued that the Thomist project represents an erotic, and perhaps the erotic strivings of the masculine intelligence are sustained in a phantasy because knowing things directly, knowing their essence, is interdicted. It is as though the natural world had been holding itself in reserve from the medieval Doctors, only to open its treasures to the true master it found in the subject of science, who knew it as it was without the interposition of any phantasies. Lacan correctly labeled this a nightmare.

How does one render a phantasy intelligible through psychoanalysis? The *locus classicus* of psychoanalytic study of the phantasy is Freud's paper "A Child is Being Beaten" (Freud SE, Vol. 18, pp. 179–204). This phrase is a phantasy, it is an image in the mind, but it is more complex than the image of a flower. Through his analysis Freud showed that the key to the structure of the phantasy is that it has a grammatical structure. It is through work on the grammar of the phrase describing it that the phantasy is rendered intelligible. So we are not moving into a world of universals, but rather into a situation where the subject will appropriate the desire in the phantasy as his. Freud remarked that the agent of the beating is erased in the phantasy and the first task of the analysis is to restore it. He discovered then that the agent was invariably the father of the person having the phantasy. Immediately we can say that the singular person seen in the phantasy, connected only with an action, is part of a structure in which there is an interaction of two people. The next step is the recognition by the person having the phantasy that he is the child who is being beaten. Thus he finds the element of the phantasy that represents him; it is not an anonymous child but he himself in relation to his father. And the next step is the recognition that this analytic construction does not necessarily represent a remembered reality but may be a desire. It need not be a desire to be beaten. As a desire it is best considered as counterfactual, and perhaps this is the reason that Freud insisted that his first hysterical patients' seduction phantasies were desires and were not necessarily remembrances. If actual fact becomes primary in the analysis then the factor of desire will be lost. And if it is lost, then a phantasy that represents a future possibility will be analyzed in terms of past fact. Thus the analysand will be led to be cured of desiring, hardly a desirable analytic result.

The ethic that informs Descartes's project is utilitarian. He justified his labor by asserting that scientific knowledge of nature will accrue to the general good of humanity by rendering us "the masters and possessors of nature." Writing of his discoveries in physics, he asserted:

I believed that I could not keep them hidden without sinning seriously against the law which obliges us to procure as much as we are able the general good of all men. For they made me see that it is possible to arrive at knowledge that is very useful to life, and that in place of this speculative philosophy that is taught in the schools, we can find a practical one, by which, knowing the force and the actions of fire, water, air, stars, skies, and all the other bodies which surround us as distinctly as we know the different skills of our artisans, we can use them similarly in all the ways that are proper, and thus to render ourselves masters and possessors of nature. This is not only to be desired for the invention of an infinite number of gadgets which would make us enjoy without effort the fruits of the earth and all the commodities that are found therein, but also principally for the conservation of health, which is doubtless the first good and the foundation of all the other goods of this life. . . . (Descartes 1953, p. 168)

For most people this is an unassailable argument; there is little that people will not give up to promote the advance of medical science. It is obvious that the exaggerated emphasis on medicine is not discontinuous with the concerns of Christian civilization. Nor is it surprising that Descartes, seeking to rationalize his method, came up with a debating point that must have seemed decisive. Its fruits are supposed to benefit a much larger segment of humanity than the speculations of the Scholastics. Descartes probably did not imagine that rendering man master and possessor of nature could have catastrophic consequences; he simply did not see the price of his call for nature to be made a slave to science. He did, of course, know what the ignorance of nature had cost in the past. His position was that if the thinking subject could become self-possessed he could then come to possess the world outside of himself.

With Descartes and with the application of mathematics, especially geometry, to the functioning of physical objects, humans found themselves in the position not only of knowing something about objects, but also with increasing power to change those objects, to alter their composition, without having to appeal to dubious intermediaries. When it came to the question of the intelligibility of the external world, Descartes suppressed the system of reference to an intelligible world, a world of intelligible ideas or meanings that was thought to exist in the beyond (Gueroult 1968a, Vol. 1, chap. 8, sect. 17). Suppressing the world of intelligibles was consistent with the suppression of the world of intelligences. So rather than have a group of angelic agents moving things according to laws that they alone understood fully, and rather than have some sort of interaction between the system of the heavens and the world of humans, Descartes promoted a world of human intelligences moving, thereby changing, things in the world without reference to anything other than God himself. It was no longer a question of learning about the movements of objects; rather it became a question of controlling those movements in the interest of the general good. Would this not be consistent with the idea that angels move whatever they move for the good of mankind? More ominously, an ethic that values utility risks promoting the goal of using nature, even of using it up. How better to demonstrate mastery and possession than to assert the right and even the duty to destroy an object?

To call this an erotic requires a considerable stretching of the imagination. Descartes has provided direct access to the body of nature and has also pointed in the direction of an intervention that does not need to pass through either the phantasm or a world of intelligibles. If phantasy sustains desire and if action to make alterations in the state of things in the external world is supported by the phantasized image, the absence of phantasy, of this mediating function, leads to a mode of intervention that privileges only the subject's enjoyment of the object. Such an intervention does not require a great deal in the nature of consent, because the argument for the utility of the intervention moves in the direction of making that consent something that cannot reasonably be withheld. Dispensing with the phantasm and the apparatus of desire, Descartes opened nature to Selfs who would master and possess it through the exertion of will. Thereby he provided a more certain mode of intervention than is provided by the phallus.

Recall that the phallus was distinguished from the time of Augustine as being the part of the body that did not respond to the commands of the will. Nowhere is the idea of self-possession more dubious. It thus was the exemplary instance of moral evil and also of human desire. Again we may say that Descartes was following the spirit of Christianity even in rejecting the doctrines of many of its greatest teachers. Perhaps he realized that the authority of a father figure was the touchstone that gave men access to the phallus. Perhaps he also saw that maintaining the phantasm as a means of having intercourse with external objects left open the path to desire for those objects. Not knowing objects directly and immediately, man could only desire them more.

The body through which the scientist studies and masters nature is not the same as the one Descartes proposed as the solution to the mind-body problem. The latter was a body in pain, a body of affects from which the mind could not distance itself. The scientist, however, studies nature through the deployment of instruments. John Locke, for one, compared this to the assumed bodies of angels. In his *Essay Concerning Human Understanding,* Locke proposed "an extravagant conjecture," namely that there is a correlation between the ability of angels to assume bodies fitted to different forms of intellection and the human capacity to create instruments like microscopes and glasses that alter the perception of the objects of the natural world. He wrote:

... that since we have some reason ... to imagine that Spirits can assume to themselves bodies of different bulk, figure, and conformation of parts—whether one great advantage some of them have over us may not lie in this, that they can so frame and shape to themselves organs of sensation or perception as to suit them to their present design, and the circumstances of the object they would consider. For how much would that man exceed all others in knowledge, who had but the faculty so to alter the structure of his eyes, that one sense, as to make it capable of all the several degrees of vision which the assistance of glasses (casually at first lighted on) has taught us to conceive? What wonders would he discover, who could so fit his eyes to all sorts of objects, as to see when he pleased the figure and motion of the minute particules in the blood, and other juices of animals, as distinctly as he does, at other times, the shape and motion of the animals themselves. (Locke 1959, p. 404)

And he concluded from this that angels and other spirits are simply projections of the human mind: "I doubt whether we can imagine anything about the knowledge of angels but after some manner, some way or other in proportion to what we find and observe in ourselves" (Locke 1959, p. 405; see also Descartes 1953, p. 1370). The victory of man over these spiritual beings resides in these passages and others like them. The path toward this victory lies in the confusion of angels with humans.

It is too facile to denounce this version of masculinity as simply diabolical. A bodily appendage that responds perfectly to the commands of the will and that serves the purpose of a healing science may as easily find its model in the holy angels. The point seems to be that angels and devils are far closer than had been thought, and that the practical application of an angelic morality yields both good and bad results (see Lacan's essay "Kant avec Sade" in *Ecrits* 1966, pp. 765–92).

What we have in the man of science who intervenes directly in nature through interposed instruments is a simulation of a masculine position. Rather than appropriate the insignia of masculinity from a father, the male subject finds the basis for his identity in something that belongs to him, of which he is certain, and which he can command. This knowledge is a function of Self, and the action of the assumed body is also considered to be his own. The Self whose source is not to be found in proper naming, the relations of kinship, or the teaching of any authority, will owe its certainty to a Mother. Effectively it is in the service of a Mother Goddess that the Self sets out to master and possess an Other (nature) that is not Her. Thereby it acquits itself of the debt it contracted in gaining Self-certainty.

We would expect that one who refused to acquire knowledge from others would also abrogate the position of teacher, fraught as it is with paternal overtones. Descartes addressed the question of the communicability of knowledge in the *Discourse on Method*. He began by saying that your concept is your own when you invent it yourself, not when you learn it from someone else. He continued: "This is so true that while I have often explained some of my opinions to very intelligent people who, while I spoke to them seemed to understand very distinctly, nevertheless, when they repeated it, changed it in such a way that I remarked that I could no longer call the opinions my own" (Descartes 1953, p. 173). This is probably considered a powerful argument for the virtue of knowledge acquired by personal experience. It also argues the authority of the author; he, as Self, is the only one who knows what he really means. Knowledge would thus be acquired by each person through the personal experience of the Cartesian method. Not only is this reminiscent of the way one gains knowledge through mystical experience, but it also rejoins the idea that in experimental science, the experiment performed by one scientist may be reproduced by any other to yield the same results. One might imagine that Descartes would be closer in his conception to the Socratic method, based as it seems to be on the fact that the interlocutor presents ideas that Socrates has not taught him.

And yet the Socratic method is an erotic; it is based on the value of dialogue, not on that of meditation, introspection, or methodical doubt.

Whatever one thinks of Descartes's method, he did in the *Discourse on Method* isolate one of the failures in the Scholastic system as a pedagogical object: for all the questions that were asked, what really concerned people was having the answers. And those answers could not contradict Church dogma. This tended to produce students, Descartes said, who were eminently capable of parroting what they had heard in courses without having the least idea of what was in question (Descartes 1953, p. 176).

The question is whether this occurred because of an excessive faith in the authority of teachers or of Aristotle, or for some other reason. That other reason must be that instead of debate and dialogue, Scholasticism, after having its day in the sun, was drawn back into the bosom of the Church. Some ideas were condemned and others became fixed as dogma. Those who deviated were obliged to recant and to watch their books being burned. In a sense Descartes was reacting against this tyranny of the Word. His retreat into a meditational mode was a response to the fact that once the oral debates of the Schools became enshrined in writing, they yielded to the tendency of writing to take on the character of fixed, immobile, incontestable dogma. And yet, Descartes did not for as much privilege speech. For all their talk about being beyond language, mystical experiences and the experiences of meditation lend themselves perfectly well to written expression. Additionally, they are eminently readable, certainly more readable than the elucubrations of an Aquinas or a Duns Scotus (See Lacan 1975, p. 71).

The activity of defending one's ideas in public debate, the adoption of dialetical strategies of question and answer, was essential to the Scholastic enterprise. We have already noted with Huizinga the similarity between these exercises and the feudal tournaments that were so important for the demonstration of virility. Are we to consider these manifestations to be an aberration in the great march of Christian theology or a manifestation of some hidden truth? I consider this moment a deviation, a sidetracking, a seduction by the power of pagan thought. The respect for the authority of teachers represented a mode of identification that corresponded to what happens between father and son—on a vertical axis. The point at which it was compromised was where there was only one woman to whom it all had to be submitted for judgment—Mother

Church. When the theology became dogma the sons of Aristotle were transformed into sons of the Mother Church, thereby to receive honor and glory and their eternal reward.

Therefore it is significant and even symptomatic that Aquinas never spoke to women; what better instance can there be of a fundamental distinction between speaker and listener than the difference of the sexes? On the other side we find the love witnessed by the extensive correspondence of Descartes with Princess Elisabeth of Bohemia. Does this show that the philosopher was able to deal with women where the Angelic Doctor was not? Or else, that for Descartes the desire of or for women was not a danger? Certainly, Descartes recognized the Otherness of the listener, but for him this meant simply that his ideas were not transmissible through speech. His belief that each person should be able to arrive at the same ideas by the personal practice of his method was simply a more effective way of creating a community of equals or counterparts. This was based on the supposition of a common experience through and of which all might gain certainty. This common experience ultimately will find its support in the fact that we are all "of woman born." In Cartesian terms this represents an appeal to common sense. We would not conclude that because Descartes had female correspondents he was willing to admit sexual difference. Quite the contrary, I believe that it was because he had succeeded in completely deeroticizing philosophy that he was capable of conversing with women, not as women, but as spirits.

Descartes was not the reincarnation of Peter Abélard; the Princess Elisabeth with whom he had a long and loving correspondence was not a new Héloïse. Both women were intellectually gifted and both were loved by their philosopher-masters, though in quite different ways. Whereas Abélard was the live-in tutor of Héloïse, a situation that lent itself to a seduction and the ensuing calamities, Descartes and Elisabeth exchanged letters from a respectful distance. Theirs was much closer to what people today would call a relationship. In his *Descartes et la Princesse Elisabeth* (1969) Léon Petit argued at length that for Descartes love was the union of the mind and the body, and that desire ought not to be part of the equation. For our purposes the following remarks of Descartes serve as an indication of the type of love he maintained for the Princess. In a letter of May 21, 1643, Descartes began by thanking Elisabeth for replying to him in writing rather than receiving him personally when he was in The Hague. He continued to describe the experience he would have had if he had seen and conversed with her. If this the counterfactual situation, described in the conditional, is his desire, we see him in this letter, renouncing it: "For I would have had too many marvels to admire at the same time; and seeing superhuman discourses coming out of a body which is so similar to those that painters give to angels, I would have been ravished in the same way that it seems to me that those coming from the earth ought to be when they are newly entering heaven." The soul of the philosopher does not see God face-to-face, but sees in the body of his beloved a female angel, an angelic woman, whose beauty is that of artistic representation. Neither of the lovers is then in a very virile position. Perhaps this means simply that the discourse in question harks back to courtly love, but where the courtly lover was aflame with desire for his Lady, awaiting only her granting his entreaty by virtue of *merci,* Descartes thanks his Lady for not seeing him, for not receiving him. He would, in effect, rather see her words than hear them, and if he hears them he will still be seeing them. He would, in effect, have been struck dumb. And so rather than confront the anxiety over speaking himself, he prefers to write.

Had the counterfactual situation taken place there would have been a risk of something erotic happening. For it to happen Descartes would have had to speak, and speech, contrary to his sense of things, does not enter the body of the listener through the eyes. Happily, Elisabeth has spared him from this experience by leaving for him only the "traces of [her] thoughts on paper." So Descartes is relieved for being less dazzled and consoles himself to have in hand a piece of writing. Through these traces he discovered that Elisabeth's thoughts are not only ingenious but are more "judicious and solid the more one examines them." Thereby he gains time to reflect and meditate and contemplate. Had he been called upon to speak to her the obligation to perform would not have given him the time for extensive examination.

One might say here, as Héloïse said to Abélard, that marriage is not conducive to philosophy. And certainly there is some truth to this: one gains knowledge of the purest and most rigorous sort if one limits oneself to dealing with a supersensible intelligence, abstracted from the limitations of empirical facts and everyday language. And yet the price of such knowledge, assuming that mathematical logic is its prototype, is that one loses the sense that it has anything to do with anything as well as the obligation to communicate it to any but the initiated. The price of such knowledge is truth.

Taking the polar opposite of such a proposition, asserting that one must have knowledge only of the empirical or of one's Self, does not resolve the problem. One has simply sacrificed a form of knowledge to wallow in what one considers to be the truth. Whether this truth derives from a face-to-face vision of God or from a face-to-face vision of empirical reality does not alter the structure essentially. As Quine stated: "Physical objects are conceptually imported into the situation as convenient intermediaries—not by definition in terms of experience, but simply as irreducible posits comparable, epistemologically, to the gods of Homer. For my part I do, qua lay physicist, believe in physical objects and not in Homer's gods; and I consider it a scientific error to believe otherwise. But in point of epistemological footing the physical objects and the gods differ only in degree and not in kind. Both sorts of entities enter our conception only as cultural posits. The myth of physical objects is epistemologically superior to most in that it has proved more efficacious than other myths as a device for working a manageable structure into the flux of experience" (Quine 1980, p. 44). Obviously, such an assertion depends largely upon what one considers human experience to be; that the myth of physical objects has provided a better structure for psychological or mental experience is extremely dubious. One might even argue that reducing psychological experience to behavioral and biochemical realities that are supposed to be empirical does not address the "flux" of human experience at all.

It is clearly not true that language always does or ought to refer to empirical realities, for this would eliminate and condemn lies, deceit, desire, and the realm of the counterfactual. And yet, as Putnam said, language is required to hook into something real at some point or other. It must also hook into those who use it. It is not so obvious that the recourse to a method of meditation based on the authority of personal experience or common sense responds to these concerns. So long as the experience is private its translation into a public medium will be problematical. As Wittgenstein pointed out in what is called the private language argument, we have no way of knowing that the sensations of one person are the same as those of another, given that sensations are private experiences and that the only way you know about my sensations, or I about yours, is through the translation of those experiences into a language whose meanings are not determined by the fact of a common experience. Having an experience in no way validates the words chosen to articulate it, and not having had an experience does not prevent anyone from talking as though he had. And if the words have something like a mind of their own they may find their resource in deceiving people into believing that their sense is common to all.

Like mystics, those who believe in the value of meditation tend to write books telling others how to have the same experience. For each his own. This corresponds, we have said, to the place of experiment in science, and it shows why a certain type of science developed. The reason was not only to give direct access to the world of empirical reality, the world of a nature that would be the same for everyone, but also to provide for everyone the same experience of that world. But if you should follow the method outlined by Descartes and arrive at the same place, is the experience yours or his? Is the sense of illumination or rapture produced by the method or is it induced by the description offered by the philosopher? And if it works how do you know that the reason does not have something to do with your wish to elevate Descartes into an authority, to validate his theory with your being?

The problem is not only the predominance of the Book as a sacred reference, but also the primacy given to the Verb. For Aquinas the problem of the possession of knowledge was covered by the fact that we say that Socrates knows, not the mind of Socrates knows. With Descartes the proper name is elided to the advantage of the verb: *cogito ergo sum*. The Latin forms seem to demonstrate that the pronoun is a function of the verb, and that it is not a substitute for a proper name. If you should be talking with someone whose name you do not know, his use of pronouns will not tell you with whom you are conversing. Not only is the reference of the pronoun essentially different from that of the proper name, but if the proper name is completely elided it is most likely that you are listening to an angel.

The position to be avoided was one that permitted Eros to enter into play. Since the Socratic dialectic was a pedagogical technique, it was necessary to establish a form of teaching that was not dialectical. What better solution could have been found than introspective meditation?

Now people have the opportunity to read the correspondence between Descartes and Elisabeth and to emulate their practice of writing in one last effort to self-deconstruct.

In the modern world the heir to the Socratic dialectic is psychoanalysis. There are very few other didactic processes that as clearly engage desire. At first psychoanalysis was attacked for its interest in sexuality; now it is rejected because of its acceptance of the division of the sexes. Have its critics truly advanced, and are they as radical as they profess themselves to be? If the division of the sexes has something to do with the division of speaker and listener in the speech act, it is all too consistent that the same people cavil against psychoanalysis because it privileges the act of speech.

It is also consistent that contemporary readings of Freud by literary scholars tend to make his case histories into moral histories—usually with Freud being cast as the villain. A civilization that was capable of turning the story of Héloïse and Abélard into a moral history through an assiduous study of their correspondence is capable of just about anything. Abélard the teacher was condemned, we have mentioned, through the efforts of Bernard of Clairvaux. To Héloïse he wrote: "Logic has won me the hatred of men. Perverse perverters, for whom wisdom is a kind of hell, are saying that I am a great logician but that I am considerably mistaken in my interpretation of St. Paul" (in Gilson 1960, p. 107).

Abélard became a man without a Church, a position, a home, and certainly without Héloïse. He was ripe to receive Christian charity in the person of the abbott of the monastery at Cluny, one Peter the Venerable. This latter caused Abélard's condemnation to be lifted, thereby permitting him to die in something like peace. Our respect for the acts of Peter the Venerable should not let us lose sight of the fact that Peter Abélard was completely broken—the better, you might say, to learn about love. Was it the genius of Descartes, then, to provide a method and a philosophy that a man can converse about and teach to women without eliciting such calamities? I leave the thought for your meditation.

SIX

MANLINESS

Within Western Catholic theology references to the virility of angels are extremely scarce—and not because they are absent from Scripture. From the cherubim with the flaming swords who guard the gates of Eden to the unmistakably virile angel with whom Jacob wrestles one night until daybreak, and even to the venerable angel of death whose night-work persuades Pharaoh to let the people of Moses leave Egypt, evidence of manly angels certainly exists. Yet when Christian authors commented on Old Testament angels, it was not these texts that drew the greater part of their attention; rather, we find in Gregory of Nyssa, Richard of St. Victor, and Bonaventure extensive commentaries on the winged cherubim Moses placed on the ark of the Covenant. Far from being warrior angels, the primary activity of these cherubim was to open their wings to cover the contents of the ark. The appearance of an angel in the burning bush also elicited considerable contemplation. The influence of mysticism is clear in the definition of angels as distant, mostly absent, beings upon whom only the most exalted and most feminine souls could look. Making the soul feminine could and in many cases did lead to a sense of the maleness of the angel or the maleness of God, but this maleness was not of the order of virility most often associated with pagan gods, demons, and genii. Even references to the armies of God, to their overthrow of the rebel angels, however much they were invoked to justify the activities of crusaders, receded into the distance as the angels fell into the abyss of their beatific contemplation of the face of God. Lacking the presence a god or goddess might manifest in a Homeric epic, angels became more an ideal form, paired with souls in something like a relationship.

Perhaps the avoidance of references to angelic virility derived from the early Christian wish to distinguish the angels from the pantheon of Greek gods. Reading Clement of Alexandria's *Exhortation to the Greeks* (1982), we find fulminations against these gods, most especially for their unbridled lust, endless fornications, unrepentant adultery, shameless worship of the phallus, and for the crimes of rape, murder, thievery, and deception. Goddesses like Aphrodite and Demeter were hardly spared the in-Clement assault on incarnate sin. A veritable catalogue of vices is attributed to the gods, and it is from this that Christianity proposed to save the world. So it is not surprising to find later Christian authors scrupulously avoiding references to masculinity among the angels, especially as demonology attributed masculine traits to those angels who had been expelled from the Heavenly City.

Despite scriptural precedence, the writers who established a Christian theology worked tirelessly to cleanse the angels of their pagan origins. Whereas these origins are evident in the Old Testament and even at times in the New, as Bernard Teyssèdre demonstrated in *Anges, Démons, Cieux* (1986), Christianity gradually removed from angels their masculine attributes. But there were exceptions. One occurred when the Church was obliged to deal with the virile ethics of feudalism. "When Saint Anselm tried to describe [God's] all-powerful existence in the invisible world, he placed him at the pinnacle of a hierarchy of homage. The angels held fiefs granted by God; their conduct with regard to him was that of vassals . . ." (Duby 1981, p. 44). While the Church accommodated itself to the knights' warrior code, whose roots were in the pagan ancestry of its participants, it was hardly at ease with such principles. In the eleventh century knights were singled out as: "a group which, in the eyes of the Church leaders, appeared to be in a state of permanent aggression and responsible for all the disorder in the world. This group represented a danger to be warded off; its destructive powers were to be contained with the help of spiritual sanctions and the terrifying threat of divine wrath. . . . It was the knights of his own diocese whom bishop Jordan of Limoges excommunicated, cursing their weapons and their horses—that is, the instruments of their turbulence and the insignia of their social position. The stipulations of the Lord's peace were like a finger pointing to one group: the men who waged war" (Duby 1981, p. 37). And also, "Although knighthood camped in the midst of Latin Christendom and held it firmly in its grip, it was the monks who reigned supreme in the enormous spiritual realm of mental anguish and religious fear and trembling" (Duby 1981, p. 58). How better to see the conflict between the knights, whose religion was filled with virile gods, and the monks, whose ideal was to become like the now-Christianized angels?

To understand why virility is such a scarce quality among angels it is necessary first to have an idea of what masculinity is. Here we may refer to the institutions of knighthood to provide a frame for what will follow. Georges Duby has chronicled the uneasy coexistence of knighthood and the Church, and it is to him that we turn first to delineate these decidedly unangelic forms of behavior. "As a masculine society, knighthood was a society of heirs. The ties of kinship built its framework. The power of the living lords sprang from the glory of those who were dead, from the fortune and renown that the ancestors had bequeathed to their descendants like a sacred trust passed on from each generation to the next. . . . Even the most insignificant adventure-seeker claimed to have a valiant ancestor, and every knight felt himself drawn into action by the cohorts of the dead who had once made famous the name he bore and would demand a reckoning from him" (Duby 1981, p. 39). Contrary to the City of God, the culture of knighthood had no interest in peace. Virtues of valor, honor and courage, to say nothing of land and titles, were gained or lost in war and in contest, in activity that was marked by the eminently virile attribute of shedding blood.

Bloodshed is at the heart of the sacrificial rituals that determine human community; Burkert even suggested that the idea of action derives from the act of killing. "Sacrificial killing is the basic experience of the 'sacred'. *Homo religiosus* acts and attains self-awareness as *homo necans*. Indeed, this is what it means 'to act' . . ." (Burkert 1983, p. 3).

Another quality central to a masculine ethic is the value placed on the honor or dishonor brought to one's name. Linked to that was the importance of one's word, of one's sworn oath. "A knight who broke his sworn faith lost the right to hold his head high at assemblies of fellow warriors" (Duby 1981, p. 41). This represents a particular form of the speech act, one in which the speaker is bound no less inextricably than he is by his name. For a knight who broke his word, the question of motivation or the state of his soul was irrelevant. His good intentions could hardly have the salutary effect that they would have within a purely Christian culture. In other than Christian cultures an agreement between men, a sworn oath, was accompanied by blood sacrifice. "Whether in Israel, Greece, or Rome, no agreement, no contract, no alliance can be made without sacrifice. And, in the language of the oath, the object of aggression that is to be 'struck' and 'cut' becomes virtually identical with the covenant itself . . ." (Burkert 1983, p. 35).

There were no woman knights. The value of motherhood, so fervently adored by Churchmen, was not a preoccupation of the chivalric ethic. The two female figures that have a place within this culture are the damsel in distress and the lord's wife. It would appear that the exclusion of feminine values inside of the world of combat permitted those values to exist and flourish outside of it. It is here that the values of erotic love were imported into the civilization.

A second group of values was added when, at a very high social level, women began to emerge from their lowliness in the southwest of the kingdom of France at about 1100. The circles of men of war first of all had to admit the lord's wife, his lady. This involved the observance of new rules of courtly conduct, before which all knights alive to fame and honor henceforth had to bow. It also invented a new order of relationships between the sexes, in other words, Western love. War and love . . . It had first found expression in song, in *chansons de geste* and *chansons d'amour*. It also developed as a form of strategy, whether in order to rout an opponent or to win and retain the love of another's spouse. In either case, the plans were laid virtually at the outset, and took shape gradually, like a game. A game governed by rules, a game which entertained, but honorably. In other words, which strictly respected a code. (Duby 1981, p. 208)

Within a masculine culture femininity is valued. What appears to be devalued is the link between mother and son, the Madonna and Infant. No man became a knight through the work of his mother. The division of the sexes is defined clearly in the culture of knighthood, and the erotics of desire exists without the moralizing that it consistently receives in Christian tradition. None of this is coherent within a world in which a maternal space is inhabited by angelic beings.

Happily enough, references to angelic virility are found in none other than Dionysius the Areopagite. Few authors wrote so extensively on the angels and few were so thoroughly respected by the medieval Doctors; to the dismay of later Catholic writers, for if any "Christian" theologian in the history of angelology deserves to be called a wicked genie it is the pseudo-Dionysius. Here is an instance of angelic manliness as he described it: "In those who are deprived a reason anger, for example, is always born in a spirit of passion and in them the irascible movement is full of irrationality. When it is a question of intelligent beings, we must give this term a completely different sense. What is understood as anger is, I believe, there virile rationality, the power which is in them to conserve inflexibly the immutable imprint of the divine form" (Dionysius 1943, p. 192). The pseudo-Dionysius even has something to say about the angelic penis: "The penises indicate royal power, sovereignty, the rectitude with which they bring all things to their conclusion . . ." (Dionysius 1943, p. 240).

Our interest in the representation of virility by the pseudo-Dionysius must go beyond the texts to reach the drama involved in the choice of a pseudonym and in the acceptance of certain texts as quasi-canonical. His place is critical because on the one hand his influence is a major inspiration of the flourishing interest in angelology in the Middle Ages; on the other the discovery of the fraud is one of the basic reasons why you are not similarly preoccupied. Here is the story.

In the sixth century, texts supposedly authored by Dionysius the Areopagite were discovered. At first their authenticity was disputed in Constantinople, but they were later elevated to a position of authority through the efforts of Maximus Confessor in the seventh century and John Scotus Erigena in the ninth. In French, the name of Dionysius was Denys and he was the patron saint of the powerful monastery of Saint-Denys. The first to shed doubt on the identity of its patron saint was none other than Peter Abélard. "Abélard had won the lasting hatred of the monks at Saint-Denys because he was the first to question whether the 'Denys' whose relics they venerated was actually Dionysius the Areopagite, and had the courage to propose another *Theologia,* in opposition to the Areopagite" (Duby 1981, p. 116).

The authority of the texts was basically unchallenged until the time of the Reformation, when Luther delighted in the discovery of their fraudulence and used it to attack the opinions of the medieval Doctors. Sterile speculations about immaterial beings were for him a waste of time, and the fraud also offered him a way to attack the hierarchy of the

Church itself, since one of its rationales lay in the comparison Dionysius made between the celestial and ecclesiastical hierarchies. It was as though God had cast a blessing on the Lutheran enterprise. According to Nygren two Catholic scholars demonstrated in the nineteenth century that major portions of one of Dionysius' texts were plagiarized from the fifth-century Neoplatonist Proclus (Nygren 1982, pp. 576–57). This much is reasonably clear.

The problem is whether or not these texts were written by a Christian theologian, and thus whether the writings have theological value despite the confusion over their authorship. This bears on the question of whether Erigena and Aquinas really believed that the texts were authentic. It is hard to imagine that such exalted spirits were duped by a ruse that was so transparent to Martin Luther. And if they were, what does this tell us about the deleterious effects of their flirtation with pagan modes of thought? These are not minor issues.

What if Dionysius was who he claimed to be? The consequences are of interest. In the first place he would have been the first Christian theologian, and the questions that preoccupied him would have been of major theological interest. His place would have been that of father to the Church Fathers, and it would have been as though in the sixth century a first father had been discovered, thereby grounding a line of fathers whose authority was based on the discovery of an intellectual or spiritual forebear. The importance of Dionysius would have been genea-logical, or better, genie-logical. For a religion whose great theorists had renounced an earthly patrimony, the discovery of their spiritual father was of great moment, to say the least.

While the early Fathers of the Church were not influenced by Diony-sius, theology in the Middle Ages attempted to stake the legitimacy of its reflections on a Christian, not a pagan, philosopher, and much of the work on angels was then understood as claiming a filiation with this father. What then happens when this father is revealed to be an impos-ter, a fraud, a plagiarist? It is not so much that the medieval Doctors did not know of Neoplatonism, nor did they have any especial fear of pagan sources. Aquinas wrote in the *Treatise on Separate Substances* that the origins of Christian ideas about angels existed in Plato, Aristotle, Pro-clus, Porphyry, and so on, authors whose value was seen in their prefi-guring the truths of Christianity while remaining pagan. The power of the Word was such that its truth shone even through pagan texts. The problem was that none of these authors was ever claimed as a father in the spirit, a father in theology. The fact that one who was given such a place was revealed to be no such thing had the effect of casting dishonor on the medieval theological enterprise, in roughly the same way that a crime committed by a father dishonors the father's name and thereby his lineage.

Who was the pseudo-Dionysius, and why did he do what he did? Even if we assume that he was inspired by the best of Christian intentions, the fact that he claimed authority by adopting a pseudonym casts doubt on his intentions, revealing a "darker purpose." There are many candidates for the identity of the author of these works. Let us examine one. The distinguished philosopher Alexandre Kojève proposed that their real author was Damascius, a student of Proclus living in Syria. Kojève made his suggestion in a note to a long discourse on the last pagan philosopher, Proclus. His point, influenced certainly by Hegel, is that pagan philosophy died out under the weight of its own contradictions, the better to open the door to the eventual development of a truly Christian philosophy. He saw the beginning of this philosophy in Descartes and its culmination in Kant. This being the case, there is no small historical gap between Proclus and Descartes, and Kojève proposed that the last student of Proclus, Damascius, conceived the plan to lead Christian philosophers astray by proposing a series of misleading theological questions. He wrote: "[Damascius] recognized the impossibility both of getting beyond the System of Proclus within the framework of Paganism and of eliminating its contradictions. But he refused to believe that a new philosophy, transformable into a System of Knowledge, could be elaborated on the base of Christianity. Or, more exactly, he did not *want* to create it. And it is to make sure of this that he seems to have tried to imprison in advance the future Christian philosophy in sterilizing Proclean frames, in presenting to posterity the System of Proclus under the cover of an incontestable Christian authority, Dionysius the Areopagite" (Kojève 1973, pp. 526–27). If this is true then Damascius would represent a wicked genie more perverse than even Aristotle, and Descartes would be the first to surmount the problem he created.

There are a multitude of other conjectures. A brief summary by Maurice de Gandillac may be found in his introduction to *Oeuvres complètes du Pseudo-Denys l'aréopagite,* written in 1943. One of the more interesting theories declares that there existed in the fourth century a bishop named Dionysius who took the name Areopagite. The use of the name of the first Athenian convert would then be an act of sympathy and filiation (Dionysius 1943, p. 23) Other authors have suggested that in fact Proclus and Plotinus had themselves plagiarized from the works of the original Dionysius without ever mentioning him and without the works being known by anyone else. This can be refuted by showing references within the text to events that occurred after the death of Proclus, but at least the suggestion has the virtue of ingenuity (Dionysius 1943, p. 20). Others have opined that the author was really a Christian who chose a pseudonym to give value to his work. Even if we were to follow the suggestion of Kojève, whose value is its refined sense of intellectual history, we might also conjecture that the intention of the author—assuming that it corresponded to what Kojève believed—was not fulfilled, and that Damascius, while thinking that he was writing a series of essays that would sidetrack Christianity, managed to trick himself, thereby writing something that was perfectly consonant with the faith he reviled. For all we know Damascius was a Christian despite and unbeknown to himself. I present these alternate explanations to show how difficult it is to have a clear and distinct idea about the matter. I find the idea of Kojève to be most interesting, but I have hardly exhausted the debate.

Let us assume that the Dionysian canon represents a literary fraud of major proportions. Its author was certainly possessed of uncommon intelligence, for he saw that the flaw in the Christian enterprise concerned questions of authority and paternity. Christianity is based on the worship of a Son-God who put an end to the line of biblical fathers. Christ had no heirs in the human sense of the word, therefore everyone is called upon the become affiliated with him spiritually. Certainly this Son was also called a King; but he is never called a father. Does this place him below the Fathers of the Church? And what sense does it have to call men Fathers within a maternal space? Is their claim to a manly role thereby rendered specious? Pagan religions, which have far more of a right to claim a patriarchal structure, admitted the existence of priestesses. Is the failure to admit them in the Catholic Church a sign of the tenuousness of the priesthood's assertion of fatherhood?

Since Christ's Queen is also his mother, this does not lend credence to his claims to manliness. Kinship then came to be based on the strength and intensity of one's faith, and for the first Christians this was shown by the willlingness to become martyrs, the emulate the sacrifice of Christ. We are not in the world of a warrior code, of allegiance to one's family or one's name, but rather in a world where the trappings of masculinity were to be sacrificed for Christ.

How does this translate into the authority of sacred texts? Why within such a religion do written words, if they are considered to have been written by the right person, become absolute and incontrovertible truth? It is not a question of keeping one's word but of believing in one word, of living a life to make that word meaningful. Where reference is not established by proper naming the connection between meaning and the world must be rendered rigid. In that case the value of one's language is a function of one's passion, of one's affective state. If, however, the private language argument says that you can never know with certainty the sensations of another, it would appear that placing a text in direct relation to its author, making its value depend on the quality of passion and belief of the person who has produced it, attempts to circumvent this argument. When a community is formed not on the basis of kinship but on that of private sensation, there are considerable problems over who has the right sensations, and who is to know?

A son is not only named by a father but is obliged to appropriate that name through a parricidal act. Within the Oedipus complex there is a conflict between father and son; the son is called upon to replace the father, to become himself a father. In Christian theology the angel who attempted to usurp the role of God was defeated and banished, thereby creating empty places in the City of God. To occupy one of these places it is not necessary to act to vacate it; any such act would guarantee that one not be admitted. Grace is granted according to the quality of one's moral passion. Humans were at one time considered to be replacement angels; they were never given the role of agent removing an angel or a god from his place.

Perhaps, as Lacan suggested, Christians have always had something of a sacred horror about what was revealed to them (Lacan 1975, p. 103). This may have led to their attempting to paper over this horror with borrowings from pagan systems of thought or even to their assertion that the faith was something that one should not think about too much. The joy experienced by those who adore a crucified and resurrected god may well be a way of distracting oneself from what is really involved in the ultimate manifestation of divine charity. To ascertain this ultimate horror we do not have to go too far. The ultimate in human horrors is incest, and it is reasonably clear that this is what is in question in the Christian Revelation. And it is an incest in which the Son is not obliged to murder and replace the Father, but where he is granted his Mother as his bride as payment for not having had such intentions. Of course, if there is no Law and if there is no kinship system, the term *incest* would be out of place. Christ does not have to take his Mother from a jealous husband; his Father gives her to him as his eternal reward.

It is essential therefore that the structuring function of kinship not exist. In its absence the conflict and drama involved in the struggle between men for women ceases to exist. The masculinity of the gods of the Greek pantheon, however immoral, did affirm the existence of laws of kinship, even, or perhaps most especially, in their transgression. And yet the moral values represented by Zeus, Hermes, or the cults of Dionysus are very far from being palatable. They were not even palatable to Plato. No one would want his son to develop the unbridled lust of Zeus or to emulate his tendency to rape women who had excited his desire. Nor would even the most zealous partisans of communication want his son to be a second Hermes, a born thief and born liar, who slaughters the cattle of Apollo in a scene that reads like a rape-murder. Instead of the glowing pictures of Madonna and Infant, some of which are at the summit of Western art, the Homeric Hymn to Hermes presents the following picture of the acts of the infant Hermes, having gone out on this own:

> While the power of glorious Hephaistos was feeding the flame,
> Hermes, endowed with great strength, dragged out of the stable
> To a spot near the fire two lowing, crumpled-horned beasts,
> And threw them, both panting, down on their backs on the ground,
> And, rolling them over, forced back their heads and bored out their
> lives. (ll. 4.115–120)

This is unacceptable because we see in the deeds of gods and angels models for human behavior. The behavior of the Christian angels is supposed to be morally exemplary, worthy of imitation. So how did the Greeks know that they ought not to go out and act in society as Zeus or Hermes act within the context of a myth? The translation of the myth into reality might have involved ritual sacrifice, but not idealization and emulation. And these myths provided matter for fictions and fantasy; they rendered certain atrocious situations thinkable, and perhaps this is preferable to the idea that one ought to police one's thoughts to repel even the least hint of immoral thought. The motto from the temple at Delphi, "Know thyself," meant for the Greeks: Know that you are not a god (Burkert 1985, p. 148).

If you know that you are not a god, and if you know that the gods are not to be imitated, how do you communicate with them, how do you negotiate the distance that separates them from humans? To answer this question we will be obliged to address the difference between the type of communication represented by the Eucharist and the type represented by animal sacrifice. Certainly there are similarities between the two, but our emphasis will be on the differences. Between communing in a sacrifice to end all blood sacrifice and sacrificing another living victim, ingesting his remains, and offering him to the gods, there is something of a difference.

Given that the sacrifice of Christ is supposed to put an end to blood sacrifice, and given that in pagan religions blood sacrifice was an essential mode through which communication existed between the human and divine worlds, Christianity was obliged to offer a substitute ritual of connection. To appreciate some of the characteristics of blood sacrifice we read Walter Burkert: "The essence of the sacred act, which is hence often simply termed doing or making sacred or working sacred things, is in Greek practice a straightforward and far from miraculous process: the slaughter and comsumption of a domestic animal for a god" (Burkert 1985, p. 55). In distinction, the Eucharist is a miraculous event in which no animal is slaughtered, and in which the matter to be transubstantiated is necessarily vegetable, bread and wine (Aquinas ST, part 3, q. 74, art. 1). Also, in the Eucharist there is no sense of nourishment; one cannot make of the Eucharist a meal. The Eucharist thus is conceived to be spiritual food. "The difference between corporeal and spiritual food lies in this, that the former is changed into the substance of the person nourished, and consequently it cannot avail for supporting life except it be partaken of; but spiritual food changes man into itself. . . . the Eucharist is the sacrament of Christ's Passion according as a man is made perfect in union with Christ who suffered. . . . the Eucharist is termed the sacrament of charity" (Aquinas ST, part 3, q. 73, art. 3). Whereas in animal sacrifice the flesh of the animal is absorbed and incorporated into the one who consumes it, with the Eucharist the communicant becomes absorbed into Christ, into Christ's Passion, in which he participates through being united with it. Blood sacrifice, where the cutting of an actual body yields blood, involves an act, a murder sanctified as part of a ritual, serving both man and god. Nor is blood sacrifice related to charity; even though the animal to be sacrificed was thought to offer consent, the intention of saving all of mankind from sin is obviously excluded. Another difference becomes clear in the following passage from Burkert: "The sacrifice, it is known, creates a relationship between the sacrificer and the god; poets recount how the god remembers the sacrifice with pleasure or how he rages dangerously if sacrifices fail to be performed. But all that reaches to the sky is the fatty vapor rising in smoke; to imagine what the gods could possibly do with this leads unfailingly to burlesque" (Burkert 1985, p. 57). It is obvious that for Christians the position of the ones who enacted the sacrifice of Christ is not to be emulated; those who partake of the Eucharist do not identify with the position of the sacrificer. Historically, whoever has been identified as responsible for the murder of Christ has been condemned to the lowest circles of Hell. The place of one who acts, which we have little difficulty seeing as masculine, is excluded and condemned in the ritual of Communion. Also, for the Greeks the effectiveness of divine intervention is more of a day-to-day affair than it is in a religion where one final judgment is to be pronounced. Blood sacrifices were local, not universal, events. Specific rituals were performed for specific purposes in specific contexts—to assure a bountiful harvest—and not to gain a taste of the promise of the afterlife.

To discern with greater clarity the specificity of Christian sacrament we note the statement of Augustine: "The visible sacrifice is the sacrament, the sacred sign of the invisible sacrifice" (CG, book 10, chap. 5). Given that it is difficult to discern the private language of invisible sacrifice, it is necessary to have sacred signs that do not deceive. Blood sacrifice is a visible sacrifice, and it is not the sign of some other invisible soulful sacrifice. The distinction is clear for Augustine: "God does not want the sacrifice of a slaughtered animal, but he desires the sacrifice of a broken heart" (CG, book 10, chap. 5). He continued to make explicit the fact that sacrifice should be understood in terms of the signified, not in terms of its signifying form. "For if he had not wished the sacrifices he desires (and there is only one, the heart bruised and humbled in the sorrow of penitence) to be signified by those sacrifices which he was supposed to long for as if they gave him pleasure, then he would certainly not have prescribed their offering in the old Law. And the reason why they had to be changed, at the fitting and predestined time, was to prevent the belief that those things were objects of desire to God himself, or at least were acceptable gifts from us to him, and to make us realize that what God required was that which they signified" (CG, book 10, chap. 5). It is noteworthy that God's desire is that you be heartbroken and depressed.

In pagan religion each sacrificial offering involves removing an animal from the commerce of human affairs. And there are other sacrifices where the object is not a living organism. Concrete objects, sometimes alive, sometimes not, are removed from human commerce to serve as signifiers of the exchange between the two realms. Christianity effaces this by introducing the priority of the signified, identified as invisible. Since the realm of the invisible is taken to be the world of meanings, it is interesting that Aquinas addressed the question of what happens when the minister at the sacrament mispronounces the words that accompany the ritual. His point is that the sacrament is valid so long as the mispronunciation does not alter the sense of the words. "But if he do this through error or a slip of the tongue, and if he so far mispronounce the words as to deprive them of sense, the sacrament seems to be defective. This would be the case especially if the mispronunciation be in the beginning of the word, for instance, if one were to say *in nomine matris* instead of *in nomine Patris*. If, however, the sense of the words be not entirely lost by this mispronunciation, the sacrament is complete. This would be the case principally if the end of a word be mispronounced; for instance, if one were to say *patrias et filias*. For although the words thus mispronounced have no appointed meaning, yet we allow them an accommodated meaning corresponding to the usual forms of speech. And so, although the sensible sound is changed, yet the sense remains the same" (ST, part 3, q. 60, art. 7). Sense has priority over sound is also stated: "As Augustine says *(Tract. 80, sup. Joan.)*, the word operates in the sacraments *not because it is spoken*, i.e. not because of the outward sound of the voice, *but because it is believed* in accordance with the sense of the words which is held by faith. And this sense is indeed the same for all, though the same words as to their sound not be used by all" (ST, part 3, q. 60, art. 7).

Even though they must be accompanied by spoken words, Aquinas considered sacraments to be something like a printing process whereby the character or characters of Christ are imprinted on the soul of the recipient, as a seal. Answering the question of "whether a sacrament imprints a character on the soul," he replied: "But a character means nothing else than a kind of sealing. Therefore it seems that by the sacraments God imprints his character on us" (ST, part 3, q. 63, art. 1). And he offered a definition of his terms: "Some define character thus: *A character is a distinctive mark printed in a man's rational soul by the eternal Character, whereby the created trinity is sealed with the likeness of the creating and recreating Trinity, and distinguishing him from those who are not so enlikened, according to the state of the faith*" (ST, part 3, q. 63, art. 3). In the next article Aquinas specified that this imprinting of a character on the soul is effected through an image. An image or character may be cut into flesh, thereby to be visible, but here the point is that no cutting is involved. The emphasis on image suggests that this process is invoked as a way out of the implications of bloodshed. This is sustained by the fact that the imprinting of characters through the sacrament of the Eucharist does not involve the slaughter of flesh; it does not involve any flesh at all. We take into account here the distinction offered by Bernard Teyssèdre between the proper name as an injury producing a scar, which occurs with certain demons or evil spirits, and the proper name as a seal, which pertains to angels (Teyssèdre 1986, p. 135).

The character imprinted on the soul of the faithful confers a moral identity, we may even say a moral character; this is in opposition to a theory that would mark the body of the bearer of the name, and would mark it differently according to sex. If the basis for the communication between the human and the divine is not an identification through images, if it is based on a ritual that cuts a piece of skin from the male sexual organ, thereby marking it visibly, then this ritual in itself divides the sexes. If naming has something to do with bloodshed, then the association of the loss of virginity with the reception of a new name would provide a ritual through which women were thought to receive names.

I am proposing that the Greek ritual of blood sacrifice has more in common with the speech act, and that it derives from a culture in which the unique value of the speech act is recognized. The conception of sacraments as imprinting derives from a culture in which both Scripture and ideas or thoughts are considered to have priority to speech. Thus Augustine privileged consistently a mode of communication that by-passes the signifying element of language, its phonetic materiality, its performing an action. The model he invoked is the speech of God to the angels: "And God does not speak to the angels in the same way as we speak to one another, or to God, or to the angels, or as the angels speak to us. . . . God's speech . . . precedes his action as the changeless reason of the action itself; and his speaking has no sound, no transitory noise; it has a power that persists for eternity and operates in time" (CG, book 16, chap 6). What Augustine held against the signifier was its transitory quality; it is not permanent like a written text and therefore does not easily lend itself to becoming dogma. Augustine was well aware of the fact that pagan societies were oral cultures, whereas the Judeo-Christian tradition privileged the written book over the speech act. He was obliged to argue the priority of writing, of the teaching of letters, as the basis for the claim that the wisdom of the Bible antedates that of the pagan divinities and philosophers (CG, book 18, chap. 39).

The Eucharist is the celebration of a blood sacrifice, but it does not involve the act of sacrificing in the sense of killing, cutting, or consuming flesh. The sacrifice of Christ is miraculously rendered present for the communicant, but it does not actually happen in the time of the perfor-mance of the ritual. The Crucifixion was a once-and-for-all event; the Eucharist is its remembrance. Certainly words are spoken during the sacrament, but these words are read aloud from a written text. While they do not have to be textually exactly the same as what is written, they must retain the sense of the original. I would suggest that the commu-nion taking place in a Church is closer to a theatrical representation of a sacrifice than a sacrifice itself. In the theatre you may well have some-thing that the spectator believes to be bloodshed through a ritual killing, but no one is actually killed at the time. If there is in fact a murder, it is not theatre, and not a sacrifice, but rather a crime.

Spoken words are heard when they are spoken. Listening is a part of the same situation as the speaking. Writing, however, provides the ines-timable advantage of your not having to come face-to-face with your listener. For a philosophical view of the place of speech in Plato and Aristotle we turn to Hintikka's *Time and Necessity:*

. . . in some obvious though elusive sense the Greek culture was largely based on the *spoken* and not on the *written* word. . . . If the spoken word is primary in relation to the written word, one is apt to think of and discuss logical and semantical matters from the vantage point of some situation in which the words in question are actually uttered. Now this situation supplies what is missing from a temporally indefinite sentence itself; it enables us to know what the moment of time actually is to which the spoken word "now" refers. . . . In a written text such words as "now" and "at the present moment" are indeterminate in a sense in which they are not indeterminate as a part of actual speech. . . . It is also remarkable that in some unacknowledged sense the spoken word was for Plato and Aristotle even logically prior to the thoughts it expresses. (Hintikka 1973, pp. 88–90).

We suggest that when certain words are pronounced at the moment when an actual sacrifice is taking place, those words have a determinate or definite reference. When, however, words are pronounced in memory of a sacrifice in a situation where the transubstantiation of bread and wine into body and blood is invisible, they have an indeterminate reference that only the faith of the communicant, the intentions of the priest, and the invisible gift of grace can render determinate. The sacrament of the Eucharist might then be considered a making of indefinite sentences definite. "In a written culture the replacement of temporally indefinite sentences by definite ones is more important than in an oral culture—to the extent that it might appear to its philosophers as the only 'correct' course" (Hintikka 1973, p. 89).

A list of the horrors of masculinity is easily assembled from stories about the Greek gods. It requires no great perspicacity to see that a denunciation of such practices is extremely appealing to civilized people. There are no more salable commodities than peace and love. And yet, it would appear manifestly unfair to say that the quality of moral evil is identical with masculinity, with acts that are the stuff of men's fantasies. If we continued on this path we would risk obscuring the amount of evil attributed in the tradition to women. The difference, however, is that there is a moral limit to their sin. Their sin is not their possession of a phallic appendage but their commerce with one. "The fact is that there comes a time when the vilest of women grow tired of the crowds of lovers they have acquired to gratify their sensuality; and in the same way the debauched soul which has prostituted itself to filthy spirits takes the greatest delight in the multiplication of gods before whom to fall and offer itself for defilement, but in the end comes disgust." (CG, book 7, chap. 24). To Augustine a mother who was honored by rituals involving bloodshed, who was supposed to promote virility, was the ultimate abomination. Given women's natural propensity to virtue, their indulgence in vice was the Supreme Evil. A believer in the integrity of the body, he had no idea that castration had to do with virility.

The Great Mother surpassed all the gods, her sons, not by reason of the greatness of her divine power but in the enormity of her wickedness. Even the monstrosity of Janus is nothing to this monster. Janus was merely hideous in his images; the Great Mother displayed hideous cruelty in her ceremonies. He had stone effigies with added members; she had living men with their organs mutilated. This was a degradation that outdid all the carnal excesses of Jupiter himself. He was a great seducer of women; but he only once disgraced heaven with a Ganymede, whereas all those professed and public perverts of hers were a defilement to the earth and an insult to heaven. In this kind of obscene cruelty we might perhaps find Saturn a match for her, or even her superior; for he, the story says, castrated his father. But in the rites of Saturn men could be slain by the hands of others; they were not gelded by their own hands. . . . the Great Mother of the gods introduced eunuchs even in the temples of Rome. And she kept up this savage custom, since it was supposed that she increased the virility of the Romans by depriving these men of their manhood. (CG, book 7, chap. 26)

Next to this passage we place the following words of Christ: "For there are eunuchs who have been so from birth, and there are eunuchs who have been made eunuchs by men, and there are eunuchs who have made themselves eunuchs for the sake of the kingdom of heaven" (Matthew 19:12).

Invoking the words of Christ here may well be considered to be the ultimate in cheap shots. Certainly Origen took them literally and so to speak to heart, but Origen was not very well-considered by theologians who followed him. In any case, the text of Augustine does invoke a horror over castration; does this have anything to do with the horror of incest as revealed in Christ? Among the things that Augustine reviled was first the place of the Great Mother, not necessarily the most powerful of the gods, but the consummate figure of wickedness. While Catholicism did eventually make the Virgin the consummate figure of goodness, it did not promote a female deity as the queen of Hell.

In psychoanalysis the sense of the castration complex is that the male sexual organ, raised to its signifying prowess, does not function as a part of the body. Of course, a eunuch is lacking in testicles, not a penis, and this does not mean that he cannot have erections or engage in sexual acts. As Luther said: "Yes, indeed, eunuchs are more ardent than anyone else, for the passion doesn't disappear, only the power" (Luther 1967, p. 176). There have been times when eunuchs were very highly valued as lovers. Eunuchs might thus resembles those phallic devils whose bodies could not produce semen. In other words, Freud's use of the term castration is not inappropriate. But even if the point of becoming a eunuch is to render sexual service, it is still clear that this practice does not make one a man among men. Perhaps this is how these practices promoted, in the minds of the Romans, masculinity. They showed that masculinity is not comprised by sexual behavior and that it is subverted by worship of a Mother Goddess.

These men who made themselves eunuchs for the worship of the Great Mother are then taxed with effeminacy, a quality that Augustine finds monumentally disgusting. The revulsion over male homosexuality is consistent within the Judeo-Christian tradition. It would be interesting to argue that this masks a condemnation of masculinity, for we may note, as Donald Symons did in *The Evolution of Human Sexuality* (1979), that male homosexual behavior has much in common with male heterosexual behavior. Or else, to be testy, we might say that the revulsion over effeminacy masks an equal horror about femininity in women. There is nothing that leads us to believe that femininity is the private property of women, any more than virility is the unique possession of men.

One doubts, however, that Augustine would have believed that men who eschew carnal relations with women are necessarily effeminate. From his point of view there must be a major difference between those who geld themselves and those who embrace the celibate life. The difference cannot be understood in terms of the production of offspring, as the effect in that context would be identical. Thus we are obliged to see a distinction on the level of bloodshed. The self-mutilation of the priests of the Great Mother involves bloodshed, whereas the renunciation of sexuality on the part of priests and monks, to the extent that it was actually practiced at that time, was bloodless.

The second difference is that the vow of celibacy does not affect the reproductive potential of the individual who takes it. It requires for its maintenance the active resolve of the soul of the celibate; this quality could well be absent in the case of the castrati. Thus being castrated in fact could lead to every sort of debauchery. The value of semen might be that its ejaculation causes phallic detumescence. In addition, castration is a very effective means of contraception; thus it is an affront to a fertility god. For Augustine men are really men when they place their sex in the service of female reproductive potential.

The contrast with Greek ritual practice is striking for its connection between castration and the phallus. "The ritual reparation corresponding to ritual castration evidently consisted of an especially striking, provocative custom. A single phallus was set up for worship and carried through the city as if in triumph" (Burkert 1983, p. 69). And while scholars have sought to label these processions "fertility rites," Burkert disagreed: "The act which alone produces fruit, that is, the union of male and female, is precisely what the phalluses do not indicate: they do not stand with their heads in the earth but, rather, upright. They are 'erected,' 'aroused,' impressive rather than reproductive" (Burkert 1983, p. 70).

In psychoanalytic theory castration is thought of in terms of a symbolic punishment inflicted on a boy as the price of his incestuous desire for his mother. The consequence is that his contribution to the production of a child is not comprised by sexual material; he becomes a father by the act of naming his child, of marking him symbolically. And his sexual experience will be defined in terms other than those of fertility. What happens, then, when the incest is not intended but is real? The transmission of names is arrested because the Law that founds it has been violated and the mother in question is rendered whole. The son becomes her phallic appendage and refuses to look at another woman. The key to this formulation appears to be that the mother is not lacking a phallus; thus what Freud called the real support of castration phantasies is lost. The genitals of the son remain intact but are not allowed to serve any function in relation to women. And the same son will remain always and eternally a son; he will never accede to the position of father, in the real or the symbolic. We remember that there is nothing in theology to suggest that Christ ever had erections.

Christianity has not done very well with the question of masculinity. It has tended to denounce most of what would be considered in other cultures as manly, without providing a very interesting or compelling substitute. The question of manliness is simply left to the side, to the side of the devils and pagans. The first family of the New Testament does not provide an adequate mythic representation of the issue. The idea that a father would allow his son to be sacrificed does tell us something about fathers and sons, but perhaps the element of sacrifice is simply a way of obscuring not only the question of that son's childlessness, but also his categorical refusal to interact with women in terms of desire. The celebration of the son's passion opens a way to the condemnation of masculinity, but also of femininity.

Perhaps with masculinity it is not so much the dying out of seed that is at issue, but rather the dying out of a name. If a name is not transmitted, it is thereby made into something that one possesses oneself, to make of it what one will; this is called making a name for oneself. To worship a name is not the same thing as to transmit it to one's progeny. I doubt that most of us have a very strong sense of the horror that accompanies the death of a name, of its being dishonored, but would that not be symptomatic of the values our civilization cherishes? Certainly no name is transmitted without there being the reproduction of the organism. And yet, the process of naming represents the transformation of something that exists merely as living organism into a human being whose place in discourse is marked by a proper name. This name will find its ultimate inscription on a tombstone. Of course, to discuss the issue of masculinity merely in relation to linguistic processes is not entirely adequate either. It is impossible to gain an adequate grasp of the issues merely on the level of language. What is required is a visual representation of the workings of language, and perhaps it is this visual representation that is presented by the stories of the Greek gods and in the drama and action of ritual blood sacrifice. The purpose of the stories would not then be to provide exemplars of virtuous behavior, but rather to permit humans to recognize the extent to which their actions are determined by the signifier.

The division of the sexes is often conceptualized in terms of activity and passivity. Such a division is not adequate to masculinity because it leaves to the side the question of naming; active and passive are functions of verbs, not names. The extent to which the verb is primary in both Jewish and Christian readings of Scripture is shown in the practice of anagogy. Even a cursory reading of one of the first and most influential practitioners of this way of reading, Philo of Alexandria, shows the constant reduction of proper names to their meanings. The stated purpose is to translate dramatic action into invisible realities. The tendency to eliminate the element of drama is also seen in the transformation of pagan gods into Christian angels.

In Greek drama the horrors we recoil from are rendered more acute for being inscribed in the kinship system. The best-known example is that of Oedipus: in particular his marriage is not in itself a criminal act. It becomes a horror when Oedipus discovers his identity, not in the sense that he arrives at any sort of self-possession, but when he discovers who his parents are. The question posed by the marriage of Christ and his mother is whether in a world in which there is no incest taboo or no names such an act is in itself a crime. The answer is that if it were not, why would anyone worship the son who had achieved it? To those who would assert that the name Oedipus is composed of words meaning swollen and foot, we reply that this does not aim at any invisible reality, but rather it points directly at the way in which his being named marks his flesh. It is bad enough that Oedipus is the murderer of Laius; his pursuit of the identity of the murderer does not make of him a common criminal. Inscribed within the systems of kinship and naming, his acts become an uncommon monstrosity. Everything that he had is instantaneously taken from him. Similarly, Hermes is not accused for the act of roasting a couple of cattle; the gravity of the act depends on the identity of the cattle's owner Apollo, his half-brother, whose age makes him old enough to be the infant god's father. The crime of theft, as opposed to murder and sexual acts, seems to be essentially related to naming, especially as to name is to mark or even to brand. Without the idea of marking one's possessions there is no such thing as theft. If whatever bears a proper name is thereby marked, this tells us that because he has a name a human being does not possess himself.

The first man to be marked in the Bible is the first-begotten human son, Cain. If the mark is something like a scar, indelible, that remains with the bearer without regard to whatever changes do or would occur in his life, it may represent the function of rigid designation in proper naming. Masculinity is the drama of proper naming. As Howard Bloch remarked astutely in a discussion of *Le Conte du Graal*: "Perceval's quest for knighthood is, at bottom, a quest for the father that is indistinguishable from a quest initially for the proper names of the father's profession and, ultimately for his own proper name. The drive toward mastery of the signs of chivalry uncovers bit by bit the traces of a lineage scattered—by the dispersion (the dissemination) associated with the Wasteland itself—throughout the Arthurian countryside" (Bloch 1986b, p. 206). And Bloch also stated that the way to masculinity in the medieval epic must pass through an unlearning of the lessons of a mother who seeks to keep her son at a distance from his father's name. "*Le Conte du Graal* is, in effect, an upside-down *Bildungsroman,* one in which learning is essentially a process of unlearning—an undoing of the obfuscating signs of the mother, her 'protective' *sens,* and, eventually, of the teaching of the spiritual father, Gornemanz. Even once Perceval's mother has accepted the inevitable attraction of knighthood, her instructions are no less misleading, no less productive of the series of misreadings that can be said to shape Chrétien's tale" (Bloch 1986b, p. 204).

A biblical text that not only concerns naming explicitly but also presents an exemplary instance of angelic virility tells of a wrestling match between Jacob and an angel. The specific virility of this angel alerts us to the fact that we may be in the presence not so much of a traditional angel, but rather of a pagan spirit who has not sufficiently well shaken off his kinship with the genii whose task is to guard specific places, to interdict access by strangers (Teyssèdre 1986, p. 15). This angel is not a messenger or minister and does not appear to be a servant of God. Also, he is not allowed to see the sunlight, in marked distinction to other angels who spend their time bathing in the Divine Light. Teyssèdre compared him to a ghost, the phantom of a lost people who had inhabited the country before Israel (ibid.). Jacob thought he was God.

The story of Jacob revolves around deception, ruses, and theft. To become the heir of Isaac, Jacob disguises himself as his brother Esau, lies about his identity, and receives his father's blessing. This blessing is like a mark: once given, even under manifestly false conditions, it cannot be retracted. Next, Jacob is deceived by his father-in-law Laban to take as his first wife Leah, sister of the woman he has worked for seven years to have, Rachel. Once Jacob has sex with Leah, thinking her to be Rachel, he is married to Leah; she is his wife because she has been marked by him. This does not prevent Jacob from marrying Rachel also, nor do these marriages prevent him from producing children with the servants of his wives. While the tradition of having a child with a servant dates to the first patriarch, bigamy is not ordinarily considered moral by the Bible. A further well-known deception is that of Jacob's sons, who through the ruse of the blood-stained coat of many colors convince the patriarch that his best-loved son, Joseph, has been killed. These events should serve as a frame for the encounter between Jacob and the angel. The struggle takes place after Jacob has dispossessed his brother of his blessing and has left the service of his father-in-law. He is in a state of anxiety over an imminent encounter with his stronger elder brother.

Here is the story in the Anchor Bible translation:

In the course of that night he got up and, taking his two wives, the two maidservants, and his eleven children, he crossed the ford of the Jabbok. After he had taken them across the stream, he sent over all his possessions. Jacob was left alone. Then some man wrestled with him until the break of dawn. When he saw that he could not prevail over Jacob, he struck his hip at its socket, so that the hip socket was wrenched as they wrestled. Then he said, "Let me go, for it is daybreak." Jacob replied, "I will not let you go unless you bless me." Said the other, "What is your name?" He answered, "Jacob." Said he, "You shall no longer be spoken of as Jacob, but as Israel, for you have striven with beings divine and human, and you have prevailed." Then Jacob asked, "Please tell me your name." He replied, "You must not ask my name." With that he bade him good-bye there and then. Jacob named the site Peniel, meaning, "I have seen God face-to-face, yet my life has been preserved." For the sun rose upon him just as he passed Peniel, limping on his hip. This is why to this day the children of Israel do not eat of the sciatic muscle that is on the hip socket, inasmuch as Jacob's hip socket was stricken at the sciatic muscle. (Genesis 32:23–33).

The angel appears in the form of a man, perhaps so as not to frighten Jacob. And Jacob considers his experience to be a struggle with God; Peniel is the Hebrew for "the face of El or God." Here he is not specifically called an angel, but the meaning is clear; when the story is recounted in Hosea 12, the word angel is used. What does the angel represent? Rashi, the greatest of the medieval exegetes, suggested after the rabbinical opinion that the angel was the guardian angel of Esau. And yet a sufficient number of the elements of this story are repetitions of the scene in which Jacob tricked his father, Isaac, into giving him his blessing, thus passing to him the rights of the first-born son, for us to offer a reading in which the angel represents a paternal and not a fraternal figure. This Rashi confirmed when he glossed the demand for a blessing: "Confirm for me the blessings with which my father blessed me, for Esau, is contesting them." And he stated that the meaning of the name change is: "It will no longer be said that the blessing came to you through insinuation and deceit, but through prevailing and openly." In this reading the repetition of the scene with Isaac is required because Jacob received the first blessing dishonestly, by declaring that his name was not Jacob but Esau. A second reason may be that the first deception of Jacob was instigated by his mother, Rebecca, and throughout that scene Jacob is described as boyish. Additionally, Jacob did not perform the act that was required by Isaac; he did not go out to hunt and did not prepare the meal his father had requested. Those acts were performed by his mother. His becoming a man through the intercession of his mother compromises his sexual identification. No boy becomes a man because a woman makes him one.

The structure of receiving a blessing thus comports two acts: deception and struggle. That the blessing be given directly according to the father's intention is excluded. In fact, as Roland Barthes noted, the blessing that the angel gives to Jacob is not only not freely given, it is given in response to a demand that resembles blackmail: the angel is obliged to give a blessing in exchange for his freedom (Barthes 1977, p. 138). We may still ask whether Jacob prevails. The text does not say so precisely; what it does say is that the angel could not prevail and therefore rendered Jacob lame by touching his hip joint. The disjointing of his leg represents a castration, providing access to the symbolic phallus. This is represented in the text by the image of Jacob limping away in the light of the rising sun. The rising of the phallus follows upon a violation of the body's integrity. The phallus is gained through a struggle with a father and the injury incurred is like a badge of courage. It is not a sign of passionate suffering or love.

Is the price of "victory" a dismemberment? This appears to have more in common with scarification than with imprinting, especially insofar as it forms the basis for a culinary taboo. The idea of the taboo suggests that the muscle belongs to the god and that the phallus is not of the same substance as other bodily flesh. If the sexual organ seeks nothing more than the pleasure of ejaculation, the phallus, meaning the organ raised to a symbolic function, has other things in mind. Masculinity is based on the fact that the phallus represents a link with something other than the body proper. We may even say that this body in its unmarked state owes its allegiance to the mother who engineered the first deception. The question then is the passage from boyhood to manhood. The first theft of the blessing was the work of a boy disguised as a man; this is obvious in the idea that the fair-skinned Jacob is disguised then as the more hirsute Esau. The second theft of the angel's blessing was the work of a man . . . up to a point.

If this structure renders the accession to manhood, it is not clear why Jacob has to be renamed. Ordinarily, a boy who becomes a man does not receive a different name. Jacob's original deception was unmanly; instigated by a woman, it placed a mother's desire above a father's. It was not unmanly for being deceptive, but rather because he did not do it in his own name. Thus it had to be repeated, and the strange thing about the repetition is that for having succeeded in his own name Jacob is given a new name. He does not end by being able to say "I, Jacob," but rather, "I, Israel." The events following this struggle, revolving around the cruel hoax about the death of Joseph, are not very encouraging. So whereas there are in this story and in other incidents in the life of Jacob clear elements of manliness, there is something else going on that is more difficult to discern.

The drama of the proper name takes place around the hole of a missing enjoyment. Is the enjoyment missing from a face-to-face encounter between father and son feminine? If that is true, manliness exists in the exclusion of the feminine. It is excluded that a son know his father through an affective tie, and it is because the enjoyment of a face-to-face encounter does not exist that the son can become a father only by replacing his father.

When Jacob steals a blessing intended for Esau he does not confront his father. More importantly, he does not perform the act of murder ordered by the father to provide food, perhaps a displacement for a patricidal wish. When Abraham is instructed to make of his son Isaac a sacrificial offering, God's last-minute intervention prevents this act from occurring. However, this does not erase the necessity to perform a sacrifice. In place of Isaac a ram is sacrificed by Abraham.

Jacob capitalizes on his father's blindness, on his flaw, and in so doing he inherits his father's failure. And that failure will be translated in his case into the idea of having seen God. Thus, like his father asking him his name, Jacob will ask of the angel his name. Perhaps this tells us that when Jacob presented himself under an assumed identity, taking credit for an act he did not perform, he did not address his father as a father. And if an important aspect of Jacob's original deception is that he does not hunt the animal (he gathers it from the flock) or prepare the festive dish, he does not in the encounter with the angel perform any sacrificial act.

The transmission of a proper name between father and son occurs because a face-to-face encounter does not. And yet, Jacob will walk away from his struggle offering an interpretation to the effect that he has seen God face-to-face. Has he thereby missed the point?

Jacob's asking the angel his name is not a simply repetition of the scene with Isaac. The angel replies with a prohibition, saying "You must not ask my name." Here the angel pronounces a prohibition, the No of the Law, from which Jacob concludes that he has seen God face-to-face. He invests the event with meaning, and that meaning asserts that faced with a prohibition against knowing the name of the being he has encountered, he knows that what he has seen is God. This seems to imply not exactly an equivalent level of familiarity, but something that may be even better than what has been prohibited.

Rashi saw angels saying the following: "We have no permanent name, our names are changed entirely according to the command of the service of the mission on which we are sent." This is a significant idea in the theory of naming. The angel does not have a name that designates him rigidly in all possible worlds. His name is a function of his activity; it is closer to a description. Let us say that the transformation of a genie into an angel has everything to do with the prohibition against the pronunciation of the Name of God. Rather than have a local genie who is part of a local drama and whose name is a signifier connected with other signifiers, we have a God who is the one and only God, for whom all other gods become angelic servants. The unspeakable name is not connected with other names; thereby, it becomes a sign, representing something for someone. The prohibition against pronouncing that name leads to the conception of a deity that is omnipresent, not in his desire but in the promised enjoyment of namelessness. This episode contains the first biblical mention of seeing God face-to-face, an experience that was later to become proper to angels, so we will dwell upon it.

What does Jacob see? And is the faculty of sight the key to this encounter? In the first place, Jacob sees someone who resembles a man; he wrestles with that man. After hearing the angel's response to his question, Jacob concludes that he has seen God face-to-face and miraculously has survived the encounter. There are other ways of reading this. In one the son is called upon to perform an act, as is Esau, and that act of sacrifice, with the animal being a representative of the god, would not be complete if the animal survived it. It would be miraculous if the man, having failed to perform the sacrifice, were allowed to survive. Perhaps this is the sense of being forgiven a failure by this God. It is not so clear why this is equivalent to seeing God face-to-face—unless, of course, the immediate knowledge of the divinity is the only condition in which the failure to communicate by sacrificial offerings would be acceptable.

Before examining the Mosaic treatment of the idea of seeing God face-to-face, we counter the Judeo-Christian reading with a description of pagan encounters with gods. Here is a summary offered by Robin Lane Fox:

Pagans kept nightly company with their gods and those who sported in dreams with Aphrodite needed no new route to heaven. Among pagans, these "visits" were freely enjoyed, and there was no restraining orthodoxy, no priestly authority which restricted the plain man's access to a nightly contact with the gods. Art and the long centuries of literature had combined with myth and the general setting of its stories to contain these visions in harmless traditional forms. Their beneficiaries took no stand against authority and did not claim to know better than their civic leaders in the matter of pleasing the gods. The divine dreams of Artemidorus and his friends sounded no call for reform or orthodoxy and took no interest in history. In Artemidorus's sample, they were not concerned to take men on a tour of the next world or to menace them with fears of what might happen after death. (Lane Fox 1986, p. 165)

After Jacob, it is Moses who is said most often to have seen God face-to-face. Examining several passages leads to textual difficulties. In Exodus 33:11: "Thus the Lord used to speak to Moses face-to-face, as a man speaks to his friend." If we assume that speaking and seeing are not the same, the following passage from the same chapter (Exodus 33:21–22) will not be contradictory: "And the Lord said: 'Behold there is a place by me where you shall stand upon the rock; and while my glory passes by I will put you in a cleft of the rock, and I will cover you with my hand until I have passed by; then I will take away my hand, and you shall see my back; but my face shall not be seen." Next to this we should consider the following from Deuteronomy 34:10–11: "And there has not arisen a prophet since in Israel like Moses, whom the Lord knew face-to-face, none like him for all the signs and wonders which the Lord sent him to do in the land of Egypt, to Pharaoh and his servants and to all his land, and for all the mighty power and all the great and terrible deeds which Moses wrought in the sight of all Israel." The question raised in these passages concerns whether seeing God and speaking with God are the same or different. Jacob does not speak with any sort of familiarity with the angel and is not told his name. From this he concludes that he has seen God, but how could he have seen clearly at night? Whereas among pagans it was a common occurrence to see gods, to be in their presence, in the Bible a very precious few are granted the experience. And we know that when Moses descended from Sinai with the tables of the Law the sight of his face was intolerable to his people. "When Moses came down from Mount Sinai with the two tables of the testimony in his hand as he came down from the mountain, Moses did not know that the face of his skin shone because he had been talking with God. And when Aaron and all the people of Israel saw Moses, behold, the face of his skin shone, and they were afraid to come near him" (Exodus 34:29–30). Does this say that Moses saw God or does it say that he spoke with him, an event sufficiently momentous in itself? Here it appears that the experience is one of speech and that this experience marks Moses, not in the sense of cutting, but in that of illuminating. And it is certainly significant that the experience is not transmissible or repeatable. Assuming that the ultimate enjoyment is not missing for Moses, it is barred to everyone else. We may ask whether an experience that is not repeatable actually happened or whether something of the experience itself has been occluded, obscured, forgotten in order that it not happen again? Those who do not speak with God are obliged to read his commandments as they are written.

In *Moses and Monotheism* Freud proposed that the events recounted in the Bible do not represent what actually happened (Freud SE, vol. 23). His idea was that Moses was an Egyptian who chose the Jewish people and adopted them as his own. Later he was murdered by them and a religion was founded on the repression of the event. This reading has been highly disputed. At the least it recommends that the events recounted in the text are not the ones that actually occurred, and that is the question that concerns us. It concerns us in terms of the question of whether all narratives have the same value and the same claim to truth. Clearly Freud believed that they do not.

What then really happened in the face-to-face encounter of Moses and God on Mount Sinai? We assume that the state of Moses' face argues for a face-to-face encounter, that only the vision of God could have produced the awesome quality of his countenance. At the same time, it is

not so clear that such a sight is possible, the opinion of Jacob notwith-
standing, and perhaps it simply means that Moses spoke with God.
Within a Freudian theory the identification of Moses with God may have
another cause, that of incorporation in the sense of devouring the body
of the murdered father. Perhaps the connection between speaking and
eating, most evident in eating disorders, finds its structure here. Is the
shift from face-to-face speech to reading a written law an indication of a
will to repress? Where men renounce the primal event, perhaps women
find themselves in the position of bringing the repression to their attention. Did Moses on Mount Sinai commit acts of patricide and cannibal-
ism? And does it make any difference? It is of course difficult to know
with any certainty. If the Eucharist is a repetition of such an act, it does
make a difference that it retains, as Freud wrote, only the affectionate
and not the aggressive meaning (SE, vol. 23, p. 87). The aggressive side
is retained in God's extensive instructions for blood sacrifice in Exodus
29. It is to reject this that the emphasis is shifted to the idea of beatific
vision.

From a Christian point of view the biblical narrative recounts what
might have happened had there not been an act of patricide. The narrative presents us with a possible world, but it is not just any event that is
occluded by the narrative. Another way of saying this is to assert that
the narrative presents a world where the incest taboo was not pronounced. Not only is a prohibition against incest not one of the Ten
Commandments, but we have it on the authority of Augustine that a
literal reading of Genesis makes it that all marriages are incestuous. Is
this a possible world? We are obliged to answer that it is not, for if it
were there would be no narratives and no proper naming. The conclusion we draw is that it is only through the act of speech, through the
part of it that is not reducible to writing and that is not acknowledged
by reading, that recognition of the founding event is granted and gained.

The cutting of the body that occurs in proper naming has its support in
the phonetic specificity of the signifier. While a proper name can be
written differently in languages with different systems of writing, its
phonetic specificity will generally remain constant. The name must be
spoken, and it is the act of dubbing that inscribes a visible marking of
the body. The body is the site in which language hooks onto the world
through the function of the proper name. The interwining of language

and a human being produces a mark on the body, and this mark shows that the human is subjected to the proper name. This marking is a making visible of the invisible, which permits a human being to navigate in whatever situations he might find himself, to couple his name with the name of the place. The cut made by the proper name is more a scar than the impression of a seal because it is not readable in the sense of having a meaning; rather it identifies the subject to himself and others. The enjoyment that is supposedly experienced in the ability to see through words to their meanings is interdicted with the proper name. To make God's proper name unspeakable is to render him the center of an unspeakable enjoyment, what Lacan, playing on words, called, *jouis-sens,* and which has been well translated *enjoy-meant.*

It is not the invisibility of meanings that is rendered visible, but rather the invisibility of the phonetic or signifying material of language. Given that a group of intermediary beings is invisible, this does not necessarily make them correspond to meaning. Signifiers as phonetic material constitute the intermediary world. To go from there to the concretions of meaning requires the introduction of the function of writing. The signifier is meaningful when it is punctuated, when, and Lacan said, it is written or conceived as written (Lacan 1975, chap. 3). In an oral culture these signifiers are called gods and demons; they are engaged in dramatic interactions with others of their kind and with humans. The meaning of those actions fluctuates as the stories, in being retold, undergo shifts. The Bible, representing one meaning fixed forever in one written text, reduces the functioning of the phonetic in favor of the written.

One problem that arises with the issue of proper names is why the function of naming should be so consistently identified as a masculine prerogative. Why is it that naming is connected with circumcision in the Jewish religion, thereby excluding female children not from having a name, but from transmitting their name to their offspring? Why should it be that a woman's receiving a name from her husband is connected with the ritual of marriage, whereby she would be marked in a way that is clearly different? And what happens when naming is identified not with circumcision but with baptism, as Christianity and many modern theorists of proper naming insist on doing?

To say that a man is marked by his name means that he is tied to it, inextricably. The idea of marking may be conceptualized in terms of knotting. Having a name comports not an accession to some sort of vision of blessedness, but an ethical obligation to bring honor to the name, thus honor to one's father and to those who also bear the same name. In effect, seeing of God face-to-face represents a moral failure to act to bring honor to one's name, to transmit one's name, this in the interest of contemplating an essence that lies beyond human naming. Immediately following the encounter between Jacob and the angel we read a chapter on the rape of Dinah. To revenge the rape Simeon and Levi, Dinah's brothers, Jacob's sons, persuade the men of the offending community to be circumcised so that Dinah can be married to the man who had raped her and who now wants to marry her. While the men are recovering from the operation Simeon and Levi massacre all the males of the community and the other sons of Jacob plunder the city and take the women and children as captives. This is vengeance, not justice; it is a conspicuous example of overkill. Through it all Jacob himself is inactive; after the fact, he is concerned that his sons have placed his tribe in danger. If there is a moral failure here it exists on the part of just about everyone involved. It is certainly significant that such a story should follow immediately after the vision of God's face.

If the ethic of the proper name seems in Judaism to concern paternity and masculinity, is the essence that lies beyond naming feminine or maternal, not a feminine position in relation to the act of naming, but an appeal to femininity taken as a maternal essence whose prerogatives surpass and encompass those of the masculine ethos? One would be hard put to imagine why a woman's achievements could not serve to bring honor to her father's or family's name. Not only that, but there are cultures where a woman has the right, even the obligation, to pass her father's name to her children, when her father has no male children. This does not mean that this relation to the proper name may be either masculine or feminine. It means that a woman may without prejudice occupy a masculine position in relation to her father's name. The problem here is that if a man is marked by his father's name in the sense of being scarred, would not a woman who is similarly marked also be in some sense scarred? We note this because the idea of scarring the female body has a negative connotation. A woman who makes such a choice will not have the same access to a feminine position as will a woman who does not.

The theoretical problem concerns the relation between the proper name and the female body. If we hesitate to prescribe for women the practice of being marked or scarred by their fathers' names, it is with some reason. At the same time we are well aware of the repugnance many contemporary women feel for the idea of receiving their husbands' names through marriage. Perhaps this is because they see it as a scarring. Where circumcision is practiced the idea involved in the transmission of a name from husband to wife seems to be that the husband's marked penis marks the wife's sex through the act of copulation. Doubtless this has something to do with those nuptial practices where the exhibition of a blood-stained sheet was held to be of great importance. The practice whereby a girl in marrying gains a proper name suggests at some level that the name she has borne up to that moment has not marked her definitively, but in a transitory way. Does this tell us that there is a second way of being named, in which a name is worn as something like a veil? Or is the idea of the name as veil simply relative to a culture in which virginity is especially prized, in which God is said to have been born of a virgin? In a previous chapter we introduced two differing views of the topology of the heavens. In the one the principle of chaining or knotting prevailed, while in the other the structure was best defined in terms of concentric spheres. Doesn't this idea of veiling correspond to the principle of the concentric spheres through which the soul travels to reach the Divine Light? Perhaps it is behind the veil of a virgin's proper name that one sees God. Such was the fate of Jacob's interpretation in the hands of Christianity. As mentioned above, and at the risk of being repetitious, it is well and good that the sex of Christ was revealed in art, was rendered perfectly visible, but it is certain that the sex of the Virgin has never been submitted to such an indignity.

For the moment we will explore the comparison between biblical and Greek thought on masculinity and naming through another scene in which a man's identity is revealed incontestably through the recognition of an injury to his thigh. I am thinking of the scar of Odysseus, the subject of a seminal essay by Erich Auerbach in *Mimesis* (1957). When Odysseus returns to Ithaca, having spent twenty years away from his home, he is unrecognizable to his wife and former nurse. The stranger they speak with resembles Odysseus, but in fact they do not know that it is he. It is only when the nurse Eurykleia, in the course of bathing his feet, touches the scar on his thigh that she knows that her master has returned.

Here the question concerns a uniquely identifying mark gained by Odysseus during a hunt after boar. In killing the boar Odysseus was gored. Thus the structure of the struggle with some sort of being who injures the hero while being injured (or threatened) by him is preserved, the difference being that Odysseus does kill the boar. The killing performed by the sons of Jacob in revenge for the rape of Dinah is not structurally parallel to the act of Odysseus. In the *Odyssey* the hunt is directly related to the original naming of Odysseus by his maternal grandfather Autolykos; at the moment of the first naming Autolykos, himself a thief and swindler, a favorite of Hermes, invites Odysseus to return to see him when grown, to receive treasures and gifts. It is during this second visit that Odysseus is injured. From a Freudian point of view the boar would represent a paternal figure and the scene the murder of a primal father.

It is interesting and suggestive to compare the revenge of the rape of Dinah with Odysseus's treatment of the suitors. Odysseus, in exacting a heavy payment for the defilement of his home, is doing something the text considers to be heroic as well as just. His action does not, as the acts of Jacob's sons, put his home in danger. Odysseus restores the tranquillity of his home. The revenge of Jacob's sons, on the contrary, not only seems excessively vindictive, but it takes place after they have gained an unfair advantage over their victims. While Odysseus, after killing the boar, went on to be a great warrior and great hero, the story of Jacob after his fight with the angel is marked for the most part by his pathos over the loss of his son Joseph. We may ask the question of whether Jacob's fight with the angel, however much it repeats mythical patterns that concern the accession to a masculine position, has not become simply a shadow of what it would have been in other religious discourse—whether, in other words, the masculinity gained in the struggle is not immediately compromised.

Masculinity and the structure of its acquisition are present in the world of the patriarchs, and yet at some level it is compromised. To understand why we look to the comparison Auerbach made between the Homeric and biblical narrative traditions. While Auerbach compared the story from the *Odyssey* to the scene of the sacrifice of Isaac in Genesis, the comparison with Jacob is equally telling. (For this and what follows see Auerbach 1957, chap. 1.)

Both traditions represent patriarchy, a world of men, a world where masculinity is valued. Yet there are significant substantive differences in the way the stories are told. Auerbach wrote that the Homeric epic is narrated "with such a complete externalization of all the elements of the story and of their interconnections as to leave nothing in obscurity" (Auerbach 1957, p. 4). The goal was

to represent phenomena in a fully externalized form, visible and palpable in all their parts, and completely fixed in their spatial and temporal relations. Nor do psychological processes receive any other treatment: here too nothing must remain hidden and unexpressed. With the utmost fullness, with an orderliness which even passion does not disturb, Homer's personages vent their inmost hearts in speech; what they do not say to others, they speak in their minds, so that the reader is informed of it. Much that is terrible takes place in the Homeric poems, but it seldom takes place wordlessly. . . . The oft-repeated reproach that Homer is a liar takes nothing from his effectiveness. He does not need to base his story in historical reality, his reality is powerful enough in itself; it ensnares us, weaving its web around us, and that suffices him. And this "real" world into which we are lured exists for itself, contains nothing but itself; the Homeric poems conceal nothing, they contain no teaching and no secret second meaning. Homer can be analyzed, as we have essayed to do here, but he cannot be interpreted. . . . The general considerations which occasionally occur . . . reveal a calm acceptance of the basic facts of human existence, but with no compulsion to brood over them, still less any passionate impulse either to rebel against them or to embrace them in an ecstasy of submission. (Auerbach 1957, pp. 4, 11)

Here we have something closely akin to what Lacan called the real. Passion and feeling are not excluded; what is excluded is the promotion of these as primary realities. Also, there is no need to interpret the text to find hidden meaning that would transport the reader into eternity. As a patriarchy, the society of Homer valued the division of the sexes; it did not exclude the feminine. The dialogue involved in the speech act requires two distinct roles. The person who recognizes the scar of Odysseus is a woman, and the dramatic complexity of the scene is in her response. To demonstrate Auerbach's points we note first the scene of recognition:

> Then he kept still, while the old nurse filled up
> her basin glittering in firelight; she poured
> cold water in, then hot.
> > > > But Lord Odysseus
> whirled suddenly from the fire to face the dark.
> The scar: he had forgotten that. She must not

handle his scarred thigh, or the game was up.
But when she bared her lord's leg, bending near,
she knew the groove at once. (Trans. Robert Fitzgerald)

Next comes the story of how Odysseus acquired the scar. Then we read of the interaction between Eurykleia and Penelope.

Her eyes turned to Penelope with desire
to make her lord, her husband, known—in vain,
because Athena had bemused the queen,
so that she took no notice, paid no heed.

Following Auerbach, we may say that there is no call here for additional interpretation; Eurykleia's desire is clear, and it is thwarted. There is a psychological complexity in the gestures, which is accounted for by the influence of Athena. The influence of the goddess promotes the drama, extends the suspense, leaves something to be desired. This goddess is not acting under anyone's orders; she has her own priorities, her own motivations, her own desires. An otherworldly being of this sort is entirely excluded from the Judeo-Christian pantheon, where one God rules one world, or better, one universe, which has one meaning.

The Judeo-Christian God is One. But there is not just one kind of Oneness. The particular kind of Oneness we find in the Old Testament is a universal encompassing Oneness, a Oneness that excludes all others, all other gods. Zeus may also be One, but he is One among others, a One that must be paired with an other. The Greek deities are much closer to mankind; their presence is apparent on earth and their influence is clear and definitive. This does not mean that they have one will, or the same will; each god or goddess has desire and engages in drama. The consequence of these otherworldly dramas is human history. And the Greek gods are anthropomorphic; they have a closer resemblance to what goes on in human life than does the God of the Old Testament. Does this simply make them projections of human actions and interactions? Probably the opposite is true. In some sense humans live their lives according to their understanding of what is going on somewhere else. However much they believe that their decisions well up from Self, the model is elsewhere. When the model is the existence of angels, this yields particular modes of human behavior. When it is the gods who are thought to provide the motivation and the reason for behavior, this leads to a world in which drama has value, not so much in providing meanings, but rather in providing ways to situate oneself in the real. Drama exists in the Old Testament, but it does not exist in the world of God; we know nothing of the lineage of this God, of how he got to be the One God, of the basis for his decisions. All this is veiled, shrouded in mystery. This leads to a demand that whatever is happening in Scripture be submitted to interpretation. One of the consequences is the existence of psychological development in biblical characters, of what people today call growth, through obscurity about motives and situational structure.

Auerbach described the psychology as follows:

But even the human beings in the biblical stories have greater depths of time, fate, and consciousness than do the human beings in Homer; although they are nearly always caught up in an event engaging all their faculties, they are not so entirely immersed in its present that they do not remain continually conscious of what has happened to them earlier and elsewhere; their thoughts and feelings have more layers, are more entangled. Abraham's actions are explained not only by what is happening to him at the moment, nor yet only by his character . . ., but by his previous history; he remembers, he is constantly conscious of what God has promised him and what God has already accomplished for him—his soul is torn between desperate rebellion and hopeful expectations; his silent obedience is multilayered, has background. Such a problematic psychological situation as this is impossible for any of the Homeric heroes, whose destiny is clearly defined and who wake every morning as if it were the first day of their lives: their emotions, though strong, are simple and find expression instantly. (Auerbach 1957, pp. 9–10)

What better way to represent psychological depth than through moral confusion? Abraham may ultimately do the right thing, but he is not sure what the right thing is; God does not explain what is going on or what his plan is. Achilles, on the contrary, knows exactly what his choice is and exactly what the consequences will be. When he is faced with the choice between engaging Hector in battle and going home, he knows that if he does the former, his life will be shortened as his glory is increased, but he is not tormented about what is going on or whether he is doing the one right thing. He knows what he has to do and he does it. There is no questioning of why he should have been placed by the gods before such an alternative.

Auerbach offered that the salient feature of the biblical narrative was its orientation toward truth.

Woe to the man who did not believe it! One can perfectly well entertain historical doubts on the subject of the Trojan War or of Odysseus's wanderings, and still when reading Homer feel precisely the effects he sought to produce; but without believing in Abraham's sacrifice, it is impossible to put the narrative of it to the use for which it was written. Indeed, we must go even further. The Bible's claim to truth is not only far more urgent than Homer's, it is tyrannical —it excludes all other claims. The world of the Scripture stories is not satisfied with claiming to be a historically true reality—it insists that it is the only real world, is destined for autocracy. All other scenes, issues, and ordinances have no right to appear independently of it, and it is promised that all of them, the history of all mankind, will be given their due place within its frame, will be subordinated to it. The Scripture stories do not, like Homer's, court our favor, they do not flatter us that they may please us and enchant us—they seek to subject us, and if we refuse to be subjected we are rebels. (Auerbach 1957, p. 12)

And also, "If the text of the biblical narrative, then, is so greatly in need of interpretation on the basis of its own content, its claim to absolute authority forces it still further in the same direction. Far from seeking, like Homer, merely to make us forget our own reality for a few hours, it seeks to overcome our reality: we are to fit our own life into its world, feel ourselves to be elements in its structure of universal history" (Auerbach 1957, p. 12).

As Auerbach described it, there is an erotic, a courting of favor, an enchantment, to the relation between the Homeric text and the reader. As with a dramatic performance, the question is not whether we believe that it is a universal truth; we are not obliged to restructure our lives and our realities to fit the universally true meaning, or to detach ourselves from the world in order to contemplate the One truth. In a sense there is a sexual division between the performance and the audience of the Homeric epic; the former is masculine and the latter feminine. It is significant that the feminine position, that of the listener, should be defined in terms of the effects produced, in terms of the fact that the listener is moved by the performance. Perhaps this is why the Homeric epics are so clearly situated within a masculine world. The importance of the effect produced in the audience is clearly represented in the scene where Eurykleia discovers Odysseus's scar. And Auerbach made clear that the assertion by the One God of a tyrannical and autocratic claim to truth changes radically not only the place of the performer, but also that of the spectator, the reader. It is no longer a question of the performer's desire for the reader, but rather of a supreme and unconditional demand for love. The love demanded is hardly erotic; it alternates between subjection and rebellion. In either case the demand remains in force. Perhaps the reason the Greek gods and goddesses do not make such demands is that they have spouses; they are always paired. The variety of interactions between god and goddess is mapped onto the interactions between performer and audience. The horizontality of pairing is excluded from the biblical narrative; the reference is always either above or below, and the meaning of the interaction between mortals is always to be absorbed in the one meaning intended by God. The biblical God is supposed to be omnipresent. Allowing nothing to escape his demands, he introduces thereby a circle of enjoyment and torment. Since his ways are mysterious, one is never quite certain whether one has responded well enough to his demands. This produces within the biblical characters the individuality that was later to become so highly prized, a psychological growth and development, a constant testing of the value of their lives in terms of their love. Writing about King David, Auerbach said: "The old man, of whom we know how he has become what he is, is more of an individual than the young man; for it is only during the course of an eventful life that men are differentiated into full individuality; and it is this history of a personality which the old Testament presents to us as the formation undergone by those whom God has chosen to be examples. Fraught with their development, sometimes aged to the verge of dissolution, they show a distinct stamp of individuality entirely foreign to the Homeric heroes" (Auerbach 1957, pp. 14–15).

Characters are who they become; they add and lose distinctive traits to change their personalities, to become different individuals. As they pass through trials they become different people. Perhaps one can trace the developmental grid that makes them what they become, as modern psychology has attempted to do for everyone. Not only do biblical characters have a history; they are history, not just theirs, but everyone's. This type of history represents something for someone, and that someone is not only you, it is everyone.

The Homeric hero fundamentally does not change, does not become a different person. This is represented by the constancy of the scar, but also by Odysseus's ability to string the great bow and to shoot as straight as he ever did. The stratagem by which Odysseus does not immediately declare his presence to his wife tells us that the joy of coming home to her is secondary to his ethical duty. The honor of his name must be established, accounts must be squared, before he merits the bed of Penelope. What we have in the difference between Homeric and biblical worlds are differing conceptions of the functioning of proper names, and to continue our discussion we are obliged to delineate the theoretical debates over this issue.

Proper naming is not an innocent matter; nor are the theoretical debates on the question academic. How proper names function has everything to do with the psychoanalytic and theological issues we are addressing. Some aspects of Kripke's theory have already been introduced; it remains for us to elaborate them. The following discussion is based on Kripke's *Naming and Necessity* (1980). In the early 1970s Kripke caused a sensation in the world of analytic philosophy by proposing that proper names are rigid designators, by which he meant that they have the same referent in all possible worlds. Since he ultimately and correctly was not pleased with the idea of "possible worlds," he later adopted that of counterfactual situations. What this means, simply put, is that if I use a proper name, say Aristotle, and what I predicate or say about the referent of that name has nothing to do with the person who bore that name, that I am still talking about Aristotle. If I were to say that Aristotle wrote *War and Peace* the name itself has the same referent as when I say that Aristotle wrote *Peri Psyche*. The descriptive traits that are said about a person are, it appears, cut off from the name's function of designating rigidly the same referent in all counterfactual situations. The proper name then represents a limit to the influence of predication on, say, a grammatical subject. Contingent facts about the person have no influence on the necessary function of rigid designation; and it appears that the function is universal. The way a proper name is fixed, Kripke said, is through an act of dubbing (or naming) which may have been inspired by some characteristic of the referent.

Dartmouth, England was so named for being at the mouth of the river Dart—but once the name is fixed, as far as referentiality is concerned it makes no difference whether you say that Dartmouth is in England or on the moon. And if you say that Dartmouth might not have been at the mouth of the Dart, you are still talking about the same Dartmouth. Whatever intention was present in the act of naming, subsequent use of the name is not linked to the intention of each speaker. If when I said that Aristotle wrote *War and Peace*, I had in fact intended to say Tolstoy or Dostoevsky, the fact that I effectively pronounced the name Aristotle determines that the name has the same referent it would have if I had been talking of *Peri Psyche.* My intention is not sufficient to make the referent of Aristotle Tolstoy.

Since this reading is a variation on the thought of Kripke, let us see how he defined the question. "It is in general not the case that the reference of a name is determined by some uniquely identifying marks, some unique properties satisfied by the referent and known or believed to be true of that referent by the speaker. First, the properties believed by the speaker need not be uniquely specifying. Second, even in the case where they are, they may not be uniquely true of the actual referent of the speaker's use but of something else or of nothing. This is the case where the speaker has erroneous beliefs about some person, but erroneous beliefs about a certain person. In these cases the reference seems to be determined by the fact that the speaker is a member of a community of speakers who use the name. The name has been passed to him by tradition from link to link" (Kripke 1980, p. 106). For Kripke the name refers to some essential quality of the referent, and he extended this to certain common nouns, called natural kind terms, like water and gold. The question is whether Odysseus's scar is a uniquely identifying mark or an essential property of Odysseus. If we were to say that Odysseus has a scar on his thigh, Odysseus would still designate rigidly in the absence of such a mark. We can certainly say that Odysseus might not have had a scar on his thigh. But does the scar not represent the fact that one man is the unique referent of the name Odysseus? For the point of the scene in Homer is not to establish a unique property of Odysseus as much as it is to show the effect of naming. The scar, to use Kripke's vocabulary, is the essence referred to by the name, or better, it provides a visual representation of the existence of such an essence. This is what the mark of circumcision does.

If it is not the speaker's intention that is decisive in the name's referring, then it is reasonable to assume that the listener holds the position of the one who guarantees the maintenance of the reference. One may want, as did Keith Donnellen (in Schwartz 1977, p. 230) to assume the existence of an omniscient listener. This tells us that the position of the listener is identified with knowing and that the listener in some sense occupies the place of language knowledge. In cases where speaker and listener are both ignorant of the referent of a proper name, the use of the name to refer to something will count as an initial naming—despite the intention of the speaker using that name—and a new chain will have been begun. This was what actually happened when Marco Polo used the name Madagascar to refer to an island off the coast of Africa. Originally, the name had been used to refer to a place on the African mainland. This does not mean that the speaker's intention determines the reference of the name; it states that the name as unique entity does not refer of itself, but refers only within the context of a community of speakers and listeners.

Such a view is contrary to one proposed by John Searle (1983) as a variation on a theory of Frege. Therein the speaker's intention is of primary importance, and the function of naming is reduced to description. This view suggests that the speaker knows what he means when he pronounces a name and that if there is some ambiguity in the mind of the listener he has only to ask the speaker for a clarification. If the proper name does not in itself have a meaning, then the context in which it is used takes on the role of providing the intention. Such a position is of course very traditional; it is consistent with views we have encountered above. How does this relate with psychoanalytic experience, where it is generally assumed that the sense of an utterance goes radically beyond the speaker's intention? Freud went to considerable lengths to show that the "excess" to the speaker's intention revealed other intentions, unconscious intentions. A pertinent question here is whether there are other minds whose other intentions disturb the subject's intention to express his thought or feeling. We would then want to know whether these other minds were human or inhuman; for if there is an intentionality that is radically other, in the sense of not being that of other people, then we would be able to exit humanism.

Searle, however, proposed the primacy of intention and meaning within the minds of people. He advised restoring the context in which the name is used, what was meant by the speaker, what was understood by the listener, through this constellation of intentions to arrive at the functioning of the proper name. Here is Searle's definition of a descriptivist position: "The descriptivist is committed to the view that in order to account for how a proper name refers to an object we need to show how the object *satisfies* or *fits* the 'descriptive' Intentional content that is associated with the name in the minds of speakers; some of this Intentionality will normally be expressed or at least be expressible in words" (Searle 1983, pp. 233–34). For Searle, a group of speakers associates a name with a certain number or cluster of descriptive traits; when the proper name is used the speaker intends to refer to the object that satisfies those traits. This assumes that the speaker has an idea of the object he wishes to refer to, thus that the description is something like a picture that has enough in common with the original for us to recognize it. Searle said that if he uses a name and knows nothing about the referent, then the fact that the name still refers to the same referent is parasitic on the knowledge of those more savvy than he (Searle 1983, p. 244).

This suggests that the specifying characteristics of the person to which the name refers have considerable weight. Kripke's reply is that whatever you have become since the moment you were named is contingent, that were you to have become someone different, were you to have had none of the personality traits or life experiences that permit someone to identify you, you would still be named John Doe, or whatever. In that latter case different traits or a different cluster would be associated with your name.

This is true, up to a point. That point is situations where people normally change their names. One might simply say that they are re-named and that the new name is as much a rigid designator as the first name. This also would be true; both Jacob and Israel are rigid designators. And yet the change of name seems to imply a change of essence, an alteration on the level of the referent. This is a problem, especially where it concerns a woman's change of name in marriage. If Jane Doe marries John Smith and changes her name, the custom seems to suggest that there is a sufficiently significant change in the referent of Jane Doe for the proper name no longer to designate the same person. Certainly the new name implies a different social and familial context. Thereby, the new name is part of a different chain of signifiers from the old.

We may ask whether it is the change in name that makes her a different person or whether she becomes a different person and then is obliged to change her name. The recent revulsion women have expressed about this custom suggests that the change in name does in fact change something essential. At the least, we can say that this is her place in the kinship system. This change must, again according to custom, be accompanied by a sexual act in which the contractual or social tie is consummated. It is not enough simply for her to change her name; if there is no consummation the marriage may be annulled, rendered as though it had never been. Nor is it enough for a woman to have engaged in a sexual act. This indicates that the referent of the name has something to do with sexual identification, and that the essential trait to which the name refers is sexual. And if it is true for a woman in marriage, the situation in which society declares that a girl has become a woman, then it ought also to be true when a boy becomes a man. The only difference is that in most cases, that of Jacob excepted, the boy does not change his name in becoming a man. And yet his responsibility to the name has changed significantly, through an event that in the case of Odysseus corresponds to a scarring of the flesh, and with Jacob through a dislocation of the hip joint. It is as though a boy becomes a man when he is subjected to the mark of castration. His name does not change function in terms of rigid designation; what changes is his acceding to the role of namer. He gains a responsibility to name others, thus he comes to know that a name is not his personal possession. Intention enters the process through the act of naming.

If it is true that the proper name marks the body universally, virginity as a representation of an untouched or unmarked body becomes an important issue. We have proposed that for the virgin the proper name is like a veil; it does not mark her beyond every contingency of her existence, since there is one experience that will change her name and also mark her body. In naming a daughter a father's intention may then be different from that in naming a son. He may name his daughter with the intention that she retain his name and that her accomplishments honor her debt to his name. This ought always to be his intention in naming a son. A second intention cannot exist in relation to a son. There he names his daughter with the intention that she take the name of her husband when she marries. In the situation where her so-called maiden name is only a stand-in for a name to be received in the future, we see that name as a decoy, a lure, or a veil. It is descriptive in the sense that it signifies within the structure of kinship that the person bearing it is marriageable. May we not extend this idea and say that for a virgin the proper name is something like a persona, a role that is adopted for a certain time and within a certain context, but which is not considered to be definitive?

Let us imagine that a young woman decides to take the veil. What is the sense of her action in terms of the function of naming? As Lacan has analyzed this, she is saying "No" to the marking function of the name, she is showing the limit to the hegemony of the performance of naming.

In brief, she is saying "No" to the phallus. The significance of this "No" is that it is the condition for the desire to name; as long as someone says "No" to the phallus, the phallus is not simply the expression of will. The virgin who takes the veil is not only declaring herself to be untouched, she is additionally saying that she is untouchable. This does not mean that she has decided to retain her father's name, to act as though she were a son or its equivalent. Her name, whether it be the first name she was given at birth or a new name gained upon joining an order, acquires a sense, which is that she refuses to be named. Thereby she becomes akin to the angels. The world within the walls of the monastery, communicating as it does with the City of God, does not know proper names as rigid designators, but rather takes names to be descriptions of a religious intention and a moral position.

It is one thing to recognize the necessary function of the virgin's refusal of the name in relation to the performance of naming; it is quite another to propose her as a model that defines the functioning of all proper names. Another way to see descriptive naming is in terms of the names of angels. According to Rashi angels have names that are suited to their functions; and such a practice certainly suggests a descriptivist theory of naming. It is consistent then that virgins and monks should model their existence, up to and including their names, on that of the angels. Since angels do not have bodies, they cannot be marked by proper names. Similarly, religious who make themselves untouchable in some sense are emulating or imitating this bodilessness.

One further way of approaching the question of the sense of the proper name is through the well-known fact that proper names do not translate from one language to another. One might even say that the proper name is rigid phonetically in all possible languages. This theory, which holds that the phonetic is primary in the proper name, was proposed by Sir Alan Gardiner as a response to the descriptivist theory of Bertram Russell. Other words of a language, words whose purpose is to convey meaning, are and must be translated. This fact was rejected by Kripke on the grounds that this does not hold for all proper names: Greece is not called Greece in Greece. He added that if Ezekiel were alive today he would probably not recognize his own name spoken in our contemporary dialect. The first point suggests that we ought perhaps to limit the idea of the nontranslatability of proper names to names of persons, or better, that we remark a distinction between names of persons and names of places. The latter are not inscribed in a kinship system and do not mark the human body. Place names have more in common with the function of proper naming as it concerns women. A woman has a supplementary function in relation to proper names; she is both person and place—the latter in the sense that she is identified with a home. This may imply that the female body is never marked in precisely the same way as the male body, but only by contiguity. And this would mean that there is something in women that falls outside of the function of proper naming, that is not designated rigidly, and thus imparts considerably more mobility to the feminine position.

As for Ezekiel, one may say that if I travel to China my interlocutors will make every effort to render my rather unwieldy name into a series of phonemes that match as closely as possible the English sound. With training I am reasonably certain that I will learn to recognize my name and that I will not think that when someone pronounces the name Mao Tse-tung he is talking of or to me. All phonemes have a range of variation within the several dialects of a language. This is not a decisive argument against the rule enounced above.

Gardiner's theory proposes that there is an aspect of language use in which the phonetic structure is cut off from meaning and sense. We call this, with Lacan, the function of the signifier, and it tells us that the phonetic specificity of any utterance lends itself to associations beyond what the speaker intends or means. It is possible, as Saussure showed in his analysis of anagrams, for a text to state one message while at the same time another pattern of sounds in the message functions to invoke something that is not named in the text (in Starobinski 1971). Such a process may certainly occur unbeknown to the speaker, as we see often in psychoanalysis. Acronyms and homonyms fall within this category.

The question is not so much how language hooks into the world, but rather how it hooks into those who speak it. And speakers articulate the boundaries of their world by naming places. Once the proper name hooks language into speakers, and places those speakers in a socially determined space, it is almost as though this action liberates the rest of language to serve functions other than to bring us into contact with empirical reality. Assuming that there was gold before there was a Mr. Gold, the common noun does not thereby become equal to its descriptive traits or predicates. Rather, the requirement that it hold fast to a common essence is loosened once there are proper names that hook language into human speakers. If the proper name is rendered dysfunctional, this produces a necessity to hook words into the objects of the world, because the world would then be an externalization of a body that has not been touched or marked by the proper name. Such a world is a body, a feminine body, preferably virginal. Some believe that this body is lying there waiting to be known scientifically, while others object to this as a violation. So rather than propose an epistemology concerning the acquisition of knowledge of things in the world, we continue with an analysis of the activity of speech.

Consider the witticism, a speech act most dear to psychoanalysts. Certainly there is an object to the joke; the joke is about something or someone. And yet the speaker's intention does not aim at this object; it concerns the effect he wishes to produce in the listener. Freud said that the joke is successful or unsuccessful as the listener does or does not laugh. However, it is not the intention of the speaker that makes the other laugh; it is the play of language or ideas in the joke itself that produces the effect. Many people fail at wit because they do not permit the language to produce an effect; they insist on producing it themselves. And there are listeners who feel obliged to laugh in recognition of the speaker's intention when the joke itself is boring and mediocre. While it is true that the laughter of one person will at times incite others to laugh by what Freud called a ricochet effect, that laughter is not the same as the one that is spontaneously released in the listener when he hears a joke. An extension of this idea is the situation where the speaker inadvertently says something funny, without intending to do so. His witty remark causes his listener to laugh, and from that fact we judge that he has permitted an exercise of wit despite or disregarding his personal intentions. While we are willing to admit the element of intention in the composition of the speech act, we do not accept that the intention is decisive in forming a judgment about the success of the act. Once the place of the listener is restored and identified with bringing judgment, things change substantially.

Psychoanalysts are very concerned with the effect produced by their words. They know that effects are not produced because the analyst intends them. They should also know that there is no way, as Lacan often noted, to predict or control the effect of one's words. The reason is that one never knows what resonance any set of words will have on any particular listener. A word or sound pattern may evoke in your listener good or bad memories depending on his personal experience. It is a simple fact of human experience that we do not learn language in a semantic vacuum; we associate words and names with experiences in our history, and the use of words and names has a tendency to evoke such experiences, consciously and unconsciously.

To move beyond this dimension let us offer the following assertion. The speaker can never precisely communicate his state of mind or body to his listener. If certain words have produced an effect in him, he can never communicate exactly the same effect to a listener. There is a dissymmetry between speaker and listener that determines the fact that whatever the state of the speaker's mind or soul when he pronounces a sentence of a language, it is never that state that is produced in the listener. Between speaker and listener, there is a radical division of labor that makes for a difference in the enjoyment experienced by the one who is pronouncing the words and the one who is listening to them. We may apply this rule to the relation between dramatist and audience; whatever the state of the dramatist writing a play, that intention is radically distinct from the effect produced. The reason is that the words produce their own effect, that they are substantial entities that carry with them connotations and sometimes even denotations beyond the intentionality of the dramatist. Only a tyrant can will a response in his audience.

One may even assert, as Socrates does in the *Ion,* that it is only to the extent that the epic poet can move out of his own mind, renounce his own intentionality, that the words can be permitted to find their own most effective mode of presentation. The epic poet is one who permits the gods to speak through him, Socrates says, and who does not allow the audience to believe that it is he, the author, who is speaking. The author of a poem is certainly not the author of the words he uses, and the place of a god or gods in this discourse is that of the author of the language. Otherwise the message the poet is communicating is personal to him, corresponds to his intention, and will not produce an effect in a group as varied as an audience. Socrates does not look very kindly on the art of the rhapsode, the man who recites poetry in public. He considers that this condition of being out of one's mind is not entirely desirable; and he adds that the knowledge required to form a critical judgment of a poem is not at all the same knowledge that animates the rhapsode. What is significant for our purposes is the division between the performer and audience. However much the rhapsode is moved by what he recites and however much his audience may share in the experience he is creating, his art depends on a knowledge that is hardly required in the audience. The performer must have some control over the instrument he employs for his performance. The audience need have no ability to use an instrument to judge of how well it is being played. And perhaps the ability to play an instrument makes one a less qualified listener; what the instrumentalist hears is not the same as what the nonperformer is hearing.

Masculinity has everything to do with the performance of acts. While there is no performance without competence, there is competence without peformance. Being a man involves knowing what has to be done and then doing it. Self-questioning and self-doubt, affective effusions and psychic torment have no place in a masculine ethos. And this does not mean that they represent the essence of femininity! The judgment of a man's act, his performance, is not his intention; it lies in the effect produced in others. And this, we will see, has to do with the extent that they are moved. Odysseus transports the suitors to another place; he himself is unmoved, he stands his ground. And his scar remains unmoved, in the sense of unchanged, in his transit of counterfactual situations.

My hypothesis is that a linguistic structure hooks into the human body through the division of the sexes. The reason for this choice is that the division of the sexes provides a visual representation of an interaction that is otherwise invisible. It also tells us that whatever goes on between the subject and predicate in a sentence, or between a speaker and listener when those roles are differentiated, is of the order of the erotic. The point at which the link is made is the male sexual organ; this may be the reason why that organ's erectile function tends to be singled out as the locus of moral evil in a world that wills a transcendence of proper naming. The hooking of names into bodies legislates against the creation of a Heavenly City; it also provides an obstacle to the obsession with the empirical. Not that the phallus alone bears the weight of such a condemnation, for the feminine sex is also condemned for its association with the phallus. As Boccaccio recounted in the famous story of Alibech and Rustico (*Decameron.* 3.10), the phallus is the Devil and the feminine sex is Hell. The monk Rustico thus teaches the innocent Alibech how to put the Devil back in Hell. A woman who renounces the phallus thereby renders it angelic. Not only is her sex not Hell, but it becomes heavenly.

Thus far we have kept reasonably close to one contemporary philosophical view of intentionality. Note that this concept has a long and interesting history and that it has applications outside the field of the philosophy of mind. It may be that a philosopher has the intention to restrict his inquiry to a particular use of the concept, but according to what we have been arguing, we are within our rights to extend it, to make use of its extension. And one of the most important places where the concept of intention has reared its head is in the field of ethics.

One can hardly say that intention counts for nothing in determining the nature of an act. Yet, the texts we have examined as exemplary in their representation of masculinity have quite a different view of intention. This point requires elaboration. Isaac intended to bless his son Esau, but Jacob was disguising himself as Esau and heard the blessing. It was the son who heard the blessing who was marked by it, not the son for whom it was intended. Again, Jacob thought one night that he was consummating his marriage to Rachel; that was his intention. But when he awoke the next morning and discovered that his partner was Leah, he found himself, despite his intention, married to the said Leah. Oedipus did not intend to murder his father and marry his mother; he intended not to do either of those things. Certainly, he had the intention to murder the man he encountered at the fork in the road and he also had the intention to marry a woman named Jocasta, but patricide and incest were not his intentions. They were his fate.

Once it was discovered that these were the acts that he had committed, there was no recourse to the notion of intention. Oedipus was an incestuous patricide, no matter what his intention was. And what made him those things was the power of his name, as the designator of his swollen foot, which was swollen by the acts of his parents, whose intention was to let him perish as an infant. And the name functions this way not because it exists in isolation, but because it is inscribed with other names in a system of kinship relations.

Perhaps this represents another intentionality, that of the gods. Perhaps the intentions of the human mind are simply shadows, dimly grasped, of these other intentions or other desires. This does not mean that the desire of the gods or even the desire that provides the linkage of the signifying chain is a projection of that of the human subject. It means precisely the opposite. Desire comes from without, not within. And masculinity has everything to do with this desire. When we say that it concerns knowing what one has to do and doing it, this means that the intelligence that grasps an ethical obligation has been transmitted from elsewhere and that the man in question assumes it as his own. Hamlet's obligation is told him by a ghost, but Hamlet is so overwhelmed by what he has heard that he cannot speak it and cannot act on it. He wallows in the position of the listener, in his having been moved affectively, and refuses to take action that would alter the situation in Denmark. Instead of the kind of external drama that existed for the Greeks, things have moved inside, to become a function of the passions of the soul. Everyone sympathizes with his plight, and this is surely symptomatic.

This is the price of making the gods into angels. Whereas the gods transmit through the medium of poets fictions and stories, humans who attain to an angelic existence within a Christian world are considered to be vehicles of the truth. They are relieved of the obligation to act. Thus Anselm said: "But I do not now see why angels only, or even angels and holy men together, are meant by the expression 'children of Israel,' as they are called 'sons of Abraham.' And they can also properly be called 'angels of God,' because they imitate the life of angels, and they are promised in heaven a likeness and equality with angels, and all who live holy lives are angels of God. Therefore the confessors or martyrs are so called; for he who declares and bears witness to the truth, he is a messenger of God, that is, his angel" (Anselm 1962, p. 235). Moral rectitude and the absolute disinterest in the affairs of the fallen world are characteristics that make of men angels. Strictly speaking there is a reduction of the element of drama in such lives, just as the invention of a single God reduces the drama of the Heavenly City. Without a spouse this God is alone, to make of the human race the ground on which his moral dilemma is played out. He has absorbed a specifically feminine enjoyment, because if he did not have it, there would be a limit to his knowledge.

The expulsion of the disobedient angels has created a harmonious space within which sensuality and violence are never again to exist. Manliness, having been expelled from the Heavenly City, continues to exist in the fallen world. Wars are still fought and there are occasions when those who fight them maintain some sense of rules. The economic world in which men have traditionally made their mark still exists. The increasing entry of women into the workforce has not changed its fundamentally masculine orientation. And the division of the sexes, a shadow of its former self, still exists with manifestations that some consider to be even more virulent than those of the past. Short of our making this earth into a replica of the Heavenly City they will probably continue to exist. Perhaps, with luck, manly behavior will at times have more than a passing acquaintance with intelligence. For better or for worse this will not happen through the restoration of pagan religion. That world, having been lost or defeated, is irretrievable. In its absence Freudian psychoanalysis is a practice that, in the words of Lacan, "re-established the bridge uniting modern man with ancient myths" (Lacan 1966, p. 402).

SEVEN

FEMININITY

Rising from the Aegean foam, metamorphized from the severed genitals of Ouranos, Aphrodite was for the Greeks feminine beauty and erotic seduction. The mortal Paris judged her the fairest of the three competing goddesses. What distinguished her from Hera and Athena was the offer of feminine beauty sustained by an act of disrobing. She revealed a beauty that was neither an idea nor a form. To keep her promise to Paris, Aphrodite gave him Helen, wife of Menelaus, thereby inaugurating the Trojan War. And even though the war did not go well for the side she championed, her son Aeneas did after a time found the city of Rome.

While Christ drew his flesh only from a female body, Aphrodite was the reverse, a female generated not from a male body, but from male genitals. And the reversal extends further: to give birth to Jesus it was required that the body of Mary be untouched and undefiled; the means by which Aphrodite was created from Ouranos required the shedding of a father's blood by his son Kronos. If these two forms of birth represent two different theories of the connection of language with the body, they state that on the one hand language through the function of proper naming cuts a father's body and takes something from it, whereas on the other the maternal body serves to produce of itself a body that the

Word or Verb comes to inhabit, in the sense of being clothed by that body.

Was it an accident, a quirk of Greek thought, that made the most feminine of goddesses motherless? The dissociation of femininity and motherhood is present in different ways in the three goddesses who contested the honor of fairest. Hera, the wife of Zeus, was the goddess especially of marriage; curiously, she was not connected with the rituals that concern motherhood. Her realm is the "consummated marriage." "One feature," Burkert declared, "strangely missing from the portrait of Hera is motherhood" (Burkert 1985, pp. 132–33). And Athena was not of woman born; she may have been conceived within a woman's womb, but she sprang from the head of her father Zeus, not from any mother.

All three were certainly mothers, but none is descended from a mother; similarly, the heroines of Shakespeare's high comedies are motherless within the context of their courtship. Placing a motherless woman in a situation where she will be courted and eventually married, thus ending the comedy, is significant. Aphrodite too is linked to courtship. Her mysteries "were intimately connected with marriage preparations" (Burkert 1983, p. 271). Is this all accidental, or does it tell us that having a mother legislates against femininity? The mind of contemporary psychology as well as that of modern feminism will balk at such an assertion. To the extent that they have wanted to present theories of femininity, these theoretical enterprises have tended to say that femininity is gained between or among women, that it arises from the identification of one woman with another. This chapter will argue that femininity is gained only through a woman's interaction with her opposite in a relation of contiguity excluding substitution and similarity.

How can we define this femininity? Martha Nussbaum provided an excellent characterization of feminine values in Greek tradition. She defined what we are calling femininity as "a kind of human worth that is inseparable from vulnerability, an excellence that is in its nature other-related and social, a rationality whose nature is *not* to attempt to seize, hold, trap, and control, in whose values openness, receptivity, and wonder play an important part" (Nussbaum 1986, p. 20). In addition, femininity is in constant strife with the masculine. As Nussbaum said: "We shall find, I believe, that at every stage in the chronological development, the picture of reason as hunter is opposed, criticized, constrained by variants of the other picture. . . ." And she added the important note that the two types of value are not polar opposites, but rather that the second combines elements of the first with those elements that the first "avoids and shuns" (Nussbaum 1986, p. 20, 20n). Thus masculinity is defined as the exclusion of the feminine, while femininity is inclusive, taking things into itself and adding to them elements that are not present in what is opposed to it.

Any attempt to gain femininity through an identification with other women, whether these other women are models of the eternal feminine or exemplars of the woman who has it all, will lead only to despair. Belonging to a group of women, taking part in and sharing experiences that are unique to women, becoming an integral part of womankind, do not give a woman a sense of being feminine. They allow her to imagine herself as womanly while producing a sense that she is not really or sufficiently feminine. Or better, the extent to which her femininity is an imitation of the appearance or activities of other women makes it impossible for her to accept her femininity as her own. Even if she were to satisfy all the predicates that are supposed to define a woman—be they associated with traditional femininity or a more modern woman—she will never from there become anything other than a generic Woman. And the generic Woman is the antithesis of femininity. If all women have certain specifying characteristics, then to have those characteristics is to be all women.

There are no insignia of femininity. Nor does one have the sense in listening to women that a feminine identity involves either anatomical or experiential constants. Assuming that a woman wants to be her own woman, to be a woman in her own right, this does not mean that she does not want any man to have a part in it. Being attractive to a man, being desired by him, seem to be essential to a woman's sense of femininity. The problem is that if she has constructed a feminine image by imitating another woman, how does she know that the man who desires her really desires her and not the other woman? To use more common parlance, it is alienating for a woman to believe that a man wants her simply for certain anatomical characteristics that all women possess. Is it any less alienating if he wants her because she typifies a role model—whether it is the Cosmo girl or the liberated woman? And it is reasonably certain that most women will balk at a man who desires them because they are so much like their mothers.

To retain inviolate the link between mother and daughter, feminist theorists have proposed as exemplary the myth of Demeter and Persephone, to make of it the model of mother-daughter relationships. There what we have is a fertility goddess, a corn goddess, who exercises her power over the harvest to cause mass starvation, thereby to extract her daughter from the hands of Hades, king of the underworld. Demeter, however, is only partially successful, for the unsuspecting Persephone, upon being ravished by Hades, has made the mistake of eating some pomegranate seeds. For this fault she is prevented from being wholly returned to her mother and has to spend part of each year with her husband. So the myth of Demeter and Persephone, which is supposed to represent womanly power, shows us a daughter who spends part of the year in an infernal marriage, and the other part in the arms of her mother. Are we to take this as a model for a woman's life? We should mention that none of the motherless goddesses mentioned above, to say nothing of Shakespeare's comic heroines, is weak, servile, frivolous; none really corresponds to the image of femininity that was so roundly attacked not too long ago. The promotion of Aphrodite as representing femininity is not a veiled effort to represent feminine women as powerless. Aphrodite's power is in her birthright: "Aphrodite's Homeric epithet *philommeides,* laughter-loving, is, in its word formation, a reshaping of the Hesiodic *philommedes,* 'to her belong male genitals' " (Burkert 1985, pp. 154–5).

Strictly speaking, Aphrodite is the goddess of sexual love. This is despite the fact that in most theories of love her place as representative of a particular kind of love is occluded in favor of her son Eros. The Greek iconography of Eros portrays a winged youth, certainly one of the types for the presentation of angels. That sexual love has its own goddess, not a god, tells us more than how powerful love can be. It tells us that a woman's love is the most powerful aphrodisiac of masculine desire. In addition, a woman's love is also the most powerful aphrodisiac of her own desire. The relation, in other words, is not symmetrical or equal, as people tend to wish.

What is it then for a woman to give her love? Lacan said it was to give what she does not have, to give a lack, in roughly the same way that Marc Antony expects that his audience of Romans will lend him their ears, to be open and receptive to his message. If the audience knows what he is going to say before he says it, or if it is simply not interested in hearing what he has to say, then it would not be giving what it does not have. So this giving is prior to a receiving, and thus femininity cannot simply be a receptive attitude, a form of pure passivity. A lack that is offered as a gift does not appear to the one to whom it is given as a lack or a void; its being offered as a gift dissimulates the void, as though the desire aroused by this love will find a place that is not nothing. What does Marc Antony seek for his speech? Evidently something that we can call a home, a place in which his words will make sense, in which they will not only come to rest, but where they will, seemingly in contradiction, produce movement. Otherwise the words will disperse in the air, as senseless as the sound of the wind.

So the question becomes one of semantics, and this, once said, leads inexorably to a consideration of the central semantic notions of truth and falsity. The relation of philosophy to truth has been dramatized by Nietzsche as a failed seduction. The opening of *Beyond Good and Evil* is justly famous; I plead its importance as reason for quoting it: "Supposing truth is a woman—what then? Are there not grounds for the suspicion that all philosophers, insofar as they were dogmatists, have been very inexpert about women? That the gruesome seriousness, the clumsy obtrusiveness with which they have usually approached truth so far have been awkward and very improper methods for winning a woman's heart. What is certain is that she has not allowed herself to be won—and today every kind of dogmatism is left standing dispirited and discouraged" (Nietzsche 1966, p. 2). Knowing this, what is there to do? One may renounce the appeal to truth in favor of the will to power, unless one is thereby hiding the belief that this is what the elusive truth has been awaiting all along. One may embrace untruth or uncertainty, thereby attempting to seduce truth by showing one's disinterest and provoking jealousy. Or else, in denouncing the ineptness of the coterie of suitors after truth, the philosopher may be taking in hand the bow that no one has yet been able to mobilize, to murder all the suitors and to retrieve the most faithful wife, Penelope, who wove and unwove a "veil" through twenty years of waiting, thereby saving the truth for the only man worthy of it. The virtue of Nietzsche's all too virile approach is placing the problem in a dramatic context; it is far from certain that he or his contemporary acolytes have thereby resolved the question or have rendered the problematic of truth a dead letter. To self-censor references to truth is to make it unspeakable, to return it to its primordial silence.

After all, this version of the seduction of truth by philosophers provides for women a very appealing position, as judges of the effect or effectiveness of a performance. The truth of a statement has something to do with whether and how it is understood by a listener; but not every listener will offer a judgment that is accurate or valuable. Nor is it very interesting to collapse the problem of the dialectics of truth by saying that there is a capital Truth, which all true statements satisfy. As is reasonably well known, that Truth runs afoul of the liar paradox. This capital Truth is the semantic version of Woman, taken to be all women or womankind. Once we have with Lacan excluded this Woman, rendered Her nonexistent, the real problems begin. No longer can one assert that there is one Truth that renders life or sentences meaningful. But if there are several, are they in some sort of competition, like the goddesses at the judgment of Paris? Perhaps there are several truths and each has her own area of influence, her own level. A statement that is false on one level may be referred to another to find its truth (See Kripke 1975).

Even more problematical is the idea that a woman's placing herself as truth in relation to a masculine performance has everything to do with her femininity. The feminine position does not merely limit itself to the kind of revelation or unveiling that constitutes the bestowing of favors; if truth is initially veiled, then that veil ought in some sense to cause and to sustain the performance. Truth must be veiled to lure the performer into coming forth with what he has to offer. Among the places where femininity goes awry, none is more enticing than for a woman to fall in love with truth, to eschew all dissembling and deceit. At that point the performer or even the philosopher does not have to seduce and win over the truth; its horror is always present before his eyes. And while he may find this an occasion for toughness, there is no guarantee that this truth is his, that it has anything to do with his performance.

If I had wanted to break with my own custom, I would have subtitled this chapter: Aphrodite takes the veil. I owe this idea to a fine article on iconography by W. S. Heckscher, entitled "Aphrodite as a Nun." In it Heckscher analyzed an iconographic curiosity he found in the best-selling seventeenth-century volume *Iconologia*, whose author was a Sienese named Cèsare Ripa. Therein as representative of the virtue of *Pudicìtia* (modesty) he found the image of Venus arrayed as a nun. Ripa's comment was: "A young maiden all dressed in white who should have on her head a veil of the same color, covering her face and reaching down to her waist. With her right hand she is holding a lily. . . . Under her right foot she has a tortoise in order to indicate that modest ladies should stay assiduously in their house, just as the tortoise stays in the house which nature has given it." He then quoted Plutarch: "Pheidias made the Aphrodite for the Eleans with one foot on a tortoise to typify womankind keeping at home and keeping silence" (Heckscher 1953, p. 109). But Ripa, Heckscher wrote, did not contract this idea directly from Plutarch; it had already been passed through Christian morality through the efforts of people like Jerome, whose views on virgins, convents, and angels we have cited above. All of which was part of a larger effort to assimilate Aphrodite to the person of the Virgin; the latter was alone in her cubicle when she received the Annunciation. She was not entirely silent, but the angel's message found in her a fertile ground in which meaning could grow. Heckscher suggested that the meaning of Plutarch's comments for the Greeks therefore would have been very different from the Christianized sense it was later to acquire. "The concept of the *manere domi* had in antiquity served merely to stress the absolute social immobility of the married woman as against the relative mobility of the hetaira" (Heckscher 1953, pp. 113–14). A *hetaira* was a woman of the world, to speak genteelly, or otherwise, a courtesan or prostitute. The idea seems to be that social immobility does not mean absolute immoblity and also that the difference between a wife and a mistress or courtesan is that the former not only makes a home but is identified in her person with that home. Of course, it is not immediately evident that making a home is the particular province of a goddess like Aphrodite. The goddess who broke up the home of Menelaus might well be considered to represent the Otherness of women.

In our time the position of wife is hardly considered to be synonymous with feminine sensuality; think of the idea of the "housewife." This is one of the reasons this position has been so roundly repugned recently. Finally, while it is useful to associate home with the role of the wife, it is equally plausible to associate it originally with the figure of the mother.

Such a series of assertions opens a number of questions concerning femininity. The first must be to note that the association of Aphrodite with sensual pleasure has been eliminated from the tradition. The Aphrodite worshipped by Sappho is nowhere to be found. The fate of Aphrodite among the Greeks was defined by Burkert: "In the iconography, the naked oriental figure was supplanted as early as the first half of the seventh century by the normal representation of the goddess with long, sumptuous robes and the high crown of the goddess, *polos*. Fine attire is Aphrodite's specialty, most notably necklaces and occasionally brightly colored robes intended to give an oriental effect. It was not until about 340 that the statue of a naked Aphrodite apparently preparing to take a bath was created for the sanctuary in Cnidos by Praxiteles; for centuries this figure remained the most renowned representation of the goddess of love, the embodiment of all womanly charms" (Burkert 1985, p. 155). Panofsky wrote that this Aphrodite was recognized by the Greeks as the Heavenly Aphrodite, the one who was later to be assimilated to the Virgin (Panofsky 1972a, p. 199). For the Greeks the Ouranian (Heavenly) origin of Aphrodite was entirely consistent with her sensuality. The representation of that sensuality concerned especially the adornment of the female body, even to the point of seeing the female body itself as adornment. This also suggests that femininity requires an embodiment, that it cannot be limited to a quality of the spirit, the soul, or the mind, to something that is invisible. The beautiful soul is a caricature of femininity.

The philosophical division of Aphrodite into Heavenly and Vulgar originated in Plato. The former was taken by Christian authors to be divine beauty, while the latter received associations with prostitution and other unseemly acts. The Renaissance Neoplatonist Ficino believed that the love engendered by the Heavenly Aphrodite permitted the possession *"ad divinam cogitandam pulchritudinem,* of divine beauty in an act of pure cognition" (quoted in Panofsky 1972a, p. 198). For him the idea that Aphrodite did not have a mother meant that she was immaterial, a pure spirit to be grasped by the intelligence. If there is something to this idea, perhaps it is that at the center of femininity there is an absence, a void, something you cannot look at face-to-face. If this is true, then the adornment of the female body would represent a dissimulation of that void, a dissimulation of the truth of the final destination of . . . one's speech, for example.

The tortoise may well be inseparable from his home, but this does not mean that he is immobile. Generally it means that he takes his home with him wherever he goes. This may represent the idea that a woman is a home, that she is the embodiment of this concept. In addition to being a person designated by a proper name, a woman becomes the place where the act of naming will produce an effect. Also, the sense of immobility as regards femininity should be understood in terms of having the potential to be moved, thus, as movable. Otherwise one would be obliged to say that a woman's being moved when she is married is the only time she is ever moved.

Why is the place of the audience immobile, as happens in many concerts? Because the audience ought to be moved, and its movement cannot be credited to the performance if it is already in motion. And also, perhaps the immobility of the audience functions as a fetish causing the performer's desire to perform. The idea that a woman should remain within the house, as it came to become a dominant image, was mixed with the state of things within the convent, and thereby with the identification of virgins with angels. Of course, this requires the qualification that nuns in convents are considered to be married to Christ. While the situation clearly resembles a harem, the difference is that in a polygamous society a certain number of men are entitled to have multiple wives, while in Catholicism only one man is granted this privilege. The fact that many modern women see the position of housewife as deeroticized also suggests a connection with the position of women in the convent. Certainly, nuns dress and comport themselves in a way that discourages all forms of erotic attention from men.

The idealization of the virginal state has kept alive a form of feminine enjoyment in "marital" sexuality that was best attained in the absence of a human husband. This in turn was accompanied by the restriction of sexuality with a human husband to the purposes of reproduction. Neither angel nor virgin is supposed to have a body, and neither is supposed to be touched. As Jerome put it: "Let her live without the flesh, though in it" (Jerome 1980, letter 107). The complexity and the importance of woman's position in relation to angels is shown by the fact that women are at different times and by different authors called upon to be like angels, to give birth to angels, and to have angels as lovers. This requires their being removed from the commerce of the male world, the better to be serve as a link between humans and the moral world of the resurrected life.

The problem and the appeal of this position is not that it represents a falsification of the feminine position; rather it is too close to the truth made into an absolute. Considering the frank condemnation of masculinity within Christian tradition, it is not surprising that a certain vision of femininity is idealized and adored. The tradition appeals most fundamentally to women, disengaging the truth of femininity from reference to men. For better or worse the price of this disengagement is the collapse of femininity into motherhood. The only way the Church found to provide for women outside of the orders a sensual enjoyment, to offer it as their birthright, and to immunize these women from the temptation of men, was to identify it with motherhood. Admittedly, this enjoyment is inferior to the one offered to the sisterhood. But the supreme feminine enjoyment did not just involve marriage with Christ; it added an identification with his wife-mother. As opposed to Aphrodite and other goddesses of femininity, the Virgin does have a mother. It is not that femininity and motherhood should be severed absolutely; that would simply be the inverse of the Catholic position. Rather motherhood and fertility function within the structure of femininity as a dissimulation, a veil, even a fetish hiding what is actually a question. The problem with the idealization of motherhood is that it takes a mask to be the thing itself.

"There is no more matriarchal image than the Christian mother of God who bore a child without male assistance. The liturgy invokes her as the *radix sancta,* the holy root of salvation, because through her the Incarnation was possible. . . . In fourteenth- and fifteenth-century Europe, the statues of the *Vierge Ouvrante,* a fetish-like Madonna whose belly opened to reveal the Trinity concealed within, became objects of devotion" (Warner 1983, p. 47). One way of looking at the problem of marriage in Western civilization has been proposed and analyzed by Marina Warner in *Alone of All Her Sex.* Where the Virgin Mother is the only womanly figure in the Heavenly City, aside from Jerusalem herself, the prototype of marriage becomes the marriage of a mother with her son. We have seen several examples of women who receive their husband Jesus Christ from his mother in an inverted marital exchange. The drama of marriage as embodied in pagan gods and goddesses is excluded from the resurrected life, and thereby the Western view of marriage is severely constricted. To be married and to be like Aphrodite makes no sense where the Mother Goddess is sexless. The problem is not so much being within or without the home. Rather, it concerns the communication and identification between matriarchs: the Queen of Heaven and the Mother Church. At that point a woman's home is her mother's and femininity is effectively excluded.

Providing the comforts of home has lately been rejected as unworthy of women. A woman who caters to her husband, who cares for her home, often has the sense that she is engaging in an activity akin to mothering and that her husband is acting like a helpless infant—at times with good reason. To make a home is a dissimulation, a play of semblances, the creation of an illusion of familiarity that covers a truth some people find unbearable. The question is whether this truth ought to be bearable or sufferable by those who seek familiarity in a home. To address it we refer to an article by Freud called *"Das Unheimliche."* The German word in the title is translated as "uncanny." What the translation loses is the sense of the literal meaning of the German, which is "unhomely." In English this word does not exist, but it is interesting that its opposite, "homely," is not very flattering when used to refer to a woman. The German word *heimlich* refers to the comforts of home. Among the definitions Freud listed we read the following: "the enjoyment of quiet content, etc., arousing a sense of agreeable restfulness and security as in one within the four walls of his house" (SE, vol. 18, p. 222). And also: "concealed, especially from sight, so that others do not get to know of or about it, withheld from others" (p. 223). The word *unheimlich* refers to strangeness, to something "eerie, weird, arousing gruesome fear . . ." (p. 224).

Simply put, Freud's argument is that anything that is uncanny had originally been familiar but has become alienated from the mind through repression (p. 241). The strange and the familiar are in some place joined, and Freud offered the following example: "It often happens that neurotic men declare that there is something uncanny about the female genital organs. This *unheimlich* place, however, is the entrance to the former *Heim* [home] of all human beings, to the place where each one of us lived once upon a time and in the beginning" (p. 245). Aside from the curious phrasing, echoing fairy tales and the biblical narrative, this most familiar place is considered to comport danger precisely because it is familiar—not so much in Freud's sense as in the sense that a child's familiarity with his mother's genitals may well be understood in an incestuous context. The place itself is not considered to be dangerous, but there is someone, a ghost, a spirit, a Sand-Man, the tutelary genie of the place, who will not allow it to be encroached upon. The connection between this father-figure and the uncanny place produces the anxiety.

Where does this leave us on the question of home? It is clear that the issue is in internal contradiction; the familiar and the unfamiliar seem to be inseparably linked. To make the choice an either/or proposition does not resolve the problem. Those who intone so vociferously what are called family values do so because the love of the familiar excludes the erotic. And those women who make every effort to eschew the familiar for love of truth tend to provoke flight in the men they encounter. The strangeness of the uncanny may provoke anxiety, but it is also a position comporting desire. If there were no desire in the Other there would be no anxiety in the subject. The comfort of home, as provided traditionally by women, tends to mask whatever it is that is frightening in the place, but this is not in itself a reason to reject the identification of wife with home for the sake of truth. Truth is not always the best of cohabitants.

Plutarch did not limit himself to the idea that women should stay at home; he also said that they should keep silent. Thus we question the value of silence in relation to femininity, especially since it is hardly univocal in its meaning (See Bloch 1986a). For some this will come to mean that women do not have the right to speak, do not have a voice; it certainly may lend itself to oppression, and this seems to be the tone or the practical consequence of the remarks quoted. This may or may not be what Plutarch had in mind; it seems clearly to be what Paul had in mind in the first epistle to Timothy: "I desire then that in every place the men should pray, lifting holy hands without anger or quarreling; also that women should adorn themselves modestly and sensibly in seemly apparel, not with braided hair or gold or pearls or costly attire but by good deeds, as befits women who profess religion. Let a woman learn in silence with all submissiveness. I permit no woman to teach or to have authority over men; she is to keep silent. For Adam was formed first, then Eve; and Adam was not deceived, but the woman was deceived and became a transgressor. Yet woman will be saved through bearing children, if she continues in faith and love and holiness, with modesty" (Timothy 2:8–15). This is a famous text; it should not be taken lightly. It links silence with the rejection of feminine adornment; the role it prescribes for women who wish to be saved is motherhood. Femininity is condemned in the interest of motherhood and the responsibility for the loss is placed with Eve. In itself this passage alerts us to the fact that it requires no small leap of faith to make Aphrodite into a nun.

Silence may also signify the position of the listener or the audience, in which case it is hardly a place comporting powerlessness. It is receptive, in one sense, but it also passes judgment on the performance, be it a speech act or a dramatic performance. Another possible meaning for silence is that it represents an experience beyond language, an area of experience that does not translate into verbal form. Since language is a public medium, the value placed on silence in relation to femininity may tell us that it represents a limit or a supplement to the domain that language covers. This corresponds to Lacan's comments on feminine enjoyment. In *Encore* he said that there was something about the experience that made it uncommunicable. From a quite different angle Donald Davidson declared: ". . . there may in the nature of the case always be something we grasp in understanding the language of another (the concept of truth) that we cannot communicate to him" (Davidson 1984, p. 29). Such statements require clarification. If the audience grasps the truth of an utterance, it may not be able to communicate this truth in words to the speaker or performer. And yet, we know that the listener of a joke communicates not what he has understood, but that he has understood, through laughter. (Remember that Aphrodite was called "laughter-loving.") It is similar for an audience through applause. Lacan deliberately chose the word *encore* as signifying a feminine position in relation to sexual enjoyment.

There is one other association with silence that has not yet been broached: the link between silence and death. Freud was not alone in noting that the life drives are noisy while the death drives are silent; the latter represent the loss of speech, the quality of muteness and even dumbness, but they also represent a return home, to a primary inorganic state. Freud addressed these issues in his paper "The Theme of the Three Caskets," and there he identified the lead casket chosen by Bassanio in *The Merchant of Venice* with the place of Cordelia in *King Lear* and also with the place of Aphrodite in the story of the judgment of Paris. All three, he declared, are instances of the Goddess of Death (SE, vol. 12, p. 291ff.). "The Goddess of Love herself, who now took the place of the Goddess of Death, had once been identical with her. Even the Greek Aphrodite had not wholly relinquished her connection with the underworld, although she had long surrendered her chthonic role to other divine figures, to Persephone, or to the triform Artemis-Hecate. The great Mother-goddesses of the oriental peoples, however, all seem to have been both creators and destroyers—both goddesses of life and fertility and goddesses of death" (p. 299). And the role of Cordelia combines what is fairest and best in women with "certain characteristics that border on the uncanny . . ." (p. 300). The goddess of love and that of death are connected because it is only the Goddess of Death who loves unconditionally, who will accept the old man Lear into her arms when no other woman will have him. This is shown no less in the Valkyrie in German mythology who "carries away the dead hero from the battlefield" (p. 301), than in the images of the *pietà* cradling the dead God in her arms.

In Freud's text the position of womanly power and mastery involves an identification with the Goddess of Death, with what Hegel called the absolute master. If this is the truth of the position of women, then femininity is a dissimulation whose purpose is to persuade men that they have some choice in the matter. And yet discourse, as Lacan said, always concerns dissembling, and it is only through the play of semblance that social links are engaged and maintained. Certainly a discourse that renounced all forms of seeming would have the effect of empowering women. The question is: at what price such enjoyment? And finally, we may want to know what God would dare be paired with this ultimate form of the Mother Goddess.

What if femininity is redefined in terms of motherhood or a biological constant? In that case it is something that belongs to each woman as a birthright received from her mother. If it is additionally, as is the case in Christian tradition, a repository of moral value, then a woman is obliged not only to express it in all areas of her life but to essay to reconstitute those areas to reflect its "virtue." It becomes an integral part of herself, and she will revolt against the social structures that manifest masculine values. For her these structures will be strictures. The values that she will then attempt to render functional in work will be those that are central to the Judeo-Christian tradition: love, care, relationships, faith, and so on. Authority will come to reside in a mother goddess. The revolution thus promoted would have as its goal the transvaluation of the values of the fallen world, to bring them into continuity with the values of the Heavenly City. Thus the distinction between masculine and feminine would be abolished and marriage as it was known traditionally would no longer exist.

Socially defined femininity derives from the structuring power of marriage, the one that does not exist among the heavenly angels. When there is no social structure that articulates femininity, then the first recourse is to motherhood, to the existence of a uterus as the defining sexual characteristic, taken to be a fact of biological nature, which all women have in common. The second is to the idea of a feminine essence, a quality that a woman may or may not have, that she may, when she does not have it, want to acquire, sometimes through identifying with other women, sometimes through a journey into the interior of her soul. This latter represents the mystical path, which contemporary psychology calls personal growth and development. It is clear that the journey's goal is a union with God, an ecstatic communion in love. The God who is love is perfectly equipped to be the object of such a quest. As with mystics of an earlier time, we find in the mythos of contemporary feminism a movement that begins with the rejection of marriage, of the enslavement inherent in domestic chores and responsibility, that moves to the reinsertion into a community of scholars and teachers, a community separated from the masculine world of greed and competition, culminating in the woman's discovery of the man of her dreams, a man who is consistently defined as an amalgam of both masculine and feminine traits: he is strong and tender, firm and sensitive, rugged and caring, he loves her for her soul and her mind, not for her yellow hair. Such a male figure represents what the mystics, both male and female, found in Jesus Christ. He is anything but the prince of a story like Cinderella. In fact, he represents the opposite. The story of the wicked stepmother and stepsisters who oppress the beautiful and more feminine Cinderella is a story in which a young woman oppressed by other women gains access to her femininity through the intervention of a husbandly man. Cinderella becomes a woman in being swept away by a handsome prince; what attracts him is not her soul or mind, but her glass slipper. Hers is the story of the oppression of a woman's femininity by other women; it represents an aspect of women's life that is sufficiently common to be recognizable.

In the meantime marriage was rejected for placing a woman's access to her femininity within a structure that defines that identity in relation to men—to two men, a father and a husband—under the sign of the phallus. Within the structure of marriage a woman is exchanged, as Lévi-Strauss said, and in the exchange she in some sense is transformed from being a girl to being a woman. The question of how a girl becomes a woman is at the heart of any inquiry about femininity, and the traditional, even universal, social structure that covers and produces this transformation is marriage. The identification of woman with wife exists in the French language, where the same word, *femme*, is used for both, and in English, where the Old English root of *woman* is *wifmon*. This is not to say that marriage is the only way for a girl to become a woman, rather that it provides the paradigm upon which other ways are based. One that comes immediately to mind is *mistress*, especially since the title *Mrs.* is an abbreviation for the former. Of course, the word *woman*, according to most dictionaries, means primarily an adult female, as *man* means an adult male. We have no intention of denouncing such meanings; rather, we assert that neither definition addresses the question of sexual identification. A woman for whom the question of what it is or means to be a woman is pertinent will not likely accept the answer: an adult female.

Defining the question of femininity in terms of marriage poses manifold difficulties. We may summarize these difficulties by asking whether it is feasible or possible for a girl to become a woman through means other than marriage, or else, whether these other means simply reproduce the structuring process in another form. Can this be done without passing through a structure in which men are the actors and in which women are in some sense the object of an exchange? Why may a girl not become a woman by being part of a community or group of women, thereby gaining a sexual identity in a way that is equal and opposite to the way that men gain theirs? These are some of the issues raised by contemporary debate on these issues. Recall Juliet Mitchell's remark from an earlier chapter: why is it that it is always men who exchange women and not vice versa? If women were to exchange men in the marriage exchange, then there would have to be some other mechanism for the accession of women to femininity. Those that are proposed place womanhood outside of male dominated discourse. The idea is that femininity is natural, not only that it is part of a woman's nature, but that it places her in direct contact with nature and her truth. If there is to be a sense of womanhood that transcends both marriage and motherhood, where better to look than to the menstrual cycle, to a natural bleeding that has nothing to do with bloodshed or any contact with a man. And the natural flow of menstrual blood is associated with femininity in many cultures, though it takes on a different significance in different traditions. But if it is denuded of cultural significance and given the task of determining sexual identity, does this not tie a woman to her body—as anatomical and biological mechanism over which she has little or no control—even more effectively than Plutarch wanted to tie wives to their homes. At least the Greeks admitted other womanly roles to that of wife, and from where we stand it appears that Aphrodite is more accurately considered to be the goddess of the Otherness of femininity. Perhaps Plutarch did not really mean what he said.

Following the examples of Jacob and Odysseus, we have said that a boy becomes a man through an action in which he is marked, preferably through a cut that sheds blood. According to the structure of the marital exchange, a girl becomes a woman by being moved. In principle this comports a change in social status and a change of place; in other times and other social contexts the two would have been identified. While it may seem reasonably evident that the audience at a performance is moved, it is not clear in our time that marriage functions to move women. This may be one reason why the institution fails them. Let us examine the concept of movement, especially as it is defined by Aristotle, who has a certain privilege in this area. Such an inquiry will present Aristotle's concept of the relation between mover and moved as a principle operative in various areas of human and nonhuman existence; it will lead us to consider whether the application of this principle to what goes on between the sexes delimits structural properties of each.

For Aristotle there are four kinds of movement: locomotion, alteration, diminution, and growth (*On the Soul*. 406b12). Something is said to be movable when it is capable of being other than what it is, when it has the capacity for change, when it is potential rather than actuality. Movement is the activation of that potential in the sense that a house before it is built is buildable (or movable) and its movement is its being built. Once it is built, once it is a house, it is no longer movable or in movement (*Metaphysics*. 9. 9). The movable is distinguished from the mover because the mover is considered to be unmoved. Motion takes place in the movable; it passes to the state of being moved by something that does not move and it is the movable that provides the principle for the interaction of movable and mover in its desire or love (*eromenon*) for the unmoved mover (see *Metaphysics*. 12. 7). The mover is thus outside of the system, a point on which Aristotle insisted, or else he acts as though he is (*Metaphysics*. 1019a15–20). The principle of the separation of mover and moved is applied even where it does not appear to be the case. After the first unmoved mover, which is responsible for the motion of the heavens, there are other unmoved movers who move the planets: "There are other spatial movements—those of the planets—which are eternal, . . . and each of *these* movements also must be caused by a substance unmovable in itself and eternal" (*Metaphysics*. 12. 7). And he added in the next chapter that these substances are gods (12. 8).

The concept of substance requires some definition. Aristotle defined it as "that which is not predicable of a subject"; this is in distinction to a universal that is predicated, usually of many subjects, but of "some subject always." Immediately preceding this definition he wrote the following: "For it seems impossible that any universal term should be the name of a substance. For primary substance is that kind of substance which is peculiar to an individual, which does not belong to anything else; but the universal is common, since that is called universal which naturally belongs to more than one thing. Of which individual then will this be the substance? Either of all or of none. But it cannot be the substance of all; and if it is to be the substance of one, this one will be the others also; for things whose substance is one and whose essence is one are themselves also one" (*Metaphysics*. 7. 13). In relation to the last chapter, substance, what something is, seems to relate to the singularity of the referent of the proper name and perhaps by extension to the referent of natural kind terms, insofar as they participate in the function of rigid designation.

The argument for the movement imparted to planets by substances taken as intelligences extends to the soul itself; if the soul moves the body then it is false, Aristotle asserted, to see the soul in motion or even as self-moving (*On the Soul*. 405b33–406a2). Here it is important to note the difference between this view of the soul and the intelligences (or minds) that move the planets and the one adopted by Christianity. In the latter theology we have seen many instances of the motion of the soul and the angels, their being attributed with potential even where they are not granted a material component. While angels are considered to be movers in some Christian writers, they are also often granted, contrary to Aristotle, the faculty of motion (CHLMP, p. 576).

The problem we see in the Aristotelian conceptualization is not so much the attribution of movement and potential to material being, first to prime matter, then to the body, but rather the status of the unmovable as object. How does it happen that the agent of movement is an object of desire and not a subject? As Nussbaum stated: "the animal is not self-moving because . . . its motions must be explained with reference to an external object of desire, which is an 'unmoved mover.' The heavenly spheres, similarly, are moved by an object of desire: this object is the unmoved mover . . ." (Nussbaum 1985, pp. 120–21). Yet at the same time the unmoved mover is an agent; it acts on the movable. There is no potential in the unmoved mover, which can never be otherwise than what it is. Clearly Nussbaum saw no problem here. Summarizing Aristotle's view of animal motion, she declared: "Aristotle calls the cognitive and orectic [desiring] factors 'movers'; he uses the active verb 'imparts motion' both for the activity of the object of desire and for the way in which the soul gets the animal going" (Nussbaum 1986, p. 277). As for the desire operative, here Nussbaum defined it as "object-directed, active inner reaching-out." It is distinguished from "being-affected" and "being-in-need" (Nussbaum 1986, p. 275). Desire is not a function of the first unmoved mover, the one that moves the heavens, but of the moved body; and this indicates that desire is "enmattered," as Nussbaum put it (1985, pp. 146, 156).

According to this point of view desire is produced in an organism by an object outside of it; it is caused by the object. Without an object to give direction there is no desire, but a vague yearning or need. Movement consists in the displacement toward the object, the effort to appropriate it. When it is appropriated the movement ceases. If the object as unmoved mover is never appropriated, as happens with the motions of the heavens, then the movement continues eternally. Our own view is slightly different. Let us say that there is an object that causes desire. To say that the body, in lacking an object, desires it, may do well when desire is thought to be an appetite. It does not answer the question of what moves the body to seek the object, unless this function is granted to the object. But if it is a separate intelligence; then this ought not to be considered to be identical with the object as unmoved mover. The intelligence must recognize that the body desires; it must recognize desire as existing outside of itself. But whose desire is it? Following Lacan's statement that desire is the desire of the Other, we say that the immaterial intelligence recognizes its own desire outside of itself and thus that it has reason to move the movable. So the work of the separate intelligence is first to read the desire and then to bring the desired situation into the real. Desire may be caused by an object, but the mover does not act to acquire the object, but rather to produce movement. Obviously this implies that there is an enjoyment in the transformation from movable to moved and that it exists even in the nonacquisition of the object. So a woman represents herself as desiring through the use of bodily ornaments. These objects are unmoved unmovers. They are for the separate intelligence a representation of his own position in the Other. Perhaps his becoming the agent of movement involves his wish to acquire the objects, but it is more reasonable to say that he aims at something else, something that adornment covers while delimiting.

Clearly this gives us a sense of why women are considered to occupy the place of the Other, as the Other sex. The lack manifested in desire maps onto the female body. The desire "enmattered" here corresponds to something movable whose mover is outside of it. If, however, the desiring body is desiring to the extent that it is separated from a subject, then that body cannot know whose desire is in question. Desire would then represent a predicate or a series of predicates in search of a signifier, in roughly the sense that the sphinx posed a question as a series of predicates of all who passed her. Those who did not provide a signifier lost their substance. If to be desiring excludes being self-moving, then the desiring Other must seek an unmoved mover; for it is the unmoved mover whose desire is realized in this Other place. The example from Aristotle that provides us with a visualization of the relations between the sexes was probably not invoked by him to that intention. "And that which offers resistance must be other than that which is moved, and wholly different from the whole of it; and what is thus unmoved must be no part of what is moved. If not, it will not be moved. Evidence for this is found in this problem: why is it that someone can easily move a boat from outside, if he shoves it along with a pole, putting it against the mast or some other part; but if he should try to do this when he is in the boat himself, he would never move it . . ." (*On the Movement of Animals,* in Nussbaum 1985, 698b18–25).

There must on the side of the Other be an object in play that designates a lack. This object, corresponding to the function of the fetish, not only designates a lack, but it functions as an impediment to the unmoved mover's making the Other into the object of his desire. His role is not to move himself, but rather to impart movement to the Other, and this involves transforming potential into activity with the end of providing for that potential a form.

The final point here is to note that the signifier, the pole of the man who is moving the boat from the shore, which imparts movement to the boat that occupies the position of the desiring Other, is the phallus. It is essential to note that it is a part of the body that acts to move but only to the extent that it functions as a signifier. However, in order to function as a signifier must it not be separated from being a bodily organ to become a part of language? From the Aristotelian point of view it is a moved mover, thereby representing the point at which the signifier hooks into the human body. It is not moved with the body as the soul is, but rather it is moved by the action of a separate intelligence. Nussbaum's description of Aristotle's approach to this question resonates with these remarks even though the Philosopher did not privilege the phallus. "Desire is an enmattered process, and we want to find out what the bodily 'moved mover' is; we need an organ, or some stuff, that is capable of receiving perceptual stimuli and initiating bodily responses. The mysterious *pneuma* is invoked to fill this gap" (Nussbaum 1985, p. 156). (For a review of the philosophical debate about the *pneuma* or breath see Nussbaum, 1985, essay 3). Let us simply quote some of the relevant remarks by Aristotle, first to see whether they sustain our understanding of what it is that serves this intermediary function, and second to note in what way breath and phallus are not exactly alike.

According to the account that gives the reason for motion, desire is the middle, which imparts movement being moved. . . . Now that which is moved but does not by nature initiate movement can be affected by an external power, but a mover must of necessity have some power and strength. It is clear that all animals have connate *pneuma* and derive their strength from this. . . . And it is obviously well disposed by nature to impart movement and supply strength. Now the functions of movement are pushing and pulling, so the tool of movement has to be capable of expanding and contracting. And this is just the nature of *pneuma*. For it contracts and expands without constraint, and is able to pull and push for the same reason; and it has weight by comparison with the fiery and lightness by comparison with its opposite. (*On the Movement of Animals*, trans. Nussbaum 1985, chap. 10)

While breath is common to all living animals, the phallus is not common to all human beings. Whereas among animals breath is the point of the juncture of body and a separate substance, among humans that function is exercised by the phallus. This is to say that human sexual desire does not function as an appetite and it is not an instinctive activity. As it happens, people are obliged to learn how to do it. Perhaps this is a consequence of the fact that for humans the function of breathing is contaminated by the transformation of breath into speech.

The discussion of movement interlaces with that concerning the identification of women with house and home. This says that the activity of building a house is the actualization of the potential, of the buildability of the house. The house itself is not this actualization, because its existence eliminates or erases its potential or possibility. And if there is no potential to be actualized there is no movement; one arrives at immobility. From this we may say that a woman who is marriageable is in a state of potential and that this potential is actualized when she is being married, that is, when she is participating in the marriage ceremony. After the ceremony she is no longer marriageable. Not only is she no longer in motion, no longer moved, but she no longer has the potential of being marriageable.

Such a line of reasoning, however imprecise its presentation here, could well lead to the idea that a married woman is immobilized because her potential is erased in the actuality of her state of being a wife. Yet if we place this idea in the context of contemporary discourse, how often does one hear from women that they do not fulfill their potential in marriage? Since I have no reason to believe that women who say that marriage does not fulfill their potential are speaking an untruth, I will modify the formula to say that in marriage a woman's potential is actualized, but not entirely. Perhaps the point is that the structure of femininity concerns a potential that is actualized, but not entirely. A woman is moved in the marriage ceremony, but are there not other experiences in the course of a marriage that move her? Sexual experience, to choose a not so random example, ought for a woman to be moving; this is the testimony of women who compare sexual enjoyment to a sensation of falling or sinking. In order for this to happen something of an unactualized potential ought to remain in play in the marriage after the ceremony.

Why does the same not pertain to a man in the marriage ceremony? The answer is that it is not marriage that makes a boy a man. It is only after he has become a man in relation to other men that he can occupy the position of the one who is supposed to act to move a woman. If a performer occupies the place of an unmoved mover, this tells us that he is not moved by his performance in the way that his audience is. Not that the performer may not be a moved mover, as in the case of the rhapsode described by Plato in the *Ion,* but in that case he is identified with the part of the body we have identified as the moved mover. The phallus as moved mover is intermediary between the performer as unmoved mover and his audience as movable.

Locating the paradigm of a woman's movement in the marriage ceremony explicates the importance of the role of the bride in religious tradition. In place of the proverb "Always a bridesmaid, never a bride," we find something like: "Always a bride, never a wife." In a strange way this seems to be the presupposition of mystics who attempt to keep their souls in some sort of motion, who wish to become a potential that is always in the process of being actualized. The mystical marriage was defined by Christianity as a subsistence of the embrace of bride and bridegroom, a timeless embrace in love. No mystic ever articulated the wish to settle down as the housewife of Christ, despite the work of nuns in convents, which has much in common with the tasks performed by a wife. Placing an emphasis on mystical experience allows us to account for the persistence of references to the bride in the tradition. It also gives an idea of the appeal of such a reference for women. Even today it is not the position of bride that women find repulsive, but rather that of wife. Even the position of mother is preferable because it gives the sense of always being moved in harmony and sympathy by the growth and development of a child.

Assume that femininity has something to do with the position of the listener and that the speaker is required through his speech to move this listener. The value of the performance is judged by the effect it produces on the listener; to the listener is granted the role of passing judgment. This produces an immediate difficulty. If the listener is a woman, let us say that the condition of her judgment is that she not judge in her own person or name, but rather in the name of something else. Such is the judgment by Antigone of the edict of Creon, which she makes in the name of the law of the gods, of their justice. Neither speaker nor listener is involved in dialogue in his own person. The appearance of the person of either can only produce the collapse of the dialectic. If, for example, the two are in love and if love is very forgiving, then at the limit the quality of the performance will be unimportant. What will matter is that it be sent as a personal communication. When charity is not involved, when the listener is desiring, then the performer is at risk. Thus the existence of performance anxiety, but not listening anxiety. The speaker is judged by the listener, but his anxiety concerns whomever he must answer to. The one he has to answer to is the teacher from whom he has appropriated his skills.

What if a woman is not the judge of the performance but rather is judged, where, in other words, the value of the performance is beyond doubt and where the listener's response can never be other than a reflection of the state of her soul. The message sent by God through the Incarnation of Christ is organized in this way. If you do not respond to it in the right way, by pledging your soul to Christ, you are condemned, either in this life or in the resurrected one—preferably in both. The question then is not whether a suitor's plea is rejected or accepted, but rather whether his beloved is innocent or guilty. The proceedings become criminal, with the recipient being guilty before the fact, by virtue of having been born. Thus the soul within such a paradigm gains an identification based on the judgment of guilt or innocence; Christianity asserts that the only way out is to accept Christ's petition for love. Within the Judeo-Christian tradition the soul is defined as fundamentally culpable, for being descended of the first sin of the first parents. Religion and at times philosophy are proposed as a therapeutic of this guilt. And the path to innocence involves learning how to respond correctly to God's demand for love. In guilt as well as in innocence the sexes are undivided. The division of the sexes is swallowed by the supervening division of angels and devils.

In relation to the Catholic Church, it stretches credulity to assert that the division of the sexes is not operative. Considering the definition that Paul gave of proper female comportment in Church, and considering that women are not permitted to administer sacraments, how can we argue that the Church is not divided according to sex? First, we note that the ministry of the priesthood is not modeled on manliness but on the ministry of the angels. Thus suggests that the function of the priest is disembodied, thus spiritual. Second, the body in question as far as Catholicism is concerned is the body of the Church. My opinion then is that it is not because the role of the priest is so thoroughly virile, but because the place of the female body is so essential as the channel of communication between Heaven and the Church.

I mean this neither as a consolation nor a rationalization. The administering of sacraments is not the same as a dramatic performance before an audience. The priest is not a performer and the audience is hardly in the position of passing judgment. The model for the interaction is neither the speech act nor the joke. Women as members of the congregation were forbidden by Paul to adorn their bodies, because adornment causes desire. Similarly they were to keep their heads covered—in order that the sight of their hair not incite the angels to desire them. Women are in Church as daughters of Eve, as culpable, and as seeking to be daughters of the Virgin Mother. They are there to submit to the judgment of their sex and to offer themselves and their bodies to Christ. The female body is not there to desire but to overcome desire in order to become the embodiment of the sacred body of the Church, not to be marked or to be moved, but to be cleansed in order to receive the reflection of the image of Mother Church and to receive the invisible inscription of the sacraments. We may grant that the experience is supposed to be moving, but that the enjoyment is submitted to an interpretation that renders it a function of reciprocated love. Communion is like receiving a love letter from one's dearly beloved. This is not the same as to be desired by a man or to be the judge of a performance. And there is no freedom to accept or reject a suit and suitor. Perhaps because Eve sinned, women in the Judeo-Christian tradition are put in a position where they are not judging but judged according to whether they are sufficiently obedient and submissive.

Through the mythic event of the temptation and seduction of Eve women have been burdened both with the guilt for mankind's access to sin and death and with the obligation to embody some sort of supernatural innocence. To counterbalance the crime of Eve, Christianity added the figure of the Virgin Mary. Thus through the act of another woman the means are provided for the redemption from the consequences of the Fall. And yet the Virgin is not a woman like other women; she is, in effect, a goddess, and this raises the question of whether Eve is perhaps a fallen goddess. Eve is not only the inverse of the Virgin, but she is also the prototype of Jerusalem, the Heavenly City exiled and reviled on earth until she regains her rightful place in Heaven. Augustine called

Jerusalem the mother of us all, and this seems clearly to be an echo of the meaning of the name of Eve, "mother of all the living."

Through Auerbach's study of Genesis we have seen the particularities and peculiarities of the biblical narrative in relation to the Homeric way of telling things. The movement into the interior, into the mind or soul, may be read as a compensation for elements of the narrative that have been elided or repressed. Let us say that there are gaps in the biblical story of Creation, and that retelling the story will afford a clearer picture of what "actually" went on. There is a substantial tradition, mostly Jewish, of filling in the lacunae in this story. So I will not apologize for the use of imaginative reconstruction of what may be a more plausible narrative, and I will leave it for others to test whether my reconstruction has any basis in other myths. I have mentioned on several occasions the simple fact that in the beginning God does not have a wife. This is a matter of no small consequence, for it requires the initial creation to be *ex nihilo*, out of nothing. This supposition was the basis for disagreements between Judeo-Christian and Greek conceptions of the world, since Aristotle, for example, believed that matter always existed and that its interaction with mind was responsible for the production of the world. The first mover could not, after all, be thought of as moving nothing. There is a significant difference between a mover and a creator.

In the opening line of Genesis God is not confronted with matter but rather with "a formless waste, with darkness over the seas and only an awesome wind sweeping over the water." This may lead you to believe that "nothing" is a bit strong; chaos seems to be a more accurate description. The quality of formlessness may have lent itself to the idea that God was faced with pure potential, but this is not the way the passage has been read. Auerbach noted the importance of psychological states in the biblical narrative and, at the risk of being blasphemous—though I have probably gone far beyond the bounds of ordinary blasphemy by now—I posit that this view of the world may well represent a state of mind. Let us call this state of mind one of anguish, of fear and trembling, mixed with some despair. I prefer anguish to despair here because of the presence of the "awesome" wind, representing a world that is out of control and threatening. It is certainly to God's credit that his response to this anguish is to act, to speak, and through his speech to transform what he sees. In the Christian version of the story God is not alone, he is accompanied by his Son, the Word. The question that now arises is how did things reach this point? I am assuming, despite what is claimed, that we are entering the narrative in the middle of things, *in medias res,* and that we may read what follows as filling in the prior events.

Imagine the following scenario. Let there be a king and a queen and two sons, two princes. One of the princes is contented with his place as prince, he has no ambition to be a king himself, and no wish to occupy his father's place. The other prince wishes for nothing else. Eventually, he revolts against his father; his revolt is defeated and he is banished in ignominy from the kingdom. You may even imagine that the good son was killed defending his father, thus to become immortalized in the memory of all of his father's subjects. And why not imagine that the wife of the king, the mother of these sons, preferred or encouraged the one who initiated a revolt, thereby to be banished herself? What remains for this king is nothing, nothing of what had been his, and it is in relation to this nothing that he will act, not only to create something new, but to create a world in which he will unfailingly gain satisfaction for the wrongs committed against him.

In part this story resembles what happens to Job, in part it echoes the story of Cain and Abel, in part that of Esau and Jacob. The rest was filled in by Christianity. With Christianity the supposition is that the Word and Lucifer are two opposing angels; the latter was banished from Heaven for revolting against God. Lucifer was identified with Satan; his name means "light giver." As was the case in some theories of angels, Lucifer was a star and his name was originally meant to apply to the morning or evening star, to Venus (Davidson 1971, p. 176; Russell 1984, pp. 11–12). If the first thing that God creates is light this may be understood as required by the loss of the light of the heavens in the death of one son and the banishment of the other. Not only would God have been required to create a new light, even to create himself as a new light, but this new light would have to be distinct from the past light, which had fallen into darkness. The distinction of light and darkness is seen by Augustine to be the division between angels and devils. "Between that light (which is the fellowship of the angels, shining with the intelligible illumination of truth) and the contrasted darkness (which stands for the depraved minds of the evil angels who have rejected the light of righteousness) God could make the division; for the evil, though in the future, could not be hidden from him" (CG, book 11 chap. 19).

We add that the Devil, expelled from the Heavenly City, established, like Cain, a kinship system in which he was the father. His position of competing with God for the place of father is clearly stated by Christ himself, who never claims such a place. Addressing Jews who are declaring that their father is Abraham and who do not accept him as god, Jesus says: "The devil is the father you belong to, and you willingly carry out your father's wishes. He was a murderer from the beginning and never based himself on truth, for there is no truth in him. When he tells a lie, he speaks his native language, for he is a liar and the father of lying" (John 8:44). This key passage points to the original murderousness of the devil, but it also seems to identify Abraham with the devil. Abraham, the father of the faith, did sacrifice a ram, identified by Lacan as a father-figure. The idea that this murder was not patricide would be the touchstone for the creation of a possible world, corresponding to the biblical narrative or the variation we are proposing. At that point the question would be whether a world in which the patricide did not take place is possible.

If we were to follow the theme of enemy twins that René Girard has extensively documented in the Bible and elsewhere, we would say that the rebellious son did not succeed in supplanting his father, but did remove the good son from the line of succession by killing him.

So far the story is reasonably plausible within the context of the Genesis narrative, but it has had too little to say about one very conspicuous element. What of the role of God's wife in all of this? Later biblical texts will promote Israel as God's spouse and Jerusalem will be considered the Heavenly version of Israel (Phillips 1985, p. 14). For the moment, in the beginning, God does not seem to have a wife, and as several commentators have noted, this is a fact of considerable significance (See Phillips 1985, pp. 6, 158). If, after all, you accept the Christian account that has God alone with his Son, the Word, at the beginning, you might also be obliged to accept that this Son must have had a mother—even if you assume that the mother of the Word could only be language, or better, a language that embodies nothing but truth.

Let us imagine that the wife of God, his consort before the calamitous revolt of one of his sons, was Eve. And let us assume either that she sided with the adversarial Satan and was therefore banished with him, or else, that she chose to leave with him. The idea of a mother siding with one son against her husband's stated wishes is manifest in Rebecca's promotion of Jacob over Esau. Interestingly, Rebecca chooses the less masculine son, perhaps as a reversal of the choice originally made by Eve, the better to assure that the same situation does not repeat itself. Her choice is that of motherhood, not femininity. Rebecca chooses the son who is more like herself. Since the adversary has more evidently masculine traits, it makes some sense to say that a feminine goddess would find him the better of her two sons.

Through the Fall the first man was seen by Augustine to have acquired desire and a phallic sexuality; we remember that a central characteristic of the male sexual organ is its congenital disobedience to the will. "Thus the result of the first man's lawless presumption and his just condemnation was not a relapse—or a repulse—into the rudimentary condition of infancy. But human nature in him was vitiated and altered, so that he experienced the rebellion and disobedience of desire in his body, and was bound by the necessity of dying; and he produced offspring in the same condition to which his fault and its punishment had reduced him, that is, liable to sin and death" (CG, book 13, chap. 3). The first man does not fall into an infantile condition that would bring him closer to Christ and that would make him like the angels; instead he falls into a state of virility that makes him kin to Satan. He represents a constant reminder of something God would just as soon forget. A man gains virility as condemnable and contemptible, as something that requires purification or redemption.

What does this have to do with God's wife? Let us imagine that a man has two sons, who differ as the night from the day. One loves him beyond reason and the other opposes him constantly. The father of these sons may easily suppose that they had been fathered by different men. Thus God's wife might have known or had another god before God. And she might even prefer the other god, for whatever mysterious reasons. We have named Eve as the wife of God. To justify such a leap of faith let us list what we know of Eve. I mention faith because Eve is a model of the unfaithful wife; she is unfaithful to her husband, the image of God, when she consorts with a serpent, who may, for all we know, be the true father of Cain. Perhaps this is why the offering of Cain was rejected. In an interesting inversion of this idea Jewish tradition has posited that Adam had another wife before Eve, Lilith, who was the mother of Cain. Lilith was also considered to be the bride of Satan (Davidson 1971, p. 174).

Sensuality exists in the encounter of Eve and the serpent, and it may be that as first wife her preference for an other god, before God, was based on reasons of sensual pleasure. The only way for the race descended from the fallen goddess to have value is morally, through a demonstration to God's absolute satisfaction that He and not some other god is the father. What matters to such a father is not whether the children are male or female, but whether they are his. In this way he emulates a mother's certainty about her offspring and identifies with the wife he has lost. When Adam is suffering for being alone of all his species, Gods knows that what he requires is a wife.

Like Aphrodite, Eve is motherless, born of a man who is the image of God, formed of a part of a man's body, which is not replaced. Fortunately for Adam he did not lose a vital part. This form of birth suggests that we are not entirely within the realm of the human; Eve is more like a goddess, or better, the human form of a fallen goddess. Eve and only Eve converses with the serpent, thus with the devil who has enlisted the serpent as his instrument. This conversation is obviously repeated in the encounter between Mary and the angel Gabriel, and it is not excessive to say that Adam is a prototype of Joseph. Both are nonparticipants in their wives' interaction with an angelic being; they accept the seduction and do not renounce their wives for it. In neither case is a husband specifically designated as the father of any child. When Eve gives birth to Cain she alone names him and she designates the father as YHWH. The difference is that Eve does have sexual congress with her husband, she is known by him, while Mary is not. Adam "falls" for his wife's offer of the forbidden fruit, thus is initiated sexually by her. Joseph requires the intercession of an angel to persuade him that his wife is speaking true; thus he is desexualized and embraces continence. Eve deploys feminine wiles to entice her husband, while Mary does not.

These points do not require belaboring. The knowledge gained in the Fall is as nothing next to the knowledge God himself requires. And that is an absolute certainty about his relation to his offspring. We have said that thereby he emulates the position of a mother, but there is more to be said. If women are granted the ability to create life, a father can assert his position only by exercising his power to take life. This is God's command to Abraham and it is God's deed as regards his only Son. There is no question of this being the accepted sense of these events. What is more commonly believed is that God is testing Abraham's faith and that he allowed Jesus to be crucified to save mankind. Thus meaning supercedes and defines an event and God in his questing for certainty becomes Woman. While Freud's reading seeks to restore the true event of patricide that these stories are designed to cover, religion has tended to fill in the gaps in the narrative with meaning.

The act of naming a child is an eminently paternal act; its significance is in its consigning the child to death. Since death is one of the faces of the Great Mother, and since the child will die whether or not it is named, the act of naming identifies the father as the agent of death. Apparently it is important that there be an agent, a mover, who effects the passage from the world of the living to the other place.

For having been seduced by a phallic creature, Eve allows sin and death to enter the world. We are less interested here in what goes on between Eve and Adam as between Eve and the serpent. Significant is the curse of the serpent: "I will plant enmity between you and the woman, And between your offspring and hers. They shall strike at your head And you shall strike at their heel" (Genesis 2:15). Not only does God sow hatred between woman and phallus, but he extends it to the offspring of each. I take this to mean that his curse creates a conflict between signifiers and the female body. Thereby the relation in question does not concern men and women but signifiers and women. It is not men themselves who are the objects of enmity, but men as bearers of the phallic trait.

The signifier is a fallen angel. Its crime is to be the unmoved mover of a woman. The problem is how to find for women something to replace their attraction to the phallus. Clearly enough the solution proposed by Christianity is the Word, not as signifying, but as full of meaning. This is not to be taken as another phallus; rather it promotes the redemptive value of the reproductive material produced by the male sexual organ. Women are supposed to suffer phallic incursions to acquire this substance. Through the process the male sex is given over to the work of fertility. Phallic creatures whose function is to provide this semen are good angels. Rather than pointing upward in pride these angels let fall their semen to cause growth in nature. The function of the female body is thereby altered. A woman will come to be exemplary of her sex for providing flesh to clothe the Word.

Of considerable import in the theorization of creation and generation is the Stoic idea of the *logoi spermatikoi,* the spermatic ratio or seminal principles. Through it the idea of fertility can be extended beyond the biological; understanding will become the product of a fertilization of the minds of listeners by seminal principles. The mixture of the material and spiritual as joined in the act of generation had considerable appeal, describing for the Stoics the "germinative forces inherent in matter" (CHLGEMP, p. 124). For them the concept functions as something of an oxymoron, representing the conjoining of matter and spirit in a permanent tension within material things. Later the more Platonic philosophers, like Plotinus, did not see these forces as inherent in nature, but rather as " 'patterns' imposed on it from without" (CHLGEMP, p. 124n). The first Christian writer to reformulate this idea was Justin Martyr: "In the second apology Justin develops an individual modification of the Stoic conception of *spermatikoi logoi* in nature, seminal principles which cause generation, and of God as the *spermatikos logos* of the world. Justin uses the idea not to explain organic birth and growth but to assert that each rational being shares in the universal Logos, of which he has a piece like a seed sown by the divine Sower" (CHLGEMP, p. 162).

The differing views are combined and synthesized by Augustine. God is the Creator of all things and he contributes to the creative process by sowing invisible seeds through the agency of the good angels.

For those seeds that are visible now to our eyes from fruits and living things, are quite distinct from the hidden seeds of those former seeds; from which at the bidding of the Creator, the water produced the first swimming creatures and fowl, and the first living creatures after their kind. . . . For, consider, the very least shoot is a seed; for, if fitly consigned to the earth, it produces a tree. But of this shoot there is yet a more subtle seed in some grain of the same species, and this is visible even to us. But of this grain there is further still a seed, which, although we are unable to see it with our eyes, yet we can conjecture its existence from our reason; because, except there were some such power in those elements, there would not so frequently be produced from the earth things which had not been sown there; nor yet so many animals, without any previous commixture of male and female; . . . For the Creator of these invisible seeds is the Creator of all things Himself; since whatever comes forth to our sight by being born, receives the first beginnings of its course from hidden seeds, and takes the successive increments of its proper size and its distinctive forms from these as it were original rules. . . . so it is not right to think not only the bad but even the good angels to be creators, if, through the subtlety of their perception and body, they know the seeds of things which to us are more hidden, and scatter them secretly through fit temperings of the elements, and so furnish opportunities of producing things and of accelerating their increase. But neither do the good angels do these things, except as far as God commands, nor do the evil ones do them wrongfully except as far as he righteously permits. (*On the Trinity*, book 3, chap. 8)

The will to synthesize God and nature through a veritable rain of spermatic principles is significant for redefining the interaction of God and the natural world in other than erotic terms. Augustine saw the linkage in terms of generation; the spermatic principles are planted in the earth to produce creatures through the agency of angels. This he deftly mixed with the idea that the angels are intelligent beings, knowing the principles of generation, which to people of his time were more hidden than they are now.

From the observation of the natural process of human, animal, and plant generation, Augustine produced an analogy of the interaction between the Divine Ideas and the material world. There is neither dialectical tension between opposing elements nor even an imposition of principles on the world; rather there is the production of something new and meaningful through the synthesis. Male generative substance becomes the model for the divine contribution to creation in the natural world, but this hardly represents a glorification of masculinity. The angels who perform the work of producing life exist within a maternal space, the Heavenly City of Jerusalem. They are the ultimate good sons who believe their sexuality is entirely in the service of fertility.

For the moment it would appear that Augustine's angels are a band of invisible floating phalloi, totally obedient to the command of their master. It would be best not to call them phalloi at all, but rather simply the invisible ideas of the male sexual organ, whose function has nothing to do with desire, but merely with the production of spermatic substances. They represent sexual organs that have been purified of desire. This has nothing to do with sexual attraction—which is one of the virtues of thinking of nature instead of women—and what it seeks is the production of new beings in a natural manner. Even the evil angels in Augustine do not act of their own volition; they act insofar as God permits them to do their evil deeds. No matter what happens God's will reigns supreme.

This does not necessarily make of God a Father. A Mother-Goddess whose domain is the natural process of generation may also be served by a band of angels, providing that these angels are not like the eunuchs who served the pagan Great Mother. These beings become the imaginary organs of this Goddess, thus to produce a rain of spermatic principles that are functions of her will and not theirs. It is interesting that when Freud articulated the female side to the castration complex, he labeled it penis envy, thus emphasizing the male sexual organ as opposed to the phallus, its signifier.

So, the Logos became flesh, as the Gospel says, and John Scotus Erigena, after Augustine, provided the provocative gloss that flesh designates the feminine sex (Erigena 1972, p. 99). Of course, by the ninth century the Logos had already become the Verbum, though Erigena, the translator of the pseudo-Dionysius, was familiar with Greek. For Erigena there is no real contradiction between Logos and Verbum. The Logos is, among other things, discourse as "saying," and thus Erigena identified it as the place of the Verb in God's saying. Thus when it is written that God said, "Let there be light," Erigena declared that God is the Father and "said" is the Verbum (Erigena, p. 143). The point, of course, is not simply that God said; it is that what he said happened as he said.

It seems clear that the Latin Verbum is not the same as the Greek Logos, and for an analysis of the Logos in Greek we turn to Heidegger's essay "Logos," which is essentially a commentary on the use of the concept in Heraclitus. Among the points that Heidegger made is that the verb *legein*, from which we have the Logos, is a principle of gathering together, or harvesting. This is quite different from creating, even generating. The issue he raised is how the elements of a sentence are held together through the effect of the Logos, how they are joined. He rejected the idea that they are unified by being placed in a single envelope, thus totalized, and also the idea that they adhere through a balancing of contraries (Heidegger 1956, p. 74). The line from Heraclitus that forms the base of his interrogation is translated by Richmond Lattimore: "It is wise, listening not to me but to the Law, to acknowledge that all things are one" (in Nahm 1964, p. 67). It is certainly significant that Logos is translated as Law, not as reason or sense. We know also that Logos may mean speech, saying, and account. The question for which the fragment poses as a response bears on what one hears when listening, and from whom. What one hears should be from the Law, not from any "me"; the suggestion is that one does not hear the sense within the words, the speaker's intention.

The fragment addresses the question of hearing, and it states that what one hears is not the sounds qua sounds, not meaning qua transcendent, but the Law renders the sounds significant. As Heidegger noted, the contrast is between hearing the speaker and hearing the Logos; thus the intention of the speaker is effaced in the interest of hearing something else, which has to do with Law. And the function of the Logos resides not only in the idea of gathering, but also in revealing or unveiling the truth. The gathering of the elements of language into a sentence fixes them and thereby renders truth present. Since the One, for Heraclitus, is fire, the function of the Logos is evident in the phenomenon of lightning. Now what does lightning represent if not a communicating between the heavens and the earth, between Zeus and mortals? Thus Heidegger added another fragment from Heraclitus, which says that the One may and may not consent to be named with the name of Zeus. Lattimore translated: "The one thing which alone is wise is willing and unwilling to be called by the name of Zeus" (in Nahm 1964, p. 72). What is in question here is the function of naming, of the Name as One; this function of naming does have a name (fire accepts being called by it), but it is also the principle through which all things are named.

Clearly the Heraclitean Logos is the symbolic phallus: taken as the flash of lightning it is a "natural" phenomenon raised to a signifying function. That this symbolic phallus marks human flesh in the male sexual organ and that this organ in its erectile prowess functions as that phallus is basic to the structure of masculinity. The Logos that becomes flesh, that becomes incarnate by being vested or clothed with flesh, is not a flash of lightning, but a supreme reason or meaning. Its point of intersection with the human body has been radically changed, and the consequence of the movement from male organ to body as flesh must alter the way in which we understand the functioning of the Logos.

The element of fire, chosen by Heraclitus as the One, has the unique characteristic among the four elements of marking bodies, even of scarring them. As the One the Logos or Law does not take all things and place them in one bag, but rather it introduces the principle of division; the one divides things and collects them in a set (see Heidegger and Fink 1973). It is consistent that the world of Heraclitus is articulated in masculine terms; even at the simplest level, it is based on principles of strife and war, on an enduring tension between contrary elements that is not resolved. Some fragments that demonstrate this are: "War is the father and king of all things. . . ."; "One must know that war is common to all, and that strife is justice; and all things both come to pass and perish through strife."; "The harmony of the world is of tensions, like that of the bow and the lyre."; "All things are exchanged for Fire and Fire for all things, as goods for gold and gold for goods."; "Fire advancing upon all things shall judge them and convict them" (in Nahm 1964, p. 68ff.) It is striking here the extent to which the Logos in Heraclitus has nothing to do with the Word that was later to become flesh.

Not only does the Logos not generate a creature in a virginal body, on the contrary, the sense of the verb *legein* as harvesting and gathering crops, and especially of putting things to rest, suggests the end of the cycle of growth (Heidegger 1956, pp. 61–62). This correlates with the idea that a flash of lightning gathers and renders present what was hidden. Speech therefore collects disparate thoughts, forms them into a grouping, and awaits a response from a listener. In this sense speech is a mover and the effect produced is motion—specifically, that the listener be moved to respond, to acknowledge reception. We have already suggested several different modes of listener response—from laughter to applause to the call for an encore. How do these differ from becoming pregnant, which event might also count as movement?

On the one hand the listener, as Virgin Mary, receives the Word, wraps it in flesh and then presents it to the world, thus creating a new being—all of this without in any way being marked. Throughout she is untouched. On the other hand the body of the listener is marked, is touched by the Law through the words, and demonstrates reception by speaking words that may be paired as are two signifiers or tokens. If, for example, a woman has a child, not only does this have something to do with her responding to a Logos and not a person, but her role will not be limited to her biological contribution. It will bear most especially on her naming or designating the father to the child.

I am not proposing this last remark as a reading of Heidegger or Heraclitus. It does, however, represent Lacan's theory on this matter.

Considering the emphasis we have placed on the father's interdiction of incest, it is good to acknowledge that the mother's word is crucial for giving a man the paternal authority to pronounce this No. Otherwise how is a child to know who the father is? When she designates her husband as father to her child, she is giving up the priority of her own link to the child, thereby to allow the child access to the symbolic order.

To say that the position of the speaker is masculine and that the place of the listener is feminine is problematic in the extreme. There is no distinction between men and women as concerns the exercise of the faculty of speech, no anatomical distinction of the organs of speech and hearing that would lead to this division. Apparently, the link is made on the basis of something like a resemblance between the emitting or extruding function of speech and the functioning of the male sexual organ, coupled with another resemblance between the receptivity of the ears and the receptivity of the female genitals. This is hardly a very strong argument. Let us provide something of a reason for this mapping. Assume that what goes on in the speech act, in the commerce between speaker and listener, is not very easy to grasp because it works at a level that is fundamentally invisible. Something may be happening in speech, but you do not see how the words do whatever they do. Imagine that in order to get a handle on the workings of dialogue it is necessary to find a visual representation of it. If the two positions—speaker and listener—are divided, then the requirement is to find a visible principle of division that applies, either to the world or to those who use language. If the latter choice is the only one that hooks language into those who use it, it seems that the anatomical difference of the sexes becomes enlisted to provide a visible support for the invisible process. As far as dividing the world is concerned, the Greeks used *herms* for this purpose. In both cases the key to the mapping is the phallus.

A division that exists in an other-than-human space therefore comes to determine the division of the human race according to sex. The initial division may be understood as intrinsic to the structure of the signifier or as determinant in a world of intermediary beings. If these beings are invisible but capable of becoming visible, this supports our argument. If the class of intermediary beings is not sexed, this has the tendency to make the mapping problematical. It does so because the sex of the angels, the gods, or the genii, offers a direction for the mapping process. It shows what gets mapped onto what and in what terms. If the angels have no sex, not only is the mapping directionless, but it does not make use of sexual difference, and thereby it tends to divide humans on moral terms. They are all called upon to be like the angels, to be unsexed, and to provide a support for the angelic condition with their lives. The question of the sex of the angels is a fundamental issue as far as human sexual identity and roles are concerned.

Like the angels, speech is invisible. You may see that someone who is speaking is moving his mouth or that someone who is listening is not, but the fact that someone is visibly moving his mouth or that someone seems to be listening does not in itself determine that a speech act is taking place. The transaction of speech, beginning with the words themselves and extending to the effect produced, is not available to sight. Yet it seems to be necessary that there be some visual representation of the transaction, some mapping of the invisible onto the visible, whether the invisible be spoken words, principles, or ideas. Nussbaum provided one good reason for this requirement when she stated that, according to Aristotle, in order for there to be a translation of desire into action a visual image must appear (Nussbaum 1985, p. 221ff.). Thus for action to take place in the world an orientation is required as well as an image of the desired object.

The principles dividing speaker and listener and even subject and predicate seem to require some way to hook into the human body and some way of being mapped onto a fundamentally visible division of the human species. It would appear that the invisible world of these structures is mapped isomorphically onto a difference between human beings that is visible on the level of genital anatomy. One consequence of this is that the assumption of a sexual identity involves the subject's taking a position on one side of the barrier dividing speaking and listening. The subject is divided not only from others, but also against himself. The role of the speaker is divided from that of the listener, and this means that the speaking subject is not the master of what he speaks; he does not determine the meaning of his sentences through his intentions. It requires an act of charity for the listener to attempt to understand what is meant by the speaker (see Davidson 1984, p. 27). Following Lacan, the function that performs the mapping from the world of structures, the world of masculine and feminine intermediary beings, onto human beings is the phallus. This represents a patrilineal descent, a transmission of not only the proper name but also the performative function of naming, and, as we have said, it marks or scars the male body preferentially. The phallus is that part of the body that functions as a signifier and whose transformation from organ into signifier lends itself to visual representation.

One way of eliminating the division of speaker and listener was to propose prayer as the paradigm of communication. There instead of a division along a horizontal axis, the vertical axis becomes primary and the speaker becomes silenced. Prayer comes closest to eliminating the interference of language, thereby making the one who is praying whole. Instead of the Platonic concept of thought as a dialogue taking place in the mind, prayer is essentially a monologue addressed to an ideal listener, one who always understands and who judges in moral terms. In the hands of Augustine the silence of the inner word of knowledge becomes more formidable, because this word in the heart is not spoken inwardly either. "We must go on, then, to that word of man, to the word of the rational animal, to the word of that image of God, that is not born of God, but made by God, which is neither utterable in sound nor capable of being thought under the likeness of sound, such as needs be with the word of any tongue; but which precedes all the signs by which it is signified, and is begotten from the knowledge that continues in the mind, when that same knowledge is spoken inwardly according as it really is. For the sight of thinking is exceedingly like the sight of knowledge" (*On the Trinity*, book 15, chap. 11). What is this "word of the heart belonging to no tongue" (book 15, chap. 23) if not an inscription, a script, as in Scripture, that is prior to speech and more perfect for enlisting the faculty of vision? It resembles what in other places is called the circumcision of the heart.

The division of subject and predicate or subject and verb was to be defeated by the unification of the two under the function of the humanized Verb. The topic of the relations between subject and verb or subject and predicate is at least as old as Aristotle and was a question of major concern for Scholastics. Among the more bizarre writers on this topic was Alain de Lille, a twelfth-century Church Doctor, who did not become a Doctor by attempting to render the laws of grammar and logic in terms of sexual morality. He did, however, provide a clear exposition of the correlation between the division of subject and predicate and sexual difference. For him the laws linking subject and predicate should reflect the "natural" connection between men and women. The goddess who commands all this must be female, since the female is the more natural of the sexes, and her name interestingly enough is Venus. His placing this under the aegis of Venus in *The Complaint of Nature* provides a link to the central concern of this chapter. For example, Alain saw nouns as representing the female sexual organ and adjectives as representing the male. Nature says: "Furthermore, my command enjoined Cypris that, in her constructions, she have regard to the ordinary rules for nouns and adjectives, and that she appoint that organ which is especially marked with the peculiarity of the feminine sex to the office of noun, and that she she should put that organ characterized by the signs of the masculine sex in the seat of the adjective. . . . And since each is influenced by the other, by the laws of necessity the adjective is attracted according to its modifying quality, and the noun as is proper in a thing retentive of substantive nature" (Alain de Lille 1908, pp. 51–52). Assume here that adjectives are descriptive characteristics that are predicated of a noun-substantive. Thereby we have the picture of something like a mother-goddess qua noun connected with things in nature, accompanied by a court of males attracted naturally to her as universal predicates, as angels. The phallic function in its connection with proper naming is clearly eluded in this scheme.

The idea that nature dictates the proper sexual relation of subject and predicate is evident in Alain's curious discussion of the erotics of syllogism. The stages comprise external connection (conversation?), kissing as part of a relationship, and finally the true "fleshy connection."

Moreover, I added that a syllogistic conclusion in the due order of three propositions should be arranged, but that it should be content with an abridgment of two terms, following none of the Aristotelian figures; being of such sort that in every proposition the major extreme should perform the office of the predicate, and the minor should be the subject, and be bound by its laws. In the first proposition the predicate should cling to the subject, not in the manner of true inherence, but simply by way of external connection, as with a term predicated from a term. In the minor proposition the major term should be joined to the minor more closely by the reciprocal pressure of the kisses of relation. But in the conclusion there should be celebrated, in the truer bond of closest inherence, the fleshy connection of subject and predicate. (Alain de Lille 1908, p. 53)

We have only to continue our reading to discover Alain inveighing against unnatural couplings of the two. And we discover such things in nothing less than metaphor and metonymy, terms we have introduced to determine the principles of the composition of a sentence according to the rule of Eros. Here is Alain: "Furthermore, just as it has been my purpose to attack with bitter hostility certain practices of grammar and logic, and exclude them from the schools of Venus, so I have forbidden to the arts of Cypris those metonymic uses of rhetoricians which Mother Rhetoric embraces in her wide bosom, and inspires as her speech with many graces; for I feared lest if, in the pursuit of too strained a metaphor, she should change the predicate from its protesting subject into something wholly foreign, cleverness would be too far converted into a blemish, refinement into grossness, fancy into a fault, ornament into a gaudy show" (Alain de Lille 1908, p. 54). What he seems to say is that metaphor and metonymy alienate the predicate from the subject, making it into an instance of Otherness. And yet, if there is to be a dialectical tension between subject and predicate, a play of attraction and division, then a model of their relations based on an equally dubious model of "fleshy connection," of becoming one flesh, ought to be excluded. The function of the Law of language is to do just that, to interdict the fleshy connection between the substantial Mother Goddess and her Verbal predicates.

It takes a certain amount of nerve to elaborate so complex and serious a topic as the relations between subject and predicate with passages that show an author at his worst. As C. S. Lewis wrote: "These conceits are now the author's chief disgrace" (Lewis 1936, p. 106). And yet, the topic of the relations between subject and predicate was of major interest in the medieval period. Within the field of medieval and premedieval semantics, one goal was to discover a type of interaction between subject and predicate that could be conceptualized in terms not of a division of the sexes, but rather, as Alain seemed to believe, of their union. Thus there was to be a harmony between substantive and its predicates, and this tended to privilege certain types of sentences, certain types of discourse. The idea was that such a harmony, which we may call love, would produce sentences that were meaningful, thus true, and thereby in direct relation with the things of the world. If things in the world are but a reflection of the real world of meanings or ideas, those sentences that presented ideas most clearly would provide access to a world of nature that was the mirror reflection of the supersensible. They would thereby replicate the knowledge of angels, knowledge of the intelligible species and other predicables.

What happened, then, when William of Ockham arrived to declare that angels as well as humans do not gain knowledge through the intelligible species? What was the consequence for the relations of subject and predicate when Ockham declared not only that there are not any species or universals outside of the mind, but also that there is no relation outside of it either (on relations, see Hyman and Walsh 1984, p. 679ff). Certainly this alters the view of angels. Previously, angels not only knew according to intelligible species, but were also identified with them. This connection may enter Christianity through Augustine's notion of the knower taking on the likeness of the known, which Ockham referred to for a different purpose (in Hyman and Walsh 1984, p. 677). The passage of Augustine is as follows: "And the true word then comes into being, when, as I said, that which we toss to and fro by revolving it arrives at that which we know, and is formed by that, in taking its entire likeness; so that in what manner each thing is known, in that manner also it is thought . . ." (*On the Trinity*, book 15, chap. 15).

William of Ockham saw truth in terms of the reference of a proposition to a thing. And since he would not in singular propositions (those that are neither modal nor hypothetical) speculate on the interaction of subject and predicate, he collapsed this relation by saying that both represent or stand in for a thing. "For the truth of such a singular proposition, which is not equivalent to many propositions, it is not required that the subject and the predicate be really the same, nor that the predicate be really in the subject, or really inhere in the subject, nor that it be really united with the subject outside the mind. For instance, for the truth of the proposition 'This is an angel, it is not required that this common term 'angel' be really the same with that which has the position of subject in this proposition, or that it be really in it, or anything of the sort; but it is sufficient and necessary that subject and predicate should stand for the same thing" (in Hyman and Walsh 1984, p. 661). For Ockham there are only substances and the intentions of speakers; there are no real extramental universals. With Ockham, rather than have a "fleshy connection" between subject and predicate to define and determine other relations, you find that outside of language the knowing subject has intuitive cognition of singular things in the world. Julius Weinberg summarized the idea: "The mind first notices intuitively a singular thing existing outside the mind and forms in itself, or receives in itself something which is similar to the external object which is the object of this intuitive noticing. This similitude of the object can serve as the object of this intuitive noticing. This similitude of the object can serve as a sign in consciousness of the object outside; and, if separated from the accidental features which *de facto* distinguish one object from another, this similitude can stand for all the objects which resemble the object which initially produced the similitude" (Weinberg 1967, p. 251). In the intuition of the thing by the intellect it is the intellect that is transformed, by absorbing the essence of the thing. Ockham wrote: "Speaking of intuitive cognition, . . . an angel and our own intellect know what is other than themselves, not through their species nor through their own essence but through the essence of the things known . . ." (in Hyman and Walsh 1984, p. 676). In addressing the question of the knowledge contained in the angelic intellect, Ockham simply erased the distinction between the angelic and the human. What is most striking here is the status of the concept of the singular "thing," the initial object of intuition, which is grasped without benefit of any sort of intermediary species. There is no need to raise the mind to the superior, angelic state. And if the universals through which people had previously gained knowledge were not real, it is not too far to saying that angels also are the intentions of the soul—a step Ockham did not take. If the Law that was so dear to Aristotelians required the intermediary agency of universals to gain any sort of knowledge, excluding out of hand the direct, face-to-face knowledge promised in the Resurrection, then the exclusion of species in favor of direct intuitive cognition represents a discarding of language in favor of concepts inextricably tied to things, which never touch them. "A concept or mental impression signifies naturally whatever it does signify; a spoken or written term, on the other hand, does not signify anything except by free convention" (in Hyman and Walsh 1984, p. 654).

Here we find a place for the important passion for etymology evidenced by many of the authors we have studied. Etymology was thought to provide a return to the original maternal language that loves nature, the language that effectively liberates man from the bondage of the signifier. What could have been more seductive than the idea of a language that had a monopoly on truth? As Howard Bloch stated:

Philo's affirmation of the initial coincidence of words and things is by no means an isolated example. On the contrary, we find the belief in the integrity of a primeval language—an *Ursprache* similar to the Indo-European of the comparative philologist—for as long as the model of universal history seems to prevail. Augustine posits the existence of an original single tongue but hesitates about what to call it, maintaining only that "if the language that Adam once spoke still survives today, it contains the sounds with which the first man named the earthly animals and the birds." Isidore follows the tradition of Alexandrian Judaism according to which "words are the indices of things," and Hebrew "the mother of all tongues." John of Salisbury refers to Hebrew as the tongue "mother nature gave our first parents." Bruno Latini considers it the "original natural language." Dante's search for beginnings leads him back through "the form of speech created by God together with the first Hebrew word . . ." (Bloch 1986b, pp. 39–40)

The idea that "mother nature" originally gave language to humans is striking for its dream of a language that would be exempt from the Law of the father. This language would be God's mother tongue. It is curious that Adam's first naming of whatever God brought before him should be considered to be intimately related with the animals themselves, for God says to Adam that whatever he calls them will henceforth be their names, as though the connection from the beginning were purely arbitrary.

Within this tradition the reduction of proper names to their meanings and of words to their etymological roots tends to erase the function of proper naming, the function of rigid designation, to make the designation dependent on the uncovering of a true meaning, as a collection of predicables. Through their functioning, in a manner that is obviously quite far from what Ockham sought, we are said to move from the common to the proper qualities of a thing. Thus a singular thing, as sole referent of an element of language, must have been seen as an aberration.

Certainly theories such as these wish to map language onto the world. To begin with the thing itself, and to attempt to see propositions in relation to things, whether real or unreal, is to take things from the wrong angle. We have asserted, with Kripke, that the significance of the function of proper naming is its designation of the same referent rigidly in all possible worlds. This means that if the descriptive characteristics a speaker intends to link with a name do not belong to the referent, then the name still designates rigidly in a counterfactual situation. The same applies to the person who does the naming in the first place. And Putnam extended the theory to the difference between expert speakers and other speakers of a language. Modifying his view, we say that the speaker may use a word without understanding exactly what it means; one may use the word "elm" without knowing all of the predicates of the word, without being able to tell an elm from an oak (Putnam 1979, pp. 227–29). This tends to link the division of the subject and its predicates to the division of speaker and listener. Where Putnam saw the role of the expert speaker as pertaining to one who knows all the predicables, we propose that to speak a language one does not need know these things. It is for the listener to judge whether the speaker is using the word correctly. The function of naming or dubbing a subject is isolated from whatever may be predicated of the term. The proper name has referentiality, whereas the predicates have truth value; the one does not assimilate with or absorb the other; the two remain separate and divided. And since the function of dubbing clearly resides within the area of masculine competence and performance, whatever the sex of the person performing, the verb phrase has to do with the feminine or with the listener.

On femininity we recall a point that Lacan made with considerable insistence, that "Woman" does not exist. This does not mean that particular women do not exist; it asserts that the generic "Woman" does not have a referent. Thereby language does not hook into its speakers through womankind but rather through mankind. The truth conditions of a sentence are altered by the situations in which a sentence may be spoken, and there is no absolute situation that renders a sentence absolutely true or false. The Woman who does not exist would, if She did exist, be the place of final judgment of truth or falsity, against which there would be no appeal. This corresponds, as Lacan asserted, to a function that is often attributed to God.

Another consequence of Lacan's statement is the following. It is impossible to generalize femininity; each woman's femininity is fundamentally hers no matter how much it has in common with that of other women. That there are certain descriptive traits often associated with femininity does not define the structure of a position that is socially determined and is based on a particular relation to being named. When feminine characteristics are gained through an identification with other women, through a girl's identification with her mother, for example, the woman in question will not know whether the feminine identity is hers or those of another woman—or her mother's. And there is no way of finding out on the level of descriptive traits or their combination. Those who believe that womanhood is gained through an identification with other women invariably arrive at a femininity that is generalized as motherhood, as though the incest taboo did not apply to mothers and daughters.

Being on the side of the predicate in a structure where the subject or substantive hooks into the real of itself regardless of its predication, a woman's position is mobile in a sense that a man's cannot be. A predicate is connected to the subject according to convention, but not necessarily to render the sentence or the dialogue productive of a single meaning. While a proper name designates rigidly no matter what the descriptive traits associated with it, it does make a difference what they are. To say that Aristotle was the teacher of Alexander is not the same as to say that Aristotle is the conductor of the New York Philharmonic. The point is not to gain knowledge about Aristotle by accepting those predicates that are true of the historical personage, for there is a context in which a historically true statement would be false and in which a false statement would be true. I am thinking of the use of coded passwords between spies. It is perfectly conceivable that one man walk up to another on a bridge in Berlin and say: "Who was Aristotle?" It may have been agreed that if the other responds "The conductor of the New York Philharmonic," this phrase is the correct complement of the first, whereas if he says "The teacher of Alexander" or any other historical fact, the transaction cannot take place. These are like the two matching tokens of the symbol, and we note that with a discursive act whose purpose is to identify the speakers to each other, it is far more astute to find a predication that would not normally be added to the subject. Otherwise, it would be impossible for the two people to recognize each other. Rather than taking the world of facts or of actuality to be the privileged place on which to map true sentences, we are recommending, again after Lacan, a dialogue that shows language affecting speaker and listener, determining their identity and their place in relation to other speakers. So a paradigm for a speech act would not be a statement that refers to a state of affairs, but something like the password you pronounce every time you decide to stop in at your local speakeasy. There it is not the meaning of the phrase pronounced or the fact that the words mean much of anything but rather the pronunciation of an identifiable grouping of sounds: "Furiously sleep ideas green colorless." The same formula will not work when you present yourself at the gates of Heaven; there the condition of your admission will be the moral content of the narrative of your history, its being meaningful within the context of meanings established by religious custom and belief, and the light this sheds on the state of your intentional soul.

In the shadow of the failure of the function of proper naming, the purpose of intelligence, must be placed in the service of the link between mother nature and mother tongue. The maternal is identified with the correct definition, the definition that permits a human being to think like an angel.

Where the maternal prevails, the conduit through which words, taken to be meaningful, are related to speaking beings is the female body, especially that part of the body associated with the creation of new beings. Whatever division is supposed to exist within the structure of language is thus obscured and erased by the recourse to meaning; instead of dialectic we have hermeneutics. Instead of opposing statements that coexist in a desiring tension, we find two statements, one of which is presented as a more precise, more correct, way of stating the other. One sees this often in psychoanalysis when it is practiced ineffectively: the analyst will provide restatements of whatever his patient says, with his being more meaningful, or else he will isolate the central meaning to the detriment of the signifying material. Such analysts see their role more in terms of indoctrination than of bringing the patient to speak and to have access to language. In such an interpretative morass the patient will be considered cured once he has become convinced of the truth of his analyst's interpretation. His access to language will be blocked along with his access to desire.

While femininity ought not to be defined in terms of motherhood, it does not exclude it either. The alternative to the worship of fertility is decidedly not the elimination of reproduction from consideration. Such a reasoning would accept the angelic and moral value of fertility as redeeming the sexual act, only to negate it entirely in an assertion of the ultimate value of sterility. In place of the angels we would have to deal with devils, fallen angels, and such a switch would do nothing more than retain masked the moral division we have opposed. Fertility has a place in sexual acts as a fetish, an object that is peripheral to the act but that may function to cause masculine desire. Obviously it is not the only suitable fetish. The masculine position is sustainable only when the truth is dissimulated. The truth must in some sense be veiled, and it appears that the place of that veil is occupied by the female body. Fertility and beauty in women are both lures, both visible attributes that allow a man to deceive himself into believing that something other than what is happening is happening.

It is a curious fact that so many great philosophers, like the Judeo-Christian God, were not married. Were they thereby simply avoiding the truth that Nietzsche saw them as wanting to seduce, or were they looking for a higher truth, Woman, which would relieve them of the requirement of confronting women? Interestingly, Nietzsche did not say that truth was Woman; he said that truth was *a* woman.

This explains why fertility can be made into the only valuable aspect of sexual desire and why it represents the translation of desire into redeeming love. It is interesting that believers insist that a worship of fertility must become universal, and that an offense against it (even by those who do not believe) is an offense against a God whose claim to oneness is his victory over death. It must have appeared at some time that the heavenly angels, even reduced to a mixture of blandness and bliss, had to be put on a shelf in order to save this God. In the effort to dissociate the angels from gods and devils, Christianity had, perhaps inadvertently, deprived them of their ability to reproduce themselves. Did this not ultimately make them unacceptable in a world ruled by a god whose claim to divinity was his providence and province over the living? This god so loved his mother that he did for her what has never been done for any human being; he rendered the act by which she was conceived free from sin and desire, and even exempted her from death. There was a risk that the desire experienced by angels would not remain entirely within the bounds Christianity had set for it, thus that the angels would revert to form and start to reproduce their own kind. For if this could happen, what need would there be for humans to be moral, for humans to make the goal of their lives filling the gaps in the Heavenly City? Besides, no one ever asked Jerusalem how she felt about all this. For all we know her desire has nothing to do with plentitude.

REFERENCES

Abbreviations
CHLGEMP: *The Cambridge History of Later Greek and Early Medieval Philosophy.*
CHLMP: *The Cambridge History of Late Medieval Philosophy.*

Adler, Mortimer. *The Angels and Us.* New York, 1982.
Alain de Lille. *The Book of Alain on the Complaint of Nature.* New York, 1908.
Anselm, St. *Basic Writings.* La Salle, Ill., 1962.
Aquinas, Thomas. *Summa Theologica* [ST]. Westminster, Md., 1948.
——. "Concerning Spiritual Creatures," in *Medieval Philosophical Texts in Translation* [CSC]. Milwaukee, 1949.
——. *Treatise on Separate Substances* [TSS]. Rev. Francis Lescoe (trans.). West Hartford, Conn., 1959.
——. *Summa Contra Gentiles* [SCG]. Notre Dame, 1975.
——. *Questions disputées sur la vérité: Question XI, Le Maître* [QDV]. Paris, 1983.
——. *Opuscules 3* (Op. 3). Paris, 1984.
Ariès, Philippe and Béjin, André (eds.). *Western Sexuality: Practice and Precept in Past and Present Times.* Oxford, 1985.
Aristotle. *The Complete Works: The Revised Oxford Translation.* Jonathan Barnes (ed.). Princeton, 1984.
Armstrong, A. H. (ed.). *The Cambridge History of Later Greek and Early Medieval Philosophy.* Cambridge, England, 1970.

Auerbach, Erich. *Mimesis: The Representation of Reality in Western Literature.* Garden City, N.Y., 1957.

———. *Scenes from the Drama of European Literature.* Minneapolis, 1984.

Augustine. "The Enchiridion," in *A Select Library of the Nicene and Post-Nicene Fathers of the Christian Church,* vol. 3. Grand Rapids, Mich., 1980.

———. "On the Good of Marriage," in *A Select Library of the Nicene and Post-Nicene Fathers of the Christian Church,* vol. 3. Grand Rapids, Mich., 1980.

———. "On the Trinity," in *A Select Library of the Nicene and Post-Nicene Fathers of the Christian Church,* vol. 3. Grand Rapids, Mich., 1980.

———. *The City of God* [CG]. David Knowles (ed.). New York, 1981.

Bacon, Francis. *The New Organon.* New York, 1960.

Barth, Karl. *Church Dogmatics III: The Doctrine of Creation.* Edinburgh, 1960.

Barthes, Roland. "The Struggle with the Angel," in *Image, Music, Text.* New York, 1977.

Becker, Carl. *The Heavenly City of the Eighteenth-Century Philosophers.* New Haven, 1932.

Bell, Rudolph. *Holy Anorexia.* Chicago, 1985.

Berefelt, Gunnar. *A Study on the Winged Angel: The Origin of a Motif.* Stockholm, 1968.

Bernard of Clairvaux. *On the Song of Songs I.* Kalamazoo, Mich., 1981.

———. *On the Song of Songs II.* Kalamazoo, Mich., 1983.

Bloch, R. Howard. "Silence and Holes: The *Roman de Silence* and the Art of the Trouvere," in *Yale French Studies* 70, 1986a.

———. *Etymologies and Genealogies: A Literary Anthropology of the French Middle Ages.* Chicago, 1986b.

Blumenberg, Hans. *The Legitimacy of the Modern Age.* Cambridge, Mass., 1985.

Boler, John. *Charles Peirce and Scholastic Realism.* Seattle, 1963.

Bonaventure, St. *Breviloquium 2. Le Monde Créature de Dieu.* Paris, 1967a.

———. *Breviloquium 4. L'Incarnation du Verbe.* Paris, 1967b.

———. *The Soul's Journey into God; The Tree of Life; The Life of St. Francis.* Ewert Cousins (trans.). New York, 1978.

———. *Questions disputées sur le savoir chez le Christ.* Paris, 1985.

Bréhier, Emile. *La Philosophie du Moyen Age.* Paris, 1971.

Burkert, Walter. *Homo Necans.* Berkeley, 1983.

———. *Greek Religion.* Cambridge, Mass., 1985.

Burleigh, Walter. *De Puritate Artis Logicae.* St. Bonaventure, N.Y., 1955.

Bynum, Caroline Walker, "The Body of Christ in the Later Middle Ages: A Reply to Leo Steinberg," in *Renaissance Quarterly* 39, No. 3, 1986.

Caquot, André. "Anges et Démons en Israel," in *Génies, Anges, et Démons,* op. cit.

Carroll, Michael. *The Cult of the Virgin Mary.* Princeton, 1986.

Cassirer, Ernst. *The Individual and the Cosmos in Renaissance Philosophy.* Philadelphia, 1972.

Catherine of Siena. *The Dialogue.* New York, 1980.

Caton, Hiram. *The Origin of Subjectivity.* New Haven, 1973.

Chenu, M.-D. *La Théologie au Douzième Siècle.* Paris, 1976.

Chodorow, Nancy. *The Reproduction of Mothering: Psychoanalysis and the Sociology of Gender.* Berkeley, 1978.

Clement of Alexandria. *The Exhortation to the Greeks and Other Works.* Cambridge, Mass., 1982.

Cohen, Jonathan and Avishai Margalit. "The Role of Inductive Reasoning in the Interpretation of Metaphor," in Davidson and Harman, op. cit.

Copleston, Frederick. *A History of Philosophy, Book 1.* Garden City, N.Y., 1985.

Corbin, Henry. *Avicenna and the Visionary Recital.* Irving, Tex., 1980.

Daniélou, Jean. *Platonisme et théologie mystique: Doctrine spirituelle de St. Grégoire de Nysse.* Paris, 1944.

Dante. *The Divine Comedy.* H. R. Huse (trans.). New York, 1964.

Danto, Arthur. "The Representational Character of Ideas and the Problem of the External World," in Hooker (ed.), op. cit.

Davidson, Donald. *Inquiries into Truth and Interpretation.* New York, 1984.

—— and Gilbert Harman. *Semantics of Natural Language,* 2d Ed. Dordrecht, Holland, 1972.

Davidson, Gustav. *A Dictionary of Angels.* New York, 1971.

de Beauvoir, Simone. *The Second Sex.* New York, 1961.

de Cusa, Nicholas. *Idiota de Mente; The Layman: About Mind.* New York, 1979.

de Finance, Joseph. *Cogito Cartésien et Reflexion Thomiste.* Paris, 1946.

della Mirandola, Pico. "Of Being and Unity," in *Medieval Philosophical Texts in Translation.* Milwaukee, 1943.

Delumeau, Jean. *La Peur en Occident (XIVe—XVIIe siècles): Une cité assiégé.* Paris, 1978.

Descartes, René. *Oeuvres et lettres.* Paris, 1953.

Dick, Steven. *Plurality of Worlds.* New York, 1982.

[Dionysius the Areopagite]. *Oeuvres complètes du Pseudo-Denys l'aréopagite.* Maurice de Gandillac (ed.). Paris, 1943.

Duby, Georges. *The Age of the Cathedrals: Art and Society 980–1420.* Chicago, 1981.

——. *The Three Orders: Feudal Society Imagined.* Chicago, 1982.

——. *The Knight, the Lady, and the Priest.* New York, 1983.

Duns Scotus, John. *De Primo Principio.* Evan Roche (trans.). St. Bonaventure, N.Y., 1949.

——. *God and Creatures.* Princeton, 1975.

[Erigena, John Scotus] Jean Scot. *Commentaire sur l'Evangile de Jean.* Paris, 1972.

Field, M. J. *Angels and Ministers of Grace.* New York, 1971.

Flandrin, Jean-Louis. "Sex in Married Life in the Early Middle Ages: The Church's Teaching and Behavioural Reality," in Ariès and Béjin (eds.), op.cit.

Foucault, Michel. *Histoire de la sexualité 1: La volonté de savoir.* Paris, 1976.

———. *Histoire de la sexualité 2: L'usage des plaisirs.* Paris, 1984a.

———. *Histoire de la sexualité 3: Le souci de soi.* Paris, 1984b.

Freud, Sigmund. *The Standard Edition of the Complete Psychological Works* [SE]. London, 1955.

Gardiner, Alan. *The Theory of Proper Names.* London, 1940.

Génies, Anges, et Démons. Sources Orientales 8. Paris, 1971.

Gilson, Etienne. *La Philosophie de Saint Bonaventure.* Paris, 1924a.

———. *The Philosophy of St. Thomas.* Cambridge, England, 1924b.

———. *Jean Duns Scot: Introduction à ses positions fondamentales.* Paris, 1952.

———. *Christian Philosophy in the Middle Ages.* New York, 1955.

———. *Héloïse and Abélard.* Ann Arbor, 1960.

———. *Etudes sur le rôle de la pensée médiévale dans la formation du système cartésien.* Paris, 1984.

Gouhier, Henri. *Cartésianisme et Augustinisme au XVIIe siècle.* Paris, 1978.

Gregory of Nyssa. *Traité de la Virginité.* Paris, 1966.

———. *From Glory to Glory.* Crestwood, N.Y., 1979.

Gueroult, Martial. *Descartes selon l'ordre des raisons. I, L'âme et Dieu.* Paris, 1968a.

———. *Descartes selon l'ordre des raisons. II, L'âme et le corps.* Paris, 1968b.

Hardy, Edward (ed.). *Christology of the Later Fathers.* Philadelphia, 1954.

Heckscher, W. S. "Aphrodite as a Nun," in *The Phoenix* 7, No. 3, 1953.

Heidegger, Martin. "Logos," in *La Psychanalyse* 1, 1956.

———. *Chemins qui ne menent nulle part.* Paris, 1962.

———. *Traité des catégories et de la signification chez Duns Scot.* Paris, 1970.

———, and Eugen Fink. *Héraclite.* Paris, 1973.

Hintikka, Jaakko. "*Cogito, Ergo Sum:* Inference or Performance." *Philosophical Review* 71, 1962.

———. "A Discourse on Descartes's Method," in Hooker (ed.), op.cit.

———. "The Semantics of Modal Notions and the Indeterminacy of Ontology." In Davidson and Harman, op. cit.

———. *Time and Necessity: Studies in Aristotle's Theory of Modality.* Oxford, 1973.

Hooker, Michael (ed.). *Descartes: Critical and Interpretive Essays.* Baltimore, 1978.

Huizinga, Johan. *The Waning of the Middle Ages.* Garden City, N.Y., 1954.

———. *Men and Ideas: History, the Middle Ages, the Renaissance.* Princeton, 1984.

Hyman, Arthur and James Walsh (eds.). *Philosophy in the Middle Ages.* Indianapolis, 1984.

Jacquart, Danielle and Claude Thomasset. *Sexualité et savoir médical au moyen âge.* Paris, 1985.

Jakobson, Roman and Morris Halle. *Fundamentals of Language*. The Hague, 1956.

Jerome, St. *Select Letters*. F. A. Wright (trans.). Cambridge, Mass., 1980.

Jonas, Hans. *The Gnostic Religion*, 2d ed. Boston, 1963.

Kahn, Charles. *The Art and Thought of Heraclitus*. Cambridge, Mass., 1979.

Katz, Jerrold. *Cogitations*. New York, 1986.

Kirshner, Julius and Karl Morrison (eds.). *University of Chicago Readings in Western Civilization 4: Medieval Europe*. Chicago, 1986.

Kojève, Alexandre. *Essai d'une histoire raisonnée de la philosophie païenne*, tome III. Paris, 1973.

Koyré, Alexandre. *Newtonian Studies*. Chicago, 1968.

———. *Etudes d'Histoire de la Pensée Philosophique*. Paris, 1971.

Kramer, Heinrich and James Sprenger. *Malleus Maleficarum* [MM]. Montague Summers (trans.). London,1971.

Kretzmann, Norman, Anthony Kenny, and Jan Pinborg, *The Cambridge History of Later Medieval Philosophy* [CHLMP]. Cambridge, England, 1982.

Kripke, Saul. "Outline of a Theory of Truth," in *The Journal of Philosophy* 72, 1975.

———. "Speaker's Reference and Semantic Reference," in *Midwest Studies in Philosophy* 2, 1977.

———. *Naming and Necessity*. Cambridge, Mass., 1980.

Kristeva, Julia. *Histoires d'Amour*. Paris, 1983.

Lacan, Jacques. *Ecrits*. Paris, 1966.

———. *Le Séminaire Livre XI: Les quatres concepts fondamentaux de la psychanalyse*. Paris, 1973.

———. *Le Séminaire Livre XX: Encore*. Paris, 1975.

———. *Le Séminaire Livre VII: L'éthique de la psychanalyse*. Paris, 1986.

Lane Fox, Robin. *Pagans and Christians*. New York, 1986.

Le Goff, Jacques. *The Birth of Purgatory*. Chicago, 1984.

Leff, Gordon. *William of Ockham*. Manchester, England, 1975.

Leibniz, Gottfried Wilhelm. *The Monadology and Other Philosophical Writings*. Robert Latta (trans.). London, 1898.

———. *Discourse on Metaphysics: Correspondence with Arnauld; Monadology*. Lasalle, Ill.

Leibovici, Marcel. "Génies et Démons en Babylonie." In *Génies, Anges, et Démons*, op. cit.

Lemoine-Luccioni, Eugénie. *La Robe*. Paris, 1983.

Lewis, C. S. *Allegory*. Oxford, 1936.

Lewis, David. *Counterfactuals*. Cambridge, Mass., 1973.

———. *Philosophical Papers*, vol. 1. New York, 1983.

———. *On the Plurality of Worlds*. Oxford, 1986.

Lindner, Robert. *The Fifty-Minute Hour*. New York, 1982.

Litt, Thomas. *Les Corps Célestes dans l'Univers de Saint Thomas d'Aquin*. Paris-Louvain, 1963.

Locke, John. *An Essay Concerning Human Understanding*, vol. 1. Alexander Campbell Fraser (ed.). New York, 1959.

Lovejoy, Arthur O. *The Great Chain of Being*. Cambridge, Mass., 1982.

Luther, Martin. "Table Talk," in *Luther's Works*, vol. 54. Philadelphia, 1967.

Mâle, Emile. *The Gothic Image*. New York, 1972.

Marion, Jean-Luc. *Sur la théologie blanche de Descartes*. Paris, 1981.

Maritain, Jacques. *Le Songe de Descartes*. Paris, 1932.

——. *Three Reformers: Luther, Descartes, Rousseau*. New York, 1934.

McEvoy, James. *The Philosophy of Robert Grosseteste*. Oxford, 1986.

Meeks, Dimitri. "Génies, Anges, Démons en Egypte," in *Génies, Anges, et Démons*, op. cit.

Meiss, Millard. *Painting in Florence and Siena After the Black Death*. New York, 1973.

Mitchell, Juliet. *Psychoanalysis and Feminism*. New York, 1975.

Montague, Richard. "On the Nature of Certain Philosophical Entities," in *The Monist* 53, 1969.

Nahm, Milton. *Selections from Early Greek Philosophy*. New York, 1964.

Nakhnikian, George. "Descartes's Dream Argument," in Hooker (ed.), op. cit.

Nancy, Jean-Luc. *Ego Sum*. Paris, 1979.

Nietzsche, Friedrich. *Beyond Good and Evil*. Walter Kaufmann (trans.). New York, 1966.

——. *On the Genealogy of Morals: Ecce Homo*. Walter Kaufmann (trans.). New York, 1969.

Nussbaum, Martha C. *Aristotle's De Motu Animalium*. Princeton, 1985.

——. *The Fragility of Goodness*. New York, 1986.

Nygren, Anders. *Agape and Eros*. Chicago, 1982.

Origen. *The Song of Songs: Commentary and Homilies*. R. P. Lawson (trans.). New York, 1956.

——. *An Exhortation to Martyrdom and Other Works*. New York, 1979.

——. *Contra Celsum*. Henry Chadwick (trans.). Cambridge, England, 1980.

Panofsky, Erwin. *Renaissance and Renascences in Western Art*. New York, 1972a.

——. *Studies in Iconology*. New York, 1972b.

Paulus, Jean. *Henri de Gand*. Paris, 1938.

Petit, Léon. *Descartes et la Princesse Elisabeth: roman d'amour vécu*. Paris, 1969.

Phillips, John A. *Eve: The History of an Idea*. New York, 1985.

Philo V. Loeb Classical Library. Cambridge, Mass., 1968.

Philo II. Loeb Classical Library. Cambridge, Mass., 1979.

Philo I. Loeb Classical Library. Cambridge, Mass., 1981.

Plantinga, Alvin. *God and Other Minds*. Ithaca, 1967.

Plato III. *Lysis, Symposium, Gorgias*. W. R. M. Lamb (trans.). Cambridge, Mass., 1975.

Plato VIII. *Statesman, Philebus, Ion.* H. N. Fowler and W. R. M. Lamb (trans.). Cambridge, Mass., 1975.

Plato I. *Euthyphro, Apology, Crito, Phaedo, Phaedrus.* H. N. Fowler (trans.). Cambridge, Mass., 1977.

Plotinus. *Enneads III. 1–9.* A. H. Armstrong (trans.). Cambridge, Mass., 1980.

Plutarch. "Advice to Bride and Groom," in *Moralia II.* Cambridge, Mass., 1971.

——. *Plutarch's Lives,* 2 vols. London, 1914–26.

Proclus. *Eléments de la théologie.* Paris, 1965.

——. *Théologie Platonicienne I.* Paris, 1968.

——. *Théologie Platonicienne II.* Paris, 1974.

——. *Théologie Platonicienne IV.* Paris, 1981.

Putnam, Hilary. *Mind, Language, and Reality: Philosophical Papers,* vol. 2. New York, 1979.

——. "After Ayer, After Empiricism," in *Partisan Review* 51, No. 2, 1984.

[Rashi]. *Rashi on the Pentateuch: Genesis.* James H. Lowe (trans.). London, 1929.

Quine, Willard Van Orman. *From a Logical Point of View,* 2d ed. Cambridge, Mass., 1980.

Rich, Adrienne. *Of Woman Born: Motherhood as Experience and Institution.* New York, 1976.

Richard of St. Victor. *The Twelve Patriarchs; The Mystical Ark; Book Three of The Trinity.* New York, 1979.

Roland-Gosselin, M.-D. "Etudes" in *Le "Ente et Essentia" de S. Thomas d'Aquin.* Paris, 1948.

Rorty, Richard. *Philosophy and the Mirror of Nature.* Princeton, 1980.

Rousseau, Jean-Jacques. *Emile, ou de l'Education.* Paris, 1961.

Russell, Jeffrey Burton. *Lucifer: The Devil in the Middle Ages.* Ithaca, 1984.

Schneiderman, Stuart. *Jacques Lacan: The Death of an Intellectual Hero.* Cambridge, Mass., 1983.

——. "Mondes impossibles et noms impropres." in *Ornicar?* 37, 1986.

——. *Rat Man.* New York, 1987.

Schwartz, Stephen (ed.). *Naming, Necessity, and Natural Kinds.* Ithaca, 1977.

Searle, John. *Intentionality.* New York, 1983.

Seznec, Jean. *The Survival of the Pagan Gods.* Princeton, 1972.

Singer, Irving. *The Nature of Love 1: Plato to Luther,* 2d ed. Chicago, 1984a.

——. *The Nature of Love 2: Courtly and Romantic.* Chicago, 1984b.

Smith-Rosenberg, Carroll. *Disorderly Conduct: Visions of Gender in Victorian America.* New York, 1985.

Speiser, E. A. (trans.). *Genesis.* Garden City, N.Y., 1964.

Starobinski, Jean. *Les mots sous les mots.* Paris, 1971.

Steinberg, Leo. *The Sexuality of Christ in Renaissance Art and Modern Oblivion.* New York, 1983.

Symons, Donald. *The Evolution of Human Sexuality.* New York, 1979.

Teresa of Avila. *The Life of Teresa of Jesus.* Garden City, N.Y., 1960.

Tertullian. *La Résurrection des Morts.* Paris, 1980.

Teyssèdre, Bernard. *Anges, Astres, et Cieux.* Paris, 1986.

Vernier, Jean-Marie. *Les Anges chez Saint Thomas d'Aquin.* Paris, 1986.

Warner, Marina. *Alone of All her Sex: The Myth and Cult of the Virgin Mary.* New York, 1983.

Weinberg, Julius. *A Short History of Medieval Philosohy.* Princeton, 1967.

———. *Ockham, Descartes, and Hume.* Madison, Wis., 1977.

William of Ockham. *Ockham's Theory of Terms: Part 1 of the* Summa Logica. Notre Dame, 1974.

———.*Commentaire sur le Livre des Prédicables de Porphyre.* Sherbrooke, Canada, 1978.

———. *Ockham's Theory of Terms: Part 2 of the* Summa Logica. Notre Dame, 1980.

Wilson, Peter Lamborn. *Angels.* New York, 1980.

Wolfson, Harry Austryn. *Studies in the History of Philosophy and Religion,* vol. 1. Cambridge, Mass., 1973.

———. *Studies in the History of Philosophy and Religion,* vol 2. Cambridge, Mass., 1977.

Ziegler, Philip. *The Black Death.* New York, 1971.

INDEX